The Victorian Countryside

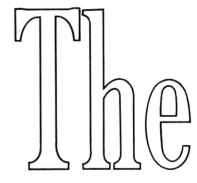

Edited by

G. E. Mingay

Professor of Agrarian History
University of Kent at Canterbury

Routledge & Kegan Paul   London, Boston and Henley

Victorian Countryside

Volume Two

First published in 1981
by Routledge & Kegan Paul Ltd
39 Store Street, London WC1E 7DD,
9 Park Street, Boston, Mass. 02108, USA and
Broadway House, Newtown Road,
Henley-on-Thames, Oxon RG9 1EN
Set in Monophoto Century Schoolbook
and printed in Great Britain by
BAS Printers Limited, Over Wallop, Hampshire
© G. E. Mingay 1981

British Library Cataloguing in Publication Data

Mingay, Gordon E.

The Victorian countryside.
1. Country life—Great Britain—1837-1901
2. Natural history—Great Britain—1837–1901
I. Title
941.08′100973′4   DA667   80-42190

ISBN 0-7100-0734-5 (Vol. 1)
ISBN 0-7100-0735-3 (Vol. 2)
ISBN 0-7100-0736-1 (The set)

Contents

Volume Two

Contents

Illustrations

Illustrations

viii

IV   Landed Society

27   The Landed Aristocracy

D. C. Moore

I

Until some eighty or ninety years ago the aristocracy were the principal English elite, in significant respects the only elite. Individually, they did many things. They had many roles. But as a group they were generally conceived in terms of two roles, that which some of them enjoyed as peers, and that which almost all of them enjoyed as extensive landowners. A half-century earlier the role as landowner had taken precedence over the role as peer. The process of change was extremely important. But it had more to do with the image of the aristocracy than with their real identity, or with their claims to a monopoly of elite status. It was a means of preserving their status in a changing social and political climate. And then, in the context of a further change of climate, a rather sudden differentiation of elites occurred and the aristocracy, whether conceived as landowners or peers, lost their monopoly of elite status.

Undoubtedly in part the loss of this monopoly was the consequence of the declining actual wealth of many landowners, the declining relative wealth of many more. Certain landowners remained very rich, especially those who owned urban land or land under which minerals had been found. But from the late 1870s, when agricultural prices broke—land values had peaked a few years earlier—landowners ceased to comprise the vast majority of very rich men.[1] Increasingly, this category was filled by men who left their money where they made it, in financial and industrial enterprises, who did not invest it in land. In part, their behaviour reflected the declining importance of land as a source of income. Even more, it reflected the declining importance of landed estates as social organizing agencies. Obviously, to some extent landed estates lost their organizing functions because other institutions stole them away. At some critical point in the long-term migrations of Englishmen into the towns, and out of the towns into the suburbs, other institutions became more important as symbols of identity to larger portions of the population. But more was involved than a simple transference of organizing function. It was not so much that urban leaders replaced the rural, or that urban institutions replaced rural institutions. Obviously, for reasons which are related to the growing proportions of the population which resided in the towns and suburbs but which urbanization and suburbanization alone do not adequately explain, major changes were occurring in the structure of authority in the kingdom in the ways in which organizing functions were performed. In many cases, until the 1870s or 1880s, the different categories of influence—political economic, social, religious—had issued from the same or related hands and this in the town as well as in the countryside. The phenomenon not only strengthened the cohesion of the operative networks and communities, it also re-enforced the private authorities of the different elites. But now, in both town and countryside, the networks through which the loyalties of earlier *pays legals* had been channelled were becoming weaker. Also, many men had acquired direct political roles who could not be reached through these networks, who were not members of the relevant communities. Whatever the nature and strength of the operative communities and networks among them—and with the adoption of the secret ballot in 1872 these are effectively hidden—their acquisition of direct political roles greatly accelerated the bureaucratization of authority, both public and private, and the growth of public authority at the cost of private. Together, these developments defined the context in which new and more specialized elites emerged whose powers and status had less to do with personal than with impersonal relationships, and who were legitimized less in terms of their actual or putative roles within one or another network or community than in terms of their wealth alone, their skills, or their actual or putative roles within one or another bureaucracy. Many members of these new elites were hangovers from the old. But their new bases of power were as different from their old as the society and state were different in which these powers were exercised. An era had ended.

II

It had been a long era. For over two hundred years England had been ruled less from Whitehall and Westminster than from a multitude of country houses, less by the Crown and its agents than by individual landowners and their agents, less in officially determined areas of administration than in areas determined by the fortuities of land accumulation, the vicissitudes of family succession, and the vagaries of estate boundaries. The principal components of this system were scarcely legal in the constitutional sense. But the events were which brought it into being. Large landowners acquired their effective powers on the eve of the Civil Wars when the Court of Star Chamber, the Court of High Commission, and the various other organs of royal power were abolished which, previously, had supervised them and restrained them. Their loss of power is not datable in the same way. Like so many other important events in the nineteenth century it had less to do with law than with the kinds of thing which most of those who drafted and enacted the law tried to prevent. To some extent they lost their powers when the state returned to supervise them and restrain them. But to put it thus risks obscuring the ironical or dialectical aspects of the state's return—the degree to which the return was prompted by the concern to perpetuate their powers. Indeed, to put it thus risks attributing to the law that which, for much of the century, the law was designed to avoid, the disintegration of the world the aristocracy had ruled.

Conceived as peers the aristocracy were both few in number and precisely definable. With the exception of those peers of Scotland and Ireland who were not chosen as representatives of their orders, their names are to be found in the lists of members of the House of Lords. Indeed, in many cases it is these who are meant when reference is made to the aristocracy. Apart from the royal dukes, the bishops, and those who were chosen as representatives of the Scottish and Irish peers, they numbered 358 in Victoria's first Parliament, 517 in her last.[2]

Conceived as landowners the aristocracy were far more numerous. But exactly how much more numerous would depend upon how much land an aristocrat-as-landowner had to possess. And to this question no simple answer is possible. But there were two boundaries, in particular, which helped define the aristocrat-as-landowners, the one between them and their poorer neighbours, the other between them and the *nouveaux riches*. This latter boundary could be eroded by time. But not the former. The differences between the life styles and powers it distinguished were far too great. On the one side were those men, sometimes described as gentry, who could only afford the pleasures and activities of the countryside. On the other were those who could also afford the far more expensive pleasures and activities of the London season. Sometimes, an income from land of £10,000 a year was used to distinguish the two groups or, what was often taken as evidence of such an income, an estate of 10,000 acres. If such a measure is used, then in the early 1870s, almost exactly nine hundred men or families would have qualified. The so-called New Domesday, the census of landownership which was taken then, did not include the metropolis. But in the remainder of the kingdom—Scotland and Ireland were included—precisely 901 men or women were listed who had properties of the requisite size.[3] Presumably, wherever their properties were located—and many of them had properties in two, some in all three kingdoms—most of them spent a good deal of their money in England, particularly in London. In this sense they were members of the *English* aristocracy. But of those whose land itself was located in England only 363 would have qualified. Of these, 186 were peers, 58 were baronets, and 177 had no hereditary titles.[4]

Conceived as peers, the functions of the aristocracy were mainly ceremonial and constitutional, or ceremonial and political, and were performed, as a rule, in court, cabinet and House of Lords. Conceived as landowners, their functions were less formal rather than informal, less constitutional than social. Also, as landowners their functions were performed more in the counties in which their estates were located than in the metropolis. As peers, they owed their ranks to the political leaders who had sponsored their promotions and to the kings and queens from whom their patents of nobility derived. In a few cases, those of the barons by writ, they owed their rank to those kings who, in the far distant past, had summoned an ancestor to a Parliament, or to what was subsequently referred to as a Parliament, which summons was later construed into an hereditary right to receive such a summons.[5] As landowners they generally owed their status to the luck or ingenuity of an ancestor who had made his fortune either by state service, commercial success, or marriage with an heiress – which latter was usually the means of enjoying the inherited consequences of someone else's state service or commercial success. But however the fortune was made, until the last quarter of the nineteenth century its investment in rural land was an all but essential step in the social transformation of the fortune-maker and his heirs into members of that aristocracy-as-landowners from which, in the course of a few generations, promotion into the aristocracy-as-peerage might be had. From Victoria's accession until the 1880s the vast majority of new peerages were granted either to existing peers—they were promotions within the peerage—or to members of long-established landed families. Only about an eighth went to persons in neither category. Then a major change occurred: the proportion granted to these persons rose to roughly 40 per cent of the total. Industrialists without land were ennobled. Also a poet, a scientist, a physician, and even an artist.[6] The practice not only reflected the abstraction of formal status and honour from political and social functions; it also reflected a fundamental change in the relationship between landownership and power which, previously, had defined the aristocracy. It was this relationship to which Meredith Townsend, editor of the *Spectator*, implicitly referred in the mid-1860s when he explained:

> The English 'aristocracy' is . . . only another word for the greater owners of
> land. It has little to do with office. . . . Still less . . . with pedigree. . . .
> Historical associations convey influence, but they cling to the property
> rather than the race, and the 'aristocratic element' of the English
> constitution is, in fact, simply the class which owns the soil.[7]

And if, in fact, he was genuinely surprised that the criterion he used to identify the aristocracy excluded all but those who had seats in the House of Lords[8] this would only testify to the completeness of that shift of emphasis and image from the aristocracy-as-peer to the aristocracy-as-landowner which was fairly complete by the time Victoria ascended the throne.

Presumably, this shift was facilitated by those peculiarities of the peerage which distinguished it from most continental nobilities. In most parts of the continent, at least until the end of the eighteenth century, members of the nobility enjoyed significant legal privileges. Also, all legitimate children of a nobleman inherited his noble rank. In these circumstances the size of the nobility grew with the simple growth of population. Endogamy, strongly encouraged by the concern to preserve privileges which marrying out might jeopardize, was not impractical. The nobility comprised a 'class'. But in Britain the peerage were distinguished not by their privileges but their constitutional role. Apart from a seat in the House of Lords the formal legal privileges which a peer enjoyed were insignificant. And their constitutional role also limited their numbers. A given peerage could not be held by more than one person at a time. Thus, whereas on the continent the passing of generations was the means of increasing the size of the nobility, in Britain it could only decrease the number of peers. Indeed, had there been no new creations, in time, the British peerage would have all but disappeared. Most peerages were held by letters patent which specified their modes of descent—as a rule to heirs male of the body legally conceived. When a peer died who had no appropriate heir the peerage simply expired. But his property passed as testamentary settlement provided. Presumably, peers and heirs apparent to peers found their spouses among the daughters of peers rather more often than did their siblings. But average endogamy rates among the children of peers were fairly low. Nor did they rise as the number of peers increased. Rather, they declined. From the early eighteenth century until the mid-nineteenth, roughly a quarter of the sons of peers found their spouses among the daughters of peers. By the end of the nineteenth century the proportion was down to an eighth.[9] In all probability, whether heirs apparent or not, most children of peers found their spouses among the children of aristocrats-as-landowners.[10] And, until the final years of the century, the status of extensive landowner was an all but essential prerequisite for promotion into the peerage. In effect, until then those who comprised the relevant 'class' were the 'greater owners of land'.

But the dynamics of the shift of emphasis from the aristocrat-as-peer to the aristocrat-as-landowner—the dynamics of the change of image—lay elsewhere, not in the recognition of the exigencies of 'class': this was minor. Rather, they lay in the working-out of that crisis of the early 1830s when the two aristocracies, or conceptions of aristocracy, confronted one another. The one was symbolized by that majority of the House of Lords whose titles dated from *after* 1783—Pitt's Peers, they were sometimes called, who identified their interests with the close or rotten boroughs, and who, presumably, would have subscribed to Wellington's description of these boroughs as the 'true protectors of the landed interest'.[11] The other was symbolized by that majority of the House of Lords whose titles dated from *before* 1783, who supported the Reform Bill as a means of abolishing the close or rotten boroughs, and who, presumably, would have regarded themselves as members of that aristocracy whose 'real interests', as Grey put it, were favoured by the Bill.[12] In various respects this crisis was extremely complex. Before it ran its course many alliances and changes of alliance had occurred. But in one respect it was extremely simple. It concerned two rival definitions of 'legitimate' political influence or power, the one essentially legal and constitutional, the other essentially social; the one identified with the aristocracy-as-peers, the other with the aristocracy-as-landowners. By and large, M.P.s were not philosophers. They used descriptions to explain what they meant, not abstractions. Russell's statements are a case in point when he explained the crisis in terms of the differences between the two aristocracies, the one which lived on their estates, 'receiving large incomes, performing important duties, relieving the poor by charity, and evincing private worth and public virtue' the other which '[did not] live among the people, . . . [which knew] nothing of the people, and . . . [which] care[d] nothing for them'. Concerning the one, he said, 'it is not in human nature that they should not possess a great influence upon public opinion'. As for the other, 'the sooner its influence is carried away with the corruption on which it had thriven, the better for the country'.[13]

The reformers could scarcely extirpate that influence which derived from property alone, that which they generally described as 'illegitimate'. But they could abolish the rotten boroughs, the main institutional symbols of this influence. Also, by franchise and boundaries, they could fashion the residual constituencies and the new constituencies so that these would provide more appropriate arenas for the exercise of the so-called 'legitimate' influences of the different local elites, the rural elites especially. In effect, they could adapt the political system to the circumstances of the aristocracy-as-landowners. The point is not unimportant that many of the men who lost powers or influence in the guise of peer retained or acquired them in the guise of landowner. But the change itself was no less real.[14] As Townsend observed some years later, the 'great governing families' had been deprived of their 'legal autocracy' but not their 'influence'.[15]

III

Each of the thirty-one families whose history was related in Townsend's book was represented at least once in the House of Lords, some more than once. But the measure of their continuing influence lay elsewhere. In particular, it lay in their presence in the House of Commons. According to Townsend's calculations, in the session of 1864 the House of Commons contained 110 representatives of these families. And, he went on, if the families of the great Scottish and Irish landowners were added to them it would be found that 'sixty families supply . . . one third of the House.'[16] Townsend's explanation of this was somewhat complex. In part, he attributed it to their wealth and the consequent advantage they enjoyed of being able to launch themselves in politics when they were twenty years younger than their possible rivals. In part, he attributed it to the charisma of their names. But even more significantly he attributed it to the 'instinct of control given to able individuals of all classes . . . [which] they alone have as a class' and, further, to 'the ability . . . [which they had] always displayed . . . to take the lead in all productive enterprise; they reformed agriculture, opened mines, built great harbours, planted forests, cut canals, accepted and profited by the railway system, and built the faubourgs of the great cities'.[17] Clearly, from Townsend's point of view it was important that the influence of the aristocracy be a measure of their personal qualities, not of the roles which institutions allowed them to perform; also, that they be involved in the various activities he specified in direct decision-making capacities, not merely as the owners of the land on which, in consequence of others' decisions, these activities were carried out. But whatever the personal qualities of individuals, institutions were crucial. Also, in most cases it was not as individual decision-makers but either as the employers of such decision-makers or as receivers of rent that they were involved. Aristocrats-as-entrepreneurs were relatively few. They became fewer as the century progressed. But Townsend's explanation is no less important for all that. While it distorts the aristocracy's real role and thus obscures much of the grounds of their continuing influence, it reveals the grounds on which, in his eyes, their continuing influence could be acknowledged.

Until fairly recently little attention has been paid to the ostensible role of the aristocracy in promoting economic growth. Indeed, they have been generally described as the inhibitors of economic growth, not its promoters: Townsend's description was rather unusual. But, essentially, the logic of the usual description was political. Both during the nineteenth century and for some years after, economic growth was generally associated with those political decisions which majorities of the aristocracy, whether conceived as peers or landowners, opposed. In particular, growth was associated with the adoption of free trade, with the repeal of the Corn Laws—and there were few policies which more members of the aristocracy opposed more strenuously. For many years the ultimate failure of their opposition and the dramatic nature of the contemporaneous economic growth seemed to provide a clear answer to the question concerning the aristocracy's general economic role: only when they had been politically beaten did real growth occur. But recently, reflecting the recognition of both the complexities of economic growth in general and the social and cultural components of the contemporary arguments about the Corn Laws, considerable doubt has been cast upon the adequacy of this answer. In consequence, questions concerning the economic role of the aristocracy have been reopened—by some, essentially, as means of studying the process of economic growth in general; by others, essentially, as means of clearing the aristocracy of the charges which previously had seemed proved against them. The logic of the one is direct and obvious. The logic of the other is less direct and less obvious. In fact, the charges derive from those utilitarian values which Townsend implicitly invoked while trying to explain the continuing influence of the aristocracy. But while the substitution of the image of the entrepreneur for that of the semi-feudal magnate may have made it easier for Townsend to acknowledge the continuing influence of the aristocracy, this substitution explains neither their behaviour nor the real sources of their influence.

In the late eighteenth and early nineteenth centuries many landowners and their agents did much to develop their properties directly. The third Duke of Bridgewater and James Brindley played important entrepreneurial roles in developing Bridgewater's Worsley mines and the canal by which his coal could be carried to

Manchester.[18] In the northern coalfield the third Marquess of Londonderry and John Buddle, and the first Earl of Durham and Henry Morton, played analogous roles.[19] And, as Professor Spring observed some years ago, 'from coal it was but a short step to railroads'.[20] In the mid-nineteenth century, on his estates in Barrow, the second Earl of Burlington, later the seventh Duke of Devonshire, was directly involved in a number of mining, railway, and industrial enterprises. On his estates in Eastbourne he was somewhat less directly involved in the building of a seaside resort.[21] In particular, wealth accrued to those families whose properties allowed them to profit most from industrialization, population growth, and the increasing concentration of population in the towns. Over the long term, until the late 1870s, agricultural rents rose—and, in part, for reasons other than those which David Ricardo had described: not only because of the simple growth of population but also because of increments of productivity. But the increased value of agricultural land was as nothing compared with the increased value of urban land or—in consequence of the statute of 1 William III which settled the question that all subsoil minerals with the exception of gold and silver belonged to the surface landowner—the increased value of land under which coal or other minerals were found.[22] Recent studies of local economic growth and recent economic studies of particular estates have shown that early in the nineteenth century the owners and agents of a fair number of estates were actively engaged as entrepreneurs. But these studies have also shown that in most cases the role of entrepreneur was abandoned as the century wore on; the seventh Duke of Devonshire was somewhat exceptional. Often at the loss of considerable actual or potential income, landowners withdrew from the role of entrepreneur to the more familiar role of *rentier*.[23] In this role they could enjoy increments of value which others produced with minimum risk and expense to themselves and minimum jeopardy to their status; also— but the advantages of this were somewhat contingent—with minimum social involvement. The question remains to what extent this tendency left later generations of James Brindleys, John Buddles, and Henry Mortons without clear institutional outlets for their energies and ambitions until the latter years of the century when joint-stock companies became numerous. But this much seems certain: at the middle of the century the assets of many estates which were comparable to those which joint-stock companies later controlled were deflected from direct productive investment. For members of the aristocracy it was essential to be rich: but to be rich in those somewhat special circumstances which rural landownership allowed, those in which wealth was both directly and 'legitimately' convertible into social control. It was this aspect of the matter which Townsend ignored. But this aspect helps to explain their fairly strong preference for their agricultural rather than their non-agricultural properties, the differences of relationship which obtained in these different categories of property, and the changes of relationship by which they tended to distance themselves from their non-agricultural properties while increasing the organizational intimacy of their agricultural properties. And, presumably, this aspect also helps to explain why for so many years the purchase of a landed estate was the symbol of success, and why, again, when the aura of landownership and the real powers which landownership conveyed were somewhat tarnished and curtailed, an increasing proportion of peers was recruited from non-landed families.

In the mid-1860s the Grosvenor family, Marquess of Westminster since 1831, Dukes of Westminster from 1874, were reputed to be the richest family in Europe.[24] There were two foundations to their wealth. The one was property in London which an ancestor had acquired by a fortunate marriage in the late seventeenth century— most of Belgravia, Mayfair, and Pimlico. The other was the building lease. Such a lease was the means by which, ultimately, a lessor could take possession of buildings which a builder had put up at his own cost. During the term, usually between eighty and ninety-nine years, the lessor enjoyed the relatively small ground rents which reflected the value of the land alone. The lessee enjoyed the other and larger rents which reflected the value of the buildings. But when the lease expired the lessor received the rents for the buildings as well.[25] The report in the mid-1860s that the Grosvenors' London properties would be worth £1 million a year when the existing leases fell in was a gross exaggeration.[26] However, while the reality of £250,000 a year[27] sufficed to set the family in an income category of their own, the family were much more affectively involved in their far less valuable properties outside of London. In the 1870s these properties amounted to under 20,000 acres, worth less than £40,000 a year.[28] But they provided nexuses which, apparently, were totally lacking with respect to the others. In 1846 when the future duke came of age, and in 1852 when he was married, there were extensive celebrations on the family's rural estates. But, apparently, none on their London estates. The Cheshire gentry and the various categories of agricultural tenant were appropriately entertained. But, apparently, not the London tenants.[29] To note that different varieties of property gave rise to different varieties of relationship is not to dispel the significance of the consequent differences in behaviour. Rather, it is to explain these differences.

The wealth of the Russell family, Dukes of Bedford since 1694, had a similar basis— building leases and mining leases applied to properties acquired by several marriages and several stints of state service. Their agricultural properties were larger than those of the Grosvenors. But their most valuable properties were located in the centre of London, in Bloomsbury and St Pancras, Covent Garden and St Martin's. In the 1880s, when various building leases fell in, these properties became worth more than £100,000 a year.[30] But a generation earlier the possible anticipation of such income had not deterred the seventh Duke, an enthusiastic agriculturist, from horrifying his agent by suggesting they be sold.[31] Nor did the differences between the incomes from agricultural and mineral exploitation tilt his preference away from the former. It was a source of considerable profit to him that the operators of one of the largest copper mines in the world were his lessees. As was the custom, these paid a fixed minimum rent designed to secure the working of the mine and royalties which varied according to the quantity and value of the minerals raised.[32] But he deplored the speculative fervour which mining encouraged and, as Professor Spring has noted, 'when ironstone was found on his Midland estates, . . . [he] refused to allow it to be mined because it would disfigure the countryside'.[33]

In the eighteenth century the Gower family, Marquesses of Stafford from 1785, Dukes of Sutherland from 1833, were directly involved in numerous mining and industrial ventures in Staffordshire and Shropshire. Indeed, the first Marquess, like his brother-in-law, the third Duke of Bridgewater, was a prototypical entrepreneur who might have provided Townsend's model. But from early in the nineteenth century, in the context of mounting problems of trade fluctuation and labour relations and competition with neighbouring producers, his heirs, at considerable loss of actual and potential income, retired to *rentier* roles.[34]

Presumably, the strong preferences which many landowners expressed for their agricultural as compared with their non-agricultural properties were neither testimonies to their dislike of money nor simple bucolic affectations, but measures of their realization that relationships having to do with agricultural property could be the source of power in ways in which relationships having to do with non-agricultural property could never be. Contemporaneous changes of relationship underline the point. While the Gower family and numerous others were substituting leases for direct exploitation of their non-agricultural properties many landowners were reinforcing the nexus which their agricultural properties provided by substituting tenancies-at-will for leases. In part, the merit of a tenancy-at-will was its flexibility. A lease specified the rent to be paid over many years. A tenancy-at-will was available for re-negotiation each year. As such it was more appropriate to the circumstances of significant price fluctuation. But in all probability tenancies-at-will were substituted for leases less for economic than for social reasons. A tenant-at-will was structurally dependent in a way a leaseholder was not: he could be evicted at six months' notice. In one respect the political importance of his precarious status was often exaggerated. Notwithstanding the allegations of various mid-century Radicals, the county voters who qualified as £50 tenants-at-will, the so-called Chandos clause voters, did not manifest any greater political agreement with their landlords than did other categories of county voter. Where such agreement obtained it was manifest by all categories. In effect, such agreement was not the consequence of the specific legal position of the individual tenant-at-will. Rather, it was a measure of the ramifications of the estate itself.[35] However, while wrong on the details of their case, the Radicals were right in the larger context. Within this context leases were symbols of tenant independence, tenancies-at-will of estate cohesion. They expressed that concept of territory implicit in the suggestion, in the early years of the century, that the owner of a great house emblazon the surrounding milestones with his coat of arms.[36] Also they expressed those concepts of status and discipline which were implicit in the description, some years later, of the sheriff, attended by forty or fifty liveried tenants on horseback, all waiting on the road some distance outside the county town for the arrival of the circuit judge. By the nineteenth century there was no longer any real power attached to the office of sheriff. It was almost purely honorary, held for a year by prominent county landowners in succession. Indeed, as the description of the waiting sheriff and his liveried tenants suggests, what made the office worthwhile was the opportunity it provided to display the symbols of personal status. The judge, when he finally arrived, moved from his own to the sheriff's carriage and the troop then proceeded into town, trumpeters going before.[37]

IV

In the mid-1830s, using a variation of Russell's argument about the two sections of the aristocracy, Archibald Alison, the Tory writer, claimed that the aristocracy had brought the reform crisis upon themselves. In part his variation took the form of describing as sequential what Russell described as contemporaneous. 'Formerly,' he declared,

> the great families lived for the greater part of the year upon their estates, and opened their magnificent mansions to all their neighbours; ... The young men of talent in their vicinity looked to these palaces as the centre of their promotion, ... and the families in the county were linked to them, not merely by similarity of feeling and principle, but the recollection of happiness, experience, and favour conferred ... under their roof. It was this mysterious compound of gratitude, admiration, and flattered ambition, which produced the influence of the great families.

But now all this was changed. The aristocracy had cut themselves off from 'their natural supporters and friends in their own counties and vicinity'. Not only did they spend more time in London, they brought their London ways back to the countryside. When the season was over and those rounds of rural entertaining were begun which took them from one great house to another, they still consorted only with themselves. In consequence, they knew 'as little of the people, whose support is necessary to preserve their own estates or honours from the clutches of the Radicals as they ... [did] of the Kalmucs or Hindoos'. Nor did their neighbours know them 'even ... by sight'. But, Alison went on, it was not too late for them to restore their influence. Indeed, as he described it, the very 'hatred at the Aristocracy' was a measure of their potential influence once they had mended their ways. For what the hatred expressed was that disappointment and anger which they could readily soothe by abandoning their 'exclusive system', by reopening 'their magnificent mansions to all their neighbours'.[38]

That the aristocracy restored their influence during the middle years of the century is beyond question. Presumably, in part, they did so by restoring the various nexuses which the 'exclusive system' had weakened. But the question cannot be answered whether they restored these nexuses for instrumental reasons of the sort which Alison described, or to accommodate themselves to the circumstances which the first Reform Act created, or because they came to share those corporate and hierarchical values which Russell attributed to that section of the aristocracy which 'evince[d] private worth and public virtue'. And, principally, the question cannot be answered because the three alternatives explain much the same behaviour. Fundamentally, the influence of the aristocracy, like that of the various other nineteenth-century elites, derived from those differentials of personal power and wealth which, until the state intruded to set the limits of contractual agreement, made one man dependent on another. The consequent networks of debt, loyalty, and animosity were the fabric of which the society was woven. They defined obligations and the limits of obligation. They provided the rationalizations of status and the grounds on which both the status and the rationalizations were criticized. And they explain the intimate connection between social relations and political action: in many cases these networks served as mechanisms of electoral recruitment. In their most dramatic form, perhaps, these mechanisms were reflected in the widespread patterns of local electoral agreement in the counties. Such agreement was most apparent on the larger aristocratic estates. But it was not limited to them. Nor were networks of debt and loyalty limited to the countryside. They existed in many boroughs, where their political impact was considerable.[39] During the middle years of the century, however, the clearest networks were those which centred on the larger landed estates; the clearest symbols of status and power were rural. As Sir Gilbert Scott, the architect, explained in the late 1850s while discussing the message which a great house was supposed to convey,

> Wealth must always bring its responsibility, but a landed proprietor is especially in a responsible position. He is the natural head of his parish or district—in which he should be looked up to as the bond of union between the classes. To him the poor man should look up for protection; those in doubt or difficulty for advice; the ill disposed for reproof or punishment; the deserving, of all classes, for consideration and hospitality; and *all* for a dignified, honourable and Christian example. . . . He has been blessed with wealth, and he need not shirk from using it in its proper degree. He has been placed by Providence in a position of authority and dignity, and no false modesty should deter him from expressing this, quietly and gravely, in the character of his house.[40]

Presumably, Scott's argument not only gratified the existing owners of great houses but those others as well who were approaching the point where they might reasonably hope to convert their own enterprise into authority. That such a conversion was considered natural is suggested by the refusal, in 1868, of the tenants on a recently sold mid-Cheshire estate to respond to election canvassers until they had received their new landlord's licence to do so.[41]

Authority was the principal adjunct of wealth and, during the middle years of the century, land was the principal symbol of authority. Presumably it was this rather than any anticipation of significant increments of rent which explains why both the prices of rural land and the numbers of great houses being built or remodelled rose into the early 1870s.[42] And presumably, too, what put a stop to these rising prices and this increased construction and remodelling some years before rents peaked in the late 1870s was the weakening of the conceptual distinction between the towns as seas of social turmoil and the countryside as a haven of calm, the tarnishing of the image of authority and dignity which the aristocracy had managed to preserve—and, it would seem, to preserve not because of their entrepreneurial roles but precisely because so many of them had withdrawn from such roles. The question remains, which was more important: the insubordination of those tenants who protested the 'unfairness' of the usual estate arrangements—those by which their landlords determined the tenants' and the landlords' rights—or that of the agricultural labourers who joined Joseph Arch's National Agricultural Labourers' Union? As an American observed at the time, the rapid spread of unionism in the countryside in the early 1870s was traumatic. For a while it was feared that 'the helots . . . [would] rise'.[43] They did not do so. Indeed, their behaviour was quite moderate. But together with that of the tenants, many of whom were demanding that their landlords' powers of determining rights be transferred to the state, it added an important condition to the message which Scott had described: there was no guarantee that what had been inherited, bought or built as an agency of social control and personal aggrandizement might not turn out to be a bad investment. The relationship between landownership and power was, in fact, contingent.

During the middle years of the century this contingency had been obscured. As long as the ultimate sources of political power were those personal networks of debt and loyalty which explain why open voting remained possible, land was the pre-eminent symbol of authority. The rituals and displays often associated with it were impressive. But these were epiphenomena—the great houses remodelled to accommodate the increased numbers of servants which custom required;[44] the *ancien régime* liveries; the practice of hiring footmen by the size of their calves, which these liveries undoubtedly encouraged;[45] even that exalted concern for precedence which was such an important social and cultural preoccupation.[46] What was crucial were the realities of relationship to which Viscount Royston implicitly referred when he observed in 1868 that his father, the Earl of Hardwicke, and the Duke of Rutland, both 'greater owners of land' in Cambridgeshire, 'were not such bigoted donkeys as to suppose they could return whom they thought proper; at the same time, they had undoubtedly the right to nominate such persons to represent the county whom they thought would be most acceptable to the constituents'.[47] According to the logic of the argument, those whom the constituents found 'most acceptable' were Hardwicke's and Rutland's relatives. One or another member of Hardwicke's family filled one of the three county seats in every Parliament between 1832 and 1879. A member of Rutland's family filled another of these seats in a sizeable number of these Parliaments. Presumably, the 'right' to which Royston referred derived in part from that combination of wealth and status which Hardwicke and Rutland both possessed in the county. It was such a combination which the editor of the North Lincolnshire poll book for 1852 recognized when he observed that 'a nobleman or gentleman representing a powerful party, and possessing the confidence of that party . . . exercises only the legitimate sway of property and character combined . . . [when he selects] a particular candidate'. But the 'constitutional power to nominate' was perverted into an 'unconstitutional power to dominate' when the necessary 'confidence' was lacking.[48] Nor was the distinction he made quite as difficult to apply as it might seem. Within limits the measure of constitutionality was political success.

To a large extent what preserved these networks were the political functions they performed—or, to put it differently, the political system in which these functions could be performed. As Alison described the first Reform Act, it was far less a threat to the powers of the aristocracy than it was to their way of life—their 'exclusive system,' he called it. Whatever the degree to which this 'system' was abandoned after 1832, at least in terms of images and the related concepts of legitimacy, power in society and state was enjoyed by those who behaved as Alison said they should. The conditions which made this possible were quite specific. Essentially they had to do with the continuing importance of patronage in all manner of activities public and private, the limited role of the state in these circumstances, and the continuing possibility of geographically separating the different gross categories of network—what was done by the constituency boundary commissioners in 1832 and what was attempted by them in 1868, by which time the earlier arrangements had lost their relevance.[49] Indeed, as the efforts and implied needs of 1868 suggest, the significance of these boundaries could no more be preserved indefinitely than the networks could be preserved whose strength depended in part upon them.

By the mid-1880s, in just about every constituency in the kingdom, the right to nominate had been transferred from the hands of the various elites who enjoyed their powers in respect of their 'property and character' into the hands of committees most of which were formally elected. In some cases the members of these committees were hangovers from the earlier dispensation. In others the very establishment of an elected committee was the means of transferring power out of the hands of such men. But whichever the case, the formation of such committees and the related emergence of mass membership political parties reflected crucial changes in the nature and locus of authority in society and state. The effective agencies of social organization and social control were no longer those which the earlier networks and the 'confidence' which derived from them had served to mobilize. A generation later, when the Parliament Act was passed, the formal constitutional implications of this were recognized. It was only possible to maintain the co-ordinate powers of the House of Lords and the House of Commons as long as the members of the one enjoyed a significant influence in the other.

These changes involved far more than the substitution of urban for rural leaders and networks. The processes are apparent in town as well as in the country-side. Many old networks of debt and loyalty were replaced by new ones. But the more important changes had to do with the replacement of hierarchical discretion by standardized wisdom and bureaucratic procedure. Within this new system many members of the aristocracy continued to claim elite status. But increasingly, those whose claims were honoured based their claims less upon their roles as landowners than upon their wealth alone or their participation in those new agencies of social control which were located in Whitehall and, in particular, in the City. And in both places, as the growing numbers of endogenous peers suggests, the role as peer enjoyed a fresh importance.

Notes

1 Rubinstein, 1977, 103.
2 *Hansard* 3rd series, XXXIX (1837); *Hansard* 4th series, LXXXVIII (1900).
3 Bateman, 1971, 495.
4 F. M. L. Thompson, 1963, 28–9.
5 Pine, 1961.
6 Pumphrey, 1934, ch. 5; Pumphrey, 1959, 9; Alfred Tennyson as Baron Tennyson, Sir William Thomson as Baron Kelvin, Sir Joseph Lister as Baron Lister and Sir Frederick Leighton as Baron Leighton.
7 Sanford and Townsend, 1865, I, 9–10.
8 *Ibid.*, I, 11.
9 Hollingsworth, 1965, 8–9.
10 F. M. L. Thompson, 1977, 44, footnote 26.
11 *Hansard* 3rd series, VII (4 October 1831), 1193–4.
12 Quoted in Butler, 1914, 255.
13 *Hansard* 3rd series, II (1 March 1831), 225.
14 Moore, 1976, especially chs 5 and 6.
15 Sanford and Townsend, 1865, I, 14.
16 *Ibid.*, I, 15.
17 *Ibid.*, I, 14.
18 Malet, 1961.
19 Spring, 1963, *passim.*
20 Spring, 1951, 6.
21 Cannadine, 1977, *passim.*
22 Stone, 1965, 338–9.
23 F. M. L. Thompson, 1963, 264–8; Ward, 1971, 72; Richards, 1974, *passim.*
24 Sanford and Townsend, 1865, I, 112.
25 Jenks, 1899, 84–5.
26 Taine, 1957, 181.
27 Girouard, 1971, 1.
28 Bateman, 1971, 472.
29 Huxley, 1967, 18, 66.
30 Spring, 1971, 41.
31 Spring, 1963, 43.
32 Jenks, 1899, 85; Spring, 1963, 43.
33 Spring, 1963, 43.
34 Richards, 1974b, *passim.*
35 Olney, 1973, 138; Moore, 1976, 50 ff.
36 Stroud, 1962, 13.
37 Howitt, 1840, 83–4.
38 Alison, 1834, *passim.*
39 Joyce, 1975, *passim.*
40 Quoted in Girouard, 1971, 2.
41 BPP 1868–9 VIII, Q. 6,427.
42 F. M. L. Thompson, 1957, 294; Girouard, 1971, 6.

43 Badeau, 1886, 288.

44 Franklin, 1975, *passim.*

45 Badeau, 1886, 20; Taine, 1957, 40.

46 Badeau, 1886, 52.

47 *Cambridge Independent Press*, 25 January 1868.

48 North Lincolnshire Poll Book, 1852, xii.

49 Moore, 1976, ch. 9.

28 The Gentry

D. C. Moore

I

In the 1830s when John Burke began publishing the directory now known as Burke's *Landed Gentry*, the word 'gentry' was not included in the title. What he published was *A Genealogical and Heraldic History of the Commoners of Great Britain and Ireland, Enjoying Territorial Possessions or High Official Rank; but Uninvested with Heritable Honours*. A decade later 'gentry' replaced 'commoners'. Whatever the specific reasons for this it is symptomatic of an important process of social redefinition and political consolidation. The conceptual boundaries surrounding the nobility were being reduced and replaced by new boundaries surrounding an enlarged aristocracy to which the gentry belonged but to which commoners did not belong.

Conceptual boundaries are important. They set limits. They imply roles. They reflect fantasies. To some extent they mirror reality and condition reality. Several generations earlier Samuel Johnson had defined a gentleman as 'a man of birth; a man of extraction, though', he added, thereby dividing the sheep from the goats, 'not noble'. His two boundaries were applied to the gentry by various nineteenth-century lexicographers. In *The Imperial Dictionary* of 1850, for example, John Ogilvie explained that the gentry were 'the classes of people between the nobility and the vulgar'. But in the eyes of John Burke, of his son, collaborator and successor, John Bernard Burke; and of numerous others, the social world was differently divided. In particular, their vision is revealed in the 'Essay on the Position of the British Gentry' by the Reverend John Hamilton Gray which appeared as a preface to the fourth edition of *Landed Gentry* published in 1862. According to Gray the restriction of the epithet 'noble' to members of the peerage was 'an abuse of terms'. The real denizens of England understood the truth, that 'the well-born English gentleman was in fact a nobleman', even though, having no title, he might call himself a commoner. But, Gray observed—and, presumably, his observation helps to explain Burke's substitution of gentry for commoner—most foreigners and many natives tended to regard all those who called themselves commoners as members of 'the "Bourgeoisie," the "Roture"'.[1] From this point of view this was an error.

To correct the error Gray described boundaries which reflect social and provincial, instead of legal and constitutional, criteria. The House of Lords scarcely figured, nor the roles of the men who received individual summons to advise the monarch; rather 'the constant marrying and giving in marriage between . . . [the gentry] and the peerage'; not the laws of succession to peerages which distinguished a single heir but the relations among the siblings from whom the heir was chosen. Time was important: the length of a pedigree. And since the length of a pedigree was really a measure of the length of time a family had owned significant amounts of land, land was important. Indeed, for the *echt* aristocracy whose definition was essential to his definition of the gentry, time and land took precedence over any other claims. As he explained,

> an immense majority of the existing peers are mere mushrooms when
> compared with a large proportion of our country gentry, who are much
> better entitled to be considered noble, because their families were
> established as a county aristocracy at a date when their lordships' ancestors
> did not possess an acre of land.[2]

As he noted, however, with obvious chagrin, what made these mushrooms less than oaks applied to the gentry as well. He admitted the point even though it 'tended greatly to complicate [his] . . . position . . .: men who have risen from humble rank to wealth [have tended] to consolidate that wealth on landed possessions'. As such, whether or not they ultimately managed 'to establish themselves among the territorial aristocracy of the country',[3] they were engaged in a process whose very recognition eroded the boundaries he emphasized. Obviously, those who claimed the pedigrees which elicited the contempt of Edward A. Freeman and J. Horace Round[4] were trying to strengthen these boundaries. Possibly Freeman was right in saying that the needs they felt 'to have come in with the Conqueror or else to be older than the conquest sap[ped] every principle of truth'.[5] But sometimes the sort of truth to which he referred is less significant than the needs which, prompting its violation, illustrate another truth.

The consolidation of wealth on land was an old practice. It was the price men paid for the status of gentleman; also, for a share of the power landowners enjoyed. Gray's insistence on distinguishing the gentry from the commoners, his refusal to recognize any distinction between the gentry and the nobility, were his contributions to the preservation of the world in which landowners retained land and power. That others contributed as well is apparent, among other things, from the fact that they continued to consolidate wealth on land. Whether they did so in spite of the accelerating growth of commercial and industrial wealth and power or because of it—whether traditional symbols were compelling because they were traditional or because the others contained too many reminders of the market place—there was no urban patrician class to speak of in Britain in the mid-nineteenth century. Possibly, for a time, the leaders of the Anti-Corn Law League threatened to create an alternative hierarchy. But this was only temporary. During most of the century real status was only available within a traditional rural context. The yearning for this status, which helped to preserve its locus and the locus of power with which it was associated, was an important political, social and cultural fact.

At one level of ambition or attainment this yearning is apparent in the observation that 'a citizen engaged in business [in a town]' would not want to build a villa from which the town could be seen.[6] At another level it is apparent in the increase in the numbers of licences issued to display a coat of arms on writing paper or cutlery. In 1830 there were roughly 7,000 or these; in 1855, 25,000; in 1868, 43,000. This was a peak, somewhat above the plateau which obtained for the rest of the century.[7] Fewer men were involved at those higher levels of which Gray spoke. The question remains how inclusion in Burke's *History of the Commoners* or his *Dictionary of the Landed Gentry* or, later, his son's *History of the Landed Gentry*, was determined. But the first contained genealogies of fewer than two thousand families. By the 1860s the son's *History* contained genealogies of more than four thousand. Whatever the real enlargement this represents—the number includes many younger sons—further enlargements were inhibited by the insistence that landownership was, as the editors of *Landed Gentry* put it in 1894, the principal 'test of rank and position'.[8] And when, on the eve of the First World War, they modified their criteria for inclusion it was not really to change these criteria. As the editors of *Landed Gentry* explained in 1914, they had abandoned their former policy of deleting families which had 'severed their connections with their ancestral homes' because of 'the vicious and crushing burden of taxation dictated by the hatred of the landowner ... [and] the nightmare of the Death duties [which] converted ... land from an investment into a luxury to be maintained from extraneous sources'.[9] Indeed, in the circumstances they described, to have continued their earlier policy would have been tantamount to disloyalty. Nor was much change to be anticipated immediately from their other decision, to assimilate the imperial consuls by according gentry status to those men 'who have never owned land, but have won their way to distinction and position in the service of the King and in other ways'.[10] Whatever was meant by 'other ways', many of the men who served the king were recruited from gentry families. Ultimately, the impact of these new criteria might be important, but less so than those which Edward Walford had described some years earlier. Indeed, in his *County Families*, first published in 1860, Walford suggested elite boundaries which did less to resist the changing distributions of wealth and power in the nineteenth century than to accommodate them. He not only included 'the titled and untitled aristocracy' in a single list, he claimed as a point of national pride that each edition of his manual would be somewhat out of date by the time it appeared. 'In a country like our own', he explained, 'mainly owing to the influence of trade and commerce, . . . [there would always be a] constant addition of fresh families.'[11] He was as eager to include these as the editors of *Landed Gentry* were reluctant. In 1860 many of his families had not yet bought land. Presumably some never bought any. Gray's stumblings among the ironies of mobility and status reveal the ambiguities of the criteria which he, the editors of *Landed Gentry* and numerous others tried to perpetuate. Whether Walford's criteria are really any less ambiguous in an ultimate sense, they have much to say about the social systems which were coming into being towards the end of Victoria's reign just as the others have much to say about those they were replacing, those which the first Reform Act reflected and reinforced.

II

The Reform Act was crucial in the history of the class Gray defined. Not only did it abolish the rotten boroughs, those symbols of aristocratic and 'illegitimate' power— the power of property abstracted from a social context—but in so far as possible it isolated rural from urban Britain, the counties from the towns. It provided the urban elites with constituencies of their own—in such a way as provided the rural elites with a respite from the political effects which the growth of towns had been having on the counties.[12] Status and class were fundamental to its formula—but these as defined in the light of rural criteria. The principal reformers' model was the landed estate, their goal the reinforcement and generalization of this model. As Lord John Russell had explained some time before, once the unrepresented towns were enfranchised the local elites would be encouraged to exercise an 'authority' within them to which their otherwise restless neighbours 'could conform'.[13]

The assumptions underlying Russell's statement acquired their logic from that society in which power was more a function of status than of money, and status was more a function of landownership than of position in court or government; from that state in which, as James Anthony Froude observed some year later, 'private ownership in land is permitted because Government cannot be omnipresent'.[14] To many men who deplored the 'illegitimate' powers of the rotten borough patrons and who feared the seemingly ungovernable multitudes of the burgeoning towns, landed estates represented symbols of 'legitimate' power and havens of social stability. Whatever the cogency of the notion that a constitutional reformation could be based on the landed estate model, Lytton Bulwer implicitly explained the notion when, in the early 1830s, he explained why many country gentlemen, when seen in London, were 'fussy, conceited . . . and pompous', who, when seen at home, were 'easy, dignified and natural'. In London the evidence of their status was lacking. But on their own estates and, by extension, in their own counties, it was not.[15] The point is

92 *right* Charles Francis Massingberd-Mundy, D.L.,
J.P. (1839–1913), photographed at South Ormsby Hall,
1900. He came from a long line of Lincolnshire
landowners noted for their work in the agricultural
improvement of the wolds (Hallgarth Collection)

93 *below left* Colonel de Burton in uniform at
Buckminster Hall, Billingborough, Lincolnshire
(Hallgarth Collection)

94 *below right* Mrs de Burton in her Victoria at the
main door of Buckminster Hall about 1898. She died in
1905 from an accident while driving in this carriage
(Hallgarth Collection)

95 *above* Family, servants and dogs at Moated Grange, Somersby, east of Horncastle, Lincs (Hallgarth Collection)

96 *above right* Conversation piece at Old Bolingbroke, near Spilsby, Lincolnshire: on the left is William Stone, the squire of the village; the flamboyant figure on the right, somewhat reminiscent of Theodore Roosevelt, is a water diviner (Hallgarth Collection)

97 *right* Hawarden Castle about 1890: servants pose with the implements appropriate to their work (Clwyd Record Office)

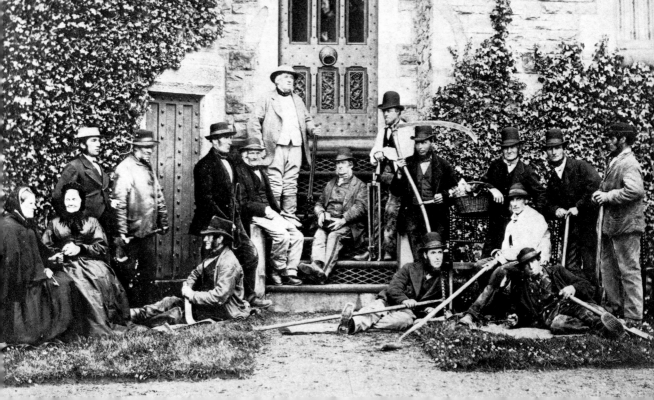

98 *above* The well-to-do farmer's domestic staff: servants at Poplar Farm, Hollesley, Suffolk, pose with the tools of their trade (Suffolk Photographic Survey)

99 *above right* Abberley Hall, Worcestershire. An Italianite house by Samuel Daukes, built *c.* 1846 with an asymmetrically placed tower (From a sale catalogue, BM Maps 137b 11 (16))

100 *right* Stoke Rochford Hall, Lincolnshire, built 1841–5 by William Burn in typically early Victorian Elizabethan (National Monument Record)

101 *above* The Hall in Hafodunos House, Denbighshire, built by C. G. Scott, 1861–6: church detail in a domestic setting (National Monument Record of Wales)

102 *below* Possingworth Manor, East Sussex, by M. D. Wyatt, 1865–70: high Victorian verticality at its most extreme (*Builder*, 1868, XXVI, 713)

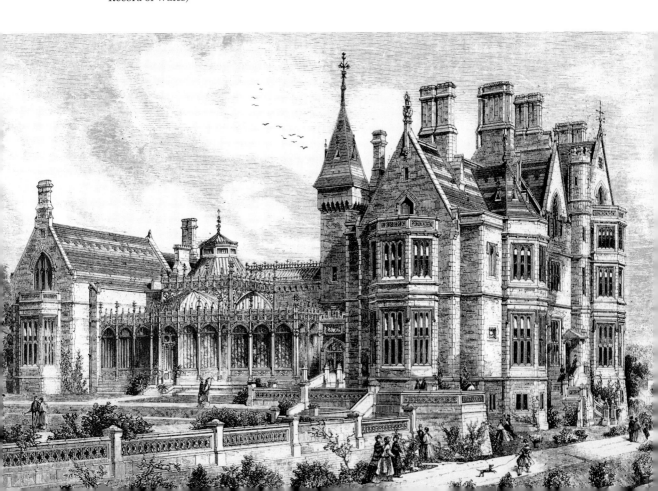

103 *above* Bestwood Lodge near Nottingham by
S. S. Teulon, 1862: asymmetry, broken outline, much
structural decoration. The 'chapel' on the left was the
servants' hall (*Builder*, 1863, XXI, 639)

104 *below* Hemsted House, Kent, by David Brandon,
1859–62: Jacobean asymmetry plus a high French roof
over the tower and a diagonal staircase window. Now
Benenden School and considerably altered (*Builder*,
1862, XX, 243)

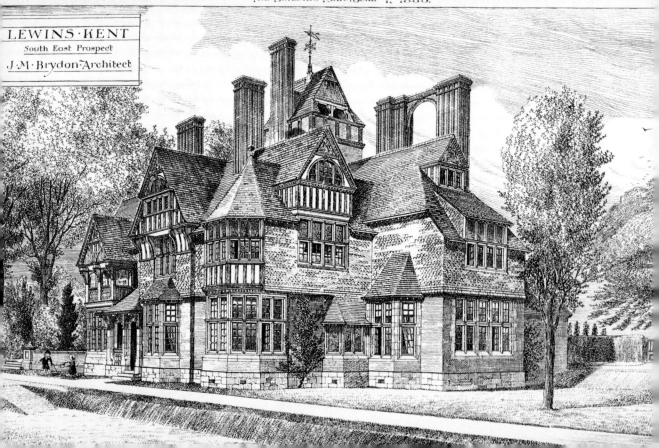

LEWINS·KENT
South East Prospect
J·M·Brydon Architect

105 *above left* Merrist Wood,
Worplesdon, Surrey, by Norman
Shaw, 1875–7: stone, half-
timbering, brick and tile hanging,
brilliantly combined (Photo:
National Monument Record:
copyright: Batsford)

106 *left* Lewins, Crockham Hill,
Kent by J. M. Brydon, 1876–83: the
same ingredients as at Merrist
Wood, used on a larger and taller
house (*Building News*, 1883, XLIV,
750)

107 *above* Avon Tyrell,
Hampshire, by W. R. Lethaby,
1891–2: a late Victorian, free
adaptation of Tudor (*Country Life*)

108 *above* Perrycroft, Colwall, Herefordshire, by C. F. A. Voysey, 1893–4. The slate roof, roughcast walls and strange chimneys are right outside the country house tradition (*British Architect*, 1895, XLIV, 437)

109 *left* Bryanston, Dorset, by Norman Shaw, 1889–94: English baroque revived for the last Whig palace

110 *above* Redcourt, Haslemere, Surrey,
by Ernest Newton, 1893–4: the beginning
of Edwardian neo-Georgian, still with
gables and some arts and crafts detail
(National Monument Record)

111 *right* Batsford Park,
Gloucestershire, by Ernest George and
Peto, 1887–93. A correct Tudor design
showing the late Victorian return to
horizontality and almost complete
symmetry (National Monument Record)

112 *above* An early Victorian version of a celebration in the mediaeval great hall of Haddon Hall (Joseph Nash, *The Mansions of England in the Olden Time*, 1838, new edition 1869, plate XXV)

113 *left* The dining hall at Bilton Grange, Warwickshire, by A. W. N. Pugin, 1841–6: an early Victorian great hall with open timber roof (*Illustrated London News* 1855, XXVI, 93)

114 The billiard room at Thurland Castle, Lancashire, by Paley & Austin, 1879–95, fitted out in a very masculine style with leather chairs and stuffed shooting trophies (National Monument Record. A Bedford Lemere photograph)

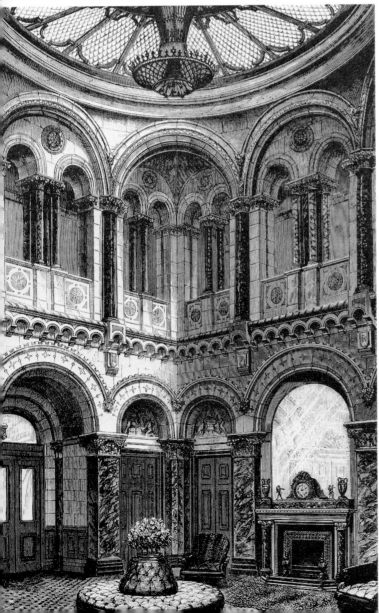

115 *above* Halton House, Buckinghamshire, probably by W. R. Rogers, 1882–8. A classical, top-lit saloon, planned in a similar way to that at Dobroyd Castle, but now used as the principal living room (National Monument Record. A Bedford Lemere photograph)

116 *left* A classical top-lit saloon at Dobroyd Catle, West Yorkshire, by John Gibson, 1865–9. Carpeted and with seats, this hall is still not really a living room. The upper galleries give access to the bedrooms (*Builder*, 1875, XXXIII, 953)

117 Rhinefeld Lodge, Hampshire, by Romaine Walker, 1888–90: a great hall in late Tudor style with hammerbeam roof. It includes a screens passage and minstrels gallery, but the small oriel window on the left opens out of the boudoir, where chaperones could sit comfortably and keep an eye on the party below (National Monument Record. A Bedfore Lemere photograph)

118　The entrance hall at Thurland Castle: a single-storey hall used as sitting room (National Monument Record. A Bedford Lemere photograph)

important not only because a good disposition is important but also because it describes the context of satisfaction of the men who were principally responsible for the legal basis of the socio-political system which came into being after 1832. Nor is it altogether surprising that most members of the real nobility were in a position to enjoy these satisfactions even more than they. Rather, it helps to explain the conceptual assimilation which Gray described. What they had in common were landed estates.

Estates were sources of wealth. Even more important, they were means of organizing and controlling large portions of the population at a time when rival agencies of organization and control simply did not exist and when government was constrained from interfering with landowners' powers both by appropriate doctrine and by the presence of many members of the aristocracy and gentry within it. As late as the mid-1880s the editor of the *Fortnightly Review* could observe, not wholly inaccurately, that 'the great landlords of England are really the rulers of principalities'.[16] A decade earlier Froude called them 'petty monarchs'.[17] Earlier still, Disraeli declared that government could not be carried on without the 'united aid and agency' of various institutions, among them 'the hereditary tenure of land'.[18] His explanation was absurdly dramatic, that 'in hours of peril and perplexity, external and domestic, landed estates offer something around which men may rally and save the State'. But the point is no less important. Landed estates were major foci of loyalty.

Alexander had noted this point in the early years of the century. As he observed, the next best thing to being Tsar of Russia was to be an English country gentleman.[19] Within the law the powers of these men on their own estates were almost absolute. They set the conditions on which others led their lives. Also, they determined who would lead these lives, who they would allow to remain upon their estates, who they would send away. Ultimately, the powers of these men were limited. But the processes by which these limitations were effected suggest that limitation was not intentional.

The man Froude cited in the 1870s to show 'the uses of a landed gentry' was a Benthamite named Smith who had taken a long lease on Crown property in the Scilly Isles. Thus, technically, in that part of the world where Froude described his activities he was not a landowner. But for the period of the lease the powers of the one were comparable to the powers of the other and, ostensibly, Smith used his powers as Froude believed he should. When he acquired his lease the islands were 'a rabbit warren of paupers'. When he died they were 'a thriving community of industrious men and women'. All this, ostensibly, because he had combined small holdings into large, had provided alternative work for those thus deprived of their 'potato patches', had built schools and chapels, had stopped drunkenness with a 'high hand', and with an equally high hand had decided who might remain on the islands, who might not. Presumably, those who remained enjoyed the conditions he set and benefited from them. Nor should the point be ignored that even though at his death the value of the islands was much greater than when he took the lease, his own profits from the enterprise had been less than his expenses. The difference was the price of that *noblesse oblige* which, from Froude's point of view, provided the gentry's essential rationale. To those who did not subscribe to the gentry ideal as Froude described it, the observation was clearly provocative: 'paternal government may be detestable when you have the wrong sort of father'.[20] Nor would they have agreed with his implication that one of the essential functions of law was to control such 'wrong fathers'.

The complete gentry role required participation in formal as well as informal government and, if possible, on the formal level in the national as well as the local arena. Thus it was only available to a few, those with large rent rolls whose debts, whether inherited or self-incurred, did not seriously limit their expenditures, and those who somehow managed to win election to Parliament. The season in their own houses in London, the rest of the year on their own estates—for this some £10,000 a year might be necessary, signifying an agricultural estate of very considerable size, or considerable income from such non-agricultural sources as urban ground rents or mineral royalties. Until the later decades of the century relatively few landowners had significant incomes from other varieties of non-agricultural source and few men other than landowners had such incomes.[21] Most of those who had such incomes were peers. But many on the fringe were not. Together, these comprised the national elite. Until 1905 members of this elite filled most of the cabinet offices; until 1888 they had an effective legal monopoly of county government; until 1880 those of them who were not peers filled most of the seats in Parliament for all but the newer boroughs, and even for some of those. Writing in the 1850s, Walter Bagehot attributed their continued political predominance to the fact that land was still almost the only investment 'not requiring sedulous personal attention, and not liable to be affected by political vicissitudes'. In consequence, he declared, 'all opulence gravitates towards the land. Political opulence does so particularly.'[22]

The point is not to be denied. But it explains rather less than it describes. Most political money was *rentier* money not because most would-be politicians became *rentiers*—although that was the case—but rather because the paths to power of many *rentiers* were smoothed both by their recognition of one another as participants in a common culture and, even more, by the willingness of others, their various dependants in particular, to acknowledge their leadership. Hence the importance of the communities in which these dependancy relationships obtained. Hence, too, the importance of the efforts to preserve these communities against the rising tide of that cosmopolitanism which, as Gray implied, was eroding the social foundations of the understanding that 'the well-born English gentleman was in fact a nobleman'. As participants in a common culture these men endured the same education, were satiated by the same recreations, worshipped in the same churches, married one another's daughters, and transmitted property by the same devices. Once the rotten boroughs were abolished they enjoyed political powers which, however these might differ in degree, tended to rise from the same ultimate source, their roles as 'petty monarchs'. In no county was it possible for an individual 'monarch' to determine the outcome of a parliamentary contest; it was possible in only a few of the boroughs. But in many counties their alliances and coalitions were crucial. In many boroughs the pattern was somewhat replicated, thus the taste developed for the enjoyment of that power which landownership itself provided. And in 1867–8 and, again, in 1884–5 efforts were made to preserve the contexts in which such powers obtained wherever it was possible to do so against the tides of social change and population movement.[23]

Obviously, the wish to play the role of petty monarch helps to explain the prices sometimes paid for rural land in the 1860s and early 1870s, thirty and even forty years' purchase of the rental value[24]—far beyond anything which rational economics might explain. Obviously, too, criticism of the way the role was sometimes played helps to explain the mounting chorus of urban complaint about the continuing influence of the aristocracy and gentry. But the real issues did not concern the behaviour of individuals. They concerned the powers of a class. The fact that many of the critics had a sneaking admiration for the class—indeed, that in some respects their criticisms were the expression of their unrealized fantasies—rendered their attacks peculiarly moderate. But they were no less clear. The class they criticized was open. But few gained admission. It was not a caste. But the admission fee was high—and high, in part, because the pressure for admission helped to drive up the price of rural land. The critics understood the social and political importance of estates. But many of them tended to regard estates more as agencies of coercion than as socio-economic communities. By the same token, they tended to attribute the aggregations of land which these estates represented rather more to the law than to the desires of those who used the law—rather more to the constraints the law imposed in cases of intestacy, when it directed the transmission of landed property to a single male heir, or, somewhat more reasonably, to the constraints the law allowed each landowner to impose upon his heirs, than to the decisions of individuals to consolidate their wealth on land or to retain such consolidations. Furthermore, they tended to claim that many estates were uneconomically large—that they were owned by men who lacked the capital necessary to enable their tenants to maximize production. In consequence—so their arguments ran—as population grew the balance of trade was adversely affected. Money was exported to pay for food which, otherwise, would have been produced domestically. Furthermore, serious problems arose as men congregated in the towns who had neither a future in the countryside nor, indeed, in the towns themselves—the one because land was inaccessible, the other because the capital was being exported to pay for food which should have provided them with jobs.[25]

In the early 1870s, in the hope that these criticisms would stop if evidence were educed to show that landownership was far more widely diffused than the critics contended, a national survey of landownership was undertaken.[26] However the folly be explained which this hope serves to illustrate, the resulting evidence scarcely proved the case it was supposed to prove. It showed that slightly more than half of England was contained in estates of more than 1,000 acres, a size often used to distinguish gentry estates from those owned by men of lesser status. Roughly 400 peers and peeresses owned estates in England and Wales which averaged somewhat over 14,000 acres; roughly 1,300 'great landowners' who were not peers owned estates which averaged somewhat less than 7,000 acres; roughly 2,500 squires or lesser gentry owned estates which averaged somewhat over 1,700 acres.[27] Most of the larger estates were some distance from London. Indeed, half of Northumberland and more than half of Rutland were contained in estates of over 10,000 acres. Estates of over 3,000 acres covered almost three-quarters of these counties and more than half of Nottinghamshire, Dorset, Wiltshire, Shropshire and Cheshire. But such estates covered less than a third of Essex and Surrey, and only 15 per cent of Middlesex. Estates of between 1,000 and 3,000 acres were somewhat more evenly distributed. But those of between 300 and 1,000 acres were less so. While covering roughly 20 per cent of Surrey, Essex and Kent, and slightly less of Middlesex, they covered only 5 per cent of Rutland and 7 per cent of Northumberland.[28]

In the 1873 edition of *Landed Gentry* families 'established' in the eighteenth and early nineteenth centuries constitute some three-quarters of the listings for Essex, but only two fifths of those for Shropshire.[29] Obviously, the home counties had become something of a dormitory area for those who hoped to achieve gentry status long before railways made such an area a real possibility. When the possibility was fully realized the rate of turnover of estates in the London area increased sharply, especially the rate of turnover of the smaller estates. Ostensibly, in the middle years of the century, in a region some fifteen miles from London, the average time an estate remained in the same family was only twenty years.[30] By and large, however, such were the smaller estates. The larger estates were rarely sold.[31] In effect, while the smaller estates, especially in the London area, changed hands in ways which undoubtedly detracted from their non-economic attributes, the larger estates tended to pass from generation to generation within a family in ways which undoubtedly reinforced the family's local associations and influence. These were the families which defined the gentry image. Those others which tried to share this image had come and gone in the past at something approximating the rate which caused so much grief to the editors of *Landed Gentry* when they surveyed the damage effected by the agricultural depression at the end of the century.[32]

But the reduced powers of the gentry in the later decades of the century were scarcely the consequence of political action. The evidence educed in the early 1870s did not intensify the criticism it was supposed to have silenced. Not that reason prevailed. When land was so largely valued for the status and power it conveyed it seems unlikely that the concentrations of landownership would have been reduced by facilitating land sales; indeed, possibly the very reverse. Nor was Britain's urban proletariat or her growing dependence on foreign food to be affected by restoring those somewhat mythical yeomen. In most cases the ability of gentry families to retain or enlarge their estates had more to do with the proportions of males among their offspring and the shortness of life of their widows than with the laws of primogeniture and settlement. A son brought home a dower; daughters took them away; and widows who survived for long to continue spending their jointures might so deplete a son's or grandson's income as to prompt him to build an increasingly precarious tower of debt.[33] Many townsmen remained convinced that if land settlement were forbidden and all landowners were free to dispose of their land at any time the concentrations of landownership would be reduced and production would be increased. But the powers of the gentry were not reduced in this way. Rather, their powers were reduced by factors which neither they nor their critics could control.

III

What is principally important in the history of the gentry is the usefulness of landownership as a test of status, the role of land in the rubrics of power. Others might acquire the cultural attributes whether in schools, universities or government departments,[34] thereby preserving the 'gentlemanly' idea and the concept of *noblesse oblige*, which provides such as effective means of rationalizing power. But their essence was not in these. It lay in the close historical relationship between land and power.

In part the weakening of this relationship was the consequence of the growing power which derived from other sources. Symptomatic of this process was the pride which Edward Walford expressed in 1860, that there would always be a 'constant addition of fresh families' in his manual, and the decision of the editors of *Landed Gentry*, in 1914, to accord gentry status to men 'who have never owned land, but have won their way to distinction and position in the service of the King and in other ways'. In part its weakening was the consequence of the agricultural depression, which reduced the incomes of many landowners from the peaks that were reached in the early and middle 1870s to the levels that obtained some years earlier and, in doing so, made life particularly difficult for those landowners whose indebtedness had been allowed to rise with rising rents. In part, as well, its weakening was the consequence of the changing organizational role of the landed estate, of the changing role of traditional status relationships in politics and government, and of the accelerating rural exodus and the concomitant growth of towns which, in the last half of the century, reduced the rural population of the kingdom from roughly half the total population to less than a quarter. There were, of course, political reforms. As with the first Reform Act, however, so with the second and third: these did as much if not more to shore up the powers of the existing elites in changing circumstances—the powers of the rural elites in particular—than to undermine them. Indeed, it was not so much legislation which affected the powers of these men as it was the growing omnipresence of government and the various changes of social relationship.

The organizational importance of the landed estate was not constant. It was considerably enhanced by land enclosure; also, in the context of declining prices in the immediate post-Napoleonic period, by the tendency to substitute tenancies-at-will, renewable from year to year, for leases which guaranteed many years' tenancy; and again, some years later, during what has been called the second agricultural revolution,[35] by the use of estate mechanisms to direct the application of the new techniques which the revolution comprised. Undoubtedly, many farmers initially welcomed tenancies-at-will. Whatever their loss of independence, such tenancies facilitated those adjustments of rent which, with fluctuating prices, allowed tenant and landlord to receive the proportionate incomes regarded as their due. But many farmers were less enthusiastic about the use that was made of estate mechanisms to encourage high farming. Possibly the growing sophistication of these mechanisms owed more to their economic rationale[36] than to their role in aggrandizing the powers of the 'petty monarchs'. But, whichever the case, these powers were increasingly at issue in consequence of their use in altering time-honoured procedures. As an estate agent explained in the early 1840s when pressed by tenants eager for the freedom which leases symbolized, once upon a time he, too, had been in favour of leases. But the price fluctuations of the 1820s had changed his mind. And now, when there were more questions than answers about what constituted good farming, he would only be willing 'to remove the screw if he knew his man and what he was doing'.[37]

After corn law repeal the problems of landlord–tenant relations were considerably aggravated: the issue was gone on which most landlords and farmers had been agreed, that which generally sweetened the principle that an estate should speak with one political voice. With the issue gone the disciplinary aspect of the principle became clearer. Possibly, with the increased emphasis upon production the disciplinary aspect became greater. When tenants were pressed to embark ever larger amounts of capital in the exploitation of their farms and rents were raised on the consequent increments of productivity,[38] the doctrine of mutual benefit was severely taxed. Similarly when tenants' crops were injured by game kept for their landlord's pleasure or, as the renting of shooting rights became more general, for the pleasure of those who rented these rights. Few landlords permitted their tenants to shoot. Thus, as guns became more accurate, permitting larger kills and encouraging more preservation, the game problem could become seriously divisive.

In large measure it was because tenants' grievances changed and estate mechanisms ceased to provide adequate means of redressing them that tenants increasingly appealed to the state. Understandably, such appeals prompted the pious observation on the part of various landowners, that 'life would be intolerable in any profession if men were obliged to be looking at everything in a barely legal or barely pecuniary point of view'.[39] But in the circumstances of the 1870s a rival source of intolerability was the reiteration of the principle that tenants had no rights other than those their landlords gave them.[40] A few years later, in the context of declining prices, many men insisted that the tenants' 'wrong fathers' were being adequately coerced by circumstance and need not be additionally coerced by legislation: to keep their land in cultivation they were now willing to accept almost any terms a tenant or prospective tenant might offer.[41] The view adds a dimension to Froude's argument concerning the role of law. But it was unavailing as a means of preserving the formal powers of the 'petty monarchs' or the quasi-legal integrity of the domains in which these powers were exercised. The Ground Game Act of 1880 gave tenants a legal right to kill hares and rabbits on their farms; the Agricultural Holdings Act of 1883 secured their ownership of the unexhausted value of their improvements. According to the editor of the *Fortnightly Review* such legislation would scarcely affect the largest estates. On these, he observed, 'custom will always assert its authority before that of positive law'.[42] But however long these estates retained their extra-territorial status, many of the others had already ceased to be foci of loyalty. They had become mere places of work and residence. They were still private property. Increasingly, however, government intruded to sort out the relationships between landowners and those who were no longer their dependants.

IV

However, the growing omnipresence of government was more clearly manifest in the roles of the various commissioners, assistant commissioners and inspectors who from the 1830s were increasingly active in advising and ultimately directing the operations of local authorities. For centuries such authorities in the counties had been the unpaid justices of the peace. Qualifying for their administrative and judicial roles in respect of their property and status, these men symbolized the very essence of the gentry ideal. But there lay the source of a major administrative, judicial and social problem. It was essential that these men perform their roles and perform them efficiently. But the very nature of the gentry ideal made it impossible to coerce them and difficult to guide them. Whatever the number who satisfied the principal legal qualification—ownership of land worth £100 a year, or ownership of a reversion to land worth £300 a year—and whatever the number who had been nominated by the various lords lieutenant, in 1851 there were almost 21,000 whose names had been placed on the Commissions of the Peace for the different counties of England and Wales. But in the kingdom as a whole fewer than 40 per cent of these had taken the trouble to qualify themselves so that they might act. And many of those who had did nothing more.[43] Early in the century in many counties such behaviour among the laity had resulted in magistrates' benches largely composed of clergy. Around the time of the first Reform Act the laity began returning to the bench.[44] The very need that they do so not only conditioned the discussion of their tasks but to some extent conditioned the tasks themselves. As the chairman of the Warwickshire magistrates explained in 1837 while opposing the suggestion that the magistrate's administrative responsibilities be assigned to elective boards, it was hard enough already to get sufficient magistrates to participate at the trials of prisoners at quarter sessions. They attended the meetings, usually scheduled during the first few days of the sessions, when administrative matters were dealt with which concerned them directly. Then they left. Thus, inevitably, if the magistrates were deprived of their administrative functions a total reorganization of the judicial system would be required as well.[45] Many M.P.s rose to protest against this slur upon the magistrates' much advertised devotion to duty. But in fact, while the presence of the magistrates *qua* magistrates was essential as a means of preserving the gentry ideal, their judicial functions were already performed by clerks and others, some of them magistrates themselves, who knew the law and whose roles were formalized during the course of the century by various court reforms. Indeed, in all probability the most important duty of those magistrates who did not know the law was that which the Warwickshire chairman said it was, 'their residence in the various places in the county where they lived, and where they were enabled to act as friends of the poor, and heal disputes as arbitrators and referees'.[46] Obviously what he had in mind, apart from their role in administering their own estates, was their role in administering the poor law. But in many cases, in consequence of the Poor law Amendment Act, these two roles had become one.

In the long term the creation in 1834 of a central commission to supervise poor law administration throughout the kingdom was a means of destroying the magistrates' autonomy. But in the short term it was a means of enhancing the powers of the 'petty monarchs'. How the one became the other provides an important part of the answer to the question why landownership became less useful as a test of status as the century wore on. Among the problems associated with the old poor law few were more troublesome than those which derived from the right of any magistrate to review the decisions of any overseer in his county. In part these problems were solved by depriving the magistrates of their powers of review. But such was done only to incorporate magistrates and landowners more directly into local poor law administration. Magistrates were made *ex officio* members of the new boards of guardians which succeeded to the overseers' roles. As landowners they had multiple votes in choosing the elected members of these boards. And, whenever possible, it was the principal local landowner whom the commissioners invited to serve as chairman. Since the boundaries of the poor law unions, the new units of poor law administration, were—again whenever possible—made to coincide with the boundaries of particular estates,[47] in many cases in the counties poor law administration became a simple adjunct of estate management.

But in time the commissioners and assistant commissioners who helped to achieve this end tended to circumscribe the areas of independent local judgment. Whatever their reasons for doing so—whether they were prompted more by their concern to protect the gentry from the results of their own eccentricities or were simply responding to their bureaucratic role—the consequences were the same. And other agents of the state behaved much as they behaved. Indeed, no sooner were the measures passed by which the gentry tried to shore up their own authority in state and society than the general responsibilities for keeping the peace of the county which the magistrate's commission placed upon them began to be defined, narrowed and vastly multiplied by the many new statutory responsibilities they were required to exercise, often under the eyes of inspectors. Furthermore, the question whether crime and social unrest were more effectively controlled through mechanisms of social network or through those symbolized by an impersonal police was increasingly answered in favour of the police.[48] And the irony at the core of the nineteenth-century revolution in government lies in the fact that many of the Members of Parliament who supported an impersonal police force, and many of those who voted to impose new statutory responsibilities upon the magistrates, and many of the inspectors under whose eyes these responsibilities were exercised, were themselves members of the gentry. Whatever their awareness of what they were doing, they were creating an impossible situation. Some men suggested that the magistrates' autonomy and status be restored by providing them with constituents for whom they could speak both to Parliament and to the small but growing bureaucracy.[49] From the other end of the political spectrum the suggestion was made that their autonomy and status be destroyed by extending representative arrangements beyond the borough boundaries. The concerns were very different: the legislative implications were the same. Whatever the relative importance of the different concerns, in 1888 most of the magistrates' administrative and supervisory responsibilities were transferred to new elected county councils, and their powers of supervision of the police to joint committees of magistrates and county councillors.

The government which drafted this measure was heir to the so-called party of the landed gentry. But, as the measure itself suggests, a significant mutation had occurred. Twenty years earlier Disraeli's assumptions concerning the crucial political role of the loyalties associated with such institutions as the landed estate had been widely shared among the leaders of the party. Indeed, they were widely shared among the leaders of both parties. But they were so no longer. Within the Liberal party their displacement was symbolized by the establishment of so-called representative organizations in the different constituencies, organizations which most of the remaining Whigs in the party refused to join—thus organizations which achieved the goal of the Radicals who established them, that of driving most of these remaining Whigs out of the party. Among the Conservatives the displacement of these assumptions was somewhat less traumatic. By and large, in the last decades of the century the Conservative leaders were drawn from the same families as before. But their powers in party, society and state derived less from extrapolations of those gentry relationships which Gray emphasized than from their roles in Whitehall, Westminster and the City. As W. H. Smith explained to Salisbury in the early 1880s, expressing the exasperation of the organization man for those whose lassitude was born of status, gentry relationships had ceased to be a source of strength to the party. Those who enjoyed them 'only want to be let alone to enjoy what they have: and [they] think they are so secure they will make no sacrifice of time or of pleasure to prepare against attack or to resist it'.[50] He was not alone in his analysis. Many of those who knew these men better than he confirmed his description even when they did not share his sentiments. It was Henry Chaplin, owner of 20,000 acres in Lincolnshire, who protested that while many country gentlemen were willing to assume arduous administrative burdens they might not be so willing if their right to do so had to be constantly vindicated. As he put it, explaining his concern that elected county councils might drive the gentry out of local government, '[they] might not care to undergo the intolerable annoyance of a contested election every three years with something in the nature of a continual canvass during the period intervening'.[51]

In fact, a sizeable number of gentry were elected to seats on county councils.[52] But while Chaplin's apprehensions were exaggerated, his observation helps to explain why the gentry as Gray defined them lost their positions of political predominance so rapidly in the 1870s and 1880s. When their leadership roles were challenged many of them simply left the game. Essentially, what prompted their behaviour was pride. They refused to play except according to those rules which recognized landownership as the principal claim to power. In many parts of the kingdom, however, the rules had been changed.

What determined the new rules, what prompted the challenges which marked their adoption, are extremely complex questions. But it is a useful shorthand to reduce these questions to those having to do with the weakening of the relationships on which landowners' powers were based, the erosion of the communities in which these relationships obtained, and the development of new institutions of politics, business and government which took the place of landed estates in organizing and controlling large portions of the population, in particular, the burgeoning urban population. The role of political reform in all this is somewhat ambiguous. The effects of the crises in which the reforms were enacted must be distinguished from the effects of the reforms themselves. Also, whatever the reformers' rhetoric, much reform legislation was designed to limit the political impact of social and economic change and population movement, in effect to preserve the context in which the old rules would obtain. But even when these impacts were limited the changes and movements could not be undone. And the crises themselves did much to change the context. What is striking is not the ultimate loss of power of the gentry, or the declining usefulness of landownership as a test of status, but the enduring usefulness of this test and the concomitantly enduring presence of the gentry in Westminster.

In the 1830s and 1840s significant landowners composed roughly three-quarters of the House of Commons. In the 1850s and 1860s they composed roughly two-thirds. Then, at just about the time when rural land prices reached their zenith, while rural rents were still rising to a peak in the mid-1870s, the sharp decline began in the proportions of landowner M.P.s. Between 1885 and 1905 the proportion was stabilized at roughly a third of the House. After the Liberal landslide in 1906 it dropped to a fifth. In 1910 it rose to a quarter.[53] The wrong things should not be read into those figures. That landowners continued to comprise the majority of M.P.s at such late dates has less to say about the chronology of economic change than about the ambiguities of response to such change, the importance of traditional social symbols and the stable nature of power relationships. In the 1830s and 1840s many landowners had interests besides their land.[54] By 1914, as the editors of *Landed Gentry* were forced to note, land was often 'a luxury to be maintained from extraneous sources'. And, in many cases, these other sources not only provided more money, they also provided more direct access to what were now the more effective mechanisms of social organization and social control. On the eve of the First World War some landowners owed their seats to the residual conditions their fathers had enjoyed: they sat for certain of those county constituencies whose continued isolation had been made possible by the adoption in

1885 of a single member constituency system. But in the larger world from which these constituencies were isolated landownership was no longer an important source of power or the principal criterion by which the powerful recognized one another. Into the new world of company directorships and formal organizations many peers and richer gentry made their way with considerable ease—but a smaller proportion of the lesser gentry. The conceptual boundaries had been eroded which the first Reform Act reflected and, for some time, reinforced.

Notes

1   Gray, 1862, ii.
2   *Ibid.*, v.
3   *Ibid.*, ii.
4   Freeman, 1877, *passim*; Round, 1901, *passim*.
5   Freeman, 1877, 41.
6   Loudon, 1846, 766.
7   F. M. L. Thompson, 1977, 31.
8   Burke, 1894, Preface.
9   Burke, 1914, Preface.
10 *Ibid.*
11 Walford, 1871, extract from the preface to the first edition.
12 These arguments are developed more fully in Moore, 1976.
13 *Hansard* NS V (9 May 1821), 615.
14 Froude, 1872, I, 130-1.
15 Bulwer, 1970, 91-2.
16 Escott, 1885, 26.
17 Froude, 1876, 677.
18 Reported in the *Standard* (London), 27 June 1863.
19 Reported in Howitt, 1840, 11.
20 Froude, 1876, 674.
21 Rubinstein, 1977, 120 and *passim*.
22 Bagehot, 1859, 233.
23 Moore, 1976, especially ch. 9; Chadwick, 1976.
24 F. M. L. Thompson, 1957, 294.
25 Such arguments lie at the core of Fawcett, 1865, and Kay, 1879.
26 *Hansard*, 3rd series, CCIX (19 February 1872), 639-41; the survey was reported in BPP 1874 LXXXII, pts 1 and 2; the evidence is most readily available in Bateman, 1883.
27 Brodrick, 1881, 187.
28 F. M. L. Thompson, 1963, 32 and 114.
29 *Ibid.*, 124.
30 Froude, 1876, 677.
31 Stone and Stone, 1972, 87.
32 Burke, 1914, Preface.
33 Clay, 1968; Mingay, 1963; Mingay, 1976a, 115.

34 Wilkinson, 1964.
35 F. M. L. Thompson, 1968b.
36 Such is an important argument in Spring, 1963.
37 Reported in *Farmer's Magazine*, 2nd ser., V, 1 (1842), 3.
38 For example, the cases mentioned in Arnold, 1877, 465.
39 Argyll, 1876, 498.
40 Reported in *Chambers of Agriculture Journal and Farmers' Chronicle*, 19 April 1875.
41 *Annual Register*, 1883, 114.
42 Escott, 1885, 34.
43 BPP 1851 XLVII 418 ff.; 1852–3 LXVIII 329 ff.; 1856 L 161 ff.
44 Quinault, 1974, 189.
45 *Hansard*, 3rd series, XXXVI (10 February 1837), 418–19.
46 *Ibid.*
47 Brundage, 1978, especially 105–44; Lewis, 1957, 254.
48 Silver, 1967.
49 For example, *Hansard*, 3rd series, CCXXXII (9 March 1877), 1653–63.
50 Smith to Salisbury, 14 August 1883, Salisbury Papers, Christ Church, Oxford.
51 *Hansard*, 3rd series, CCCXXIV (16 April 1888), 1371.
52 Dunbabin, 1965, 358.
53 Thomas, 1939; 1958.
54 Aydelotte, 1962.

29 The Victorian Country House

Jill Franklin

I

Victorian country houses are little known or visited, though well over a thousand are documented,[1] perhaps twice as many were built, and a very large number of them survive. They are extraordinarily varied in appearance, yet all of them make use to a greater or lesser extent of architectural elements borrowed from an earlier period, just as Georgian country houses had done. Fashion in historical style changed far more rapidly in the nineteenth century than it had done in the eighteenth, moving in sixty years from Italianate classical or Tudor and Jacobean to various kinds of Gothic, then on to English vernacular and finally round again to the classical English baroque. None of the new fashions completely ousted the previous ones, so that belated Italianate overlapped with the earliest neo-Georgian, while Elizabethan remained popular throughout the reign and after.

The great variety of styles in use at one time—and by no means all of them have been named—suggests that none was as universally satisfactory as Palladian had once been. Rapid social change had left country house owners as a class uncertain and divided over the image their houses should present, and in a single decade they could house themselves like feudal, Christian lords of the manor, classic squires, French renaissance monarchs or yeoman farmers. Yet although period styles were sometimes copied so faithfully that it can be quite difficult to distinguish fifteenth- from nineteenth-century work, more often the total effect is as unmistakably Victorian as that of Rossetti's paintings after Dante or Tennyson's *Morte D'Arthur*.

399

The early Victorian house, whatever its style, normally had a rectangular main block two or three stories high, with a low even roof or identical Elizabethan gables, beneath which were regularly spaced rows of large sash windows. The elevations might be symmetrical or asymmetrical, but in any case were built up on a system of balancing horizontals and verticals, often with a single tower offsetting the low bulk of the house. Abberley Hall (*c.* 1846) (Plate 99) and Stoke Rochford Hall (1841–5) (Plate 100) are in different styles, yet still have much in common. Ashlared stone was still the favourite building material, external colour was uniform and decorative trim thin and rather meagre. With certain exceptions, such as Anthony Salvin's Peckforton Castle or Sir Charles Barry's Cliveden,[2] houses of this period have a slightly tentative air despite their size, as though their designers had lost momentum in the gap between the fading of classical ideals and the arrival of Gothic ones.

By the 1860s, more than half of all new country houses were being built in a Gothic style,[3] but it was different from the early Victorian variety for it was no longer chiefly surface decoration but had become to many architects the only possible means of expression. Yet Gothic architects faced the major difficulty in designing country houses that little medieval domestic architecture of any kind survived and even less could serve as a direct model, so that everything had to be adapted for modern use, and even then much had to be borrowed from ecclesiastical buildings. However, conviction prevailed over common sense, and neither architects nor owners saw anything incongruous in furnishing the hall with a portion of thirteenth-century nave arcade, as at the Hall in Scott's Hafodunos House (Plate 101), or in lighting the gentlemen's cloakroom with a lancet window, as was done at G. Somers Clarke's Milton Hall in Kent.[4] It was no odder, they might have said, than living behind the front of a classical temple.

The real force of Victorian Gothic came not from its church detail but from characteristics that it shared in varying degrees with other current styles. The most striking of these was a tremendous emphasis on height and a consequent narrowing and constriction of all proportions. It was accompanied by marked asymmetry and broken outline, as well as by what was called 'truth', which meant giving full expression on the outside to the function of the rooms inside. Consequently country houses were no longer four-square and spreading, but piled up and aspiring. Roofs became higher and more steeply pitched, the skyline more romantic than ever before in England. Fantastic spires and tourelles, wedges, pyramids and hipped gables might be clustered together in one house over an equally varied façade, whose many kinds of windows were composed in asymmetric diagonals and triangles and in many different planes. The front door was no longer in the centre, and instead of windows matching left and right an oriel might be answered by a chimney breast or even by blank wall; sometimes the base of the staircase window rose diagonally. 'Truth' also affected the attitude to materials. Stucco was a sham and rough-textured stone often thought preferable to ashlar because of the 'interesting variety' it could give.[5] Exposed brick was now seen as honest and might be handled with considerable virtuosity. Decoration had to be 'structural', that is, differently coloured, and sometimes aggressively contrasting building materials could be used to form stripes, diapers and banded window heads. The Gothic country house looks tense and often restless; it lacks either classical magnificence or comfortable domesticity, but it has a powerful and dramatic quality all its own (Plates 102, 103 and 104).

Gothic for country houses held first place for little more than twenty years. By the 1870s owners were beginning to want to incorporate a suggestion of comfort and cosiness. Norman Shaw, the greatest of Victorian country house architects, was the key figure in evolving out of Gothic a new style to answer this need.[6] It was called 'Old English'[7] and took its motifs from the cottages and farmhouses of the home counties, exploiting tile-hanging, half-timbering, casement windows with small leaded panes and tall Tudor chimneys; or red brick might be set in friendly contrast to newly rediscovered white paint. All this variety would be assembled into a deceptively casual-looking asymmetry, as though the house had grown up at random over the years. Roofs were still broken up, windows were of all shapes and sizes but the ensemble was more informal, spread out and welcoming than in Gothic (Plates 105 and 106). It was also more bourgeois, so that those who chiefly wanted to look imposing still opted for stone-built Tudor.

Old English could be delightful, especially for houses that were not too big, but after a while there was a reaction in favour of a more unified, coherent look. It could be expressed in two ways. Some architects continued to use Tudor or vernacular motifs, though with less emphasis on correct period detail, building free and asymmetric compositions that were less cluttered and more abstract than those of the previous generation. Many of Edwin Lutyens's early country houses were designed in this so-called 'free' style (Plate 107). However, clients who liked the style mostly wanted small to medium-sized houses: C. A. Voysey and Baillie Scott, who each developed a personal version of it, were never commissioned to design a really big house (Plate 108). Where formality or grandeur was required, architects and their clients, feeling the need for strict symmetry and classical discipline, turned to the English baroque of Wren and the early eighteenth century. Norman Shaw's flamboyant Bryanston (Plate 109) of 1889-94 and Chesters of 1890-4 were influential in setting country house fashion in this direction. Ernest Newton, Shaw's pupil, preferred a rather quieter Georgian or Queen Anne (Plate 110), and Lutyens, too, added English classical to his repertoire. At the same time, Tudor and Jacobean houses became correctly symmetrical again (Plate 111). So what with the various free styles, the ever-popular Tudor, and once again classical, the client of 1900 had as wide a choice for the style of his house as had his predecessor in 1837.

II

All Victorian country houses were planned in two virtually separate parts, the main or family block and the service wing. Each part occupied much the same ground area, but while the main block was designed to be conspicuous and elaborate, the service wing had to be 'invisible' like the servants themselves. For the sake of convenience the Victorians invariably put all the 'offices' on one side, where they might be screened off by bushes or banks of earth and were usually hidden from the principal garden. Complete concealment of the service wing was often impossible on the entrance front, in which case it was considered essential to be able to see instantly 'the one part of the edifice as superior and the other inferior'.[8] So the service wing was normally lower than the main block, often brick-built where the house was stone, and with all its detailing faithfully reflecting the social gradings within (Plates 104, 109 and 111).[9]

Coming inside the early Victorian country house, the caller would find himself in a formal entrance hall, possibly top-lit and with a first-floor gallery giving access to the bedrooms. Several large and high reception rooms, all simply shaped, well-lit and of classical proportions, would open off it on a clear and axially arranged plan. One of them would almost certainly be a billiard room, virtually a standard feature by the 1850s. Smoking in the main body of the house was still out of the question, and though a few early smoking rooms date from the later 1840s[10] they were well-secluded, probably in the tower, for no taint of smoke must reach the principal rooms. The main innovation of the time, pioneered by Edward Blore, Anthony Salvin and A. W. N. Pugin, was the revival of the medieval great hall, which was usually fitted up in Gothic, but could be Jacobean.[11] At first owners were a little uncertain how it should be used, so that in some houses it became the main hall, in others the dining room or a free-standing room kept for entertaining and various social functions.[12] Initially, it did not matter if the great hall had no very obvious function: at a time of social tension it evoked a comforting if unreal vision of feudal order, the lord and his docile peasantry carousing in harmony together (Plates 112 and 113).

By the 1860s the country house interior had altered. The plan became non-axial and a great deal more complicated; routes were more confusing; corridors had more turnings and rooms now included a variety of oddly-shaped bays and were apt to be darker and gloomier than before. Whereas in the eighteenth and early nineteenth centuries saloons and suites might be included purely for display, each Victorian reception room was planned for a single precise function. The living areas for the different sexes and groups in the house were systematically sorted, and segregated accommodation was provided for each.

On the ground floor a masculine suite developed as a counterpart to the drawing room, which had always been feminine territory. Each sex might use the rooms in the other domain, but it was on sufferance rather than by right. The male suite developed round the library, which had been common ground in Regency days but gradually grew more masculine in furnishing and atmosphere, so that ladies seemed less in place there.[13] Then the billiard room, which in the 1830s and 1840s was often linked to the drawing room, as at Osborne, came to be regularly placed next to the library, even though in some social circles ladies were always free to play (Plate 114).[14] These two rooms, along with a gentlemen's cloakroom and a separate entrance, formed the nucleus of the suite, and the owner's study might also be included in it. By the late

1860s, when smoking in the main house had become more acceptable, the smoking room normally adjoined the billiard room. Finally, the gun room, a typical example of Victorian specialization, appeared about this time and often, though not invariably, formed part of the suite.

Between the gentlemen's rooms on one side and the ladies' rooms on the other, lay the neutral territory of the hall. At the beginning of the period it was still the little used, formal entrance; by the 1850s it had begun a remarkable transformation into the favourite family living room; Mentmore was one of the first houses whose hall was planned as a living room from the start.[15] By the 1870s many new country houses had an adaptation of a medieval great hall or classical saloon as their principal, most used reception room (Plates 115–118). To us these halls feel too high and usually too public to make acceptable sitting rooms; to the Victorians they had the over-riding advantage of being the only place in the house that was open-plan and available at any time of day for use by members of either sex, by family or guests, dogs, even children (Plate 119).

According to Robert Kerr, author of a weighty book of 1864 on house planning, the Victorian gentleman's first requirement at home, which easily outweighed elegance, importance or ornament, was 'quiet comfort for his family and guests'.[16] By 1900 it was easy for him to be very comfortable indeed, far more so than in 1837.

The most important single element in country house comfort was warmth, which was achieved by a mixture of traditional and new methods. English rooms had always been warmed by individual open fires and continued to be so throughout this period. Consequently every living room and every bedroom had its separate fireplace, whose grate had to be cleaned, its fire laid and lit daily, its coals carried and put on at frequent intervals. The Victorians loved their cheerful, glowing fires and saw no reason to economize either on fuel or labour; but even from their point of view the system had the great drawback of leaving the corridors and outlying corners unheated. The hall, too, was often difficult to keep warm: Mrs Charlton of Hesleyside, for instance, described her downstairs as 'a cavern of icy blasts'.[17]

This changed with the gradual introduction of central heating, starting with a few installations at the end of the eighteenth century. Hot air, hot water, and steam systems were all tried, but without any pumps to aid circulation it was necessary to rely on convection, so the pipes had to be two or three inches in diameter and the radiators or grilles of immense size. Controlling the boiler and maintaining an even temperature was extremely difficult and demanded considerable intelligence and skill. Central heating remained rare in the early nineteenth century, but despite the technical difficulties it was increasingly often included in new houses from the 1840s on, though at that time it was almost always confined to the hall and corridors. However, as more of the problems were solved principal rooms, too, were provided with radiators to supplement the fires, until by the end of the century heating could be taken for granted in a new house, though certainly not in an old one. The combination of central heating and open fires was, of course, hugely extravagant, but without doubt it was luxuriously comfortable too.

Heating problems were closely allied to those of ventilation. The Victorians were newly and fully aware of the importance of fresh air; they considered that breathing 'vitiated' air was dangerous to health, even to life, and one of their objections to full central heating was that it made the air unpleasant and stuffy.[18] But they were in a dilemma since they also hated draughts. So first they made doors and windows as tight-fitting and draught-proof as possible and reinforced them with screens and thick, heavy curtain materials, but then they had to reintroduce fresh air, not only for health but even more importantly to prevent the horrible discomfort of smoking chimneys: even the best-designed chimney will smoke if the only outside source of air is down the flue. So an enormous number of patent grates came on the market, designed to draw in air and consume smoke in a great variety of ways. None was ideally satisfactory. At the same time several systems of ventilation independent of the heating systems were invented. These often involved air ducts hidden in the walls or set in free-standing pipes; open grilles in cornice or ceiling, acting as outlets for vitiated air, were common.

Owners were probably wise to be cautious over central heating in its early days. They were less conservative about new forms of lighting. In 1837 country houses were still lit by a combination of candles and oil lamps, and many continued to be so. Gas light was already available, but it was far from satisfactory. Each country house had to manufacture its own gas in its own gas house and the resulting product was so dirty, hot and smelly that it was unacceptable in the family rooms. However, it was considered good enough for the servants and was installed in service wings and corridors at least from the early 1840s.[19] Various experiments and improvements culminated in the invention of the gas mantle in 1886, by which time a high proportion of new houses had at least partial gas lighting; but by then it was really too late, for electric light had become practicable for domestic use in 1879 and was already being used in a few country houses by the 1880s.[20] Ten years later it was still far from reliable and extremely expensive to run, but when working it clearly outmatched all older forms of lighting in brilliance, cleanliness and convenience.

Plumbing arrangements also improved markedly during this period. Every Victorian country house had its own, usually abundant, water supply, and this was piped right round the house, but at first with only a few outlets apart from the w.c.s and the housemaids' closets. The gentlemen's cloakroom probably had a basin with a cold tap, but there were no other plumbed-in washbasins anywhere. The bathroom was reserved for the master and mistress, with perhaps a second one for the nurseries. Guest bathrooms did not exist, and a guest washed with jug and basin and slop-pail in the bedroom or dressing room, and bathed in a hip bath in front of the fire. Every drop of hot water had to be carried up the back stairs from the kitchen, and one manservant remembered carrying forty cans night and morning.[21] Piped hot water in the country house is not recorded in the architectural press until the later 1860s, and although there are probably instances of its being installed earlier it did not become standard even in new houses until the late 1870s or early 1880s.[22] Once piped hot water had arrived a few more bathrooms were usually, though not invariably, provided. Guests could now expect one to every two or three bedrooms, though only exceptionally one to every suite. Even the men and maidservants would have one apiece.[23] Plumbed-in washbasins never reached the bedrooms; it was felt that sleeping in a room with a plug-hole connected to the drains was an unacceptable risk to health.

The Victorians had become very conscious of the connection between health and sanitation and gave much thought to the w.c.s which were provided in generous numbers. They invariably had an outside window and usually a connecting lobby. Nor were the servants stinted, though as a precaution against smells in the house, they often had to make do with closets outside the main body of the house.[24] Drains and sewerage, too, received a great deal of attention. Glazed and impermeable drain pipes, pioneered by Henry Doulton, were obviously less hazardous to health, and there were advances, too, in the design of valves, traps and devices for eliminating 'effluvia' or dangerous smells.[25]

III

Victorian country houses were built to last. They were intended as permanent family possessions and represented a long-term investment: part of the return was to be a conspicuous and powerful position in county society, in the future if not immediately. So they were constructed as solidly as possible; building methods were sound and careful, materials durable, nothing was shoddy or sham.

Costs varied enormously, naturally. As was only fitting, the Duke of Westminster spent the most: Waterhouse's remodelling of Eaton Hall cost over £600,000; but the Duke of Northumberland paid £250,000 for Salvin's remodelling of Alnwick Castle, Earl Manvers £170,000 for his new Thoresby Hall, also by Salvin, and Viscount Portman at least £200,000 and probably much more for Bryanston.[26] Several commoners' houses also cost huge sums. R. S. Holford's Westonbirt, built by Lewis Vulliamy, cost over £125,000, and John Walter's Bearwood by Robert Kerr over £120,000.[27] Lynford Hall by William Burn for Lyne Stephen, said to be the 'richest commoner in England', was reported, when up for sale in the 1890s, to have cost £145,000 to build, and the figure is by no means unlikely.[28] Others that must have cost as much or more include Waddesdon and Rhinefield Lodge.[29]

At the other end of the scale it seems to have been impossible to build what the neighbours would have recognized as a country house for less than £6,000 or £7,000. A farmer in Hertfordshire became suddenly and unexpectedly richer when his land was found to yield coprolites or fossilized dung, used as a fertilizer. He decided to build a country house, Pirton Hall, for £5,000. 'I must beg to disabuse you of the notion of a *Mansion*', wrote his architect. For that price he would simply supply 'a good Country gentleman's house, plain and unpretending'. The final total was nearer £10,000, including stables, lodge and kitchen gardens.[30] S. S. Teulon's Enbrook, near Hythe, which was only just large enough to be reckoned as a country house at that date (1853–5), cost about £7,300 for the house alone.[31]

With such a price range no single house can be taken as entirely typical, but David Brandon's Hemsted House in Kent (Plate 104) can stand for many. The owner, Gathorne Hardy, later Earl of Cranbrook, bought the estate of just over 5,000 acres for £124,000 with money he inherited from his father's Staffordshire ironworks. The accepted tender for the house was £18,000, the final cost £23,000, but that sum did not include such items as the gasworks, grates and furniture, which brought the complete bill to almost £33,000.[32]

Few really detailed sets of building accounts survive, but both at Westonbirt and Bearwood a little over half the building money went on wages, the balance on materials and transport. Wages ranged from £2. 12s. 6d. per week for the most highly skilled men to 10s. per week for labourers; but since the building process was hardly more mechanized than in the Middle Ages and very few items were prefabricated, huge numbers of men were needed on the site. Well over 400 men were employed at various times on Westonbirt, and 110 men sat down to the 'roofing supper' at Hemsted.[33] The size of the house was only one of the factors affecting the final price. Stone naturally cost more than brick, and stone itself varied in price according to quality; Chilmark was more expensive than Bath stone, for instance.[34] Bearwood, which was brick-built with lavish decorative trim in stone, can suggest relative costs. Some 4,250,000 bricks were made on the estate at a cost of £6,400 and the total bricklaying bill was just over £17,000. The stone, Mansfield for trim and York for paved floors, was just over £17,000, plus £850 for cartage, and the complete stonemasonry bill was over £26,000. Country houses needed huge amounts of timber, and at Bearwood the total figure for joinery work was over £40,000, nearly as much as the brick and stone together. Ironwork cost £9,000, including £4,000 on rolled iron joists, £4,600 went on plumbing and leadwork, £6,000 on the stoves and heating apparatus. Painting, glazing and gilding came to only £7,000 together and plastering the same. The architect's commission was the standard 5 per cent of the cost of the house, plus travelling expenses.[35]

Most houses bear witness to the Victorian preference for durable materials. Many have no external paintwork at all: Mentmore had copper window frames, other houses had unpainted oak or teak. Indoors the servants' wing would have its walls plastered and painted, but in the reception rooms wood panelling or tooled leather hangings were often preferred (Plates 113, 117 and 118). Consequently far less maintenance was necessary than in the days of stucco outside and lavish paintwork inside.

After an owner had decided how much to spend on building his new house, he next had to work out the maximum number of servants he could afford to keep. The plan of the house was geared to this figure. Of course servants were essential to domestic comfort, but above a certain size of household, say fifteen indoor servants, the precise number made little difference to the family's standard of living, though a considerable one to its status. Thus livery servants, who for much of the time were of little practical use, had a function merely in being conspicuously on view. Such an attitude to domestic service was possible and even made sense because throughout the nineteenth century domestic servants, women especially, were cheap and available in huge numbers; and of all the domestic jobs to be had those in the country house were among the most sought-after.[36]

Consequently, although a great deal of thought was given to the smooth running of the house, good planning had absolutely no connection with labour saving, at least until towards the end of the period. Running hot water in the bathroom was a success not because it saved the servants carrying the cans but because it saved the guests having to wait for them. A well-planned house was one where the work could be reasonably shared out between a fixed number of servants, and so organized that each servant could carry out his duties without getting in another's way. To achieve this the Victorians classified the various jobs, providing a separate and appropriate place in which each was to be carried out. In earlier times the brushing of the family's clothes had been done in the servants' hall; a Victorian house had a separate brushing room.

One aim of the planning was to ensure that men and women servants had no unnecessary contact with each other, not only in the sleeping quarters but also in the course of their work: segregation would promote efficiency and propriety at one and the same time. It was equally important that the servants should not disturb the family's illusion of privacy, even though everyone knew they were there and that it was impossible to keep secrets from them.[37] Separate entrances, staircases and corridors brought home who was who and prevented unnecessary contact. The architect of Rhinefield Lodge noted that 'an important feature of the planning of this house is that no servant's room or office, with the exception of the attic dormers, can overlook the grounds at any point'.[38]

The work of the country house was organized, as in the eighteenth century, into three departments, headed by the cook, the butler or steward and the housekeeper. These three, and personal servants such as the ladies' maids, were known as 'upper servants' and were sharply differentiated in duties and status from the under servants, who did the really hard and menial work. Demarcation lines were rigid and no servant, even the lowliest, could be asked to do the work of another.[39] Also, in any large house much of the servants' time was spent in waiting on each other. T. F. Buxton, the owner of Easneye, near Ware, had twenty-three servants and reckoned that fifteen waited on the family and eight on the fifteen.[40] It is no wonder that from 1830 to 1870 or later the service wing grew more elaborate and occupied more space in relation to the main house than ever before.

One early Victorian house can give an idea of the general principles of layout. Stoke Rochford Hall in Lincolnshire (Plate 100) was built in 1841–5 at a cost of some £60,000 for Christopher Turnor, a hereditary landowner.[41] His architect was William Burn, famous for his skilful planning.[42] Each household department had its own cluster of rooms. The butler, who had five menservants under him in 1871, had his section in the basement under the main house.[43] This arrangement gave the footmen easy access to the hall and front door, though the basement bedrooms for the menservants were much disliked.[44] Next came the housekeeper's section, placed beneath the exclusively family part of the house, known as the 'private wing', so that the housekeeper had easy communication with her mistress in the boudoir overhead. The housekeeper's room was used as her office and sitting room, and often as a dining room by the upper servants. In 1871 the housekeeper had under her four housemaids, two still-room maids and three laundry maids. Further on came the kitchen department, staffed by the cook, two kitchenmaids, a scullery maid and a dairymaid. It was arranged round a kitchen court, one side of which held the servants' hall, the only room where the under servants could legitimately spend any time in the company of the opposite sex. The laundry and the brewhouse were the furthest from the main house because of the smell and steam.

Perhaps the most remarkable feature of the plan to modern eyes is the distance from kitchen to dining room, some 40 metres. This was no lapse on the architect's part but rather an instance of good planning, since the Victorians were terrified of kitchen smells, cabbage water above all.[45] Far better for the footman to walk the length of two cricket pitches than risk tainting the dining room. Then each staircase has its meaning and function. Only guests and adult members of the family might use the principal staircase from the hall to the first floor; housemaids, footmen and children were relegated to different and minor backstairs. A little later houses could have a staircase reserved for visiting bachelors, a nursery stair, a young ladies' stair.[46] All this multiplication made still more work. It was only towards the end of the century that planning sometimes became a little simpler: the kitchen could be a little closer to the dining room, the service wing contracted slightly, staircases were fewer. But where comfort was concerned labour saving meant nothing.

IV

Before he reached the comforts of the house the visitor had to pass the lodge, whose style would warn him what to expect of the mansion, then drive through the park or grounds. Few of the landscaped parks surrounding the Victorian country house were entirely of Victorian creation. So much landscaping had been done in the eighteenth century that after 1840 comparatively few large new estates were assembled from untouched or agricultural land. Among the exceptions to this are Bylaugh Hall, Norfolk, a house of 1849–52, built in the middle of turnip fields and landscaped by W. A. Nesfield, the best-known landscape designer of the time; Waddesdon Manor, where the planting of well-grown trees created an instant park out of an outlying portion of the Stowe estate; and Cragside, where William Armstrong made a romantic Rhineland forest grow on a bare Northumberland hillside.[47] But Aldermaston Court, Tortworth Court and Bearwood were more typical (Plate 124): each replaced an earlier house whose park had been landscaped in the eighteenth or early nineteenth century, leaving the Victorians to make only comparatively minor alterations.[48]

In any case, whether it was an entirely new creation or not, the Victorian park would have startled an eighteenth-century gentleman a good deal less than its mansion. It was likely to reflect the ideas and practice of Humphry Repton and the effect aimed at in the wider landscape was still one of heightened naturalness. The free outlines of the planting emphasized the contours of the slopes and opened up views to the distant horizon, suggesting or exaggerating the extent of the estate. If nature permitted, a river or stream was dammed to form a sinuous lake in the middle distance, its banks partly shaded by trees and shrubs.

The Victorians liked to use a great variety of species in their planting and were particularly fond of conifers and plants with dark shiny leaves, such as laurels and rhododendrons. Many new species from all round the world became available in the early Victorian period, including hollies, weeping trees, conifers, bamboos; monkey-puzzles were in plentiful supply from 1843, Wellingtonias from 1853.[49] Their novelty of form or exotic colour were always eagerly welcomed, but plants were now juxtaposed with a botanist's eye rather than a painter's. J. C. Loudon thought Kent and Repton had 'indiscriminately mixed and crowded together' their bushes and trees, and that it was better to arrange them by species according 'to their kinds and forms' in the way that would 'best display the natural form and habit of each'. He called this the 'Gardenesque' style, and it led on to the fashion for specimen gardens and the planting of specimen trees (Plate 122).[50] The Victorians also liked strong colour contrasts and a romantic overall effect. The eighteenth-century grounds of Stourhead were designed to be neat, trim and idyllic. By the nineteenth the outlines were blurred, the planting was lusher and denser, and far more dark-leaved plants were used; the rhododendrons were Regency but the peak years for conifer planting were the early 1850s.[51]

The treatment of the approach altered too. The Victorian country house was not for public viewing, as the eighteenth-century one had been. Privacy was now much more important than grand initial display, and in order to keep the park and the garden front of the house secluded the Victorians made the carriage drive wind round the edge of the park, so that the visitor caught his first sight of the gardens, lake and main prospect only after passing through the house. Many older houses, Hatfield among them, had their main entrance moved round to what had once been the back.

The immediate surroundings of the house altered much more than the outer park. Repton had often used terraces and flower gardens as a transition between the man-made bulk of the house and the apparently natural park, but now a formally planned, carefully detailed, small-scale foreground became one of the most characteristic, if impermanent, features of early and mid-Victorian grounds. Sir Charles Barry gave many of his houses a setting or intermediate zone of Italianate terraces bounded by stone balustrades at different levels, often linked by formal stairways and punctuated by urns and possibly statuary. He called it 'architectural gardening'[52] (Plate 123). The terraces themselves were laid out with elaborate and symmetrically designed parterres, edged with box, and filled with coloured stones or tightly packed, highly coloured bedding plants. Beyond the parterres would be shrubberies, rose gardens and specimen gardens, until finally the park proper was reached.

In the later part of the century bedding-out became rather less popular, and the parterres were often replaced by borders that were still formally and symmetrically laid out but were now planted with what were referred to as 'old-fashioned flowers', hardy if humble perennials, freely arranged as in a cottage herbaceous border.[53] William Robinson and Gertrude Jekyll were the principal propagandists for such planting, advocating softer and subtler colour schemes and stressing the importance of attractive foliage and good ground cover.[54] Architectural features such as pergolas, stone-bordered pools and garden pavilions were often included, and as the zones were no longer so rigidly demarcated the flower garden took on some of the manufactured naturalness of the park. At the very end of the century another reaction brought a revival of formal and symmetrical gardening in keeping with the new symmetry in architecture.[55] Both kinds of garden design flourished until the Great War.

V

By 1900 there was little demand for landscaping on the grand scale. The number of houses built, like Hemsted, as the centre of a landed estate had reached its peak in the 1870s, and it dropped continuously from then on.[56] The agricultural depression and the competition of cheap foreign food had caused a considerable fall in rents and the sale value of land, especially in arable country. Many owners of large estates who were dependent on their rents had to cut expenditure; others were forced to try and sell out altogether. The result was something of a glut of country house estates on the market.[57] By the 1890s it was easy and far cheaper than formerly to buy or rent a period house. Such famous houses as Houghton Hall, Hesleyside and Apthorpe were up for sale in the 1880s and remained on the market for years.[58] This naturally made it even harder to sell modern country houses. Octavius Coope, M.P., the brewer, paid £120,000 for his estate in 1878 and spent £30,000 on building his house, Berechurch Hall; but when he put the estate up for sale ten years later the best offer (not accepted) was £80,000, and in 1894 he had still not disposed of it.[59] In these circumstances the idea of building a new country house inevitably lost much of its glamour.

At the beginning of the reign hereditary landowners had built three times as many houses as the *nouveaux riches*. By the 1880s they were building only half as many, and by the 1890s fewer than a fifth.[60] Those of them who could still commission large houses almost certainly had non-agricultural money, like Lord Portman, paying for Bryanston with his London rents. New men were still building very large country houses, though fewer than before, but towards the end of the century their money probably came from different sources too. They were now more likely to be in biscuits, general groceries or soap, like G. W. Palmer of Huntley & Palmer and Marlstone House, Berkshire, Hudson Kearley (later Lord Devonport) of International Stores and Wittington House, Buckinghamshire, and his neighbour, Robert Hudson of

410

Hudson's soap and Danesfield. South African gold paid for Cavenham Hall in Suffolk and for Tylney Hall in Hampshire. Shiplake Court was built by a stockbroker, Wightwick Manor for an ink and paint manufacturer. And, as before, bankers, shipowners and brewers all built country houses.

It was nothing new for rich and successful members of the middle classes to move into the country, but now, instead of transforming themselves into landed gentry with country houses surrounded by estates of hundreds if not thousands of acres, they often preferred a medium-sized house with grounds of tens of acres, grounds which in all probability had originally belonged to some great landowner forced to sell off outlying parcels of land in order to keep going.

Professional men, as well as business men of all kinds, now commissioned these houses in the country. Much of Norman Shaw's work in the home counties was for successful Royal Academicians, Philip Webb's last house, Standen, was for a solicitor, Leonard Stokes's Thirteover for a barrister, Voysey's Greyfriars for the writer, Julian Sturgis. Although Shaw and Lord Portman ensured that no one could make a mistake about Bryanston, the look and style of a house in the country such as Redcourt (Plate 110) was often indistinguishable from that of a newly built, modest country house with a proper estate. True, the grounds were small and the owner could not hope to move in county society, but still his house was a well-built and valuable piece of property and he could live in it in the greatest comfort without having to worry about tenants and rents. No wonder that by 1900 many owners preferred the appearance of a country house to the reality.

Notes

1 Principally in the architectural journals: *Civil Engineer and Architects' Journal*, 1837–67; *Builder*, 1843–; *Building News*, 1855–; *Architect*, 1869–; *British Architect*, 1874–; *Academy Architecture*, 1889–; *Studio*, 1893–; *Builders' Journal*, 1895–; *Architectural Review*, 1896–; *Country Life*, 1897–; and in Pevsner, 1951–74.

2 Peckforton Castle: British Architectural Library, Drawings Coll., W8/12 (1–15); *Country Life*, 1965, CXXXVIII, 284–7, 336–9; Girouard, 1971, 73–7. Cliveden: *Builder*, 1850, VIII, 318; Barry, 1867, 119–22.

3 Franklin, 1973, 15, 19.

4 *Building News*, 1874, XXVII, 254.

5 *Civil Engineer* 1860, XXIII, 129.

6 Girouard, 1971, 44–9, 141–6, 158–60; Saint, 1976, 24–53.

7 Eastlake, 1872, 110, 131, 135, 339.

8 Kerr, 1864, 226.

9 Scott, 1857, 157; Stevenson, 1880, II, 142; *Civil Engineer*, 1864, XXVII, 181.

10 Osborne House, 1845: Girouard, 1971, 25; Abberley Hall, *c.* 1846: sale catalogue, BM Maps, 137b, 11 (16); Bricklehampton Hall, 1848: sale catalogue, BM Maps 137b 11 (17); Mentmore Towers, 1850–5: *Builder*, 1857, XV, 738–40.

11   Blore: Goodrich Court, 1828–41, V & A Drawings 87430, 1–40; Nash, 1845, 12. Moreton
      Hall, 1841–3, BM Add. mss 42027, vol. 28, 15–17. Salvin: Harlaxton Manor, 1828–38,
      Country Life, 1906, XX, 522–32; 1957, CXXI, 704–7; Hussey, 1958, 239–48; Pevsner,
      Lincolnshire, 1964, 561–5; Pugin: Scarisbrick Hall, 1837–45, Pevsner, *North Lancashire*,
      1961, 218–23; Stanton, 1971, 28–33; Girouard, 1971, 60–4. Bilton Grange, 1841–6,
      Stanton, 1971, 176, 200.

12   Dining room at Great Moreton Hall and Bilton Grange, free-standing at Bayons Manor
      and Hall, Barnstaple (see Pevsner, *North Devon*, 1952, 92).

13   Loudon, 1833, 796; Gore, 1849, I, 288; Kerr, 1864, 129; cf. Eliot, 1876, Bk 5, ch. 6.

14   Fullerton, 1847, I, 9; Ticknor, 1864, 358; Yonge, 1853, 35; Cavendish, 1927, I, 145;
      Knightley, 1915, 226.

15   Disraeli, 1938, 159; *Builder*, 1857, XV, 738–40.

16   Kerr, 1864, 73.

17   Charlton, 1949, 176.

18   *Builder*, 1854, XII, 288; Stevenson, 1880, II, 221.

19   For instance at Worsley Hall, Lancashire: British Architectural Library, Drawings Coll.,
      Worsley Account Book, 12–23 October 1843.

20   Girouard, 1971, 17.

21   Lanceley, 1925, 177.

22   Didsbury Towers, 1865: *Builder*, 1873, XXXI, 222, 722. Crown Point, Norwich, 1865: 1872
      sale catalogue, Norwich Public Library. Bayham Abbey, 1869–72: *Builder*, 1871, XXIX,
      985–7. Wykehurst Park, 1871–4: *Builder*, 1872, XXX, 565–7; Murphy, 1883, 90.

23   Stevenson, 1880, II, 75; Muthesius, II, 56.

24   For instance at Clouds, plans British Architectural Library, Drawings Coll., V14
      (11–216). Cf. Westonbirt, British Architectural Library, Drawings Coll., R.S. Holford,
      letter 16 November 1865.

25   Stevenson, 1880, II, 265–74; Saint, 1976, 180–4.

26   Eaton: Smith, 1971, II, 387–99. Alnwick: Pevsner, *Northumberland*, 1957, 69. Thoresby:
      Thoresby Account Book, Nottingham University Library. Bryanston: Saint, 1976, 432.

27   Bearwood: Berks. RO: Walter Papers, Building Accounts, 1864–70. Westonbirt:
      Westonbirt Papers and Fortnightly Returns, 1864–71, British Architectural Library,
      Drawings Coll.

28   *Estates Gazette*, 31 December 1898.

29   Waddesdon: Fowler, 1894, 171–2. Rhinefield: *Builder*, 1889, LV, 121–2.

30   Herts. RO: Pirton Papers, 71830–72035; Hanscomb, 1967, 159.

31   *Builder*, 1854, XII, 486–7.

32   *Builder*, 1862, XX, 242–3, 259; first Earl of Cranbrook, *Private Diaries*, and Hemsted
      Account Book, East Suffolk RO: HA 43/T501/286–306 and 178.

33   Westonbirt computed from Fortnightly Returns, see note 27; Hemsted: Cranbrook
      Diaries, 28 October 1860, see note 32.

34   Estimates and correspondence for Pangbourne Tower owned by Mr J. V. Hamilton.

35   Kerr, 1864, 223; *Builder*, 1884, LXVIII, 549; F. M. L. Thompson, 1963, 187.

36   Franklin, 1975, 221.

37   Disraeli, 1845, 157; Trollope, 1869, II, ch. 51; Kerr, 1864, 75; Lethaby, 1935, 99.

38   *Builder*, 1889, LV, 122.

39   Dana, 1921, 40.

40 Information from his grandson, Mr J. Buxton.
41 Pevsner, *Lincolnshire*, 1964, 644.
42 Kerr, 1864, 476; *RIBA Transactions*, 1869–70, series 1, XX, 121–4.
43 1871 census, PRO: RG 10/3357. (In the 1851 census, the jobs of the menservants are not given, and in 1861 the family and many of the servants were away.)
44 Horne, 1930, 236.
45 *Builder*, 1886, L, 87; Cholmondeley, 1897, 52.
46 Early bachelor stairs at Bearwood: Kerr, 1864, 3rd edn, 1871, plates 35, 36; Westonbirt: British Architectural Library, Drawings Coll., V7/3 (1–17); nursery stair at Highclere Castle (Sir Charles Barry): plans at house; young ladies' stair, Bearwood.
47 Bylaugh Hall: *Builder*, 1852, X, 517–9; *Building News*, 1869, XVI, 272 ff.: Waddesdon Manor: Fowler, 1894, 171–2; *Gazette des Beaux Arts*, 1959, series 6, LIV, 13–16: Cragside: Girouard, 1971, 143–4, 293–9; *Country Life*, 1969, CXLVI, 1640–3.
48 Aldermaston Court: *Country Life*, 1899, VI, 240–2; 1907, XXII, 54–9. Tortworth Court: *Country Life*, 1899, V, 592–6: Bearwood: *Country Life*, 1969, CXLIV, 964–7.
49 Hadfield, 1960, 314, 322–3.
50 Loudon, 1840, VIII.
51 Woodbridge, 1971, 14–18, 28–30.
52 Barry, 1867, 113–19.
53 Girouard, 1977, 152–8.
54 Jekyll, 1899; 1900; Jekyll and Weaver, 1912; Robinson, 1883; Clifford, 1962, 206–11.
55 Blomfield and Thomas, 1892.
56 Girouard, 1971, 6.
57 *Estates Gazette*, 8 January 1881, 14 October 1882, 14 July 1883, 6 February 1892, 4 January 1896.
58 *Estates Gazette*, 31 October 1885, 15 October 1887, 7 January 1888, 7 January 1893.
59 *Estates Gazette*, 7 January 1888, 6 January 1894.
60 Girouard, 1971, 6.

30   The Model Village

Michael Havinden

In discussing model villages it is as well to be clear at the outset what we are talking about since the term can be used to describe a wide variety of settlements. Probably the most generally recognized would be a planned village, such as Nuneham Courtney in Oxfordshire or Milton Abbas in Dorset. These were completely new villages, established on fresh sites because a landowner wished to remove an older village which had become an unsightly impediment to the development of his garden or park. These might perhaps be regarded as the ideal types, but they are not typical model villages. The typical model village would be more like East Lockinge in Berkshire (now Oxfordshire), which was an ancient historic village dating back to Saxon times; but which was partly resited and subjected to large-scale redevelopment, modernization and 'prettification' by its owners, Lord and Lady Wantage, in the mid-nineteenth century.[1] The motives were partly aesthetic, partly philanthropic, and also practical—the belief that a well-housed and contented labour force would be more stable and more efficient than a miserable and discontented one.

However, although the typical Victorian model village was probably the handiwork of a paternalistic landlord, there were also other important types. These included co-operative settlement schemes inspired by people like Robert Owen and even Tolstoy; and the settlements established (albeit briefly) by the Chartists around the mid-century. There was also another type of growing importance: the model industrial village (of which Owen's New Lanark was perhaps the archetype) later developed in the direction of garden suburbs, such as Bourneville, near Birmingham; New Earswick, near York; and Port Sunlight, near Birkenhead. The term 'industrial'

414

may also be understood quite broadly; it comprised villages devoted to mining and railways and also newly established small ports. Finally there were the seaside resort villages, of which Thorpeness in Suffolk was a representative type.[2]

If there was such a wide variety of model villages it is not surprising that the motivations and inspirations behind them should also have been many and varied. Before looking at these in more detail the chronological question should be briefly disposed of. Strictly speaking, a Victorian model village should be one built between 1837 and 1901; but these dates have no significance for the subject. The inspiration for builders often lay in changes of taste which occurred in the late eighteenth century (especially the rise of Romanticism and the passion for the picturesque); whereas motivations like the desire to improve living standards, which were powerful in the late nineteenth century, continued on beyond 1901 without any break. So for purposes of convenience we shall take the century of peace between 1815 and 1914 as our time period. Although it was a period which witnessed more rapid and more profound changes than at any preceding time in British history, it was at least unified by one important influence which did not greatly change: namely the economic, political and social ascendency of large (and frequently titled) landlords throughout the countryside.[3]

I

As we have seen, eighteenth-century model villages like Nuneham Courtney, Milton Abbas, and New Houghton, Norfolk, were really by-products of the landscaping activities of people like 'Capability' Brown and Nathaniel Kent. They excited no particular interest in themselves, and no powerful social, humanitarian or aesthetic interests were involved in their construction. But by the nineteenth century this attitude was beginning to change. The villages were becoming objects of interest in themselves, although the aesthetic pleasure they were intended to give their owners was still a very much more powerful motive than any desire to improve the comfort or the well-being of their inhabitants: that was to come later.

It was the rise of the 'picturesque' movement in aesthetic fashion, and particularly the new interest in cottages as a specially important symbol, which seems to have been the initial inspiration for the early nineteenth-century model village. Many artistic trends, like the poetry of Byron and Wordsworth, and the landscapes of Constable, no doubt contributed to the generalized development of the mood, but it seems to have been the specific influence of two theorists which gave the movement its real driving force. These were William Gilpin and Sir Uvedale Price. Gilpin made tours in the latter part of the eighteenth century to encourage people to visit romantic and remote areas, such as Wales or north Devon, where wild and picturesque elements of an older age still survived. The enthusiasm of Wordsworth and Coleridge for Lynmouth gorge, and later the Lake District, were part of this development. Gilpin was bored by the classical regularity of a village like Nuneham

Courtney, which, although he admitted its superior convenience, seemed to him to lack the charm of the picturesque village. This charm was essentially based on a variety of styles in cottage building.

> When all these little habitations happen to unite harmoniously and to be connected with the proper appendages of a village—the winding road, a number of spreading trees, a rivulet and a bridge and a spire to bring the whole to an apex—the village is compleat.[4]

Sir Uvedale Price elaborated these sentiments in his *Essay on the Picturesque* (1794) where he encouraged landlords to remodel their estate villages along these lines, saying,

> there is, indeed, no scene where such a variety of forms and embellishments may be introduced at so small an expense, and without anything fantastic or unnatural, as that of a village; none where the lover of painting, and the lover of humanity, may find so many sources of amusement and interest.

Price's vision of the ideal village is well illustrated by his later comments on some cottages painted by van Ostade:

> Their outline against the sky is generally composed of forms of unequal heights, thrown into many different degrees of perspective; the sides are varied by projecting windows and doors . . . [and they demonstrate] what still may be shown in the playful variety and intricacy of buildings and their appendages, where space, elegance and grandeur are unthought of.[5]

It was not long before this alluring seed bore fruit, and strangely it was one of the masters of classical architecture, no less a person than John Nash himself, who designed the prototype for all later picturesque villages—Blaise Hamlet. The site was a few miles to the north-west of Bristol in the parish of Henbury, outside Blaise Castle, the mansion and park of the patron, the wealthy Bristol Quaker banker, J. S. Harford. Fortunately the nine ornate cottages built by Nash round a green in 1810–11 now belong to the National Trust, which has saved them from becoming totally engulfed in the surrounding suburbs of Bristol. Each cottage was built to a separate design and every device of the picturesque was employed to maximum effect—steeply pitched thatched roofs, dormer windows, rustic porches and luxuriant creepers abounded; but Nash's greatest pride was in the lofty and elaborately ornate brick chimneys. Yet although Harford prided himself on his humanitarian interests (and campaigned against the slave trade) the accommodation offered in these cottages was extremely meagre. Admittedly they were intended for elderly people, but one small, dark living room downstairs and a couple of bedrooms in the eaves were all they provided—plus exterior wash-houses and privies tucked away at the back. Clearly, aesthetic interests had triumphed over the residents' convenience, and this unfortunate example remained powerful throughout the nineteenth century.[6]

However, its influence declined from the 1840s when awareness of the appallingly bad housing conditions prevailing in so many rural areas became more widespread, and the desire to improve standards began to prevail over purely aesthetic considerations—although it was still hoped to combine the two. A leader in the movement for better standards of convenience and hygiene in cottages was Prince Albert, who became the active patron of the Society for Improving the Condition of the Labouring Classes, established in 1848. The society circulated plans for model cottages (see Plate 151) and, using the Prince Consort's example of improvements on the Crown estates, inspired landowners to rebuild cottages and remodel villages. The prince was responsible for improved cottages at Windsor, and for model villages at West Newton (Sandringham estate, Norfolk) and Whippingham (Osborne estate, Isle of Wight). Soon some of the wealthiest landowners, like the dukes of Bedford, Devonshire and Northumberland, were following the prince's example and setting a fashion which others were eager to emulate.[7]

There were, however, a number of problems which could easily deter all but the very wealthiest enthusiasts. The first was economic: cottages were a bad investment. Some figures from the Duke of Bedford's estates in the 1890s, relating to fifty-two cottages, show that the average cost of construction was £296. It was generally believed at the time that the gross rent should be about 10 per cent of the capital to cover rates, repairs and incidentals, and allow some measure of profit on the investment. This would imply a yearly rent of £29.60. In fact the duke drew between £2.60 and £5.20 a year from these cottages, depending on their size. If we regard £4 a year as an average rent, the return on the investment was only about 1.3 per cent.[8]

This economic problem was compounded by the fact that the inhabitants of model cottages, or model villages, were frequently not the employees of landlords but of tenant-farmers. Hence the landlord had no direct interest in subsidizing their wages. Where the model village was built primarily for domestic servants or estate employees, as at Edensor on the Duke of Devonshire's Chatsworth estate, this problem was minimized; but it must generally have acted as a deterrent. Another linked factor was the fear of erecting cottages whose occupants might become unemployed and hence fall on the poor rates. Indeed, so great was this fear that many landlords were more concerned with pulling down cottages than with erecting them. Villages of this type were known as 'close' villages, and a vigorous controversy raged on their relative merits and demerits as compared with 'open villages', which became correspondingly overcrowded and insanitary.[9] In fact, in view of the strength and pervasiveness of the deterring factors, it is surprising that so many model villages were built.

The desire to retreat to a self-sufficient, co-operative rural settlement is very ancient. No doubt it embodies a faint folk memory of ancient village communities, as well as a reaction against the pressures and tensions of city life (which were reinforced in the nineteenth century by the dirt, disease, noise and squalor of so many new industrial towns). Robert Owen was an early enthusiast, though most of his

417

attempts to found rural settlements, both in England and America, were disastrous failures. One of his dissident disciples, William Allen, had better fortune though with Lindfield in Sussex, founded in 1831, and successfully based on smallholdings.[10] Fergus O'Connor tried to lead the Chartists in the same direction in 1848 after the failure of their mammoth petitions demanding the suffrage; but the few settlements which were established, like Charterville in Oxfordshire, Great Dodford, Worcestershire, and Snigs End, Gloucestershire, soon failed as social experiments, though they struggled on as centres for a few smallholders.[11]

Finally, there were the quite different motivations which inspired the builders of industrial villages. Their problem was usually to provide accommodation for a workforce which had to be attracted to a new site convenient for the mill—whether it was water or steam. Some of the early industrial villages like Turton and Egerton, Lancashire, which were built by the Ashworths for their employees, were relatively utilitarian,[12] but if the manufacturer were very successful, elements both of philanthropy and desire to make a mark entered his motivation, as can be seen with Sir Titus Salt's Saltaire (1850s) near Bradford,[13] and Lord Leverhulme's Port Sunlight (1890s) near Birkenhead.[14]

II

As we have seen, the 'picturesque' style reigned almost unchallenged in the early nineteenth century, and only gave way slowly, and in scattered places, to rival styles. Some notable picturesque villages after Blaise Hamlet were Somerleyton in Suffolk, Ilam in Staffordshire and Old Warden in Bedfordshire. Somerleyton, near Aldburgh in east Suffolk, was built for the great railway contractor, Sir Morton Peto, and was largely designed by the architect, John Thomas, in the 1850s. It is described by Gillian Darley as perhaps the most successful functioning picturesque village today.[15] Another good example is Ilam, set magnificently on a site in the Pennine dale country of north Staffordshire. It was designed by George Gilbert Scott in 1854 for a wealthy manufacturer, Jesse Watts Russell. Its garishly coloured tile-hanging is quite out of character with the vernacular architecture of the area, but gives the village an unmistakably 'picturesque' stamp.[16] Old Warden, Bedfordshire, built for the Ongley family around the middle of the century is another example well worth a visit, with much pretty thatch and elegant decorations.

One of the first rivals of the picturesque was eclecticism, which by its very nature can hardly be regarded as a style, and has, inevitably, produced some of the most extraordinary and eccentric of all the model villages. The picturesque style emphasized variety, but variety within the confines of a certain unity of approach and treatment. Eclecticism took this variety to its logical conclusion and removed all restraints. The best example is probably to be seen at Edensor, by Chatsworth, where the Duke of Devonshire built a remarkable collection of cottages in contrasting

119　Masons at work on the construction of Waddesdon (*Gazette des Beaux Arts*, 1959, series 6, LIV, 15)

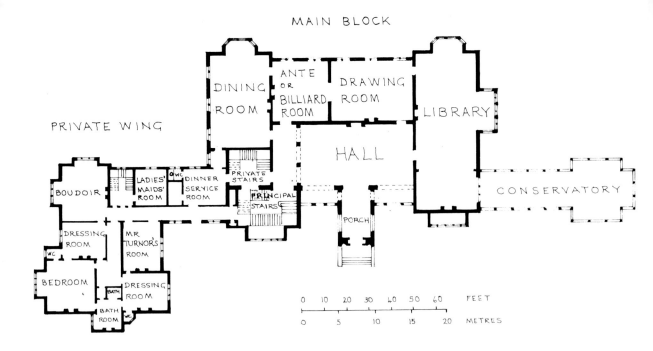

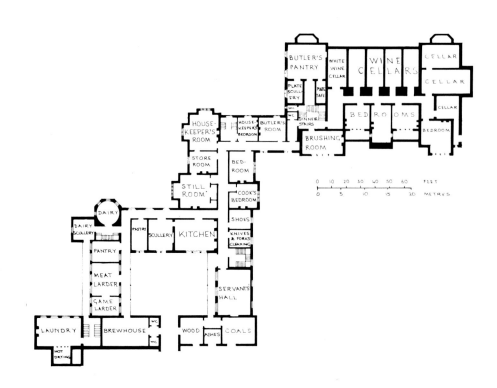

120 Stoke Rochford hall, plans of the principal floor and the basement (Redrawn from plans in RIBA Drawings J12 (1 and 2) British Architectural Library, Drawings Collection)

121 The kitchen at Minley Manor, Hampshire, part of the additions of 1885 and later by George Devey to a house of 1858–62 by Henry Clutton (National Monument Record. A Bedford Lemere photograph)

122 *above left*   A Victorian fernery: one kind of
specimen garden (Alfred Smee, *My Garden, its Plan
and Culture*, 1872, pl. 10)

123 *above right*   Architectural gardening by Sir
Charles Barry at Shrubland Park, Suffolk, 1848 (Alfred
Barry, *The Life and Works of Sir Charles Barry*, 1867,
pl. 17)

124 *opposite above*   Parterres in Trentham Park laid
out by W. A. Nesfield in the 1830s and 1840s,
photographed at the end of the century (*Country Life*,
1889, III, 273)

125 *opposite below*   Tortworth Court. The park was
landscaped in the eighteenth century, though the
conifers and specimen trees are younger. The formal
terraces lie between the house and the park (*Country
Life*, 1899, V, 592)

126 *above* East Lockinge, Oxfordshire. This view shows the main street after it had been re-aligned by Lord Wantage in 1860 to remove it from the view of Lockinge House. The model cottages with their mixture of traditional Berkshire and Victorian Gothic styles were designed by Lord Wantage himself (Museum of English Rural Life)

127a, b and **c** *below and opposite* Somerleyton, Suffolk. Built for Sir Morton Peto, a successful building contractor and Liberal MP for Norwich, about 1850, Somerleyton contains 28 cottages and a school built round a large green. It is perhaps the best surviving example of a 'picturesque' model village, still remote and rural

128 *left* Scene at the homecoming of Lord and Lady Heneage of Hainton, July 1896. The venerable figure standing close to the carriage is Mr Harrison, the oldest tenant on the estate (Hall Collection)

129 *below* An estate banquet for tenants held in the forecourt of Coleorton Hall, 1849 (Leicestershire Museums, Art Galleries and Records Services)

130 *above left*   Drinking a stirrup-cup at a meet at Culverthorpe, near Sleaford in Lincolnshire (Hallgarth Collection)

131 *below left*   The eighth Earl of Harrington with his hounds. The Earl brought hounds from Nottinghamshire to hunt part of the Quorn territory in Leicestershire (Leicestershire Museums, Art Galleries and Records Services)

132 *above right*   Two gentlemen pose with their bag, at Hainton, a village on the Lincolnshire wolds south-east of Market Rasen (Hallgarth Collection)

133 *below right*   A shooting party pose at Holton le Moor, Lincolnshire (Hallgarth Collection)

134 The squire and friends wreak havoc among the partridges. This scene of 1895 shows a breech-
loading shotgun in use (*Illustrated London News*)

styles for his estate employees. The cottages are mostly detached and are well-built of local stone, but their styles range from mock-Tudor, castellated Gothic and Italianate renaissance to sturdy Swiss 'chalets', with a weird variety of intermediate decoration attached. In some ways it is the ultimate in model village architecture.[17] Although the picturesque and the eclectic were perhaps the most characteristic architectural manifestations of model villages, they did have some more sober rivals. An unadorned utilitarianism inspired Henry Roberts's cottage designs for the Society for Improving the Condition of the Labouring Classes, and it had a widespread influence, notably in villages on the Duke of Bedford's estate, and also those of the Duke of Grafton, like Potterspury in Northamptonshire.[18] The revived classic and Gothic styles had only limited influence, being too imposing for cottages; though elements of the former may be seen at Saltaire, and of the latter at Akroyden, near Halifax. These styles were not only too imposing but also too expensive.[19]

A more sensible response to the question of style was employed by those architects who sought to conform to the local vernacular style prevailing in the district while adding any minor improvements which may have seemed necessary. Thus at Penshurst in Kent the nineteenth-century additions conform more or less to the prevailing timber-framed Tudor style; and this approach was also adopted by Lord Wantage at East Lockinge, although admittedly some picturesque additions (particularly in the strange shape of dormer windows) were allowed to creep in.[20] This modified vernacular approach was fairly widespread. At Baldersby St James in Yorkshire William Butterfield adapted a local vernacular style in brick which was neo-Georgian except for its steeply pitched roofs. An even more modern type of vernacular was used by Raymond Unwin and Barry Parker at New Earswick, built for the Rowntree chocolate workers outside York, *c.* 1901–10. Here steeply pitched tiled roofs were combined with simple, often whitewashed, exteriors and fairly large windows, which were characteristic of what was then regarded as 'modern' architecture. As a garden suburb New Earswick, of course, occupies an intermediate position between village and town. Its ambience and feel are rural, but it is in fact part of the urban area of the city of York.[21]

Standards of housing varied very much from village to village, but with a tendency towards improvement as the nineteenth century progressed. The earliest picturesque villages, like Blaise Hamlet, provided only rather limited, dark and poky living space, but after the middle of the century most cottages offered a living room and kitchen downstairs, and three bedrooms above. The moral aspects of overcrowding particularly alarmed the Victorians, and it became increasingly seen as important that children should not share their parents' bedroom and that separate bedrooms should be provided for boys and girls. As families tended to be large this could still mean that three or four boys or girls might share a bedroom, but it was a great advance on the conditions which had often existed in the early part of the century.

An example of earlier conditions is provided by Ardington and Lockinge in 1860, before Lady Wantage and her husband started their work of amelioration. In later life (1907) she pungently described the old-world cottages as 'fast-decaying hovels

through whose wattle and dab walls a walking stick could easily be thrust'.[22] When
it was decided to remove part of the village which was too close to the Wantage
residence to a more congenial site, Lady Wantage described the part to be destroyed as
'farm sheds, muck yards and hovels'.[23] The Wantages set about building the new
model cottages with enthusiasm; and it may not be a coincidence that Lord Wantage
had previously served as an equerry to the Prince of Wales, a position for which he
had been selected by Prince Albert, some of whose enthusiasm for model cottages may
have rubbed off on the young equerry. Lady Wantage stated:

> An architect was rarely employed; plans of buildings have always been
> made and executed under Lord and Lady Wantage's own superintendence.
> The picturesque character of the old style of cottage building, with its
> 'wattle and dab' walls, rough timber beams and thatched roofs, has been as
> far as possible retained, with the view of preserving the irregular character
> and charm of the old Berkshire villages.[24]

By the standards of the time these were sturdy and roomy cottages. Downstairs they
had a living room 15 feet square and 8 feet 6 inches high, a small kitchen and outhouses containing a coal-stove, a built-in copper with fireplace beneath for boiling
water for washing, and an earth-closet. Upstairs they had three bedrooms, one
measuring 15 feet by 12 feet, and the other two 12 feet by 8 feet.[25] However there was
one aspect of residence which never occurred to the Wantages: present-day residents
find great difficulty in getting any furniture into the upstairs rooms because of the
steep roof gables and narrow twisting stairs.

Modern sanitation was inevitably a late development since very few villages had
piped water supplies, but it is interesting to note that Henry Roberts's 1848 design for
model cottages contained water-closets if only with outside access, whereas when
Prince Albert and Roberts designed a pair of model cottages for the 1851 Exhibition
water-closets were provided with internal access, not only on the ground floor, but
upstairs as well. These cottages were reconstructed at Kennington in south London
after the Exhibition, where they still stand.[26]

However it is unlikely that many villages had piped water before the twentieth
century, and it was in the industrial villages close to towns that progress was most
rapid. In 1859 Akroyden was supplied with water and gas, and drainage was by
'sanitary tubes'. Bathrooms were still unknown, but an interesting variation on the
usual tin tub before the fire was provided at Bourneville (*c.* 1895) where a sunken bath
was built in the kitchen floor in front of the range. When required its cover was
removed and it could be filled from large kettles warmed on the range.[27]

Generally speaking, model villages almost certainly provided above-average
accommodation by the standards of the time, and usually supplied it at an artificially
low rent as well. If the quality of the housing seems inadequate today that is merely a
reflection of how much the general standard of living (and its associated
expectations) have risen since Victoria's time.

III

The greater wealth (and often the greater needs) of industrialists enabled them to pioneer some of the improvements in housing standards and introduce them before they became practical in agricultural villages; but conversely it may have been the latter which inspired some industrialists to provide housing for their workers in the context of a village or garden suburb rather than in the densely packed urban tradition.

An interesting example of the industrial village approach is provided by Street in Somerset, now a small town virtually attached to Glastonbury, but for many years a model industrial village. Street is the home of the shoe-making firm of C. & J. Clark Ltd, one of the largest shoe manufacturers in Britain. This is very much a family firm, founded by Quaker farmers in 1825 when Street had a population of around 800 people. Shoe-making was at that time a cottage industry which provided employment for people living in Street and a number of surrounding villages. Clarks, however, were so successful with their shoes that it became necessary to bring in machinery to meet the expanding demand of the 1850s, and by 1861 the firm was producing 208,000 pairs of shoes a year. The population of Street was then 1,900, of whom practically all worked for Clarks. By 1901 the population had reached 4,000 (and shoe production 800,000 pairs), but Street still retained its village character.[28]

The Clarks had built their factory in 1857 right next to their own house in the main street, and there it still stands, though considerably enlarged. From the beginning they decided to provide housing for their workpeople, and the roads and houses were carefully planned and laid out to ensure that ample gardens and recreation space were left. The local lias stone (called blue, but actually a light grey) provided an excellent building material, and the company houses were built in a modified vernacular similar to that which is so attractively displayed in nearby towns and villages like Somerton and Compton Dundon.[29]

Although now too big to be regarded any longer as a village, Street yet retains the physical limits and the small community atmosphere which the more widely celebrated industrial garden suburbs, like Bourneville, Port Sunlight and New Earswick, have to some extent lost because of their proximity to large cities. The outward sprawl of Birmingham, Birkenhead and York has threatened them with encirclement and absorption, and although they have managed to retain a semi-rural atmosphere the village community aspect has inevitably tended to wither. However, all these industrial communities (Street included) share with traditional model villages the overriding influence (though not always the dominance) of one employer family. Lord Leverhulme at Port Sunlight clearly revelled in his paternalistic role, though the other three, the Cadburys at Bourneville, the Rowntrees at New Earswick and the Clarks at Street (all Quakers), were more concerned to try to reduce this aspect of their role so as not to induce hostile reactions amongst their employees. For the feeling of resentment at obligation, which can arise even towards the most beneficent of patrons, has always been the most troublesome fly in the ointment of the model village. With this aspect of the subject we may conclude this chapter.

IV

In a situation where a landlord was providing the housing and, as frequently happened in model villages, other amenities as well, such as allotments, sports grounds, clubhouses ('reading rooms' as they were often called) and generally a well-organized and pleasant environment, he would inevitably expect to receive the gratitude, respect and obedience of his tenants. Equally inevitably they were inclined to feel a sense of being manipulated and a loss of self-respect. This feeling was no doubt accentuated in cases where the landlord disapproved of public houses (as many did), or expected regular attendance at church (as Lady Wantage did). At Selworthy in west Somerset Lady Acland provided red cloaks for the old-age pensioners to wear. This may have made the rural scene more charming, but must also have added to the feeling of diminished independence.[30]

All these issues were ventilated in a pointed way in relation to the Lockinge estate in an article which appeared in the Liberal *Daily News* of 25 September 1891. It was written by a 'special commissioner' who paid a visit to the estate, and appeared under the title 'Arcadia Realised', together with Lord Wantage's reply. The main points are given in the following quotations.

> One of the most interesting and instructive scenes of rural life in England may be found in the villages of Lockinge and Ardington. . . . I went over yesterday because two or three years back I understood that the owner of this vast estate was going to crown and complete the remarkable little social system he has created here, by admitting his people to a share in the profits of his farming, and I wished to learn a little about the result of it. . . .
>
> 'These villages of Ardington and Lockinge' the special commissioner went on,
>
> are well worthy of a visit. Seen in the early summer especially, as I saw them on a former occasion, they strike one as quite a little rural paradise. The estate is beautifully timbered; the cottages with their ornamental eaves and pointed gables, their fanciful chimney-stacks and pretty porches overgrown with ivy and roses, their grassy slopes and lawns and shrubs and flower-beds, all present innumerable points of view with which the artist would be enraptured. Every villager has, or may have, his allotment. There is an admirable reading room and a public house in charge of a salaried manager who has no interest whatever in pushing the sale of drink, but who is especially required to provide soup in winter, and tea and coffee and other non-toxicants at all times. There is a first-rate co-operative store, with commodious

premises, at which the people can get all the necessaries of life, clothes, grocery, bread, meat, and provisions, on profit-sharing terms. The bakery is a beautiful little place, with patent ovens and the newest machinery. In addition to all this, over a hundred villagers are employed in municipal workshops, so to speak—shops fitted with all kinds of the latest machinery and the best appliances—saw-mills, carpenters' shops, blacksmiths' shops, painters' shops, wheelwrights' shops—all for the building and repairing and general maintenance of the property on the estate. There are two churches and an excellent school. In short, it is a little self-contained world in which nobody is idle, nobody is in absolute want, in which there is no squalor or hunger, while in the midst of it all is the great house of Lockinge the beautiful home of Lord and Lady Wantage, always ready to play the part of benevolent friends to all who need their help, and who indeed, by all accounts, seem sincerely desirous of promoting the happiness and well-being of their people. The regular pay of the labourers on the estate is not higher than elsewhere. I understand that it was a shilling or so higher at one time, and that in consequence Lord Wantage has the very cream of the labourers in that part of the world, but that it was reduced to ten-shillings a week when the profit-sharing scheme was promulgated the expectation being that this reduction would be more than counterbalanced by the dividend that would be distributed when the farm accounts were made up.

Having found so much to praise at Ardington and Lockinge the special commissioner turned to what he thought 'radically rotten and bad':

The whole system of things here is another illustration of that 'model' village life which is merely another name for social and political death. Lord Wantage is not to be attacked. He stands high in the esteem of all his neighbours and friends—unless maybe some of the tradesmen in the little town of Wantage, who are naturally angry with co-operative supply stores—and he has most laudably and consistently carried his Conservative principles into action. Materially, the result on the face of it is delightful and as a means of keeping the control and management of the people by the aristocracy nothing could possibly be better. But for all the purposes of political life and social progress and human development it is utterly bad. Lord Wantage has done for the people, in the true spirit of benevolent Toryism, what the people ought to be able to do for themselves—not individually, of course, but collectively and unitedly, and by their own sturdy independent and manly effort. I don't know what Lord Wantage's personal wish may be with regard to the voting power of his own people but I am sure that those people themselves have no idea whatever that they are free electors. 'Any politicians here?' I asked an old man as I walked up the road with him through Lockinge. 'What's them?' said the man with a puzzled air. 'Politicians,' I bawled, thinking the old man was a little deaf or very stupid—'Politicians—you know what politicians are'. 'Be-em animals they goes out to shoot?' said the old fellow. Then I saw the waggish twinkle of his eyes that told me plainly enough he was only making a fool of me. He knew very well what politicians were, but he wasn't going to talk about such matters at Lockinge, and I couldn't induce him to. All around I heard Ardington and this village spoken of as a political dead sea, in which no public opinion ever was known to manifest itself. Nobody would say that Lord Wantage was a man to exercise any improper influence on his people; but he is a strong Tory, has been a member of the Tory government, his agents are Tories, and he owns all the land and houses, and can give or take away employment. I could not find anybody who knew of a political meeting having been held in these places. I heard it rumoured that there was one man who dared avow himself a Liberal, but I couldn' find him. 'O yes, Sir', said a woman in the place, 'they all votes Lord Wantage's way, of course. It wouldn't do for em to go again 'im.'

And according to the *Daily News* reporter, many of the amenities of Lord Wantage's villages were accompanied by irritating restrictions on individual freedom:

I am assured that the admirable little public house in Ardington is to a great extent a failure, because the men find that they are not free to talk there, and that whatever they say is liable to be carried by the birds to the agent's or bailiff's ears. The people are managed and governed and controlled without the least voice in their public and collective affairs, and, though they undoubtedly have strong opinions on certain matters, they dare not give expression to them. For instance, the people have allotments for growing their own vegetables, but they must not keep a pig. They have flower gardens in front of their cottages; if they don't keep them in order the bailiff will be down upon them. A labourer doesn't quite like his cottage; there is no possibility of shifting without the bailiff's consent and arrangement. 'They daren't blow their noses over at Ardington without the bailiff's leave,' said a labourer in the neighbourhood. The people control nothing, have no part whatever in anything like public life, nor any voice in matters directly affecting their own welfare. . . .

For their village stores the men ought to subscribe their own capital, pay interest, if at all, into their own coffers, and pocket the profit of the whole business. The management would, of course, be in the hands of the people

themselves, who would elect their own officers and control their own affairs.
Whatever advantage there might be would be public advantage, and it
would all be consistent with everybody's perfect freedom and independence.
There need be no fear of anybody, no cringing to agents, no concealment of
opinions—absolutely nothing inconsistent with free, individual, manly life
and sturdy citizenship. . . .

To the Editor of the '*Daily News*'

    Sir, . . . It is not my desire or intention to enter into any controversy;
but I feel it would be unfortunate if some of the systems in operation on
my estates, which your commissioner describes, were to be discredited
by erroneous statements which would have the effect of discouraging
their adoption elsewhere.

    A correspondent of yours who signs himself 'Lockinge' makes many
and varied complaints on behalf of the labourers of this district. Among
these the allegation that the 'bonus' system has caused universal
dissatisfaction among the labourers on this estate can only have a
misleading and mischievous effect. In spite of what this correspondent
says, I strongly (after experience of some years) recommend the system
as an incentive to industry, and as conducive to a widening of interest
on the part of the labourers in the prosperity of the farm on which they
work. The bonus is, as your commissioner points out, given over and
above the regular wages paid to farm labourers on this estate, which
are in no way affected by it, and which rise and fall according to the
fluctuation of supply and demand. It is not intended that the bonus
system should be worked on strictly profit-sharing principles, which at
present involves considerable practical working difficulties, but which
further experience may possibly overcome. But the amount of bonus
given is dependent on the profit realised. Certain farms of mine, which
till recently made no profits, and consequently gave no bonus, have
since last year paid their way, and have yielded a bonus, which I hope
may be gradually increased in amount as the farm profits improve. The
enforcement of sanitary regulations naturally falls upon the landlord,
whether he happens to hold town or country property, and the
insurance of healthy conditions by means of estate rules must in some
cases override other considerations. The convenience of a pig-sty close
to the cottage backdoor is more than counter-balanced by the
contamination of the neighbouring well. But it by no means follows
that, because a pig-sty is not allowed close to a cottage, the cottager is
forbidden to have one elsewhere. The allotment is the most suitable
place for a pig-sty, and on this estate every man, can, if he wishes, have
one put up at cost price, and removed at his convenience. Allotments

should, where possible, be in near proximity to the village. Such is the case on this estate, and the proof that they are not 'failures' is that the demand for them is such that none are ever vacant. The management of the public house is so well described by your commissioner that I need say no more about it, except to observe that the sole restrictions enforced are such as the law of the land imposes, namely, those restricting the supply of liquor when men are in a state of drunkenness. The co-operative stores established in these villages distribute the whole of the profits among their customers, being worked on what is known as the Rochdale co-operative system. This mode of distribution was adopted, after full consideration, in preference to another plan, also on the Rochdale principle, which disposes of the profit in the shape of dividends, among the shareholders. But when there are shareholders who take these dividends, the money returned to the customers on their purchases is to that extent diminished, and this consideration has guided the managers of these stores in their adoption of a system which is working very satisfactorily.

It has been said in your columns that it is easy to draw pleasant pictures of the condition of the agricultural worker under the care of a beneficent landlord. But why assume that such a condition can only be purchased at the expense of freedom to think and act for himself? The fact that we live in democratic days is no reason for disparaging and discouraging the legitimate influence landlords may exercise over their neighbours and tenants by helpful supervision and by friendly interest in their affairs which ought not, and which do not, interfere with the freedom of speech and liberty of action which are the right of all alike, of labourers as well as landlords.

I am, Sir, your obedient servant,

Wantage

Lockinge House, Wantage, Berks, October 3 [1891].[31]

These two quotations provide such an excellent summary of the conflicting contemporary views of model villages that further comment is hardly necessary; except to point out that the economic advantages of residing in one could be very real. Those who wished to maintain a more independent and self-reliant way of life had a high price to pay.

In conclusion it should be noted that model villages (both rural and industrial) had a far wider influence than their limited numbers would imply: for if a few landlords could aspire to remodelling a whole village, there must have been hundreds who were inspired by the example to tackle the housing problem on a smaller scale. New cottages were built to ampler and more convenient standards, and older cottages, which might otherwise have been neglected, were refurbished or extended. Thus was the influence of the model villages filtered through the whole of the Victorian countryside.

Notes

1   See Havinden, 1966, for a general history of Lockinge and the Wantage estate.
2   See Darley, 1975, for an excellent and wide-ranging discussion of the many types of model village.
3   See F. M. L. Thompson, 1963, *passim*.
4   Cited by Darley, 1975, 8.
5   Cited by Cooper, 1967a, 1454.
6   Pevsner, 1958, 468–9.
7   Darley, 1975, 45–7.
8   *Country Life*, 10 December 1904, 881–2.
9   Holderness, 1972b, *passim*.
10   Allen, 1846, *passim*.
11   Alice M. Hadfield, 1970, *passim*.
12   Boyson, 1970, 115–40.
13   Holroyd, 1871, *passim*.
14   Wilson, 1954, I, 142–58.
15   Darley, 1975, 30.
16   Cooper, 1967a, 1456.
17   Pevsner, 1953, 129–31.
18   Cooper, 1967a, 1456.
19   Darley, 1975, 67.
20   Havinden, 1966, 105–11.
21   Darley, 1975, 92–4.
22   Havinden, 1966, 54.
23   *Ibid.*, 68.
24   *Ibid.*, 69.
25   *Ibid.*, 95–6.
26   Darley, 1975, 45–6.
27   *Ibid.*, 67, 70.
28   Clark, 1975, *passim*.
29   Little, 1974, 129–34.
30   Acland, 1976, 9.
31   Havinden, 1966, 113–18.

31   Landlords and Tenants

T. W. Beastall

I

The landlord–tenant system depended upon the great wealth of landowners and the security, coupled with a freedom to make the best of their farms, that this gave to tenant-farmers. Landlords were expected to put their capital into their estates, to protect their tenants in bad times, to stand for fair or sympathetic conduct towards farmers and to eschew all appearances of rapacity or ruthlessness. Not all landlords were wealthy but their conduct had to suggest that they were, and their standards in estate management were set by those who from agricultural rents, woodlands, mines, railways, docks and urban building, were possessed of great incomes and vast assets.

Many landlords had gradually developed a relationship with their tenants which was relaxed, interested and encouraging. Showing concern for the condition of one's tenants was as essential a part of rural life as participating in the many sporting activities that went with the ownership of a great, or indeed a small estate. The landlord owned the soil, and through his agent made sure that it was kept in good heart by holding his tenants to certain conditions of practice. It had to be as well-drained as possible, enclosed, served by convenient roads or lanes, protected from the ravages of rabbits, and its function as a crop- and livestock-raising asset reconciled with the claims of hunting, shooting and fishing. The farmhouse and buildings, with walls and some hedges, were usually the landlord's responsibility. Perhaps his chief contribution for being spared the direct risks of farming was that in capitalizing the holding he was enabling the farmer to use all his resources for implements, seeds, fertilizers, the purchase or hire of better livestock, the use of more horse power, and the employment of good shepherds, wagoners and labourers. This made possible the traditional aim of tenant-farmers, the one held in the 1840s by occupiers on the north Lincolnshire uplands, who tried to make in a year at least three times the amount they had to find for rent and tithes. If rent and tithes stood at £1,000 a year, then that sum could be spent on labour, fertilizer and family living costs, and £1,000 would be looked for in addition as profit.[1]

Cottages for the farm's labourers were often built and maintained by the landlord. Sometimes he would keep them in his own hands and let them to farm workers himself. On other estates cottages were let with the farm and the tenant had control of their occupation. For tenant-farmers there were advantages in not owning the land they farmed. It was easier to raise the capital to rent a farm than it was to buy one, and cheaper to set up one's sons as tenants than it was to buy holdings for them. Mobility in bad times was easier for tenants than for owner-occupiers, and yet ownership of land could be combined with tenancies. When prices fell during a run of bad seasons the landlord acted as a buffer between the tenant and the adverse conditions of the time. Rent reductions or returns eased matters until the crisis passed.

Residence was another feature of the landlord-tenant system that gave to English farming an enviable degree of stability and commitment by both farmers and owners. Tenants were expected to live in the main residence of a holding or to install there a responsible member of their families. Landlords, whose seasonal migrations took them to London and elsewhere, were expected, nevertheless, to spend part of the year on their estates. The Dukes of Devonshire had to know about their tenants in Ireland and in eight English counties. The better communications of Victorian England enabled landowners to keep in close touch with the affairs of their estates, and to have early reports on the meetings between their agents and the tenants at events like the biannual rent or audit dinners. Many landlords maintained a home farm, from which to feed their households at cost price and to practise farming themselves with the aid of farm managers or bailiffs. This tradition brought them into contact with their tenants, but movement about their estates in the course of hunting and shooting probably did as much or more to familiarize them with the farmers' mood and the condition of their farms. Landlords had to make some effort to provide balanced holdings. They had to break up inconveniently situated farms, and attempt some redistribution of difficult land so that those with capital and skill could tackle it successfully. The purchasing policy of many estates was to buy up the land of interlopers and round off the property in a ring-fence layout. A resident landowner was of value to a tenant, too, in dealing with difficult neighbours.

Through his landlord a tenant enjoyed access to political affairs and business knowledge. For example, landlords appreciated that Repeal of the Corn Laws would affect their estates, and some provided leadership for their tenants in preparing for it. Under the Land Improvements Acts landlords negotiated loans for draining and building. New ideas were introduced through agricultural shows and ploughing competitions. Aristocratic owners recommended practices found in distant counties, and urged upon their agents comparisons which otherwise would not have been readily available to the local tenantry. The earls of Scarbrough, for instance, made comparisons between their tenants in Lincolnshire, Yorkshire and Durham. Lord Willoughby d'Eresby would call for the use of hedge bills on his Lincolnshire estate such as he saw in Scotland, and he could show his staff on the Grimsthorpe estate the 'Scotch method of sowing turnips upon ridges'.[2] Size and diversity gave to large owners and their agents a breadth of knowledge which must have benefited their management. The advice of a landlord was useful, too, when railway promoters were seeking support for their schemes. He usually had knowledge of alternative proposals and his response to overtures was likely to be more discriminating than that of an owner-occupier who lacked his contacts and his political influence. The tenth Earl of Scarbrough wrote to his Yorkshire tenants in 1900 telling them to be on their guard when railway promoters approached them. The demands of the coal interest were strong in the county at that time, and it was important for agriculture to speak with a single and influential voice.[3]

The landlord–tenant system as represented by the great estates of the aristocracy was not spread evenly over the country, but since it was to be found in all geographical and farming regions its example and influence were strong. In Victorian England most counties had from one fifth to a half of their total acreage farmed under the system. While there were counties like Kent, Surrey, Essex and Middlesex where London's purchasing power had prevented the creation of really great estates, there were others like Lincolnshire where formerly poor land had been bought cheaply, welded into estates, and improved. The north and the west of England were more influenced by the landlord–tenant system than the south and the east, but the style and the assumptions of the system were widely known and served as standards of comparison, if not always of imitation, in areas where great aristocratic estates were few.[4]

II

That on the whole good landlord–tenant relationships were the norm is confirmed by the substitution in the second quarter of the nineteenth century of tenancies-at-will or annual tenancies for leases of three, five, seven or twenty-one years. Farmers were willing to risk their capital at a time of uncertain farming prospects on the strength, sometimes, of nothing more than a verbal agreement with the landowner. Of course, there were strong economic forces supporting this informal arrangement. Tenants with capital and skill were hard to find, and they knew that an annual agreement left them free to move if they were not making a profit, and moreover the landlord was unlikely to hazard having to take his farm in hand by evicting his tenant. Leases had been useful to both tenants and landlords when waste land was being broken into tillage, but after the Napoleonic wars farmers had to watch profit margins carefully as cereal prices levelled out well below the inflated peaks of wartime. They did not want to be tied to the terms of a lease, and the freedom to assess their position each year at Candlemas or Michaelmas appealed to them. Not only were landlords denied access to their farms by a lease, but when prices fell tenants would throw up the lease unilaterally. This left the owner with either the unwelcome prospect of accepting the situation or exacting some form of penalty; a time-consuming and unpopular activity. For him, too, the annual agreement was therefore more acceptable. It was for these considerations, which made good sense in the early Victorian farming context, that leases fell into disfavour, and it was not a crude attempt to wield political power over a proportion of the electorate enfranchised by the Chandos amendment in the 1832 Reform Act. The new importance of the tenant with the ability and capital to tackle large farms now that price levels were lower and the protection of the Corn Laws might be removed was in itself a good reason for enfranchising a vital interest in rural society.

Tenancy arrangements varied within farming regions and even within individual estates, but while encouraging the tenant to invest in his holding most agreements were designed to preserve ancient or valuable pasture, keep the arable in good heart, and ensure that when vacated the farm was fit to hand over to a newcomer. A smooth take-over, an absence of disputes, and a short period of dual occupation of either farm buildings or the land, were also important in any agreement. On the Durham, Lincolnshire and Yorkshire estates of the Lumley family new annual agreements were drawn up in 1864. Six months' notice on either side was to be given, and mineral, timber and game rights were reserved by the landlord. In Yorkshire land was let on 2 February and farm buildings from 1 May. Written consent was needed before pasture could be ploughed: a fine of £10 an acre could be imposed on a tenant ignoring this clause. Rents were to be paid biannually, and the occupier had to meet all other outgoings, except the landlord's property tax. Tenants were also to keep a foxhound free of charge. The land was to be farmed according to the best methods of the district, and no straw, chaff, hay, fodder or turnips sold off without permission. A four-course rotation was to be followed, and no two white crops sown in succession. On leaving, the tenant was to be compensated for his improvements under the terms of the local custom. In 1897 an amended form of the agreement required the tenant to insure his stock and produce, to live in the farmhouse or to place a member of his family there, to paint the buildings every fourth year, trim hedges and clear ditches every year, and, for the convenience of hunters, remove all barbed wire between 1 November and 1 April.

The first twenty-five years of Queen Victoria's reign saw much investment by tenant farmers in bones, guano, marl and lime. Many developed mixed enterprises, balancing their resources between stock-rearing and cereal-growing, and by keeping their sheep in the fields to eat clover or turnips they consolidated the soil, manured it and raised its fertility. Cattle were fed artificial 'cake', the manure from which, when collected in the fold or crew-yard of a farm, became a valuable commodity. Farmers were willing to put their capital into horse power, labour and farm carts to transport the manure to their hungry croplands, and in some of the upland regions of Yorkshire and Lincolnshire even to help their landlords build new barns and crew-yards out in the fields so that mixed farming could advance. But some farmers grew difficult as their leases ran out. William Dawson was the tenant of the 2,300 acres of Withcall farm, near Louth on the Lincolnshire wolds, under Lord Willoughby d'Eresby. In 1842, with six years to run, he became anxious to buy his farm, which stood detached from the other estates of his landlord. He threatened to spend no more on bones, linseed cake, artificial manure, draining, building or fencing, and threatened, too, to sow the whole acreage with wheat. Leases, in fact, might encourage an occupier to think that he had a right to be given a first refusal to purchase his holding at a low price; or that as he had enjoyed a long lease the landlord was bound to refuse him a renewal and offer it to a newcomer for a higher rent. Tenancies-at-will, on the other hand, could continue indefinitely in a flexible arrangement undisturbed by the crisis which inevitably came when a lease was due for renewal. The Earl of Yarborough boasted that he did not *get* tenants in Lincolnshire, he *bred* them! Many of the families listed late in the nineteenth century as walking puppies for the Brocklesby hunt were already there in 1754. This continuity of association with the estate, if not occupation of the same holding, was achieved by a system of mutual respect, relatively low rents and tenancies-at-will. In Nottinghamshire, too, by the 1840s leases were neither wanted nor expected as sons succeeded fathers on farms in many cases.[5]

Farmers were willing to exchange leases for annual tenancies because county customs for tenants' compensation ensured that investment in their holdings would be safeguarded. Compensation varied within counties and even within farming regions, however. In parts of the West Riding tenants were paid for what they had put into the land by way of seed and fertilizers in their last year of occupation, and for half their costs in the penultimate year. This strong custom meant, it was believed in farming circles, that a tenant could fail in Yorkshire, set up again in Nottinghamshire with his tenant-right award, fail again and set up once more in Lincolnshire. Heavy tenant-right payments discouraged younger applicants for farms who had skill but little capital. On the other hand, the custom encouraged tenants' investment, gave security to the tenant-at-will, and helped the landlord in that fewer farms were run down. Landlords could buy up the tenant-right of an outgoer and offer the farm to a newcomer without a demand upon his capital. The tenant-right would then be paid off over a period of years as part of the rent. It also saved landlords the unpopularity of taking action against a man who left owing large arrears of rent. Although landlords were possessed of considerable powers in law to seize the goods of defaulting tenants, they were reluctant to exercise them, and the spectacle of a tenant committed to prison was not one that many landlords would contemplate. By deducting some or all of the arrears of rent from the sum to be paid the outgoer by the new occupier, the landlord could recover his rent without attracting adverse publicity in the press.

In the Lincolnshire uplands farmers were prepared to take large farms without even a compensation clause in their annual agreements. Their security, they said, rested in the high repute of valuers, the strength of local custom and goodwill. William Loft of Trusthorpe, who farmed 500 acres of wold and 500 more of marsh, converted his fourteen-year lease into an annual tenancy in 1847.[6] On the Leveson-Gower estates in Shropshire and Staffordshire farmers were not interested in leases in the years after the Napoleonic wars. James Loch, the agent, believed

> The attention and capital of the landlord should be bestowed upon the permanent improvements which, in their execution, would withdraw too large a portion of a tenant's capital from the cultivation of the land . . . this is the landlord's proper line of duty, and well suited to his station and position in society.

The landlord having helped the tenants to weather the difficult years for farming in the 1820s, the Lilleshall and Trentham estates were praised by James Caird when he saw them in 1850. Loch was delighted by his verdict. By then his work of over forty years was having its effect. Lilleshall was thought to be the lowest-rented estate in England and arrears were few. During the 1840s the agent had thought the farms were under-rented, but because of uncertainty about the future of the Corn Laws the landlord was prepared to bear some of the cost of Repeal by forgoing the rent increases. He pointed out to another landlord that the Leveson-Gower rents had been reduced by about 26 per cent in the late 1830s: 'no wonder your tenants bellow and scream'.[7]

Landlords were reluctant to raise rents until tenants had reaped the reward of their improvements. So in districts where tenants had helped bring marginal land into cultivation rents were allowed to remain low. In addition, though between 1815 and 1840 rents went up by only small amounts or not at all, prices fell, and therefore in real terms landlords were not losing and were willing to postpone rent increases. On the Brocklesby estate of the Earl of Yarborough wold land was let at 10*s*. to 12*s*. an acre in 1833 when on a valuation it was deemed to be worth from 20*s*. to 27*s*. Yet within roughly the previous forty years the gross income of the estate had increased three-fold, an increase which in real terms was even higher. Nevertheless, rent took only about a third of the returns accruing to the tenant-farmer. James Caird thought in 1850 that rents were a function of landlords' attitudes and of those of their agents, rather than of the land's intrinsic value or the ruling level of prices for agricultural produce. On the larger estates rents tended to be low: the owners had other sources of income. Where a few large estates dominated a district then the 'custom of the neighbourhood' was to offer and ask for low rents. In Lindsey the 40,000 acres of wolds land owned by Lord Yarborough influenced rents in the whole region. Although land was generally low-rented, the agent said of one tenant on land worth 34*s*. or 35*s*., 'I cannot think how Atkinson can have the conscience to accept it at 25s an acre which is what he pays.'[8]

In the 1850s, when the shock of Repeal had receded and some of the benefits of improvement showed returns, rents were raised on many estates. In 1850 an applicant for a farm on the Cowdray estate in west Sussex was refused a low rent on the ground that other tenants would be encouraged to ask for the same. When rent abatements were discontinued or rents were raised agents tended to record their relief in letters to their employers. In September 1854 there were fifty-six tenants at the Cowdray estate audit dinner and thanks were conveyed to Lord Egmont for the previous rent abatement 'and not one remark on its discontinuance'.[9] In July of the same year, after attending a dinner at the White Hart in Lincoln, Weston Cracroft Amcotts noted: 'Cordial reception from my father's Hackthorne tenants at their rent dinner . . . —not a murmur at having their rents raised.'[10] At Cowdray on 13 September 1853 Lord Egmont was told by his agent of a good rent audit. There were few arrears, and at the Angel, Midhurst, there was 'quite a roomful, and all were gratified with the treat your lordship gave them, the buck was a very fine one, and the grouse in fine perfection'. The workpeople on the estate had a dinner of beef in October, 'and all were highly gratified and very thankful, the high prices will make the coming winter a severe one for the working people'. This was a time of agricultural prosperity, however, when rents climbed back to the levels of 1815, arrears were few, and the high noon of Victorian farming was enjoyed by both landlords and tenants.[11]

III

The golden years of high farming ended with a succession of bad seasons in the late 1870s. Heavy imports of cheap grain shook the confidence of farmers, and landlords were again obliged to help. Rent returns and reductions, with drainage schemes and measures to convert arable land to pasture, were employed to ward off the nightmare of landlords—the taking in hand of untenanted farms impossible to let without massive capital expenditure. In Essex extra out-buildings for milking parlours were built as dairy farming was introduced to traditionally arable districts.[12] On the Bedford estates the nature of the land precluded a swing to pastoral or mixed farming, and on others the management's assessment of how best to help the tenants reinforced the traditional style of farming. Estates in livestock-raising counties fared better. Landlords avoided having to make large reductions in rent, and by keeping up expenditure on buildings, drainage and other land improvements, they obviated a steep fall in net incomes. This was true, for example, of a property in Northumberland, the Earl of Harewood's estate near Leeds, and Lord Fitzhardinge's estate in Gloucestershire.

On the Duke of Bedford's estate near Woburn the cost of farms in hand between 1879 and 1896 worked out at £1,284 a year. But on the Duke of Sutherland's estates in Staffordshire and Shropshire, where a change away from cereals to mixed farming was actively encouraged, the burden of farms in hand from 1880 to 1899 was only £220 per annum. Dutch barns for the storage of winter fodder were provided. These, with their galvanized iron roofs on iron pillars, were cheap to erect and maintain, and saved the farmer the cost of thatching his hay ricks. Covered fold-yards were built to help the winter fattening of cattle, and, where possible, heavy land was drained and put down to permanent pasture at a cost of £10 to £15 an acre. This was preferable to allowing tenants to let uneconomic arable tumble down to poor grassland.

On the whole, landlords had been quick to make use of public funds to help drain the heavy clays which were so expensive to farm. The Duke of Cleveland spent great sums on draining his Northamptonshire estate on boulder and Oxford clays. In Northumberland, on the estate of Earl Grey, much had been done in the 1850s and 1860s to drain the heavy land, while near Alnwick on the Duke of Northumberland's farms draining had been carried out without a change to permanent pasture. In Devon tenants on the Duke of Bedford's estate were enabled to grow better turnips, and others, also thanks to better draining, could turn to a wider variety of green crops. Landlords helped tenants to meet the difficulties of the period 1873–96 by creating confidence where possible, dealing promptly with complaints, and encouraging the enterprising. Even so, landlord–tenant relationships were put under considerable strain. Edward Heneage said in 1886 of his tenants on the central wolds of Lincolnshire: 'I am afraid I shall lose some tenants of the larger farms even at reduced rents.' Of his neighbours he observed: 'Landlords are in such a panic that they are letting at any price and giving thirty and forty per cent reductions ... farmers will not be practicable and reduce their own expenditure.' By 1881 his own rents had to follow the levels of 1847 despite the £100,000 spent since then on improvements.[13]

On the estate of the Foljambe family in north Nottinghamshire the larger tenants suffered most and their farms were the hardest to let. Those with farms of under 150 acres who relied on family labour and combined dairying with cereal production needed less assistance from their landlords. While one good tenant on the Scarbrough estates in 1885–6 was given a rent reduction and an installation of water power for chopping and grinding, with no interest charged, a neighbour was refused a rent abatement: his land was 'full of twitch and altogether unfit to grow anything. The fences are neglected and full of gaps', the agent observed. In November 1886 some Yorkshire farmers meeting near Doncaster passed a resolution claiming:

> The present low prices of corn and stock and the prospect of agriculture in general warrants a substantial return on the rent and they trust that landlords will make their tenants large returns ... the whole half year's rent will not compensate for the loss sustained through the depression in value of farm produce.

By the 1890s, however, tenants were coming to see that rent reductions alone would not solve their problems. Lord Scarbrough's agent told him in 1892: 'All paid up and there was no feeling expressed asking for a reduction of rent—the general impression was that your lordship had met them fair as to rent and they must look to some other source to improve matters.'[14] Although numerous tenancy changes were not averted, the estate's management did give confidence to the more resilient of the tenants, and those who held on until the 1890s survived to enjoy a limited prosperity in the new century.

IV

Though disputes about annual tenancies, rent, leases and compensation for improvements strained landlord–tenant relationships, they were internal stresses within a paternalistic society. To its critics from the industrial and urban classes, rural England presented a united front. Loyalty, custom and a genuine wish for guidance at election times caused tenants to welcome advice on how to vote. Many had little time for, or interest in, politics, yet in the days before universal suffrage to cast a vote was a privilege not to be forgone. Traditions of voting for the landlord's candidate went with the handing down of farms from father to son as a natural expression of a mutual interest. Only when a landowner switched from one party to another had he to be explicit about his expectations at the polls. And when parties divided, as did the Liberals over Irish Home Rule or the Conservatives over Imperial preference, landlords made their wishes plain, as some of them were to do again in 1931 when their tenants faced the prospect of a national government.

Guidance was expected, too, on ceremonial occasions. In 1894 the agent at Cowdray wrote to the tenants telling them when they were to present plate and addresses to Lord Egmont on the occasion of his silver wedding, and when the gifts would be on view. In September 1897 they received instructions about attendance at the earl's funeral.[15] National and family occasions were marked by well-ordered ceremonies. Seating plans were drawn up in estate offices and the steward would be their unobtrusive stage manager. These gatherings always helped to bring an estate together, but the activity that above all others emphasized the leadership of the aristocracy was fox-hunting. Tenants were expected to help protect foxes, and to shoot one was an outrage in most English counties. Tenants were invited to subscribe to hunts, and the sixty or seventy well-mounted farmers in scarlet who followed the Brocklesby were living proof of the success of improvement on the north wolds of Lincolnshire. Yet in the last quarter of the century there were complaints about the cost and the risk of keeping a foxhound puppy. A tenant in Yorkshire, who had lost 'into teens' of lambs and two ewes, refused to repair a bridge on his farm 'owing to the foregoing losses, high rent, bad seasons, bridge more convenience to hunters than self . . . I absolutely refuse to do more because I cannot afford to or I should not stick at such a trifle'. His confidence that his complaint would meet with a sympathetic response was justified.[16]

Shooting was wholly reserved for the landlord and his friends, but occasionally leading tenant farmers would be invited for a day with the guns. Although a radical observer of the rural scene emphasized the damage done by corn-eating pheasants, tenants objected more to the losses inflicted by rabbits and hares. The last, with a taste for the crops of improved husbandry like turnips and carrots, were the subject of bitter complaints, especially in times of low prices. The Ground Game Act of 1881 allowed tenants to destroy rabbits and hares without their landlord's permission, but traditions of deference made many occupiers rely upon a drive against rabbits by their landowners' keepers or compensation in the shape of lower rents. The custom of giving game each year to tenant-farmers and parsons as a seasonal present was well-established by Queen Victoria's reign, and the worst features of game preservation, savage sentences on poachers and the use of spring guns, became things of the past. On many estates tenants were allowed to shoot freely once the flying game season was over, but landlords were suspicious of farmers whose sporting interests might conflict with theirs; and a strong reason for rounding off estates by the purchase of inlying fields was to exclude the guns of owner-occupiers or urban speculators. A 'quiet' applicant from Pulborough for a farm on the Petworth estate in 1850 was eligible in every way except that he wanted to keep two greyhounds for coursing on the farm and the common. In October 1850 at Rufford Abbey in Nottinghamshire a great £100-a-side, two-day shooting match between a team from Melton Mowbray and another from Market Harborough saw the shooting of 172 brace of partridges by one side and 132 brace by the other. Squires led the teams and the Earl of Scarbrough provided 'sumptuous entertainment', though he did not take part in the competition. Steeplechasing, considered a plebeian diversion, might be patronized by land agents and stewards but was not thought suitable for their employers. Landlords would play cricket with their tenants, gamekeepers and local clergy, but hare-coursing, appropriate enough for estate servants, was not indulged in by landowners and leading tenant-farmers.

Deference to the landlord's wishes in sport and personal conduct could be irksome, but in return the tenant could expect an active interest in his welfare. The reports of nineteenth-century land agents included many personal details about tenants and their families, and for those who were content to live and work within the social assumptions of the Victorian estate there was a degree of security that counted for something in an age of accelerating change. When, at the turn of the century, a duchess addressed a gathering of tenants' children on an estate in Yorkshire, she said that it was nice to cross the county border to see 'other people's people'. Though later generations might think it a patronizing observation, they could not, with justice, see in it indifference or lofty disregard.[17] Landlords and tenants worked within an informal partnership which took account of both social deference and economic reality. There were limitations as in all partnerships, but it produced social stability in the English countryside and improved standards of farming—advantages which drew favourable comment from observers of the agricultural scene, both in bad times and good.

Notes

1   Perkins, 1976, 130–1.
2   Lincs. RO: 3 Anc. 7, 23/33/44, 34/55.
3   Lumley MSS, Letter Book 1900, 761.
4   F. M. L. Thompson, 1963, 27–44.
5   Lincs. RO: 3 Anc. 7/23/7/18; 23/43/16; Collins, n.d., 17; BPP 1848 VII 409.
6   BPP 1848 VII 7160–2, 7163–4, 7698.
7   Richards, 1974c, 11, 105, 116.
8   Lincs. RO: Yar. 5, 25 September 1841; Perkins, 1976.
9   Dibben, 1960, No. 1907, 4, 22.
10   *Lincolnshire Life*, September 1974, 48.
11   Dibben, 1960, No. 1906, 14, 15, 20, 22, 28, 41.
12   Gavin, 1967, 86; BPP 1896 XVI R.C. 1894–7, 4; Perren, 1970.
13   Lincs. RO: 2 Hen. 5/14/39, 42, 44, 96; 2 Hen. 5/8/63.
14   Beastall, 1975, 163–9.
15   Dibben, 1960, No. 1899.
16   Beastall, 1954, 137.
17   Author's conversation with member of a Yorkshire farming family.

32   The Land Agent

Eric Richards

I

The foundations of country house life in Victorian Britain and its splendid façade of conspicuous consumption and social ritual rested upon an elaborate structure of rural management, with, on a large property, a bureaucracy of bailiffs, stewards, ground officers, clerks, mineral managers and sub-agents of all sorts. At their head stood the land agent, sometimes referred to more grandly as 'commissioner' or, in Scotland, as 'factor'. Land agents were the men who administered rural Britain in the age of the great estates and their managerial responsibilities were heavy by any standards: the great landed estate was one of the largest business enterprises of the Victorian economy. Between 1816 and 1895, for instance, the agents of the dukes of Bedford presided over the expenditure of £4¼ million on the equipment of the Bedford estates.[1] By the middle of the century turnover of rental income on several large estates exceeded £200,000 per year. And in many respects the management of an estate was more complex and subtle than that of a factory or railway company or house of commerce.

Many proprietors handed over to their agents almost all responsibility for running their properties, to the point where the agent became the *alter ego* of the landlord. 'Sometimes, when that owner is an absentee, almost the whole power and control conferred by the possession of such a territory is vested in the landlord's representative.'[2] He could influence the direction and volume of agricultural investment, modify the entire social climate of an estate, manipulate electoral behaviour and greatly affect the level of efficiency and welfare in the landed community. Some agents behaved with as much patrician style as their masters; others were of a rougher breed, technicians with plans to pursue, men who enjoyed the daily exercise of authority. A few agents managed to tyrannize entire rural populations, creating riot and an undying legacy of hatred. But most were honourable, serious and trustworthy men, key managers in the growth of the Victorian economy, and they were not easily found or trained. In an age when many estates diversified their enterprise into industry, mining, transport and urban development, the versatile skills of the agents were visibly stretched. Yet they were also a vital link which sustained the traditional framework of rural Britain, that element which David Spring called 'the coherence of landed society'.[3] Their conviction in this system was sometimes even greater than that of their masters, and their identification with the old agrarian order made them its stoutest defenders. At the end of the Victorian age they mounted a noisy corporate resistance to the impending break-up of the great estates.

A good agent was a man who improved the agricultural practice and value of an estate, who was self-effacing enough to channel all public credit to his employer, and who cultivated the expected reciprocation of respect between the landlord and the community. His work was most easily performed in modern farming areas in prosperous years; it was most difficult among the congested, poor and mutinous populations on the peasant fringe of the Victorian economy. In England the land agent was often regarded as the respected, knowledgeable and even impartial conductor of the rural scene. In Ireland he was as likely to be the hated symbol of landlord neglect and exploitation. Captain Boycott was the best-known agent of the century, mainly because his name has passed into the language. Most agents lived less dramatically and with less controversy. It is a testament to their ability to organize paper that much of the history of modern agriculture is derived from land agency records.

The public reputation of the land agent was extraordinarily mixed. Professionalism and a high moral responsibility, together with expertise in man-management and technical mastery, were the virtues to which the leaders aspired. But the business was too varied to allow a stringent and uniform code of conduct, and land agents at all times had the greatest difficulty in creating a collective professional identity. They were, inevitably, the instruments of unpopular agricultural change, and it was an acknowledged part of their function to absorb as much of the obloquy as they could manage. It was expressed in an Irish opinion that 'the landlords were sometimes decent men, they will tell you, but the agents were devils one and all'.[4] It was a profession which probably attracted more than its share of unsavoury characters. In part this was a consequence of the open nature of recruitment to its ranks: virtually anyone could set up as an agent. In part also it reflected the lack of systematic training in the business of land agency. The problem was compounded by the rapid increase in the demand of the Victorian economy for the skills of managers. The scale of management, in terms of turnover and investment, continued to grow at a time not only of rapidly changing technology but also of shifting assumptions about social, political and economic roles on the land. For instance, many agents in the middle of the century found themselves saddled with the task of managing political influence, while their masters equivocated about the morality of the exercise. Moreover, the organization of farming created problems no less than those of industry and, after Repeal, agriculture was more vulnerable to seasonal and external instability than any other part of the economy. Able and trustworthy agents were always scarce. When the superintendent of the Bridgewater Trust was asked if he could recommend a man for a position on another estate, he replied of agents in general:

> If he is clever and has learned his business, he is tempted away by high wages . . . and if induced to stay he immediately supposes we cannot do without him and becomes an idle, impudent Rogue—*au contraire*, if he turns stupid and incompetent for any situation, he is sure to remain on our hands, and I can readily send you half a dozen of this sort.[5]

It was a scarcity reflected also in the very substantial salaries commanded by the elite of the profession. As early as 1811 Earl Fitzwilliam's agent was paid as much as £1,200 per annum, while in the middle of the century Christopher Haedy, chief agent to the Duke of Bedford, received £1,800, salaries comparable with the top railway managers of their day, and which understate the value of a position which was normally associated with lucrative perquisites.[6]

II

Regular methods of land management had emerged by the end of the eighteenth century and the land steward was one of the main instruments in the rationalization of technology and tenure. While there remained a great deal of overlap between the trades of agent, surveyor and lawyer, on the larger estates management became more systematic, even scientific. Smaller estates tended to be administered either by the owner himself, or by a local farmer, an attorney or a clergyman, usually on a part-time commission basis. In the Victorian age there were endless efforts to gain professional recognition for land agents, and a dissociation from the previous low opinion of lawyers and attorneys—partly incurred by well-known cases where local land markets had been manipulated for the personal gain of the landlord's representative, or where bribes had been taken from tenants in return for special favours. Large estates required residential agents who gained in both income and prestige since they deputized for the landed aristocracy: men 'for social and political reasons who could be continuously on the spot to demonstrate the owner's authority'.[7] The employment opportunities for land agents, and consequently for their professional status, were much advanced by the tasks generated by the great body of legislation associated with parliamentary enclosures and tithe commutation, measures which drew upon the accumulating expertise of land agents. In the late nineteenth century the spate of land legislation and regulation persuaded more landlords to reform the administration of their estates and this had a favourable effect on the public esteem of land agents.

Adam Smith had warned landlords against over-enthusiastic agents who took over too much of the initiative and enterprise in agriculture. The danger, he wrote, was that eventually

> the country (instead of sober and industrious tenants, who are bound by their own interest to cultivate as well as their capital and skill will allow them) would be filled with idle and profligate bailiffs, whose abusive management would soon degrade the cultivation.[8]

J. R. McCulloch, by contrast, thought that landed estates (and indeed the nation) were generally better placed when the landlord was an absentee and the management left in the hands of intelligent agents with whom the tenantry preferred to deal.[9] In reality land agents provided much of the driving force behind the remarkable improvements in agricultural productivity, partly as managers, but also as technicians and propagandists for the ways of improvement. The duties of agents were never-ending: letting farms, keeping accounts, drawing up leases and tenancy agreements, checking farming practice among the tenantry, evicting the recalcitrant and the bankrupt, presiding over institutions of local government, encouraging improvements, supervising plantations, keeping the peace between tenants, labourers and cottagers. These were likely to include also the supervision of domestic arrangements of the landed proprietor and the complex delegation of authority for the exploitation of urban, industrial and transport resources of the estate. It was hard work and it broke the health of many good men. They took few holidays, often worked on Christmas Day, and normally spent a large part of their life on horseback dealing with every mundane detail. Sometimes their employers sensed the strain and packed them off, perhaps to Harrogate, to renew their energies. The very large agencies often managed, in a general supervisory fashion, many different estates. Thus Messrs Rawlence & Squarey in the 1890s supervised about a quarter of a million acres in twenty-four counties.[10] On the great estates there was usually a complicated hierarchy of offices, with a central office in London which co-ordinated the diverse estates. Some properties, such as those of the dukes of Bedford and Sutherland, would daily generate small mountains of correspondence. At the local level there were two functions of surpassing importance. One was rent collection, which required the efforts of sub-agents, auditors and bailiffs, helped along by a modest degree of hospitality to ease the money from producer to rentier. Here it was important to judge the degree of rigour appropriate when dealing with tenants in arrears. The second vital task was the selection of tenants: the highest bidder was not necessarily the best, for an estate would need men of capital, technical ability and general reliability rather than mere speculators. An informal network between the large estates helped in the vetting of tenants.

Most land agents were drawn from the middling ranks of society, younger sons of country gentlemen, or farmers, lawyers or clergy. Many agents had no formal training at all, and some of those who specialized in the management of mining property in the early Victorian period were barely literate. But informal solutions emerged, particularly in the form of unofficial 'schools' of agents. The best training was an apprenticeship in the offices of one of the top managers of the day, with Clutton or Sturge or Squarey or Woolley or Thomas Smith or the Lochs—all of whom raised a stream of articled pupils who were able to move into senior positions on other estates.[11] There were internal controversies about the relative importance of theoretical knowledge and practical experience; there was unanimity that the profession was continuously undermined by the easy entry of amateurs and incompetents. In the early nineteenth century Scottish agents enjoyed an unusual prestige which was partly based on the fame of Lothian farming, but they never came to dominate the profession. The most important source of talent was hereditary: there was an extraordinary number of sons and nephews of agents. As Edward Hughes put it, 'Like the civil servants they not infrequently died in harness, and in the hope that the mantle would eventually fall on their sons or relatives.'[12] There were many instances of dynasties of land agents whose hereditary claims on the position were almost a parallel to those of their patrons.

Aspiring to a status comparable with the medical and legal professions, the leading land agents were endlessly indignant at the dilution of their reputation by untrained interlopers. C. G. Grey of Dilston fulminated at the regiments of retired soldiers, sailors, butlers and house stewards who inhabited the profession, the failed farmers, pernickety lawyers, and former head clerks. Worst of all were the relatives of the landowner: 'Poor relations, for whom some provision is desirable, would generally cost an owner less if he were to make them an allowance to live at Bath or Cheltenham.'[13] James Caird, perhaps the most penetrating observer of land management at the middle of the century, castigated some of the weaker arrangements of the day. In Oxfordshire, for instance, he blamed landlords for their ignorance of agriculture: 'And what is equally unfortunate . . . they have not yet seen the necessity of making amends for their own defective knowledge by the appointment of agents better qualified.' In Northamptonshire some landlords were merely interested in rent returns and employed maximizing agents who had no expertise and felt no responsibility for the care of the soil: 'Some employ men of low standing with a small salary, and in a dependent position, butlers, gardeners, and sometimes gamekeepers, performing the function of land agent. Lawyers are employed by some, but merely receive the rents.'[14]

Incompetent agents, wrote Caird, were a menace to the agricultural community. The weakly old gentlemen and the retired officers in charge of valuable property could easily let slip the reins of improvement and eventually rents would decline. A good agent would provide the foundation for a general improvement of productivity and rising rents from 'an active and intelligent tenantry'. Some agents were paragons: Bright, Lord Hatherton's man, not only managed to double the stock and the output of the home farm in Staffordshire, but invented a revolving harrow and a furrow press which sowed and rolled seeds in one operation. Caird warned landlords against expecting such services too cheaply. Even the most bigoted landlord, he said, knew that rents could only be maintained if the tenantry were given the facilities and professional advice that were required. 'An experienced sensible agent, with the aid of a willing tenantry, will effect as much with £100 as an inexperienced or incompetent man can with £200.' G. C. Brodrick[15] calculated the costs of management in the 1880s and found them extremely variable. On large, well-managed properties in the Midlands costs could be as little as 4 per cent of the rental, compared with more than 20 per cent in other places.[16]

John Lockhard Morton also railed against the type of ignorant agent who had no science, no knowledge of the land, and whose one idea was 'that the exaction of exorbitant rents from the tenantry is his chief business'. Morton would not absolve a landlord from the responsibility of management for otherwise he would be at the mercy of his agent:

> Then, in such a case the landlord is separated from his tenants by an
> impossible barrier, and, in most cases, can only reach them at second hand.
> He wants that knowledge of the farmer's life, habits, modes of thinking, and
> general hopes, which are necessary to create a sympathy between him and
> them.[17]

In rare cases, such as that of R. H. Bradshaw of the Bridgewater Trust, an agent could manipulate his masters and tie them in such legal knots that quite extraordinary stratagems and inducements were required to dislodge him.[18] In the 1860s most landed property in England remained in the hands of solicitors 'who are usually little more than receivers without much knowledge of the details of management',[19] and there were frequent public criticisms of bad agents who 'would wish to act a despotic part towards tenant farmers'.[20] Even at the end of the century the profession had made little progress in its efforts to control entry. Henry Herbert Smith observed that agencies were overstocked with 'a large body of persons who have failed in every other walk of life, or have been obliged . . . to retire from other professions . . . the waifs and strays of the professional world'. Anyone could walk into the agency trade without qualification or restriction: 'The most incompetent tiro can advertise himself as a learned specialist', he wrote, and the worst sort were attracted by visions of an agent's life full of hunting and shooting. Worse still were the retired military men whose background disqualified them 'because they are accustomed to handle men like machines'.[21] Ireland appears to have suffered more than its share of this sort of recruit.[22]

There was no separate Land Agents' Society until 1902, although the elite of the profession had gained entry to the exclusive Surveyors' Club formed in 1834. In 1886 it was claimed that the great majority of the leading agents of the day were members of the Surveyors' Institution.[23] There was no separate category of agents in the Census, but there were informed guesses that in 1877 about sixty agents controlled approximately two-thirds of England,[24] and though this may have been an exaggeration it pointed clearly enough to the concentration of ownership and the extent of the authority wielded by agents. By the end of the century the levels of education had probably improved; in 1882 the Royal Agricultural College at Cirencester reported that most of its students became land agents.[25] There was also an evident decline in the importance of solicitors doubling as agents; by the 1890s, it was said, the 'times have beaten that class of men', and 'their places are taken by practical men who are able to farm the land for the landlord when he gets it in hand'.[26]

A recurrent theme in the credos of the most influential agents was that they should strive to transcend the raw fact that they were the creatures of the landlords and that they should administer the rural community with Olympian impartiality. It was an ideal of moral responsibility emphasized by Thomas Smith Woolley in 1871. Estate agents, he thought, should not regard themselves merely as 'machines for carrying out their own wishes and decisions of landlords'; they should indeed have equal regard for 'the rights or claims of their tenants or dependants'. Thus, as he phrased it,

> he should regard all questions between them with judicial impartiality,
> being neither led by amicable weakness, or a desire for popularity, into
> trifling away his employer's rights, nor by even less worthy motives, into an
> unjust or arbitrary dealing with his neighbours.

Land agents very rarely questioned their belief that, of all forms of rural property, the estates of the landed aristocracy were the best managed. Nor did they doubt that this happy circumstance rested ultimately upon a natural sympathy and understanding between the strata of rural society. It was striking that, after a century of agrarian rationalization, land agents were advised against too rigid an application of the rules of political economy, and against that polarization of rural society which was associated with 'the further development of the terrible tendency of modern society to crystallize as it were into a few strata, more or less bitterly antagonistic to each other'.[27]

III

Land agents managed all aspects of estate business including the mobilization of electoral support and political information. After 1832 the exercise of political influence became less obvious and, indeed, more ambiguous. Symptoms of independence among the tenantry raised the blood pressure of many estate agents, but most landlords by the middle of the century appear to have relied upon a continuing tradition of deference in rural society: 'the tenant voted with his landlord not out of fear, but because he accepted the traditional nature of authority, unquestioningly'.[28] It was a tradition, however, reinforced by the informal powers of influence exercised in practice by the agents. In the parliamentary inquiry into electoral proceedings in 1868 there was investigation of a case which involved the mass switching of votes to a landlord in Cheshire. Asked if direct pressure had been applied by the landlord, the local magistrate replied to the contrary, but explained, however, that

> he allows his agent to go to the tenant, and he allows him to say how much it would please the landlord, if the tenant voted in a certain way, and gives hints that if the tenant does not vote as his landlord wishes, all sorts of petty indulgences, in the shape of small repairs, additional gates, and perhaps a little time to pay his rent, will be withdrawn, and the landlord, except in very few cases, has not the straight forwardness to say 'You may vote as you please'. He stands by and lets the agent hint all these things.[29]

In 1859 it was reported of a Buckinghamshire election that

> Mr. H. Bull was a land agent, and had considerable influence at Aylesbury. He had an opportunity of being of service to small farmers in many ways in regard to loans, mortgages etc., and by merely lifting his finger and saying for whom he could vote, he would probably carry between thirty and forty voters with him.[30]

There was similar evidence for Wales in the 1890s. One witness before a parliamentary committee remarked that he had 'known agents going around to the tenants to tell them how and for whom to vote. I have also known them to meet tenants and walk them in a body to the polling booth.'[31] In Ireland the exercise of political manipulation was less veiled and the role of the agent more muscular. The landlord was less able to draw upon the assumption of deference, and there was more blatant resort to the threat of eviction at times of electoral conflict. When Lord Hertford came to recognize the practical independence of his tenants he took the logical step of raising his rents to the full value of the land. The land agent in Ireland was thus the 'physical reminder of proprietorial power . . . . As members of a notably beleaguered profession, they stood at the intersection between landlord and tenant, a location at once exposed and dangerous.'[32]

There was always a social distance between land agent and master; even the brilliantly successful agents like James Loch and Rowland Prothero, men who became lesser gentry in their own right, maintained a dutiful deference that seems mildly incongruous in retrospect. Very often such men dealt with employers who were wilful, prodigal and unintelligent, who had to be mollified and coaxed into commonsensical ways. Agents like Loch and Haedy perceived their function as, in part, to preserve the aristocratic empires over which they ruled, rather like ducal prime ministers, despite the recurrent waywardness of some of their patrons. Some agents acted as highly respected consultants to other estates, called in for overhauls of administrative structures and for major policy changes. The country house network facilitated this important interchange of expertise. Sometimes an agent would plead for retrenchment with superhuman stoicism. The Duke of Bedford observed the extraordinary efforts of his family auditors, the Adams, who 'continued for more than thirty years to remonstrate with his father (and in pretty strong terms too) at his annual excess of expenditure over income and his consequent increasing debt. It is very creditable to them.'[33] At the other end of the scale from the great ducal commissioners were the unglamorous agents of the very small landlords, one of whom was pictured at breakfast with his employer by Richard Jefferies:

> The steward was usually in attendance. He was a commonplace man, but little above the description of a labourer. He received wages not much superior to those a labourer takes in summer time, but as he lives at the Home Farm (which was in hand) there were of course some perquisites. A slow quiet man, of little or no education, he pottered about and looked after things in general.[34]

The devotion of many land agents to efficiency, good relations and profit made possible the pursuit of pleasure and extraordinary feats of consumption by their masters. There is little evidence of the attitude of agents to this curious arrangement though many of them seem to have regarded it as the natural ordering of society.

IV

Individual land agents of the Victorian age are remembered because they were successful, notorious or simply well recorded. Francis Blaikie, steward at Holkham, represents the early nineteenth-century model. Previously agent to Lord Chesterfield, he entered Coke's service in 1816 and set about the regularization of some of the famous Holkham innovations. Within a few years he was receiving a salary of £650, and in charge of a substantial bureaucracy of sub-agents. He was a proselytizer of improvement, a writer of treatises, a Scot who considered it 'a duty incumbent upon man to diffuse to his fellowmen the fruits of his experience in this life. All men have not the same advantages in acquiring information. Those advantages are bestowed upon us by the providence of God.' Blaikie was exceedingly expert in the details of agricultural method, a penetrating critic of bad practice, a somewhat solemn figure of efficiency and rectitude, and inexhaustibly devoted to his employer. His was a total identification with the interests of the Coke family and he saw his role as that of saving his masters from their best instincts. During one financial crisis Blaikie remarked with some feeling that 'Mr. Coke's benevolent mind outstrips his resources.—It is a virtue in him carried to excess, and for which I see no remedy in this world', and he felt intensely frustrated that Coke could not see the matter in the same serious light.[35]

The Oxley Parker agency, a dynasty which spanned most of the nineteenth century, was developed by Christopher Comyns Parker, a member of the select Surveyors' Club, and second son of a Chelmsford attorney. The Oxley Parkers became substantial country gentlemen in Essex society, men with a superb grasp of the details of how the country worked and of the vagaries of agriculture. They managed many estates and trained themselves to the task. Their business was greatly enhanced by work associated with tithe commutation and their success depended on accumulated trust and reputation with landowners. They took virtually no holidays and frequently worked more than twelve hours in a day, much of it in the saddle. John Oxley Parker, the son of the founder of the land agency business, began his day early, and a visitor wrote: 'Being aware of your early rising habits will plead an excuse for my making an appointment with you at your House at 5 o'clock tomorrow morning.' His biographer described his work in this way:

> He served landlords who often expected to reap where they they had not sown, parsons who depended on his services for their livelihood, parishioners and tenants who relied on him somehow to save them from ruin in evil days, companies established to make new railways, and landowners who wanted to make a profit out of them, and all the time he had to hold in his mind one prime consideration—not just what was expedient, but what was right.

When the Oxley Parkers selected a tenant, possibly the most important task, they looked for sobriety, a good churchman and communicant, preferably married and of a good family, Conservative in politics—'A fast young man would terrify us quiet people' was a typical comment. The Oxley Parkers made considerable money both as farmers and as land valuers. Conservative though they were, they felt it necessary to remind their patrons repeatedly of their social obligations and their identity of interest with the welfare of all classes on the land. No agents were more conscious of the fragile basis of trust upon which all relations in agriculture rested.[36]

Some land agents became national figures in the Victorian countryside. John Grey of Dilston (1785–1868) took charge in 1833 of the Greenwich Hospital estates in Northumberland, over which he presided for thirty years. In this case the agent possessed considerable effective autonomy: 'He was as free in action as if he had been an independent Landlord . . . it was for the interest of the Hospital as well as for the tenantry under his control that he was left thus unfettered.' A dynamo for improvement, Grey developed the estates with enough success to increase the rental by £20,000, and its food output by half, while simultaneously enchancing the condition of its people. He reduced the number of sub-agents from twelve to three, and it was widely claimed of him that he was 'guide, philosopher and friend to all the tenantry'. 'He constantly bore in mind the real and fundamental identity between classes which becomes more marked in an advanced and complicated social system, where everything is mutual and reciprocal.' He established agricultural societies, farmers' clubs and libraries; he often spent between five and eight hours a day on horseback. His great reputation as an agent reflected upon his own trainees, whose services were solicited by proprietors across Britain as well as by the Emperor of Austria and the manager of Public Works in Sardinia. 'He sent many a stalwart

Northumbrian in this way to disseminate his advanced notions in different parts of the world, or to carry out the plans of enlightened noblemen on their parks.' And in 1858 the French government asked him to estimate the effects that free trade in corn had wrought on England. He was described on his death as 'a leading name in English agriculture, a leading exemplar of the duties of landowning, a leading teacher by example and precept, of good farming in every department of it'. He had the unusual habit of making extremely frank public statements which were critical, for example, of absenteeism and the poor provision for cottagers on many estates. In 1840 he expressed displeasure at the 'grandees who lavish expense upon their castles and deer-parks but disregard the dwellings of the cultivators of the land'. In 1846, at a meeting of the Royal Agricultural Society in Newcastle, he told the Duke of Cleveland that he was wrong to think that there was a limit to improvement—such a limit could never be reached while unimproved properties and annual tenancies persisted, and he went on to remind landlords of their palpably unfulfilled obligations to the working classes, notably in the provision of education and accommodation.[37]

One of the best-known agricultural writers and ideologues of the old rural order was Rowland Prothero (created Lord Ernle in 1919) who became agent-in-chief to the Duke of Bedford in 1898. This was after a diverse career in law, academia and literature. He had been editor of the *Quarterly Review* from 1893 to 1899, but he had a passion for agriculture which the Bedford appointment brought to a focus. He recalled the suggestion that his new employment would entail a loss of social status, that he would indeed 'be lucky to get a glass of sherry in the dining room'. This fear was outweighed by his sense of the challenge of the huge Bedford estates. The terms of his appointment also helped. In addition to his salary Prothero was given a rent- and rate-free country house in Bedfordshire, a staff of three indoor servants, seven gardeners and three keepers. Heating and lighting were also free; moreover

> Cream, milk and butter were supplied every day from the dairy at Woburn. Game and the produce of the fine garden were at my disposal. Port, whisky and mineral water were all allowance, and I was given the run of a cellar of Vintage Hocks.

The hunting was excellent, too, and Prothero had the use of two tennis courts and a squash court. Much of this comfort was duplicated at the second country house he was given in Cambridgeshire. Prothero administered a structure which delegated much authority to local agents, 'men at the top of the tree in their profession', and he exercised control 'mainly through the financial checks on independent action'. His most important function was probably that of defending the system of vast aristocratic estates, especially their role, as he saw it, of nursing agriculture through the many years of adversity, and in which the Duke of Bedford had been 'typical of the standard of social and moral obligation towards the tenants and workers'. He particularly sought to improve the comfort and security of cottagers, and attempted to act as a benevolent buffer between workers and farmers. He was a great believer in the powers of cricket as a social solvent, for 'no better opportunity exists for making

449

real friends with rural workers than that afforded by a village club for which you play regularly'. He thought that the old integrity of English village life had shrivelled into a mockery of its former self. 'Sober and industrious, the . . . villagers lived narrow, self-centred lives, knowing no interests outside themselves. They seemed to be passing through life without really living. They were my neighbours. Could I do anything to vary and widen their experience?' One of his answers was to offer village talks on historical figures such as Bunyan, Wesley, Wyclif and Savonarola. Prothero subsequently entered politics at the request of the duke. In his first campaign his opponent described him as 'the pampered pet of a Noble Duke'. In fact Prothero's agency spanned the period of the dissolution of half of the Bedford estates, and he found increasing opportunity to develop his public career. In the First World War he became president of the Board of Agriculture and was charged with the responsibility of organizing the food supplies of the nation. He is now best remembered for his classic and controversial history, *English Farming, Past and Present*, which accurately reflected his own conservatism and nostalgia for a bygone harmony in the countryside.[38]

V

In Wales land agents seem to have come into their own during the time of the enclosures, and there was a current of nationalist feeling against those brought in from England and Scotland to administer the large estates. They had 'a passion for raising rents, shortening leases, consolidating farms, and enclosing land hitherto little used'.[39] In general the Welsh estate agent was more unpopular than his English equivalent: it has been said that

> As representatives of a largely anglicized and Anglican landowning class, some of whom were absent from their estates for a greater or lesser part of the year, the agents were frequently the recipients of abuse and vilification, both from radical writers and from the chapel pulpit.[40]

One English agent, Thomas Cooke, remarked bleakly in 1842:

> My English ways do not suit Welsh customs, and my opinion of the Welsh farmers generally is that they know less than their horses. They are too ignorant to be taught. They are a hundred years behind the worst English districts.[41]

The tradition of anti-agent criticism found voice in the Welsh Land Commission of 1893–5. It was said that the influence and social status of the agent in Wales were greater than in England because the gulf between the landowning and tenant classes was greater. Daniel Jones remarked in evidence: 'We are of opinion that the management of estates is too often entrusted to men of other nationality than our own, inasmuch as difference of language between agents is a source of great inconvenience.' One agent was remembered as the great tyrant and depopulator of the Mostyn estate, another as 'the curse of the country', while another was reported to have vowed an intention 'to exterminate Nonconformity in Cardiganshire and starve the damn preachers'. The report of the commission noted such allegations and remarked:

> There is an impression in Wales, as elsewhere, that owners sometimes employ as agents men of a hard and grasping temperament, strict in their view of the duties of others with the intention that they should act in a way more rigid and exacting than they as owners should venture to act without incurring censure or resentment—men willing for the gain of office and its individual profits to run the risk of any amount of unpopularity and to take upon their own shoulders the social obloquy that rightly should fall upon their employers.

Although Welsh agents were generally absolved of charges of merciless rapacity, the commission did not scotch all the adverse criticism of ignorant, corrupt and truculent agents in the country, and it expressed the view that the level of competence of agents was generally inadequate.[42]

Some agents in Victorian Britain behaved like colonial administrators or missionaries, as though they were carrying the benefits of civilization to retarded outliers of the world. This was especially irksome when the agent was a stranger, vested with powers to bring about radical changes, and yet worse if he could not speak the language of the people involved. Agents from the Scottish Lowlands often possessed such a reputation. James Loch (1780–1855) was probably the most influential estate administrator of his day. The son of a bankrupted proprietor in Kinross, Loch was given a legal education during Edinburgh University's golden age. In 1812, instead of entering politics, he took over the supervision of the vast Sutherland estates, and remained at the helm until his death in 1855, when he was succeeded by his son, George. The Sutherland estates were among the greatest managerial challenges of the Victorian age. In Scotland were the million acres of unreformed Highlands, seething with poverty, corruption and discontent. Here Loch found a bickering and astonishingly prodigal body of factors mismanaging the colossal process of clearance and the associated regeneration of the coastal zones. In England were three substantial estates, full of coal and ironstone, potentially very productive and ripe for zealous improvement. There were four large family seats to maintain and a level of consumption to be made properly conspicuous. And as well there was the Bridgewater Canal, which gave the Sutherland family a vast income, in all more than £2 million net over a period of thirty years. It was an inherited asset, fraught with difficulty because Loch had no control in the management of the wonderfully lucrative canal. Moreoever, he felt impelled to seek terms with the impending competitors—the Liverpool and Manchester Railway in the teeth of total opposition from the canal managers. Steeped in classical economics, liberal in politics, Loch was also for many years in Parliament and was widely consulted on

451

political and legal matters throughout his career. Lord Wharncliffe was told that a few minutes of conversation with Loch 'would be worth guineas of manuscripts'.[43] He wrote books and pamphlets in defence of his Sutherland policies, and he faced the grilling of the House of Commons on the question of the Highland clearances. He acted in the management of five other large aristocratic estates, and spent much of the rest of his life in public service and antiquarianism, and in raising a large family, the sons of which became notable figures in late Victorian life.

Loch was totally dedicated to work; he stated many times that it was his function to shield his masters from any odium connected with the policies pursued by the family. All the estate administration was made systematic and centralized; the tenantry were required to communicate only through the agents and factors. Loch indeed had said that 'His Lordship's territories are a kingdom and ought to be considered in this light by those he employs', and he undoubtedly cast himself in the role of prime minister. His conviction never dimmed that aristocratic landed estates were the first instruments of progress, and he could not understand his own unpopularity, a matter which hurt him deeply. After the era of James and George Loch the Sutherland estates were administered by a succession of unhappy commissioners: Sir Archibald Kemball, a soldier-diplomat disappointed in his career, and then R. M. Brereton, a civil engineer and agent with experience in India, North America and Norfolk. Both found the crofter question almost impossible to cope with. Their resignations were mainly occasioned by interference from the Sutherland family, especially from the heir, Lord Stafford, who took over the administration in 1880 and tried to model it on the pattern of a railway company with regular board meetings. He lasted almost two years, his resolve defeated by bitter quarrels with his father. The turbulence of management in this period served to emphasize the previous achievements of the Lochs.[44]

James Loch had recruited many Lowland agents for both England and the Highlands. In the Highlands factors inevitably wielded great local authority and, in many instances, misused their powers. Sir John Sinclair in 1795 had warned that 'a Highland estate is populous and extensive, it ought never to be put under the management of one factor', and he believed that all factors ought to be held within a system of restraint.[45] Such men were charged with the responsibility of clearing large populations from extensive areas in the Highlands and many were hated figures; others agonized over the tasks they performed and wept for the people caught in their tragic economic dilemma.

As the crofting community developed means of political and physical expression in the last quarter of the century, the task of the factor became extremely difficult. One of the best-known, indeed notorious, factors was Evander MacIver of Scourie in Sutherland, a man of robust views and a sense of traditional order in the north. He refused to believe that the crofter system could be either profitable or prosperous, and he was angered and appalled by the rebellious attitudes of the people. A Lewisman, with a command of Gaelic, he reigned for half a century over a population which he regarded as far too large for its own comfort and too susceptible to infections of Irish land leaguism. He was highly critical of his superiors—men who, he believed, were too often ignorant and unfitted for their work, and a duke who thought more of his yacht than his estates.[46] In the evidence before the Napier Commission in 1883 a Free Church minister described the Sutherland family as benevolent, but 'the agents of his Grace are his hands, his eyes, his ears, and his feet, and in their dealings with the people they are constantly like a wall of ice between his Grace and his Grace's people'.[47] The factors came to feel much tension during the crofter agitation. One of them remarked in 1885 that 'every eye is upon the Factor, and his every action is liable to be construed as hostile to the Crofter Class'; it was a time when ground officers resigned for fear of their lives. 'To suit the present crisis', wrote another, 'a Highland factor would require to have a head of brass, and feet of iron.'[48]

Irish land agents enjoyed higher social status than others, mainly because they were more effectively substitutes for absentee landlords, and were the centre of the local community.[49] But they were also more exposed to abuse and actual danger than those elsewhere, and bore the main brunt of the controversy and disorder of the Irish countryside. In Ireland, it has been remarked,

> the post of the land agent itself conferred that kind of status i.e. of the gentry, and any Irish land agent moved virtually as a matter of course into the magistrate class: he lived, entertained, and hunted like a gentleman, and he took his part like a gentleman in displaying the authority of the established regime, and in maintaining order in a much troubled country. With this social and administrative position, Irish land agents were members of the upper class.

Their belief in the philosophy of the great estate was yet more total than that of their counterparts in the rest of Britain, and their fear of its break-up reached a proportionally higher pitch. Irish land legislation eventually left them redundant and without compensation.[50] Of W. Steuart Trench, land agent to several landowners in Ireland, and a man whose name is said to be abominated still in popular tradition, it was claimed: 'So evil was he that the rats invaded his grave and devoured his body.' His *Memoirs* were designed to place before England the serious problems of land management in mid-century Ireland. Nevertheless, he retained a note of optimism: Ireland, he considered, was not 'altogether incapable of management' because 'justice fully and firmly administered is always appreciated in the end'. His introduction to Ireland had been dramatic enough. He arrived at the Shirley estates in March 1843 to find the tenantry still exultant at the death of his predecessor, an agent named Mitchell. On the night of Mitchell's sudden death they had

> lighted fires on almost every hill on the estate; and over a district of upwards of 20,000 acres, there was scarcely a mile without a bonfire blazing in manifestation of joy at his decease. So remarkable an occurrence as this could not pass unobserved by one who was about to succeed him.

The tenantry then embarked on a campaign to demand rent reductions from the landlord, Shirley, by intimidating the new agent. Trench faced the people in tight-lipped, uncomprehending attitude. Kicked, beaten, punched, hat knocked off, threatened, prayed against, assaulted, his clothes stripped from his back, dragged across the main street of Carrickmacross, sticks whirling over his head—Trench (by his own account) came close to death in his resistance to the demands of the people. He eventually out-bluffed the amassed tenantry, following advice from other agents that any compromise on the question of rent would endanger every other proprietor and that the 'barony would be completely disorganised'. Trench stood firm and Shirley's rent roll, apparently, was preserved.[51]

For a later period in the century Samuel Hussey's *Reminiscences* serve to illustrate the extreme dangers facing many agents in Ireland. Hussey was described as 'the most abused man in Ireland', a man who survived attacks on his life including an elaborate dynamite attempt on his house in Kerry in 1884. A substantial owner in his own right, he was especially conscious of the elevated status of agents. His multiple agency was one of the largest in Ireland, and he appeared before no fewer than seven commissions. His *Reminiscences* thundered against what he termed the copious mendacity of the enemies of Anglo-Irish landlords, and he blamed Gladstone for creating most of the trouble in Ireland. The danger was so great that

> I never travelled without a revolver, and occasionally was accompanied by a Winchester rifle. I used to place my revolver as regularly beside my fork on the dinner table, either in my own or in anybody else's house, as I spread my napkin on my knees.[52]

The experiences of Trench, Hussey and Boycott were, no doubt, more memorable than most, but the life of an Irish land agent was not easily compared with that of his English counterpart.[53]

VI

It would be impossible to estimate with any degree of accuracy the independent contribution of land agents to the economic and social life of the Victorian countryside. There is no doubt that, in the highest ranks, the profession was peopled with men of considerable distinction and great ability. In terms of the organization of agriculture and the ownership and use of land, they were an extremely conservative force. The fact that they wielded such large measures of authority with, outside Ireland at least, relatively little social friction, was a tribute to their skills and to the resilience of agrarian traditions in Britain. Their extreme diligence, loyalty and identification with their masters certainly sustained the old aristocratic order and permitted many landowners to follow careers of extraordinary leisure or of political and social leadership. F. M.L. Thompson has argued, however, that the professionalism of land agents, and the diminished interest of the landed class in the actual work of the countryside, helped to hasten the eventual disintegration of rural society, that the 'roots of deference in a personally administered paternalism were being sapped'.[54] It is sometimes argued that land agents were powerful initiators of the rationalization of agriculture in the early nineteenth century, that they were a managerial elite who achieved rapid gains in food productivity. By the same token it is possible that their collective dedication to technical perfection *per se*, and to very high levels of investment, encouraged over-capitalization in agriculture in the last quarter of the century. Their acceptance of the assumption that the return on capital on the great landed estates should naturally be lower than elsewhere in the economy may have helped to undermine the competitive capacity of British agriculture. And, indeed, it is not self-evident that these attitudes were fully in conformity with the 'national interest'.

Notes

1 Bedford, 1897, 76.
2 Smith, 1898, 311; BPP 1896 XXXIV 249.
3 Spring, 1963, 53.
4 Quoted in Hughes, 1949, 186.
5 Quoted in Richards, 1974, 107.
6 F. M. L. Thompson, 1963, 161–2; Spring, 1963, 133.
7 F. M. L. Thompson, 1968a, 32.
8 Quoted in Hollander, 1973, 234.
9 Robinson, 1826, 58.
10 BPP 1894 XVI, Pt I, 451.
11 F. M. L. Thompson, 1963, 157.
12 Hughes, 1949, 198.
13 *Transactions of the Surveyors' Institution*, 1871–2, IV, 282–3.
14 Caird, 1852, 27, 417.
15 *Ibid.*, 493–5.
16 Brodrick, 1881, 422n.
17 Morton, 1858, 7–9, 23–9.
18 Richards, 1973, ch. X.
19 *Transactions of the Surveyors' Institution*, 1868–9, I, 60.
20 Morton, 1858, 29.
21 Smith, 1898, 295–9.
22 Donnelly, 1975, 183.
23 *Transactions of the Surveyors' Institution*, 1886–7, XIX, 3.
24 F. M. L. Thompson, 1968a, 32, 97.
25 BPP 1882 XIV 192.
26 BPP 1894 XVI pt II, 235; BPP 1894 XVI pt III, 265; BPP 1896 XVII, 141.
27 *Transactions of the Surveyors' Institution*, 1871–2, IV, 271–2.
28 Nossiter, 1975, 48–9.
29 BPP 1868–9 VIII 250.
30 Davis, 1972, 163–4.
31 BPP 1895 XL 2.

32 Hoppen, 1977, 90–1.
33 Spring, 1963, 34–5.
34 Jefferies, 1880, 182.
35 Parker, 1975, 189; Spring, 1963, 130–1; F. M. L. Thompson, 1963, 156.
36 Parker, 1964, *passim.*
37 Butler, 1869, *passim.*
38 Ernle, 1938, *passim.*
39 Jones, 1973, 7.
40 Colyer, 1977, 403.
41 *Ibid.*, 413.
42 BPP 1896 XXXIV 250–8.
43 Spring, 1963, 89.
44 Richards, 1973, *passim.*
45 Sinclair, 1795, 136.
46 MacIver, 1905, *passim.*
47 BPP 1884 XXXIII 2594.
48 Stafford R. O.: Sutherland Papers, D593/K/1/3/73, Purves to Kemball, 23 February 1885;
    Gunn to Kemball, 16 March 1885.
49 Donnelly, 1975, 187.
50 F. M. L. Thompson, 1968a, 259 ff.
51 Trench, 1868, VII, 64–78.
52 Hussey, 1904, 67, 235.
53 Maguire, 1972, ch. VI.
54 F. M. L. Thompson, 1963, 183.

33 Landowners and the Rural Community

F. M. L. Thompson

I

As the twentieth century knows very well, it is not too difficult for any tolerably well-organized and disciplined group in authority, adequately furnished with jackboots, machine guns, and bully boys, to hold the populace in thrall, extracting an outward show of respect and obedience from the inward experience of fear. One strand in the rural literature of the nineteenth century asserts, or implies, that rural communities were held in thrall to the superior and possessing classes through the exercise of analogous coercive power and the fear of the consequences of disobedience, even though these might be exercised in a more decentralized, more civilized, and less obtrusive fashion. It is a view which sees agricultural labourers and village folk harbouring a sullen resentment, dislike, and hatred of farmers, parsons, and squires, nurtured on poverty, oppression, and regimentation, which for most of the time slumbered and grumbled under the surface, and occasionally flashed out in explosions of violent words or deeds at moments of acute crisis.[1] The idea of the undeclared war of the countryside with scarcely veiled jackboot social relationships is vividly expressed in a well-known passage by Joseph Arch:

> We labourers had no lack of lords and masters. There were the parson and
> his wife at the rectory. There was the squire, with his hand of iron
> overshadowing us all. There was no velvet glove on that hard hand, as many
> a poor man found to his hurt. . . . At the sight of the squire the people

trembled. He lorded it right feudally over his tenants, the farmers; the farmers in their turn tyrannised over the labourers; the labourers were no better than toads under a harrow. Most of the farmers were oppressors of the poor; they put on the iron wage-screw, and screwed the labourers' wages down, down below living point; they stretched him on the rack of life-long abject poverty.[2]

A second view portrays the rural relationship not so much as one of conflict contained by coercion, as of potential disaffection or awkward independence massaged away by social leadership, social conditioning, and paternalism. In this version the underlying relationship is also one of conflict, but vigilance and calculated manipulation on the part of the gentry normally succeeded in mediating it into an outward social harmony resting on deference and obedience, although periodically the conflict broke surface in protests, riots, or strikes.[3] A third view, singing the praises of the happy harmony of village life, of simple thatched-cottage contentment nourished by landlord kindliness, is barely credible in the light of today's conviction that all societies function with tensions and frictions, but was nevertheless widely held by contemporary apologists for the existing social order.[4]

The attraction of all these views is that, in their different ways, they present the relationship between landowners and the rural community in a satisfactorily positive way, involve the attribution of clear-cut, strongly motivated, and purposive actions to the landowners and equally clear-cut and intelligible responses from the villagers, and lead on into exciting abstractions about social control or class collaboration. The difficulty with them is that they rest on assumptions about landowners' behaviour and attitudes, and precisely about the extent to which the effects of their actions were calculated and intended, and about the degree to which they felt any commitment or involvement—whether defensive or benevolent—with the rural community at large, that make the theories conveniently self-validating. There were certainly many individual landowners whose sense of the duties and responsibilities of their station led them to minister to the moral and material welfare of what they thought of as their people, in ways which they decided were most suitable and proper, discharging what was felt to be the pastoral care of their flock so as to condition, discipline, perhaps control, the recipients of attention and mould them into dutiful, God-fearing, obedient, industrious, useful, law-abiding, and quiescent people who knew their place, kept it, and did not question the social order which made it a humble one. There were also, no doubt, a few who did similar things more explicitly out of fear of social disorder and rural unrest, conceiving the effects of their actions on the minds and lives of the community as measures of moral police in support of formal civil authority. But many more, the silent majority as it were, were not sufficiently active, imaginative, responsible, or assertive to try to use their power and position to influence the rural community in any systematic way. They were narrowly self-centred in their interpretation of what was required to protect their interests, they were concerned to look after their own ease and comfort, to keep up appearances, and to look after their immediate dependants; beyond the park walls, figuratively, if not indifferent to wider issues of the social order in the countryside and how best to preserve it, they did not regard it as their business to make any special contribution. Those who could not be bothered much with the schools, churches, reading rooms, sick clubs, soup kitchens, drinking places, or recreations of the lower orders were the saving grace of the rural community. It was their indifference, quite as much as the inability of the methods of social control, if there was indeed such a deliberate effort at social management, to achieve their proposed ends, which preserved the capacity of the rural population for independent development. Liberty, after all, depends not only on eternal vigilance, but also on eternal sloth and inefficiency on the part of those with power and privilege.

II

Sloth, however, was not exactly what farmers and labourers felt to be the hallmark of the preservation of game, which was the most widespread and most rapidly growing country pursuit of the greatest number of landowners, the activity which more than any other made country life and the ownership of country estates gratifying, and the point at which landowners mobilized their maximum amount of directly coercive power and displayed most nakedly the legal and physical force which maintained the rights of the propertied over the propertyless in the countryside. A Scottish tenant farmer might 'call a gamekeeper's work doing nothing; the principal part of his business is tormenting the tenants. . . . I say that gamekeeping is an idle trade and an idle class of men go into it', but he meant not that gamekeepers were indolent but that they were interfering busybodies engaged in an unjustifiable, unproductive, and vexatious activity.[5] The systematic preservation of game, the employment of armies of keepers, the formation of special game departments in the managerial structure of large estates, the controlled and costly rearing of birds and the provision of special coverts for them to inhabit, the organization of large shooting parties, and the culminating attainment of grand *battues* where the hundreds or thousands of brace were carefully noted in the game record books, were essentially Victorian developments. As the earlier, more informal and less effective shooting of game that was wild-bred and not too thick on the ground developed into the formal Victorian shoot, with its improved shotguns, regular shooting attire, and increased numbers, landowners took increasing trouble to protect their stake in cash and in pleasure. The custodians of these investments multiplied, from about 8,000 at the beginning of Victoria's reign to over 17,000 at its end. In the rural districts there were, by 1911, more than twice as many gamekeepers as country policemen;[6] the popular impression, in any case, was that the rural police helped at public expense in the struggle to keep poachers away from private preserves, an impression which the 1862 Night Poaching Act did nothing to allay. It may well be that this Act, which gave the police powers to search on suspicion of poaching, was passed at the request of the chief constables who were alarmed at the growing number of bloody affrays between poachers and keepers, and wanted firmer legal grounds on which the police could intervene to keep the peace by anticipating such conflicts;[7] that did not alter the fact that the police appeared to be assisting the keepers in putting down poaching, rather than engaging in the neutral task of preventing bloodshed and murder.

The ordinary countrymen's view was that of Joseph Arch: 'They object very much to being subjected at any time to be assailed by a police officer and searched; they do not like that idea of the law.'[8] The Act was looked on as blatantly discriminatory class legislation, since it was only the poor man on foot with bulging pockets who was liable to be searched, not the gentleman in his carriage; and it, and the whole parcel of game laws to which it was but a refinement, were regarded as draconian and unjust since wild animals ought not to be, and could not become, private property. Arch again expressed the general view: 'We labourers do not believe hares and rabbits belong to any individual, not any more than thrushes and blackbirds do.'[9] He was quite right in law: the offence in poaching was in trespassing on private land in pursuit of game, not in the mere taking of a wild animal that could not have a legal owner. Such niceties did not make the game laws any more acceptable. They were generally held in contempt by countrymen, who failed to see anything morally reprehensible about poaching, and who regarded poachers as heroes or resourceful and daring hunters who brought valuable and tasty food to meagre larders, not as villains, criminals, or sinners. Poachers themselves, apart from the professional gangs who lived by supplying the urban markets with illicit game, and which were thought to be particularly active and well-organized in the 1820s and 1860s, were the braver and more independent village men, who regarded themselves at one level as engaging in a battle of wits with the keepers, at another level as fighting a secret, just war against the tyrannical selfishness of the wealthy.[10] For once the radical politicians who denounced the game laws, from John Bright in 1845 to Joseph Chamberlain in 1885, were voicing a deeply felt grievance of genuine countrymen rather than expressing an urban radical's notion of what countrymen ought to be feeling.

There was no respect for the game laws, and gamekeepers were disliked and detested by farmers and labourers alike. Here was one way in which the landowners were doing what they could to unite the rest of the rural community against them. 'Gamekeepers are generally troublesome to farmers,' said a Norfolk farmer from one of the most highly preserved and most favoured sporting regions in the country, 'breaking down fences, leaving gates open, prowling about. They are generally men of bad character.' Clare Sewell Read, a Norfolk M.P., confirmed that 'gamekeepers are generally very much disliked by farmers'.[11] The interference by the keepers was one irritant; the interference by the hares, rabbits, and game birds themselves was another, breeding a long story of protests against crop damage and loss, which were reduced but not stilled by the Gladstonian 1881 Ground Game Act that gave tenant farmers the right to take hares and rabbits on their own holdings. If the evil repute and bad blood caused by game laws and gamekeepers are not to be doubted, however, the extent to which these infected the countryside is still worth examining. All regions, all climates, and all types of farmland and woodland were not equally suited to game or equally favoured by sportsmen. Grouse were partial only to the bare, uncultivated moors and fells of the northern uplands and the highland zones; they shared some of the bleaker and more remote parts of the kingdom with deer, for whose stalking men were already prepared to pay as much as £2,000 a week by the 1870s.[12] In these thinly populated and infertile parts there was little competition with agriculture and little contact with communities except for those who lived by gillying; there were vivid folk tales of brutal clearances of poor crofting families to make way for the deer, but the actual culprits were more often sheep. It was in the lowland areas that game and people came together, and here the partridge and pheasant needed ploughland and grain crops while hares and rabbits, though ubiquitous, thrived best on light and well-drained soils. The sporting map followed landowners' tastes as well as natural habitats, and hence the distribution of game preservation observed man-made as well as natural contours. It shows that preservation, and therefore the community's experience of game laws and keepers, varied widely from one part of the country to another.

The gamekeeping force, and hence presumably game preservation, reached its peak in the early 1900s, a fitting reflection of the opulent pursuit of amusement in the Edwardian countryside. The 60 per cent growth in the number of keepers since the 1860s is perhaps surprising, across the years of depression; but it suggests the switch from basic agricultural production towards the provision of leisure activities as the role of the land, and emphasizes the degree to which shooting rents supplemented or surpassed farm rents as sources of income from land in some areas. It is no surprise that, in 1911, predominantly rural and agricultural counties such as Hereford, Norfolk, Suffolk, Dorset, Shropshire, and Westmorland had twenty to thirty gamekeepers to every 10,000 inhabitants, while highly urbanized and industrialized counties like Middlesex, Lancashire, Durham, or the West Riding had only one or two keepers per 10,000 population, since this is simply a slightly eccentric way of measuring the difference between rural and urban communities.[13] It is of more significance that the heavily keepered counties also had six or seven times as many keepers per head of total population as did other almost equally agricultural counties such as Leicester, Cheshire, Essex or the East Riding, and over three times as many as deeply rural Cornwall, Devon, Lincoln and Bedford. Keepers, however, in so far as they were not merely private policemen, were more concerned with the population of game animals in their charge than with the size of the local human population, and a more functional measure of their presence is their relation to land area as the basic determinant of game population. On this scale Suffolk, at the top, with ten keepers per 10,000 acres of land in the county, had over five times the keeper density of Cornwall, at the bottom. The densely keepered areas, on this reckoning, were Norfolk, Suffolk, Hampshire, Hertford, Surrey, Sussex, Berkshire, Dorset, Kent, and Shropshire; the agricultural counties where keepers were comparatively sparse, less than half as common as in the strongly guarded counties, were Northampton,

Huntingdon, the East Riding, Devon, Leicester, Cumberland, Cambridge, Westmorland, Lincoln and Cornwall. A similar analysis can be made for the Welsh counties, where only Flint, Anglesey, and Denbigh had high scores on the Suffolk or Hereford level, and all the other counties, most noticeably Brecon, Merioneth, Carmarthen, and Cardigan, were thinly keepered on the Cornish model.

Both measures confirm the supremacy of Norfolk and Suffolk as shooting counties where there were three or four gamekeepers in every village, and they outnumbered the police by two or three to one; here the iron of the game laws and the bitterness of the keepers' war was likely to have entered most deeply into village life. The home counties, perhaps, required particularly strong protection to ward off marauding Londoners, and if they are set aside in a special category the other most popular preserving areas with high rates of contact with keepers were Hampshire, Hereford, Dorset, and Shropshire, closely followed by Sussex, and with a large group of middling counties headed by Buckingham and Oxford. Much of the best hunting country of the midland shires—Northampton, Leicester, Nottingham—had low keepering ratios, because foxes and pheasants were not compatible, and enthusiasm for the one tended to exclude the other.[14] Otherwise there was no special logic about the distribution of the under-keepered areas: there were some in the south west, in the east, in the west Midlands, the east Midlands, the north west, and the north east, in most cases rubbing shoulders with highly preserved counties; there was no particular correlation with the presence or absence of aristocratic or gentry estates. If, however, it is assumed that one gamekeeper could manage about a thousand acres with efficient care and protection of game, and perhaps twice that area with something short of perfection, then the figures mean that in more than half the counties of England and Wales, comprising nearly two-thirds of the countryside, at least half the fields and woods never knew the attentions of gamekeepers. It is a fair guess that some very large proportion, approaching half, of the rural population also never encountered gamekeepers or needed to take careful steps to avoid them.

There is some evidence that the regional contrasts, already apparent in the mid-Victorian years, became more marked in the later nineteenth century; in 1861 individual counties ranged 50 per cent above and below the national mean of keepers per 10,000 acres, while by 1911 the variance had grown to over 100 per cent. The widening differences were perhaps due to improved upper-class railway mobility that encouraged specialization on the best endowed and most favoured areas, perhaps to expansion of shooting in the counties most affected by falling grain prices, perhaps simply to the quirks of individual tastes. As a straw in the wind, Cheshire, a dairying county which maintained its agricultural prosperity, marked time in its appointment of keepers and dropped from the premier position in 1861, more closely watched even than Norfolk, to a middling position in 1911. It is likely, therefore, that what had been a general if somewhat thinly spread experience in the mid-Victorian years, became a much more localized and concentrated confrontation in the later nineteenth century. Perceptions of the inequity of the game laws became more vivid just at the time that practical encounters with their enforcement were becoming less typical.

III

The shooting gentry pursued the protection of their pleasures with no less zest than they devoted to the shooting itself, heedless of the social cost. That cost included the spread of animosity, encouragement of contempt for the law, and threats to public order; it also included the fostering of a popular poaching culture which lived on pub stories of daring feats, narrow escapes, and cunning ruses which outwitted gamekeepers, which embodied the local lore of the virtues of living independently and defying authority, and whose standards were those of the superiority of the rights of free men to take free, natural goods over the rights of private property.[15] The keenest shots, game preservers, and employers of keepers would have argued, no doubt, that their sport was such an integral part of landowning, and indeed constituted the chief benefit and reward from the possession of landed estates, that any hostility and alienation engendered by its full and proper enjoyment, although naturally misguided and regrettable, had to be accepted and countered just as any other anti-landlord tendencies were to be countered—by leadership, example, education, and Christian morality.

It is, nevertheless, one of the ironies of the countryside that the ardent game preservers, who had strong motives for residence on their estates and intimate knowledge of their locality which should have nourished close ties with the local community, in fact made a major contribution to creating frictions and inflaming passions. Hunting, that other sporting interest which brought landowners into the country, was generally held not to produce similar socially divisive effects, except among the ranks of the upper class themselves where foxhunter and game preserver were not infrequently at loggerheads. Great trouble and offence could be caused when either fox or pheasant was killed outside the ordained course of pleasurable pursuit, and preserving landlords who took stern measures to exclude the hunt from their properties and to destroy the foxes were likely to attract pungently expressed local disfavour. This conflict was never general, partly because there was to some extent a separation of hunting and shooting areas, and mainly because many sporting landowners both hunted and shot, either in succession on different days in the week or in succession in different stages in life, taking to shooting as they became too old and portly to continue riding to hounds. Where it did break out, however, the conflict could be decidedly sharp, rising to its peak in the early 1900s as the enormous Edwardian shooting parties mounted to a crescendo of slaughter and were bitterly blamed for a growing scarcity of foxes. The hunting community, with its effortless assumption of prior and superior rights, denied responsibility for causing these frictions which disrupted the solidarity of the landed classes and complicated, if they did not frustrate, the task of keeping rural society in order. Hunting literature, indeed, especially hunting fiction, gave a strong impression that there was a real hunting community, cutting across class lines, bringing together the rural classes, and acting as an important agent of social harmony. There is abundant evidence that many farmers regularly rode to hounds, from the wealthy Yarborough estate tenants who hunted with the Brocklesby in the late nineteenth century to the hundreds of Leicestershire farmers with the Quorn, and the Gloucestershire farmers who virtually controlled the running of the Vale of White Horse.[16] It was certainly not a gentry preserve or a male preserve—unlike shooting—but apart from local farmers, and large numbers of outsiders who flocked to the fashionable hunts, it is not clear that other social groups were much represented; country doctors and parsons maybe, but the hunting village blacksmith or carrier must have been a rarity, and other village workers, let alone farm labourers, were hardly in the hunt. If it is more than doubtful whether hunting was an all-class affair for rural society, its close dependence on a landlord–farmer axis was of considerable importance in bringing together those two groups which otherwise were socially distanced and liable to have some conflicting economic interests. Certainly some farmers were obliged by the terms of their tenancies to support the local hunt, by walking hound puppies and by allowing the hunt over their fields; and others showed their discontent at the considerable damage to fences and growing crops that a field of hundreds of horses could easily cause, by exercising their right to warn the hunt off their farms. These, however, were a minority; eased by the diplomacy and cash of hunt committees, and by masters of foxhounds who gave annual dinners to the farmers, paid some compensation for damages, and took trouble to cultivate friendly relations, hunting enjoyed the goodwill and support of the majority of farmers, without which it could not have existed. As for the majority of the local community, labourers may have derived some pleasure from the colourful spectacle of the meet, or a glimpse of a large field at full stretch, and relished the chance that persons of high degree might be levelled by falling into ditches, but at best they were bystanders with no place in the hunting network, and the goings on of the hunting folk did not affect them one way or the other.

In the eyes of the generality of landowners the function of their estates was to provide the income to support their life style; the function of the countryside was to provide good sport. If the sport was hunting, it did something to unite the upper reaches of rural society, bringing together landlords and tenants, and at least did nothing to antagonize the labourers. If it was shooting, on the other hand, it emphasized and exacerbated social divisions, irritating the tenant-farmers and imbuing the labourers, who felt the direct consequences of game preservation and game laws, with a sense of social injustice and a contempt for the law which the wealthy used to oppress the poor. In such a situation the rational and efficient behaviour for the landowners as a class would have been to make sure that in those regions where their own actions tended most to undermine social order and their own authority, counter-measures designed to neutralize such influences were most actively promoted. Direct strengthening of the power of the law by maintaining more rural police in the disturbed than in the quiet areas was one possibility. Such a course was indeed implicit in the advice of the chief constables of rural counties in 1859, whose figures of savage attacks on gamekeepers not surprisingly showed a clear correlation with the main game preserving counties.[17] It was not, however, followed

464

in practice. It was true that in 1861, when county police forces had not been long established and many were still in their first few years of feeling their way towards a desired size, the leading game and poaching county, Norfolk, had marginally more policemen per head of population than a hunting county like Leicestershire; but it was scarcely a significant difference that could suggest any deliberate reinforcement of coercive power.[18] In the next fifty years, as game preservation intensified and became more elaborate, the numbers of rural police were everywhere increased; but they did not increase as fast as total population, and in the great shooting counties police forces expanded markedly less than elsewhere. The result was that by 1911 policing ratios were practically identical in all the more agricultural counties, with only Cornwall, Rutland, and Shropshire apparently more law-abiding than the rest in so far as they had one third fewer policemen in relation to the population than the others. East Anglia functioned with exactly the same policing ratio as the great hunting shires, and indeed of the ten counties where gamekeepers were thickest on the ground only three—Hertfordshire, Kent, and Surrey—had a high police presence, twice that of the other seven, and that was accounted for by their large urban populations and proximity to London. There had clearly been no effort to match heavy concentrations of gamekeepers with heavy concentrations of police to contain the extra lawlessness engendered by strict preservation; rather, the reverse had happened, and the great shooting landowners, by multiplying the number of keepers they employed at least by two, had enabled their counties to economize on police, patrolling their covers with their own staff, perhaps consciously in order to avoid the unpopularity of being responsible for putting more policemen on the public rates.[19]

IV

Such figures might suggest that it was no more difficult to keep order in the areas of greatest exposure to the game war than anywhere else. Conceivably contemporary opinion exaggerated the popular hostility to the game laws and sympathy with the poachers, and there never was any particular problem in maintaining authority and landowner superiority in the affected areas, but this seems unlikely in the light of the clear-cut testimony. It is possible that the resentment was indeed widespread, but remained sullen rather than overt because of other pressures which were effective without there being any need for the display of extra physical force. Among such influences education took pride of place as the panacea prescribed by Victorians in authority when they sensed any whiff of social or moral decay or collapse in the populace, and was indeed frequently regarded as a more effective and enduring instrument of social order than troops, police, or magistrates. Support of village schools was one of the most typical activities of Victorian landowners, and the visit to the schoolroom, more often by the lady than the master of the big house, was the most common form of contact of the possessing classes with the generality of the lower orders outside the ranks of immediate employees and dependants, at least with

465

the younger members of the general community. Support was typical, but not universal. It is not in doubt that before 1870, when popular education depended on the voluntary schools, these were two or three times more numerous, in relation to the population of school age, in the rural and agricultural than in the urban and industrial areas; this meant that rural communities subscribed more generously than urban ones to the building of schools. Which members of rural communities subscribed is, however, in some doubt; and while there were considerable variations in school provision among the predominantly agricultural counties themselves, it is more than doubtful whether these variations conformed to any scale of differing degrees of exposure to the risks of disaffection.

The history of education has been so preoccupied with questions of policy that the geography of schools has not been much studied. Kay-Shuttleworth's view on the extreme educational backwardness of East Anglia in the 1830s, where he found little except 'a lawless population of paupers, disbanded smugglers and poachers', may be only a small straw in the wind, since on his way to becoming the country's leading educational pundit he was biased towards noticing whatever proved the need for more schools; it does not look, however, as if the shooting squires were at this time aware of any particular call to concern themselves with educating the people.[20] A generation later the Newcastle Commission on Popular Education provided a more objective measure of the variations between counties in the support of voluntary schools, when in 1861 it published a table ranking the counties in order of the proportion of children on the books of their schools in relation to total population. This has been accepted 'as an index of the eagerness or reluctance with which local persons were prepared to subscribe to the building of the schools'.[21] After twenty-five years of considerable effort and achievement by the voluntary societies, during which the numbers and capacity of their schools had been increased four- or five-fold, this index recorded that the greatest eagerness had been shown by Wiltshire, Westmorland, Oxfordshire, and Rutland, and the most reluctance by Cornwall, Northumberland, Warwickshire, and Durham; the best performers were nearly three times more generous than the worst in finding funds for school building. The table does not distinguish between rural and urban areas, and it is arguable that the eduationally neglected counties were predominantly those with large industrial and urban populations: Lancashire, Yorkshire, Nottinghamshire, and Staffordshire did not appear far from the bottom of the league. On the other hand, decidedly rural and agricultural counties might be either very keen on schools, like Wiltshire and Westmorland, or definitely unenthusiastic, like Worcestershire and Devonshire; while the indifferent to mediocre performance of Norfolk, Suffolk, Hampshire, or Sussex suggests that the strong shooting interests of those counties had still seen no need to show any special interest in rural schools. They were indeed comfortably outclassed by the great hunting shires, all of which supported more schools. Hence, if there was any connection at all between the sport-based social characteristics and needs of a district, and the level of interest in and support for schools, it seems possible that the greater friendliness, neighbourliness, and comparative absence of

466

social friction in the hunting shires, and indeed in counties not notable for any kind of sport, disposed the propertied classes to an active interest in the educational welfare of their communities, while the frictions and disaffections of the shooting counties, far from causing the landed gentry acute anxieties about the local moral order and inducing special zeal for carefully managed schools as a corrective, served to make them tight-fisted, suspicious, uncooperative, or even hostile towards the idea of helping ungrateful and disaffected people to better themselves.

In the final phase of voluntary activity, before rate-financed schools established effective control of elementary education, it is possible that landowners in some of the previously laggard areas were shamed or provoked into making good some of their earlier neglect and indifference. Leaving aside those cases where there was a stampede after 1870 to safeguard Anglican and paternalist interests by hastily founding new National Society schools within the few years' grace allowed by the Act, in order to ward off the threat that school boards would be set up to provide for local deficiencies of school places, there is some evidence of more sustained efforts. By the end of the 1880s the dust had more or less settled on the controversies over the establishment of school boards, and where none had been set up, either compulsorily or voluntarily, it is safe to assume that the voluntary schools were adequate in size and quality and were tolerably well supported by their communities. In 1889 school boards looked after the education of 62 per cent of the population of England, but there were extremely wide regional variations in their distribution: 95 per cent of the population of Middlesex came under school boards, and 80 per cent in Surrey and Warwickshire, but only 3 per cent in Rutland and 10 per cent in Dorset. Many of the counties which, by this standard, had the poorest record of support for voluntary schools merely confirmed the indifference that they had already demonstrated by 1861: thus Devon, Cornwall, Durham, Nottinghamshire, Yorkshire, and Staffordshire were at the bottom of the 1889 league just as they had been towards the bottom of the 1861 table. Similarly, Rutland and Dorset, Berkshire, Hertfordshire, Oxfordshire, and Wiltshire appear at the top of both tables. There were, however, some counties in which an apparently sharp change in attitude towards voluntary schools occurred between 1861 and 1889: there seems to have been a notable increase in the liberality with which schools were supported in Cheshire, Herefordshire, and Shropshire, that had transformed them from middling to poor performers in 1861 into front runners in 1889; and while Lancashire, Northumberland, and Worcestershire reached the middle of the order only in 1889, they had moved up from very lowly positions. On the other hand, support seems to have contracted severely in Gloucestershire, which dropped from ninth to thirtieth place, and to have dwindled significantly in Essex, Northamptonshire, Norfolk, and Westmorland, whose relative standings deteriorated markedly.[22]

The regional pattern of concern for education is an interesting one, not least for its failure to conform with the distribution of large or gentry estates, or with distinctions between pastoral and cereal areas, let alone with distinctions between hunting and shooting counties. Since it also shows, albeit tentatively, that it was possible both for counties which cared about schools and those which did not to manage with unusually small numbers of rural police, it suggests that education did not necessarily turn out the superior law-abiding citizenry it was intended to produce. It is, above all, an awkward pattern for any thesis which places landowner support at the centre of Anglican school expansion or regards an interest in the village school as a typical landowner activity. The implication that landowners as a group were erratic, unsystematic, and unreliable in their concern for local schools, however, accords well with the opinions of contemporary administrators, who saw the local parson as the key figure in initiating and sustaining the local school, and the local landowners as a set of potential but reluctant subscribers which the clergy had to struggle hard to mobilize. The conclusion of the assistant commissioner for the eastern counties, reporting to the Newcastle Commission on Popular Education, was that

> Farmers seldom feel any interest in the school, and seldom therefore subscribe to it. Landowners are often non-resident, and if they subscribe, do so to a very insufficient amount. Where landowners are resident and study the welfare of their tenants and labourers, they usually take an interest in the school and contribute liberally, if they do not wholly support it. But these cases are not frequent.

The assistant commissioner investigating a sample of parishes in the western agricultural counties found more than a third of the local landowners 'to whom the school in the parish from which they derive their income is a simple matter of unconcern'. The Newcastle *Report* itself summed up the situation in a passage which was sternly critical of the landowners:

> [The clergyman] is the man who most feels the mischief arising from want of education. . . . He begs from the landowners; if he fails to persuade them to take their fair share of the burden, he begs from his friends, and even from strangers; and at last submits most meritoriously, and most generously, to bear not only his own proportion of the expense, but also that which ought to be borne by others. It has been repeatedly noticed by the school inspectors, and it is our duty to state that as a class the landowners, especially those who are non-resident (though there are many honourable exceptions) do not do their duty in the support of popular education, and that they allow others, who are far less able to afford it, to bear the burden of their neglect.[23]

On this view the regional and chronological variations are to be explained largely in terms of the chance distribution of zealous, conscientious, and persuasive clergymen rather than in terms of differences between landowners in their perceptions of their self-interest or their ideas of their social responsibilities. The often passive role of landowners is a warning that the frequent references in family and estate papers to annual subscriptions of a few guineas to local schools are not to be taken as evidence of active involvement, but may more likely indicate no more than a token, and often perfunctory, compliance with the importunings of the local clergymen. The school managers, and of course the parson, would be well aware of which local landowners did subscribe and which did not, and the annual subscription was no doubt a small price to pay for securing freedom from vexatious calls, and a reputation for basic attention to a social duty, and as such served to smooth relations with that level of rural society. Those at the receiving end of education, however, the schoolchildren and their parents, are most unlikely to have known who the subscribers were, so that simple subscription offered no dividends of deference or obligation to the landowner, and provided him with no paternalist satisfaction. Active involvement, of a kind likely to be noticed by the villagers and to reinforce their attachment to the local gentry, required considerably more effort: the donation of a site, financing of the school building, or support of the teacher's salary were the material contributions likely to accompany a keen and continuing interest in a school and to bring a patron into direct and impressionable contact with the children. Many landowners did indeed contribute on this scale, like Lord Shaftesbury, who within three months of inheriting the family estate in Dorset had launched three schools where before there were none, and ended by meeting the salaries of six or seven school masters and mistresses; less pious peers did no less, like the Duke of Bedford, Lord Pembroke in Wiltshire, or Lord Cholmondeley in Norfolk. The example, however, was far from widespread. A sample of seven recent volumes of the *Victoria County History* mentions 118 National Society schools; 68 of these apparently had no particular patron worthy of mention, while of those which were substantially supported by individuals only 21, or 17 per cent of the total, had patrons from the landowning classes.[24] This is probably a reasonable measure of the extent of serious, as distinct from superficial, landowner contact with the education of rural labourers.

V

As with schools, so perhaps with churches, closely linked as they were as the centres of authority and social discipline in village life. Unfortunately there are no sources which permit a ready assessment of the extent of landowners' activities in church building, extension, and restoration, let alone of their involvement in the life of the church and the conduct of its parishioners. There were some, like Lord Tollemache at Helmingham in Suffolk, who insisted that all the farm workers attend church every Sunday; and others like Sir Tatton Sykes who rebuilt or restored twenty churches in the parishes near his seat of Sledmere in the East Riding.[25] It is not likely, however, that such individuals were typical of their class, which by inclination would regard such matters as the parson's business, to attend to as best he could. If concern with succouring and supervising the main agencies which were held to mould the morals and behaviour of the rural labourers was a minority pursuit for landowners, it is possible that concern for their material welfare was more widespread. Next to their wages, which were directly controlled by farmers, not landowners (except for household servants and estate workers), and were effectively determined by the market, housing was the labourers' chief concern. The condition of their home profoundly affected the welfare or misery of a labourer's family; many social observers believed that it was also a decisive influence on their morals. Rural overcrowding was commonly held to encourage immodesty, licentiousness, promiscuity, and incest; a typical view was that 'in the villages where the cottages are most crowded there are the greatest number of illegitimate children'.[26] While overcrowding was also thought to cause intemperance, by driving men to the beer-shops, the drive for cottage improvement was no doubt more strongly nourished by the desire to eradicate incest and promiscuity, an object to be attained by providing enough rooms to separate the sleeping arrangements of the sexes. Success in such endeavours was probably never very great, since the incest taboo seems to have been as firmly held by the labouring as by other classes, and despite the prurient shock with which country parsons and doctors claimed to have observed incest it is unlikely ever to have been anything but exceptional; while there are no grounds for supposing that rural fornication fell out of favour.

Even if the desired effects on sexual behaviour may not have been realized, cottages were none the less built. Among a certain group of landowners discussion of cottage improvements and the merits of two- or three-bedroom designs, and the exchange of restrained complaints about the meagre financial returns on cottage building as an investment, became as absorbing as the talk of record bags or record runs among other groups. Many individuals, from Lord Shaftesbury in Dorset—who in spite of his initial confession on inheriting the estate that

> surely I am the most perplexed of men, I have passed my life in rating others
> for allowing rotten houses and immoral, unhealthy dwellings; and now I
> come into an estate rife with abominations! Why, there are things here to
> make one's flesh creep; and I have not a farthing to set them right,

in the end managed to find the money to build many cottages[27]—to the Duke of Northumberland in his county, from the Earl of Leicester in Norfolk to Lord Dartmouth in Staffordshire, acquired considerable reputations in the middle years of the century as builders of model cottages. Some, like the Earl of Leicester, went further, and as well as building cottages, let them direct to the labourers instead of following the normal system of letting cottages along with farms to tenant farmers, who might then use their power to threaten eviction from tied cottages to intimidate their workers; the earl's arrangement turned cottage-owning to paternalist account by interposing the landowner as the labourer's protector in this sector of the conflict between farmer and labourer, although it may not have done much to help agricultural efficiency. Individual instances, however, are an unsatisfactory foundation for any generalization; if it is accepted that, by 1914, landowners as a group had built some 22,000 cottages for farm workers, cottage-building is revealed decidedly as a minority pursuit.[28] Several individuals are known to have built two hundred or more cottages on their estates in the period of greatest activity, between 1850 and 1880, so that the total may have represented the work of no more than one or two hundred landowners. In any case, even in relation to an agricultural workforce which had shrunk by about one third between 1851 and 1911, these cottages cannot have contributed as much as 5 per cent of its housing; it was a rare and untypical labourer's family that experienced the joys of living in a model cottage, or whose home harboured reminders of landowner influence.

With landowner attention to basic living conditions confined to such a limited scale it is hardly likely that their provision of such frills in the way of village amenities as reading rooms, village halls, or playing fields was more lavish or widespread. Some individual landowners did indeed provide some or all of these things as part of their concept of social duty and leadership, although the impression conveyed by country house literature is that gentry-sponsored sport for the locals was confined to an annual cricket match between the big house eleven and the servants and labourers, played on a pitch in the park, until in the early twentieth century the idea of more permanent and specialized playing fields began, especially under the influence of football, to be imported into the countryside from the towns.[29] An even more casual impression is that the great majority of villages went without any public meeting places until the crop of memorial halls began to appear after 1918. It may be that the less expensive and less capital-intensive forms of helping the local community—running a village clothing club, distributing blankets and coal, opening a soup kitchen in winter, subscribing to a local benevolent or friendly society—were more widely practised by landowners. Such help for the needy and encouragement to the thrifty, whatever the explicit, conscious motive for giving it, no doubt helped to establish the character, influence, and authority of the donor and thus to preserve his position at the head of the social hierarchy in his country; one might expect it to be given above all to the villages which stood directly outside the park gates, living in the shadow of a big house.

VI

It might seem, indeed, as if all the evidence of landowners' involvement in providing the material equipment of village life—schools, churches, cottages, and clubs— pointed towards the conclusion that their horizons of social responsibility and spheres of active social leadership and control were limited to the villages and parishes that they held in sole ownership. Such an explanation would dovetail neatly with the strong mid-century concern over the distinction between open and close parishes and the differences in their states of misery or well-being. Open parishes were those with no dominant landowner, in which property ownership was diffuse and sites for cottages could be readily acquired; they were overcrowded, overpopulated, poorly housed, heavily burdened with poor rates, and the source of much of the labour, which commuted daily on foot, for working the farms of the close parishes. These, by contrast, were in single ownership, or at most in the hands of two or three owners; the numbers of cottages were carefully controlled and restricted in order to keep population below the labour needs of the parish and thus ensure that poor rates were kept low. It would not be unreasonable to expect that close parishes were the ones to receive close attention. The object of close parishes was to keep down expenditure on the poor, however, and this could be achieved by simple restriction of numbers without any need for the restricted number of cottages to be better than those elsewhere, or for the inhabitants to be better looked after. It could be argued, indeed, that from the point of view of a landowner concerned only with the essential requirements of keeping social order and preserving deference the powers of property were so complete and unchallengeable in close parishes by virtue of their monopolization, that there was less need than in other places for deploying the more subtle instruments of control through benevolence. Hypotheses aside, the available figures do not support the idea of an association between close parishes and paternalism. In the country as a whole close parishes amounted to perhaps 20 per cent of the total in rural areas at the middle of the century, a proportion much in excess of those which saw any cottage building by landowners. The regional variations in 'closeness', moreover, which range from high points of 33 to 43 per cent of all townships being close in Norfolk, Leicestershire, Rutland, Lincolnshire, and the East Riding, to low points of 6 per cent in Essex, Cambridgeshire, and Hertfordshire, with much of the midland shires and west country in the middle of this range, do not correspond at all with the variations in the support of village schools, unless they hint vaguely at an inverse correlation.[30] There were too many close parishes, in the wrong places, for these to have been necessarily the places where village life was most dominated, regulated, nursed, and cosseted by a powerful landowner.

That there were many villages in which there was much doffing of caps, either because people did not dare risk giving offence by doing otherwise or because they wished to show appreciation of favours and good works received, is not in doubt. If the distribution of good works, embodied in churches, schools, cottages, clothing clubs, free coal, soup kitchens, and, towards the end of the century, patronage of healthy recreations and the occasional cottage hospital, was not determined by a random scatter of individual landowners and their wives who happened to have lively social consciences, it may well have depended on the residential habits of landowners and the extent to which particular big houses were identified with immediately dependent villages. A map of rural communities which were particularly under the eye, or thumb, of a landowner patron might well, therefore, be very similar to a map of estate villages, defined as those which, although not necessarily custom-built in uniform style, adorned and complemented the big house and housed estate workers, pensioned dependants, and some of the outdoor servants as well as the more typical village population of farm labourers and village workers and tradesmen. The map would have many large blank areas, for all the general evidence indicates that paternalism was restricted and localized in its appearances, and above all that it was not systematically deployed in those places and situations where the traditional social order and respect for the law were most threatened by social stresses and strains. It is possible to conclude either that the benefits and comforts of social services provided by landowners were reserved for a privileged minority in the countryside, or that only a minority were unlucky enough to be subjected to the constraints of social discipline and control imposed from above; either that the majority of landowners neglected their social responsibilities towards the majority of the people living on their estates, because they were indifferent, lazy, or self-centred, or that the majority declined to abuse the power of property by interfering in other people's lives. Either way, for most country folk landowners were remote figures who left them to fend for themselves, living their own lives and fighting their own battles with farmers and other employers. Pockets of sheltered, protected, and regimented rural communities studded a landscape populated by much more independent, self-reliant, and exposed villages; which set of communities were more contented, or more resentful of their lot, is an open question.

Notes

1   E. P. Thompson, 1965, ch. 7; Green, 1913.
2   Arch, 1898, 55.
3   Dunbabin, 1974, 14.
4   Howitt, 1838, I, 286., quoted in Horn, 1976b, 5.
5   BPP 1873 XIII, Q. 3028–30.
6   1911 Census, England and Wales, occupation tables, rural districts.
7   BPP 1862 XLV.
8   BPP 1873 XIII, Q. 8067.
9   Arch, 1898, 159.
10 The chief constable thought there were 300 men in Hertfordshire who maintained themselves for several months each year by commercial poaching: BPP 1873 XIII, Q. 240.
11 BPP 1873 XIII, Q. 1616–27, 6653.
12 *Ibid.*, Q. 6637.
13 Statistical information is from the occupation tables of the 1861 and 1911 censuses.
14 Itzkowitz, 1977, 146–50.
15 Sources as far apart as Engels, 1950, 266, and the chief constables in Memorial, BPP 1862 XLV 2, agree, approvingly and disapprovingly, that poachers were generally regarded as 'village heroes'. See also Samuel, 1975a, 207–27.
16 *Victoria County History: Lincolnshire* I (1906), 494; Itzkowitz, 1977, 172–3.
17 BPP 1862 XLV.
18 The figures were 19 police per 10,000 inhabitants in Norfolk, 15 in Leicestershire.
19 The normal ratio in 1911 was 11–12 police per 10,000 inhabitants in the agricultural counties; in Cornwall, Rutland and Shropshire it was 7–8, and in Hertfordshire, Kent and Surrey 19–21.
20 Hurt, 1971, 22.
21 Hurt, 1968, 6.

22 BPP 1889 LIX, 6–7.

23 BPP I 1861 XXI, II 157, 74; I 78.

24 *Victoria County History: Essex VI; Gloucestershire XI; Middlesex V; Oxfordshire VIII, IX, X; Wiltshire X*. A complete count of the National schools mentioned in these volumes shows that the sites were provided, or the costs of building largely met, by

Members of landed aristocracy or gentry	21
Wealthy non-landowners	15
Local clergy	10
Oxford colleges, and bishops	4
No particular individuals	68
Total	118

25 Evans, 1970, 123–4; Pevsner, 1972, 43.

26 Quoted in Burnett, 1978, 45.

27 Hodder, 1887, 449.

28 Whetham, 1978, 48.

29 Girouard, 1978, 271, 285.

30 Holderness, 1972b, especially 135.

34   Country Sports

Raymond Carr

Country sports were dependent for their development on a series of interlocking variables: forms of land tenure; techniques of farming; changes in transport facilities; technical innovations in sportsmen's instruments—both animal and inanimate. They also reflected, and were an index of changes in, income distribution and social mobility. Some sports were socially divisive—shooting for instance. Some were generally popular as creating the sense of a coherent rural community, as was hunting—with some startling exceptions. Some were socially neutral, as was fishing. Some—horse-racing, cock-fighting, pugilism—were regarded by the respectable as degrading and vicious; others—rowing and cricket—as manly exercises. All were regarded as typically British. When Queen Victoria died Britain considered itself, and was considered by others, as the greatest sporting nation in the world.

I

The simplest elements to isolate are technical changes in farming methods and the effects of the 'railway revolution', as sporting writers referred to the mid-century development of the railway system. Technical innovations revolutionized shooting, whereas there were few technical advances in hunting. The railways changed the face of the hunting field; they had a less dramatic effect on shooting.

Shooting changed completely in the Victorian period as a consequence of successive improvements in guns; it is characteristic of the mentality of sportsmen that each of these improvements was fiercely resisted by the old school, accustomed to the old guns. After 1815 even as obvious an improvement as the percussion cap to replace the flintlock was criticized because it sometimes failed. By the 1860s the superiority of the breech loader over the sometimes dangerous and certainly slower-firing muzzle loader was evident; it was resisted because it threatened to change the nature of the sport. In early nineteenth-century prints the sportsman is pictured with a friend shooting over pointers at birds flying *away*, a relatively easy shot; rapid-firing guns (and the increased killing power of the choke bore after 1874) made it necessary for 'sport' to make birds more difficult to hit and led to *battues* in which pheasants were driven *towards* the guns. Old-fashioned sportsmen criticized *battues* as little better than massacres and as un-English. In November 1867, with an unwilling Emperor of Austria as his guest, Napoleon III, in violet velvet with precious stones as buttons, used 250 beaters to kill 3,829 head of game. If English gentlemen did not indulge in such 'burlesques' they did begin to keep game books and look on the number of birds killed as an index of the sport enjoyed.

Changes in the way England was farmed—reflected in the landscape itself—lay at the root of the changed patterns in hunting and shooting. The primacy of the midland shires as a fox-hunter's paradise—the 'eye of hunting England' as the hunting journalist Nimrod (Charles Apperley, 1779–1843) called it—was advanced by the enclosure movement and better drainage. The new hedges created the jumps that made shire hunting a unique experience; better-drained pastures created splendid scent-carrying turf that sent bitches screaming over the grass and enabled a field to gallop up to them, and sometimes, to the horror of successive masters of the Quorn, over them. 'In proportion as the agriculture of the country is improved, the speed of the chase is increased.'[1] Throughout the century the supply of good grass to gallop over depended on the relative profitability of arable farming and grazing. The post-war depression in 1815 increased pasture; so did the agricultural decline of the 1880s. What was bad for farmers was good for fox-hunters.

Later another change, the use of wire, and especially barbed wire, as a cheap method of fencing, was regarded by hunting men as a major disaster in that it could bring down a horse. In 1862 the Duke of Rutland stated bluntly that 'unless wire fencing was done away with, fox hunting must cease in Leicestershire'.[2] Since wire was cheap farmers wanted to use it, and the outrage of fox-hunters threatened to ruin the 'harmony' between them and the farmers. In the end, as so often in the history of fox-hunting, harmony was saved by hard cash: the farmers were paid to take down wire in the hunting season.

High farming and enclosure changed the pattern of shooting. The old, thick, pre-enclosure hedges held game that could be flushed out by spaniels, as did the stubble of corn fields where pointers were used, before the advent of the mechanical reaper. This encouraged, if it did not cause, hand-rearing of game and intensive preservation.

'This trebly accursed revolution of railroads', argued Delmé Radcliffe, would end fox-hunting. It would turn rural England into 'one vast gridiron'. It would drag the fox-hunting squire to London—and it was a consistent argument of fox-hunters that only a resident gentry saved England from a 1789 or 1848. In fact fox-hunters like

Surtees became railway enthusiasts; railways brought new, rich subscribers, expanding the hunting field socially and geographically; and they took hounds and horses to distant meets.

II

The rural sport *par excellence* was fox-hunting. With some exaggeration the novelist Anthony Trollope—himself a brave hunter, since he was shortsighted and could never afford good horses—called it *the* national sport.[3] This claim was only credible given the absence of rivals: cricket and golf were still geographically limited, and the great spectator sports and club activities of the twentieth century—except, perhaps, for rowing—were still in their infancy. Fox-hunting, on the other hand, had become by 1860 more than a private diversion; it was 'a highly organized, extremely influential public institution . . . with a significance out of all proportion to its role as a mere sport'.[4]

The fox-hunter's claim that his sport was 'national' was based not merely on its geographical ubiquity—all England except near the great industrial towns was hunted. The ultimate justification of fox-hunting in the eyes of its supporters was that it was 'democratic', that it involved *all* social classes, that it was a Platonic image of a supposedly harmonious rural society, an institution that bound together farmer and landlord while excluding the common enemy of both—the agricultural labourer, consistently portrayed in hunting literature as a brutish clodhopper who merely interfered with sport.

Hunting on horseback with hounds was, in its origins, an exclusive royal and aristocratic pursuit and the quarry was the deer. With the shortage of deer in the seventeenth and eighteenth centuries the fox (hitherto a despised vermin and the quarry of village hunts whose activities persisted in remoter regions to distress early nineteenth-century masters) became the prime quarry. The hare was a popular rival. It was the great aristocratic families—the Spencers, Somersets, Fitzwilliams, Pelhams, Manners—who financed and organized the 'smart' packs of foxhounds of the later eighteenth century. It was a fashionable midland squire, Meynell, who revolutionized the technique of fox-hunting during his mastership of the Quorn (1753–1800) and established Leicestershire in the eyes of the sportsmen as the 'Vale of Cashmere'. But beside these magnates and rich landowners modest squires all over England were turning from hare-hunting to fox-hunting in the early years of the nineteenth century; and though the old generation of enthusiasts believed that hare-hunting was more technically exacting, their sons preferred the faster, more exciting sport. At the bottom end of the social scale there remained local farmers' packs and the scratch packs near the large towns. Surrey fox-hunting allowed London merchants to get back to the city in order to catch the evening post. For early Victorian fox-hunting was not even exclusively rural: it entered into the life of market towns, and the stockingers of Leicester still came out for a day with the

Quorn. The artist George Morland (who died of drink in 1804) lost all his sitters to a local meet. 'Last Monday week almost everyone in Margate was drunk by reason of the Freemasons' meet and fox hunt.'

When Queen Victoria came to the throne fox-hunting therefore embraced a varied and wide social spectrum, from the Duke of Wellington to George Morland's Margate inebriates and John Peel (d. 1854), who kept his pack on an income of £400 a year. It is characteristic of the snobbery so evident in *Punch* that her reign showed a process of social contraction at the lower end of the scale and inflation in its middle ranges. Though scratch packs persisted in the provinces, the tone of fox-hunting as a whole was set by the smart midland packs. Mr Jorrocks, the city grocer who, as a master of foxhounds, was not above peddling tea to his field, called himself a 'Post Office Directory man'. Very few packs by 1850 would have taken on such a master. R. S. Surtees (1803–64), the greatest of hunting novelists, was an incurable romantic describing a rapidly vanishing scene; the young blades who people the novels of Whyte Melville (thrown and killed stone-dead, in 1878) are socially respectable, with little of the old-fashioned countryman's knowledge of the ways of hounds and foxes. They are out, by 'jealous riding', to show off their expensive horses. They take tea with vicars' daughters.

The early Victorian hunting field still exhibited in the morals and life style of masters like Osbaldeston (1787–1866) and Jack Masters (1777–1849) the social promiscuity and rough manners of Regency England. Masters was a compulsive womanizer; Osbaldeston lost his fortune gambling. Victorian respectability came with the most professional of all early nineteenth-century masters, Assheton Smith (master of the Tedworth, 1826–58). He was a regular church-goer (though he held up the congregation by talking with his huntsman in the church porch), a classical scholar, and an astute businessman who administered a vast fortune founded on Welsh slates supplied to the new industrial towns.

Field sports, at least from the sixteenth century, had been an arena of social mobility. To take over the local pack, put on a red coat, provide drink and food for a lawn meet, was to become socially acceptable in a rural society of which the local master of foxhounds was a dominant figure. In Surtees's greatest novel, *Mr Sponge's Sporting Tour*, Mr Puffington, the son of a starch manufacturer, takes on a pack of hounds 'because he thought it would give him consequence'. Already in the eighteenth century ironmasters and cotton-spinners had bought landed estates for sporting and social purposes.[5] In the mid-nineteenth century the arrival of the 'purse proud *parvenu*' distressed conservatives and led to an unfortunate outburst of anti-Semitism. But by the 1860s *British Sports and Pastimes* talks of sport—above all of hunting—as a 'most serious influence on the lives of Englishmen of the upper *and middle classes*'. It was part of the process that so distressed Cobden in 1863; it led 'manufacturers and merchants . . . to prostrate themselves at the feet of feudalism'.

This advance was facilitated by the most fundamental change in the economics of fox-hunting. In the 1830s to maintain a midland pack in style cost between £4,000 and £5,000, when a peer's average income was £10,000.[6] By the 1860s, and even more so after the agricultural depression in the 1880s, only the richest of magnates could continue to supply free hunting for their neighbours. A contribution from the field was inevitable. With the advent of the subscription pack, if what Trollope called 'feudal grandeur' vanished, the hunting field was open to all who could subscribe. Combined with the 'railway revolution' this meant an expansion of the field both numerically and socially. Sir Robert Foster, Member of Parliament for the City of London, arrived at Paddington to hunt with the Beaufort: hacking back to the local station he amused himself by reciting the third chapter of Hallam's *Middle Ages.*

This expansion of the field tested the central alliance which supported fox-hunting: the alliance of farmers and fox-hunters. Fox-hunting meant licence for fields of galloping horses to crash across land they did not own, a licence freely granted to known neighbours but which was less easily given to large, 400-strong fields of 'strangers'. Since the legal right to cross other people's property was never established by fox-hunters—their claims to do so were dismissed in the Capel case of 1808[7]—the freely given permission of the occupiers was vital. When the bankrupt exiles in Dieppe and Boulogne set up a fox-hunt, the local peasantry called out the gendarmerie. That English farmers as a class never sought to challenge fox-hunting is one of the strangest features of rural life.

Fox-hunters were sometimes warned off by shooting landlords, and very occasionally challenged by individual farmers. Many tenant farmers were bound in their leases to allow hunting, many more were wary of annoying a landlord who might let him off lightly in a bad year. But the evidence is overwhelming that farmers either actively supported hunting—Cobbett had earlier noticed a deplorable propensity in farmers to take up hunting themselves—or accepted it as part of the unchallengeable hegemony of the landed gentry. Fox-hunting was not merely a symbol of that hegemony; it was consciously used as a form of political patronage, as George Osbaldeston found out to his cost when he criticized an innkeeper out with the Duke of Beaufort—the brewer was an important voter. Conscientious masters, like the Dorset squire Farquharson, spent a great deal of their time and energy fostering good relations with farmers, presiding over endless farmers' dinners and patronizing agricultural shows. They usually succeeded. It was where such assiduous cultivation was impossible, or where intensive farming made hunting particularly damaging to crops, that fox-hunters were cursed, as when they were pursued with pitchforks in Harrow.

The alliance of fox-hunters and farmers resisted both the propaganda of urban radicals and, more surprisingly, the strains of the agricultural depression of the 1870s and 1880s. Nevertheless, it survived in an altered form as the depression eroded the— always idealized—image of a harmonious rural society. The supposed community of interests between landowners and farmers was under increasing attack from radicals aiming at 'the utter abolition of the present landed aristocracy'.[8] With falling rents, landlords found it harder and harder to bear alone the costs of a hunt. They were forced either to cut costs or accept a subscription; one of the severest shocks to the hunting community came when Lord Yarborough—whose family had maintained the

Brocklesby hunt since the eighteenth century—was forced to sell his dog pack in 1895, keeping only the bitches. And even the Duke of Rutland cut back to four days a week.

If landlords were feeling the pinch so were the farmers, and falling prices made them less willing to accept the damage inflicted on their crops and fences by large fields, and on their poultry by preserved foxes. Just as magnates were forced to accept subscription, so farmers demanded heavy compensation for damages. The old alliance was saved by cash—wire and poultry funds rose dramatically. On these conditions farmers still tolerated fox-hunting; but they now demanded a say in its management. In 1878 the Quorn farmers acted in one of the recurring disputes over the right to hunt a country; by 1887 they were on the hunt committee that selected the master—and this in the smartest hunt in the country.

Thus the fox-hunting society was changing. Subscription became *compulsory*. The idea of a sport open to all was, in the words of the editor of the *Field*, 'a pleasant fiction'. It was open to money, and with money came a new influx of moneyed upstarts—the financial saviours of late Victorian hunting. Farmers no longer accepted fox-hunting as being in the unchallengeable order of things; they had in many areas, though by no means all, to be paid indirectly for preserving foxes and refraining from actions for trespass and damages. 'Almost at the end of Victoria's reign, hunting society was taking on the connotations of "Victorian" that we associate with business and industrialization.'[9] Yet there can be no doubt that hunting remained not merely a central feature of rural society, but for those outside it who wished to be accepted in it an activity to be supported. As Professor Thompson argues, as long as the horse and carriage remained symbols of social standing, so the landed aristocracy retained its predominant place.[10] A magnate master like the Duke of Beaufort was still a great figure in his country; and there were still toadies and snobs like Mr Jawleyford with social pretensions, ready to flatter a red coat in the hopes of a smart marriage for their daughters.

There can be little doubt that the fox-hunter's claim that his sport was 'democratic' was even less well-founded in 1901 than it was in 1837. But fox-hunters were never at a loss to find new social merits in what they could never look on as a mere amusement. To its defenders, the hunting field became an instrument in the formation of an imperial class. In 1899 the historian of the Belvoir claimed that on 'sharing the sport of his superiors the young middle-class Englishman began to acquire the virtues and good qualities of a governing race' by combining his 'sturdy common sense' with 'aristocratic boldness', thus filling out a class that could rule 'an immense dependency of mixed races'. Fox-hunting, by 'the grafting of aristocratic virtues on a democratic polity', was thus the secret of the 'peculiar strength of English character and power of rule'.[11]

III

There is a sense in which racing spanned the widest social spectrum of all sports.

480

Newmarket had been made famous by the Stuarts; it was the seat of the ruling oligarchy of the Jockey Club; yet like every other racecourse, Newmarket attracted crowds of all classes. Many of the Victorian owners—particularly in the later years of the reign when a good stallion cost £12,000—were great patricians. The Duke of Westminster owned Bend Dor who sired Ormonde; the Duke of Portland the faultless St Simon, sire of Persimmon, who won the Derby for the Prince of Wales in 1893; and yet Eclipse, the greatest eighteenth-century horse, was bought by an Irish adventurer who had once been the 'legs' of a sedan chair. The punter who had lost his all could feel in the same boat as that inveterate loser, Lord Glasgow; the more fortunate could share some of the elation of Henry Chaplin who won £115,000 on the Derby of 1857 from Lord Hastings—who had just run off with his fiancée.

The racing community was not snobbish—on the contrary, it was the familiarity between well-born and 'vulgar' which was regarded by the snobs and prigs of Victorian England as the great social vice of the sport. It did, indeed, see some curious and unsavoury examples of social mobility. John Gully was the son of a bankrupt Bristol butcher: prize-fighter and publican, he became a prosperous bookmaker, ending up as M.P. for Pontefract in 1832 and an owner with three Derby winners to his credit. But he remained what he had always been—a crook—and in 1854 he was warned off the course at Epsom.

Racing not only united a curious variety of social classes, it was the only sport that united country and town. In the early years of the reign a host of small race meetings still took place all over the country—much disapproved of by Surtees as shoddy affairs run by landlords and bookies. But the great racecourses were mostly in or near towns (Doncaster, York, Chester, Aintree). Indeed, many nineteenth-century municipal corporations established racecourses in the hope of attracting trade: Epsom was established, as was Cheltenham, to improve the trade of the spa. Most of these municipal ventures collapsed; but the great race meetings—particularly in the north—brought farmers and squires to the town where, at parties and balls, they mixed with the citizens.

Apart from during the Interregnum, racing had developed continuously since the days of James I under royal patronage. George IV was a keen racegoer and owner; William IV considered patronage of racing a duty, until hit in the eye at Ascot by a gingernut. Queen Victoria went to the Derby only once, and abandoned Royal Ascot after the Prince Consort's death. The eighteenth century had established the thoroughbred horse, the three great classic races, the Jockey Club dominated by the humourless, obsessed Sir Charles Bunbury, *Weatherby's Racing Calendar* (1722) and the *Stud Book* (1796), and the professional jockey. Nevertheless, when Queen Victoria came to the throne the sport was discredited. It was, in the words of its most recent historian, 'at the lowest moral ebb of its history'.[12]

The reason for this discredit was evident to all—gambling. This surrounded racing with petty crime: 'crimped' matches fixed by the owners, pulling (checking) horses (even the great George Osbaldeston confessed to this), breaking into stables and feeding horses with lead shot or opium. In the 1820s Mr Thornhill, a Yorkshire squire and member of the Jockey Club, got Sam Chiffney to win races only by offering him more to win than the bookmakers offered him to lose. Such practices persisted even amongst the most respected owners.

But it is typical of Victorian attitudes that society was less repelled by gambling-inspired crime than by the effects of gambling on the class structure. Young aristocrats would fall into the hands of common 'legs' and money-lenders, as Osbaldeston's autobiography and John Mytton's death as a discredited bankrupt prove. Gambling attracted a crowd of undesirables to racecourses: the throng of tipsters, card-sellers (called *spivés*, the origin of 'spiv'), gipsies, acrobats, made Epsom 'disgusting' to Disraeli.

The racing world attempted to reform itself. Lord George Bentinck, himself a great 'plunger', attacked the betting fraternity with the hatred of familiarity. In 1844 he exposed the 'Running Rein' scandal, the most notorious fixed Derby; he made Goodwood an ordered affair in contrast to the 'obscene Bohemianism' of Epsom. Later Admiral Rous cleaned up handicapping and improved starting; but though he detested heavy betting, he refused to join Sir Joseph Hawley and *The Times* in a crusade against betting as such. It was, he saw, the life-blood of racing. Without it, the sport would become the profitless private concern of a few aristocratic *aficionados*.

The onslaught of outraged morality on flat racing was as nothing compared with the attack on the more truly rural sport of steeplechasing which had developed out of riding matches between friends across country. The organization of steeplechases by publicans with aristocratic backing disgusted Nimrod as cruel to horses and unfit for women to watch; above all, it entailed undesirable contact between the nobility, whom Nimrod loved, and the 'vulgar', whom he hated as only a successful social climber can. 'The most *cocktail* pursuit', he called it, 'ever entered into by English gentlemen.' The *Liverpool Courier* came out against Aintree as 'wanton torture'.[13] Again it was the 'barefaced swindling' of the gambling world surrounding steeplechasing that almost killed it. However, by the 1870s the National Hunt Committee began its fight against crooked practices, and in 1885 the Heythrop organized the point-to-point, later to be a pillar of hunt finance and a means of winning local support—it was still a rough affair, and the saddle and bridle of a fallen horse were stolen by the crowd.[14]

IV

Those who shot could never even pretend, as fox-hunters pretended, that their chosen recreation contributed to some ideal of rural harmony. It was, by late Victorian times, deeply divisive. It not merely divided rich and poor, landlords and tenant-farmers: it divided the sporting community itself with a bitter war between fox-hunters and game preservers. Even before the mass shoots of the 1880s and the introduction of the breech loader, shooting was unpopular. The laws that restricted

the shooting of game to certain income groups and forbade the public sale of game—
the absurdities which encouraged poaching and covert sale on a huge scale to supply
the new rich of London with a game course at dinner—had been savagely attacked by
Sydney Smith. But even after the repeal of the laws the terms of the farmer's lease still
usually ensured that the shooting of game was confined to the landlord.

This quasi-monopoly, as it applied to hares and rabbits, was the most resented
feature in the rural hegemony of English landowners, and an irritating source of
friction between landlords and tenant-farmers (though there were other and more
serious conflicts—compensation for improvement, for instance). Rabbits—preserved
in warrens in enormous numbers—and hares did a great deal of damage to crops and
even to bank hedges. This grievance was not removed till the Ground Game Act of
1881. It is a curious proof of how ingrained and enduring are traditions of aristocratic
privilege that, as a boy on a farm, I still believed we must not shoot hares, and indeed I
was once beaten for so doing.

As we have seen, the driving of large numbers of game—pheasants and
partridges—*over* guns, the 'much vituperated system of *battue* shooting',[15] was
deplored as a mere 'massacre' by conservatives bred on walking up game with dogs.
By the end of Victoria's reign the country house shooting weekend, to become an
institution in Edwardian England, was already well established. Huge bags became a
necessity and a source of pride. At Holkham, in 1790, 3,000 birds were shot in a year;
by 1880 the same number were shot in a single day. Payne-Gallwey considered 1,000
birds a day normal for a good shoot; Lord Walsingham quoted the game book of a
Norfolk estate: in 1821, 39 pheasants; in 1875, 5,069.[16]

Preservation made landlords much more particular about any rights of the general
public to cross their land, disturbing 'their' game, even taking the occasional pot-
shot. By closing up old rights of way landowners were 'on the eve of losing the
sympathy of a very important class'; outraged countrymen would join 'vestrymen in
black satin waistcoats and black cloth boots who slobber over their soup', i.e. the
urban radicals, in their crusade against 'feudalism'.[17] Nothing revealed more clearly
the tensions between shooting landlords and the rural community than poaching.
While few countrymen sympathized with the town gangs who fought pitched battles
with keepers and policemen, the individual poacher became something of a folk hero.
Such a poacher was James Hawkes. His journal reveals him as an intelligent man,
opposed to drink, an organizer of bicycling clubs, a radical in politics and a supporter
of Bradlaugh. He saw poaching, which was his passion, as a legitimate means of
feeding the poor and as a protest against 'the Class'.[18] He clearly enjoyed the
sympathy and respect of his neighbours who took his view that birds were a gift of
God not the property of the landlord. When they were involved in heavy expenses in
preserving and hand-rearing—it was estimated that each preserved pheasant cost
£1—landlords took the opposite view. Birds they reared were their property,
poaching was robbery with violence; this was particularly the case with night
poaching which was severely punished under the act of 1844. On the big shoots of East
Anglia, and near Yorkshire mining villages, a minor guerrilla war was waged.

The complications of the Game Laws made the gamekeeper's task a difficult one. 'The number and intricate arrangement of the Statutes at present in force make it very difficult', ran a manual first published in 1889, 'for any one, not a practical lawyer, to obtain such a knowledge of their varied provisions as to ensure that the right thing shall be done at the right time.' Some of these complications were the result of the ingenuity of the poachers themselves. Since killing game on land was illegal, poachers trained their dogs to drive game onto the public highway: thus killing game on the public highway had to be made an offence (7 & 8 Victoria, cap 29), but the powers of arrest on the public highway remained obscure.[19] That these laws were enforced in rural districts by magistrates in whose interests they had been drawn up made them seem even more intolerable. Town magistrates simply refused to transport men for night poaching.

In the later years of the reign landlords were encouraged by royal example. The Prince of Wales bought Sandringham in 1863 and turned the estate into one of the finest shoots in Europe. The prince rode roughshod over his tenants, driving one of them, Mrs Cresswell, who wrote a bitter attack on his 'sport', to emigrate to Texas in desperation at the Sandringham agent's indifference to farming profits.[20] Queen Victoria was disturbed. She asked the prince to stop his excesses 'and to do a little away with the *exclusive* character of shooting'. Here the queen, as she so often did, put her finger on the real issue: shooting was a minority sport. Its only conceivable social benefit was the employment of keepers and of villagers as beaters. Their wages were not handsome: even in the 1920s I was paid sixpence a day as a beater. One of my beater friends, who amused us by digging shot out of his arm with a penknife, was given £1 by the landlord as compensation.

Shooting divided not merely rich and poor—it divided the sporting establishment. Game preservers did not welcome the local hunt disturbing their birds. To a fox-hunter vulpicide was a crime; to a gamekeeper concerned to provide a bag for his master and his shooting tenants, the fox was a vermin which devoured expensive birds. Coverts were drawn blank or found replete with mangy 'bag' foxes after all the wild foxes had been poisoned. The war between the two sports became bitter. Foxes were disappearing at such a rate in shooting counties that a well-informed journalist could argue that 'hunting has become [by 1908] little more than a farce'.[21] In the end a solution was found by paying gamekeepers to preserve foxes; but it was often an uneasy compromise enforced, as that inveterate pheasant-slaughterer, Lord Walsingham, admitted, 'because of the amusement [fox-hunting] afforded *all* classes of society'.

It was in Scotland that shooting was at its most exclusive. Grouse-shooting (birds were driven after 1870) was a rich man's sport at £1 a brace and bags of 300. Deerstalking was 'a millionaire's sport', though physically extremely strenuous; shooting stags in a first-class forest might cost nearly £100 a day.[22] Both had been made more easily accessible by the railway revolution. 'On one day you may be lounging along the hot pavements of Pall Mall ... the very next afternoon you may be in the heart of the Highlands.'[23]

Hunting, shooting, and racing were all in their different ways contentious: all, for instance, were attacked by Evangelicals as wicked, and by radicals as relics of feudalism. All enjoyed upper-class patronage. Fishing was never aristocratic, but there was a division between coarse fishing and fly fishing. Coarse fishing became more popular with cheap railways fares and more organized after the establishment of angling clubs with an annual subscription of 10*s*. 6*d*. Fly fishing became steadily more expensive, both in terms of tackle and rents, as it became, like shooting, preserved. The technical revolution came with F. M. Halford's *Dry Fly Fishing* in 1889. The very rich went to Scotland to practise their art. It was expensive—£5 per salmon caught in the 1890s when a season's rent might be £1,500. More modest fishermen could get their fishing at hotels at £1 a day all found.[24]

V

How had the social composition of field sports, particularly the hunting field, changed in Victoria's reign? It had both contracted and expanded.

One of the first recorded fox-hunts started from Preston; by 1900 there was no hunting in industrial Lancashire. The same process of urbanization had eaten up good hunting country round London. This meant that the occasional middle-class city fox-hunters—Engels had been such a one—vanished. The 'purse proud *parvenus*' were buying up the manor houses and had become residents. The fox-hunting businessman was becoming a rarity, though Mr Brassey, son of the railway contractor, was to keep the Heythrop in great style. The stayers were the rich: banking families like the Drummonds, the Barclays—for a long while masters of the Puckeridge in Hertfordshire—and the Rothschilds. The invasion of the rich and the expansion of subscription certainly tended to drive out the less affluent from the *smart* packs, but in Devon and parts of the north old traditions persisted of hunts composed of gentry, farmers, solicitors, and corn merchants. Everywhere a great magnate—such as the eighth and ninth dukes of Beaufort—was the natural master if he was willing to serve; but in the 1870s Moreton Frewen sensed the changes at Melton Mowbray, capital of hunting England: 'I arrived to find no oligarchy; but vast numbers of rich, well-dressed, absolutely idle people who constituted the society of the day.'

Army officers—particularly cavalry officers—hunted and were given long leaves so to do; the local garrison was a valued support, however much the jealous riding of young officers—and also of young undergraduates—distressed masters. Hunting parsons were a less steady support. Their numbers were always exaggerated by sporting journalists and fox-hunters engaged in proving the respectability of their sport. As the clergy became more professional and were less often recruited from the landed gentry, so the supply of hunting parsons dried up as incomes declined. Moreover the ecclesiastical climate had turned against fox-hunting: Bishop Phillpotts of Exeter waged an unsuccessful campaign against west country hunting parsons in a diocese where the Reverend Jack Russell (a guest at Sandringham, and on one occasion ready to hack seventy miles to a Salisbury meet) rather than the bishop set the tone; but elsewhere, as Trollope sadly admitted, 'he [the hunting parson] is making himself to stink in the nostrils of his bishop, and is becoming a stumbling block and a rock of offence to his brethren'.[25] Charles Kingsley gave up hunting as 'not a suitable occupation for a parson and anyway I am too proud to ride unless I am as well mounted as the rest'; this latter condition he could not fulfil on his stipend. When the Bramshill hunt servants turned up at his funeral they stayed discreetly outside the churchyard.[26] By 1900 the hunting parson was a rarity.

He was replaced in hunting literature and on the hunting field by the woman fox-hunter. The objections of conservatives were based on the moral hazards of aiding a lady who fell off, yet the long skirts that preserved decorum were very dangerous in jumping country. The improved side-saddle and new designs in skirts solved the conflict between morals and safety. By the late 1860s women feature in all hunting literature, and it is in order to become respectable that Trollope's Lady Eustace takes up the sport. If some of the women fox-hunters were high-class tarts like Skittles, when so eminent a personage as the Empress of Austria hunted regularly with the Pytchley the hunting woman was royally sanctified. It must be painful to proponents of women's liberation that it was in field sports that women achieved equality with men. This was less true of shooting. Ladies were essential ingredients of the country house shooting weekend; but they were less welcome in 'the actual shooting party'.[27]

VI

I have dealt in detail only with hunting and shooting, the field sports *par excellence*. Coursing and otter-hunting were popular in many parts of the country. Stag-hunting was recovering once more in the west after its near collapse after 1825 when the last English staghounds were sold to a German buyer. Nor have I dealt with those sports which were practised in the country but which did not involve either the breeding of animals, as with racing, or killing of animals, as in the case of fox-hunting or shooting. Cricket began as a rural sport and was spreading out from its old homes in Kent and Hampshire. It united country gentlemen like Osbaldeston and Assheton Smith and professionals who were not gentlemen; but its Mecca was, after all, London. Rowing was popular in a way that is hard to imagine today. Osbaldeston tried his hand at it, as he did at everything else from billiards to walking races. The day of the Regency all-rounder was vanishing and sport was becoming pro-fessionalized. Nevertheless, the hunting, shooting, and fishing countryman, the sporting squire, has come down to us as an enduring image of the Victorian age.

Notes

1   Egan, 1836, 197.
2   *Field*, 7 November 1863.
3   Trollope, 1868, 71.
4   Itzkowitz, 1977, 1.
5   E. P. Thompson 1965, 218.
6   Carr, 1976, 116, 124.
7   Bovill, 1962, ch. 4.
8   Carr, 1976, 149 ff.
9   Itzkowitz, 1977, 175.
10 F. M. L. Thompson, 1963, 1.
11 Dale, 1899, 40.
12 Longrigg, 1972, 115.
13 Seth-Smith, 1969, 22–64; Blew, 1901, 1–70.
14 Hutchinson, 1935, 94.
15 *New Book of Sports*, 1885, 35.
16 Longrigg, 1977, 250–1.
17 Gale, 1885, 139, 142.
18 Christian, 1961, 20.
19 Porter, 1907, 30–1.
20 Chenevix-Trench, 1967, 173.
21 Richardson, 1908, 26–50.
22 Grimble, 1886, 58.
23 *New Book of Sports*, 1885, 22.
24 Aflalo, 1899, 75.
25 Boyd, 1934, 75–6.
26 Chitty, 1974, 163, 297.
27 *New Book of Sports*, 1885, 35.

V Labouring Life

35   The Workfolk

W. A. Armstrong

I

The stages by which the medieval English peasantry disappeared, and the impact of successive phases of enclosure, continue to be debated. However, it is clear that the classic tripartite division of rural society (landlords, tenant-farmers, landless labourers) had already made its appearance by the early eighteenth century. To the extent that it could not be met by creating new holdings on hitherto uncultivated land or by an unthinkable restructuring of land tenure, the ensuing growth of the rural population after about 1740 brought about an inexorable increase in the ratio of labouring men to farmers and landlords. This outcome has been observed in a number of European countries as well as in England and Wales. As was certainly the case in the Scandinavian countries, population growth was primarily induced by falling death rates, a consequence of a distinct abatement in the incidence of epidemic disease, and, in some parishes, a noticeable improvement in the survival of infants.[1] In the early nineteenth century land drainage schemes were another factor deemed to have exerted a favourable influence, for example at Wisbech, Dunmow, Newhaven, Ongar, and in east Kent where the marshy land bordering the Isle of Thanet was effectively drained.[2] Thus, by the mid-nineteenth century low annual rates of mortality were a matter of common observation: 19 per 1,000 at risk (Cranbrook, Pateley Bridge, Romney Marsh); 18 (Farnham, Liskeard); 17 (New Forest, Bideford, Hendon); 16 (Builth, Holsworthy); and even 15 (Glendale).[3] Although these figures relate to rural districts as a whole, farm labourers had shared in the favourable trend.

According to statistics collected by the Manchester Unity of Oddfellows, only carpenters among twenty-five occupational categories had a higher expectation of life than labourers, and at twenty the farm labourer could anticipate 45.3 further years, at thirty 30.7; at forty, 29.9; at fifty, 22.2; at sixty, 15.8.[4] These advantages extended to their offspring. Although women's work in the fields evidently had a tendency to increase infant mortality, the long-run trend was unmistakable. By 1911, when the national infant mortality rate was 125 per 1,000 live births, the level in families of agricultural labourers stood at 97, compared with dock labourers (172), carters and carriers (147), bargees (161), and bricklayers' labourers (139).[5] Of course, this is not to suggest that there was no preventable wastage of life among them (comparable figures for the offspring of solicitors and clergymen were 41 and 48 respectively), but such levels supported very considerable rates of natural increase when their comparatively high rates of fertility are taken into account.

There was a widespread impression that the usual age at marriage for both labourers and their brides was falling in the late eighteenth and early nineteenth centuries, associated with the decline in indoor service and, in particular, with the nefarious influence of the Old Poor Law, which was believed to encourage improvident unions and reckless breeding. These suppositions, which persisted well after 1834, often depended upon highly untypical illustrations. For example, a contributor to the *Cornhill Magazine* in 1864 invited his readers to picture the labourer 'some fine morning, before he is two-and-twenty, on his way from church, with his bride, who is only seventeen'.[6] However, there is remarkably little evidence to support the idea of a change in their usual age at marriage, and in point of fact a much more plausible argument is at hand to suggest a higher level of rural fertility. From the 1861 census (which gives details of proportions ever-married, convertible to mean marriage ages), Anderson has inferred that in agricultural registration districts under 15 per cent 'traditional' (i.e. where labourers were abundant and correspondingly less of the labour force consisted of farmers, their relatives, and servants), the mean age at marriage was 26.6 (males) and 25.6 (females). Conversely, in districts more than 45 per cent 'traditional', they were 28.4 and 27.0 respectively, indicating differences in marriage ages of nearly two years (for males) and seventeen months (females) respectively. A structural shift involving only 20 per cent of the labour force thus had the capacity to raise potential marital fertility by some 6 per cent.[7] What probably occurred between, say, 1750 and 1860 was a relative increase in the number of those who at all times had tended to marry comparatively early. It will be noticed that far from invoking a shift in marriage habits, the argument assumes a degree of inertia in behavioural patterns. Moreover, it would appear that this extended to the labourers' reproductive characteristics, for during the second half of the nineteenth century they were comparatively slow to reduce marital fertility rates. Flora Thompson offers some interesting comments on the moral precepts which influenced procreation. On the one hand it was reckoned unseemly for grandmothers to bear children ('when the young 'uns begin 'tis time for the old 'uns to finish'). Yet marriage subsequent to conception was 'a common happening at the time and little thought of', and the control of births within marriage seems to have been frowned on in village circles. An admission of recourse to coitus interruptus met with the comment, 'Did you ever! Fancy begrudging a little child a bit o' food, the nasty greedy selfish hussy.'[8] At all events, according to evidence gathered in 1911, completed fertility per hundred wives of agricultural labourers, standardized for marriage age, was 7 per cent above the all-class average for marriages taking place before 1851, and while the all-class average moved down by 21 per cent when the marriages of 1881–6 were compared, that of farm labourers was reduced by only 16 per cent, their fertility now standing 14 per cent above the all-class average,[9] so that in a sense, relative to the rest of society, it was actually increasing.

With a sizeable gap between fertility and mortality, rapid rates of natural increase were apparent both before and during the Victorian period. Between 1750 and 1831 the population of sixteen 'agricultural' counties rose by 1.75 millions (88 per cent), notwithstanding a net loss of 0.75 millions by migration. In the Shropshire village of Moreton Say, where the population doubled between 1680 and 1800, the number of labourers quadrupled: at Ash (Kent), which also experienced a doubling of population between 1705 and 1842, the number of holdings did not keep pace, in fact they declined by a quarter.[10] Save in the exceptional circumstances of the French Wars of 1793–1815, the forces of natural increase constantly threatened to swell the number of labourers faster than new employment opportunities could be created, and the danger was still very much in evidence in Victoria's day. In the words of Dr Hunt, this was an 'uncalled-for increase' which imposed strains on all rural economies,[11] most obviously in the south where the alternatives were fewer. The implications of demographic increase in any case, were serious for the labourers' standard of life; it does not take much imagination to see that had there been no migratory outlets the outcome would have been economically and socially disastrous.

II

By comparing the educated guesses of Gregory King for 1695 with information from the 1831 census, Clapham reached the plausible conclusion that the ratio of labourers to all occupiers had moved from about 1.75:1 to 2.75:1 over the intervening years—or 5.5:1 in relation to occupiers known to be employers.[12] Corresponding figures for 1851, the point at which the agricultural labour force reached its recorded zenith, are 3:1 and 5:1 respectively.[13] There was, of course, a good deal of regional variation reflecting prevailing patterns of farming and land-holding, so that in Wales, where 72 per cent of all holdings were below 100 acres, the percentage of farmers with more than two labourers was only 17, and outdoor agricultural labourers accounted for but 36 per cent of all males engaged in agriculture. By contrast, in south east England where 22 per cent of holdings were over 500 acres, 59 per cent had more than two labourers, who accounted for 82 per cent of all males in agriculture. At the national level, the 1851 census enumerated nearly a quarter of a million farmers and graziers

(226,000 males, 23,000 females) as well as 112,000 male and 269,000 female relatives including farmers' wives. Their hired employees numbered 1,125,000 males and youths (chiefly outdoor labourers but including 102,000 described as servants) and 144,000 females, mostly indoor servants who numbered 99,000. After 1851 the number of employees began to fall.

Table 35.1   *Employees in agriculture in England and Wales, 1851–1911**

Thousands

	1851	1861	1871	1881	1891	1901	1911
Males	1,124.5	1,114.0	939.6	850.6	776.5	637.5	674.4
Females	143.5	90.6	58.1	40.4	24.2	12.2	13.6
Total	1,268.0	1,204.6	997.7	891.0	800.7	649.7	688.0
% change since previous census:							
(i) males	–	−9.3	−15.7	−9.5	−8.7	−17.9	+5.8
(ii) females	–	−36.9	−35.9	−29.8	−40.1	−49.6	+11.5
Ratio of employees to farmers and graziers	5.08	4.82	4.00	3.97	3.58	2.89	3.00

*Derived from Taylor, 1955, 36–8. *N.B.* the table includes farm servants but seeks to exclude such categories as estate managers, gardeners, agricultural and forestry pupils, machine proprietors and attendants, woodmen, dealers, land proprietors, etc., as well as farmers' relatives. A few retired persons were included among the occupied before 1881.

Although there appears to have been a slight reversal of established trends during the Edwardian period, the pattern is otherwise consistent. There was a declining labour force in relation to farmers, whose numbers sank by only 10 per cent down to 1901, and thereafter rose by 2 per cent. This contraction was especially marked with respect to females, whose participation had hitherto been encouraged by the increasing neatness of agriculture (affording more hoeing and weeding); by the erosion of alternative opportunities in activities such as hand-spinning, and, perhaps was prompted by the more stringent conditions of relief after the Poor Law Amendment Act of 1834.

So far as women were confined to mainly indoor service, including such tasks as firelighting, cleaning utensils, preparing meals, milking cows, and making butter, there could be no objection to female employment. However, their systematic deployment on outdoor work presented a society of increasing moral rectitude with a dilemma, noticed especially at two points. One was localized, namely the situation of the 'bondagers' of Northumberland, where the hinds were often required to provide an extra female labourer for farm work. These women, sometimes although not invariably female relatives, excited admiration for their versatility and strength, and stimulated as well a good deal of concern about their moral welfare and apparently

494

feudal status. A more widespread problem was the employment of women and children in public gangs, particularly in the eastern counties. Although there was no evidence of unusual ill-health among them, the system was roundly condemned in the 1843 inquiry on women and children in agriculture on account of the loss of educational opportunities for children, 'impudent' behaviour among the women, and the unbridled power it gave to gang-masters frequently described as 'low' and 'hard'. In 1867, following further inquiries by the Children's Employment Commission, a new Act sought to prohibit the employment of children under eight and gangs of mixed sex, and to license gang-masters. This did not apply to the private gangs employed by farmers which were in any case more numerous, and indeed, some of the twenty-two public gangs said to exist in Lincolnshire towns became private by the simple expedient of the farmer paying their wages directly.[14] But the employment of juveniles came to be further curtailed with the Agricultural Children Act (1873) and the Education Act of 1876.

Factors other than legislation were primarily responsible for an increasing reluctance on the part of women to engage in field work, in gangs or otherwise. Those encountered by F. G. Heath in 1874, stumbling along the road between Dorchester and Milborne in heavy boots 'with a sodden and sulky expression of weariness', were becoming less and less representative.[15] In the late 1860s Farmer Rollinson of Igburgh in Norfolk had been unable to get a woman worker 'in the last three years', whilst at Felthorpe able-bodied women preferred to walk three miles to the paper mill at Taverham, and at Salhouse it was remarked that the women 'did not care to come out' as their husbands' wages improved. Likewise in the Westhampnett Union in Sussex female labour, 'once largely used', was now rarely employed outside haytime and harvest, and at Slinfold there was scarcely one tenth of the employment of female field labour characteristic of twenty years before. By the 1880s it had become largely a memory at Lark Rise in Oxfordshire.[16] Meanwhile, bondagers were disappearing as the image of the institution became increasingly unpopular and the hinds voiced the grievance that they had to keep the woman for a year but were paid only for the days when she actually worked. By the 1890s this, too, had almost vanished, at any rate from the Glendale Union investigated by Wilson Fox.[17] Even female farm service was in headlong decline. It is possible that the figure of 99,000 female farm servants of 1851 exaggerated their numbers by including a good many who were primarily domestic servants, but there can be no doubt about the trend, for their numbers were reduced to 24,000 in 1871, and by 1891 they were no longer separately distinguished within the agricultural category.

In one respect, the declining role of women in agriculture was part of a more general trend to decasualization. This is not a process upon which the census statistics in Table 35.1 can throw much light, partly because the returns must be presumed to show a man's main occupation, although not necessarily his only one. In practice, a variegated pattern of employment was facilitated by the prevalence of piece rates and short—frequently weekly—engagements. Moreover, since they were invariably taken in late March or early April, the censuses did not reflect either the size or the complexity of the labour force at peak seasons when the farmer's outlay on labour might well double or more.[18] To some extent these abnormal requirements were met by a redistribution of labour within the agricultural sector itself. Collins has identified one category of movement from grass and woodland pasture to arable areas, for example from the Vale of Gloucester and the cheese districts of north Wiltshire to the southern chalklands; from the Yorkshire dales to the East Riding; from the pastoral districts of Devon and Somerset to the Isle of Wight. Another category aimed to exploit the different timings and sequences of work between hill and vale, light and heavy land, and different farming systems, with a view to taking two or more harvests in a season. Yet a third category, and quantitatively the most significant, was between the 'small-farm subsistence and large-farm capitalist sectors of British agriculture'.[19] In the west Midlands this had formerly come chiefly from the hill counties of Wales, and in northern England entailed a flow of crofter folk from the counties of Argyll, Perth, and Ross and Cromarty, but by the Victorian period Ireland was a much more important source. The number of recorded immigrant 'harvesters' peaked in 1846–8 at the time of the Famine, and thereafter tended to decline, with a tendency for the Irish to fall back on those areas where wages were highest, such as Yorkshire, Lincolnshire and the fen country.[20]

Traditionally, rural domestic industries such as hand-weaving had been another important source of seasonal labour, and through much of the Victorian period the polyglot armies of casual workers in towns, including many women, remained so, as Samuel has shown.[21] In the long run, and particularly after 1870, the importance of these 'wandering tribes' declined, for a number of reasons. These were in part technological, occasioned by increased use of the scythe and fagging hook in place of the sickle, and later the adoption of reaping machines which tended to lower the earning capacity of part-timers who were increasingly confined to the subordinate tasks of gathering and binding. Other factors included the greater regularity of employment in towns at wage-levels which came to be higher than those which could be earned in the harvest field, and the gradual divorcing of an increasingly street-bred urban population from rural contacts.

However, the process of decasualization was far from complete by the end of the century. In the Monmouth Union in 1893 many of the labourers were reckoned to rely for nine months in the year on other work, such as quarrying and mining, and in 1913 the Land Enquiry Committee guessed that some 100,000 farm workers (about one tenth of the total) could fairly be described as casuals.[22] This figure did not include those who continued to venture into the countryside to engage in market gardening, hop-picking, and fruit-picking, activities which were expanding their labour requirements through the Great Depression period as the arable acreage contracted. For those who in the 1890s worked in such disagreeable metropolitan industries as fur-pulling, match-making and white lead manufacture, the attractions of hopping in Kent were obvious, and this particular seasonal influx remained in being until after the Second World War. But in agriculture proper there was no doubt about the trend. Agricultural commentators had long realized the value of the farmer's 'constant men' and advocated long engagements for specialist workers such as ploughmen.[23] Even in Wiltshire in the 1840s, where the overall situation of the agricultural labourer was poor, farmers would provide ten to twenty perches of land, ploughed and manured, together with a cottage and a good garden at 30–50s. rent per annum.[24] It is fair to assume that the easing by migration of the rural labour surplus would have had the effect of gradually increasing the regularity of employment of those who remained on the land, thereby increasing the farmer's reliance on his regular staff. In a sense, Wales offered the extreme case. Here the social distinctions between masters and men were very much less marked than in England and outdoor labourers were very hard to come by. In a primarily pastoral region requiring constant supervision for livestock, indoor service became the increasingly dominant form of hired labour in the later nineteenth century.[25]

III

The labour surplus apparent in southern England during the early Victorian period seems to have favoured a tendency on the part of farmers 'to pay low wages in order to maximise employment for the men with poor-law settlements in the parish because the economic alternative of paying low wages for a small marginal product was unremunerative expenditure on poor relief'.[26] Against such a background cash wages showed no significant sign of advance before the middle of the century when the national average, according to Caird, was 9s. 6d. — no higher than in 1824. Thereafter it moved to 11s. 6d. in 1860–1; 12s. 5d. in 1867–71; 13s. 9d. in 1879–81; 13s. 4d. in 1892–3, and 14s. 5d. in 1898.[27] Mechanization seems to have had little impact on wages except in as far as it served to benefit a small number of operatives, such as the sixty 'formerly ordinary but intelligent farm labourers' employed by the Northumberland Steam Cultivating Company, whose wages had risen, in consequence, from 15s. a week to 20s. or 23s.[28] Nor did the organization of labour have a lasting impact. It is true that between 1871 and 1873 advances of 2–3s. a week were frequently achieved without industrial action, for example on the farms of Lord Braybrook at Audley End and Viscount Dillon at Ditchley in Oxfordshire, whilst in an essay on *The Dorsetshire Labourer* Thomas Hardy noted an average increase of some 3s. in this notably backward county.[29] But wages rose by at least as much in northern England, where there were very few trade unionists, and also in Wales, where it was said in 1892 that there was no trade unionism and nothing in the nature of a strike had ever been known.[30] Moreover, the waning agricultural unions proved powerless to resist effectively the loss of at least part of these increases as employers, beset by falling prices, retaliated in the later 1870s and 1880s. Rather, the long-term improvement was primarily due to changing conditions of demand and supply. Against a background of 'improved cultivation, more general and thorough management of root-crops, the extension of sheep farming, and winter feeding of stock' in the 1850s and 1860s, migration began to deplete the number of workers on offer so that by 1871 Dent considered over-supply to have become unusual.[31] As it gained further momentum migration frequently brought about a situation where the supply of labour was reckoned hardly equal to demand, as at Bryngwyn near Hereford where the counter-attraction of industrial employment in south Wales was keenly felt.[32]

However, nothing could be more fallacious than inferring earnings exclusively from the cash wages so far considered. Perquisites and allowances in kind played a large, if slowly diminishing part in the labourer's gross income. Notwithstanding the near-universal condemnation of the practice of supplying alcoholic beverages to field workers in the *Reports of the Special Assistant Poor Law Commissioners* (1843), beer continued to 'appear in the accounts of every farmer as an addition to his labour bill' in East Anglia,[33] and the practice remained very common in the southern, western, and south Midland counties. It was made illegal with the passage of the 1887 Truck Act, but continued nevertheless, as Rider Haggard was informed in the neighbourhood of Bridgewater in 1900.[34] Drink apart, the 'privileges' noted in 1867 in Devon and Dorset included the provision of a potato patch and cheap fuel or wheat although, as Hasbach points out, no farmer provided all together;[35] whilst in the 1893 Labour Commission there is evidence of the survival of various payments in kind.

If perquisites, and along with them extra harvest earnings, are reckoned as additional to cash wages, other factors worked in the opposite direction as potential deductions. One was simply loss of time in bad weather, although there was considerable variation of practice. From Wiltshire in 1893, it was reported that many farmers tried to keep their men on, wet or dry, in order to have a sufficient supply in the busy season. On the other hand, as Spencer observed after driving through the Essex villages of Latchingdon and Steeple on a wet day, 'most of the male occupants of cottages appeared to be at home or in the public house'.[36] Probably, as Clifford contended, the larger farmers were more ready in wet weather to pay their weekly men at any rate, if not those engaged in task-work.[37] The most comprehensive evidence on the subject, collected by the Land Enquiry Committee in 1913, suggested that time was lost by inclement weather in 47 per cent of parishes, ranging from 19 per cent in the north to 68 per cent in the south Midlands and eastern counties.[38] Loss of work through illness was another obvious way in which wages could melt away, and injury another, for sadly, accidents could give rise to atrocious conduct on the part of employers. In illustration Canon Girdlestone pointed to the case of an unfortunate carter who having saved a valuable team and waggon when they bolted, at the expense of having his ribs crushed, received from his ungrateful master neither wages, a visit, nor as much as a quart of milk for his children.[39]

So far as such factors could be taken into systematic account, Wilson Fox concluded that the earnings of ordinary labourers stood in a ratio of 119:100 to current weekly wages, although the variation was vast, ranging from 148 (Pewsey) to 106 (Uttoxeter and Wetherby).[40] Undoubtedly, as the Land Enquiry Committee maintained, labourers' earnings (as distinct from cash wages) were by far the more important figures,[41] and, whilst the earlier wage material does not lend itself to comparison, they appear to have moved on the lines indicated in Table 35.2.

Table 35.2 *Agricultural labourers' earnings by region**

	1867–70	*1898*	*1907*
London area and home counties	16s. 6d.	18s. 5d.	18s. 6½d.
South west	12s. 5d.	15s. 7d.	16s. 10d.
Rural south east	14s. 4½d.	15s. 9d.	16s. 5d.
South Wales	12s. 7½d.	17s. 0½d.	18s. 2d.
Rural Wales and Herefordshire	13s. 0d.	16s. 1½d.	17s. 8d.
Midlands	14s. 1d.	17s. 10d.	18s. 4½d.
Lincolnshire, Rutland, Yorkshire (E. and N.R.)	17s. 1d.	18s. 0d.	18s. 10d.
Lancashire, Cheshire, Yorkshire (W.R.)	17s. 1d.	18s. 8d.	19s. 7d.
Cumberland and Westmorland	18s. 6d.	18s. 9d.	19s. 2d.
Northumberland and Durham	18s. 9d.	20s. 5½d.	21s. 5½d.
England and Wales, average of the regions	13s. 9d.	16s. 0d.	17s. 11d.

*Based on Hunt, 1973, 62–4. The unweighted average relates to fifty-four English and Welsh counties.

To what extent did such earnings support a rising standard of life? Prior to 1870 it is probable that any improvements were slight, and contingent upon a greater regularity of employment than had been obtainable in the 1830s and 1840s, coupled with an increasing solicitude for the welfare of their shrinking labour force on the part of more enlightened landlords and employers.[42] But with wages failing to fall commensurately with prices in the years that followed, there was a more noticeable advance. The falling cost of necessities was reflected in many ways. In 1893 Chapman noticed that on clothes lines good linen appeared instead of rags. The cottages contained a better standard of furniture, and every young man over sixteen carried a watch. Butchers' carts called in the villages at least once a week, and not the least significant sign of progress was the appearance of lamps fuelled by cheap paraffin putting an end to the old habit of going to bed (or the public house) as early as seven or eight o'clock. At Chatteris a great many labourers took a weekly newspaper and patronized seaside trips, whilst there was a noticeable increase in the consumption of tobacco.[43] Although such comparisons were by no means entirely novel, in districts where small units prevailed, such as the Isle of Axholme, in Cumberland and in Wales, the situation of the labourers was often favourably contrasted with that of the farmer himself.[44]

These impressions of a rising standard of comfort have to be qualified in several important respects. One critical factor, as Rowntree was so effectively to demonstrate in his study of York, was the family life cycle. Given the most favourable auspices (i.e. where there were adult children living at home) it was pointed out that gross family income could compare with that of a city clerk or a poor curate;[45] but as Rowntree's own excursion into rural sociology made clear, the presence of a large brood of younger children was a very significant factor in rural poverty,[46] and, as we have seen, the fertility of farm labourers was definitely on the high side. Secondly, even if we disregard significant local disparities at the district or parish level, there were well-marked regional variations in earnings, as is apparent from Table 35.2. From at least the 1780s wages in the north of England had tended to pull away from those in the south. In 1850 Caird suggested that the difference was of the order of 37 per cent, and confidently ascribed this to 'the proximity of manufacturing and mining enterprise'.[47] There were differences of opinion among contemporaries about subsequent trends, as well as the importance to be attached to 'indulgencies' as a countervailing factor. In fact, Hunt's researches suggest that the percentage (of the British average wage) by which the maximum regional wage exceeded the minimum fell from 44 in 1867–70 to 28 in 1907. The important point to note is the persistence of variations, and his striking conclusion that 'wage differentials at any one time were as great as the overall improvement in wages between 1850 and 1914'.[48] Nor did the employment of women and children offset these differences, even when it ran at its height in the first half of the Victorian period. Hunt concludes:

> Four shillings is probably a generous estimate of the average gross earnings of wives and children in the 1850's, and this was no more, and in many cases less, than the margin between farm labourers' wages in the north and south . . . [and] whatever residual compensations the rural south may have enjoyed at the beginning of the period were not enduring.[49]

IV

With the southern labourer in mind, Hunt has argued elsewhere that 'sectors of the English agricultural labour force were living at a standard which, whilst adequate to sustain life, fell short of the level needed to ensure maximum labour efficiency', and that low wages were a consequence as well as a cause of low productivity.[50] This state of affairs was mitigated only slowly after 1870 as agricultural wages rose and regional variations became less marked. It is true, as his critics have pointed out, that as well as the varying quality of land, the relative amount of capital per worker would tell on labour productivity, and that his argument depends heavily on the citation of mainly impressionistic comments.[51] Yet it is striking how consistently the grain of this evidence runs in the same direction, that is, if one compares adversely the quality of labour in the south and east with that obtainable in Scotland, the north of England, and the north Midlands. In cases where southern labourers were transferred to the north it was often observed that they found difficulty in staying the pace. Thus in 1855 George Grey had attracted some two hundred southern labourers to dig drains in Northumberland by the prospect of earning 20–25s. a week by the piece. Within a short time only ten remained, and they never succeeded in making more than 15s. 'There was not a man among the whole importation that had legs and shoulders to compare with our lads of seventeen years of age.'[52] Caird, Clifford, Culley, Read, and Brodrick were but a few of the experts convinced of such disparities in labour efficiency, and Wilson Fox in 1906 was following a well-established tradition in ascribing them to the cumulative effects of 'generations of bad feeding' in the south.[53]

Poor nutrition, presumably, should be reflected in an above-average rate of sickness among farm workers, and there are conflicting impressions in the literature. On the one hand, Flora Thompson's recollections of Lark Rise in the 1880s are favourable: the doctor was rarely seen there and the general state of health was excellent owing to the 'open-air life and abundance of coarse but wholesome food'. At the other extreme we have Canon Girdlestone's view that the labourers of north Devon in the 1860s did not live, they merely 'didn't die'.[54] As we have seen, the rates of mortality prevailing among farm labourers were low by contemporary standards. Yet the Yorkshire doctor, Charles Thackrah, had emphasized in the 1830s that they were 'far less robust in figure than we would expect from the nature of their employ', and a few years later the published statistics of the Manchester Unity showed that although farm labourers enjoyed outstanding longevity, nevertheless they experienced 'an aggregate amount of sickness of 6.2 per cent more than the whole of the rural districts'. At age twenty the average was 4 days, 2 hours sickness; at age thirty, 6 days, 5 hours; at forty, 8 days, 2 hours; at fifty, nearly 14 days, at sixty, nearly 27 days.[55]

The relationship between age and sickness revealed in these figures of Ratcliffe takes on further significance when the age structure of the agricultural labour force is examined, for as a result of age-selective migration it had come to be characterized by a comparatively high proportion of very young workers and an excess of the elderly, with a great dearth of men who who were at once fully experienced and still in the prime of life, say, between twenty-five and forty-four. Notwithstanding comments like that from Zeal (Devon)—'our young men have all gone, only old people and cripples left'[56] W. C. Little contended that a comparison of the census returns for 1871 and 1891 gave no support to the prevailing impression of an ageing labour force; likewise the Registrar General was of the same opinion and succeeded in misleading Hasbach entirely.[57] In fact, a lateral rather than an historical comparison was more appropriate since the ageing process had been going on for many years. Such an approach reveals that in 1891 elderly workers (i.e. those aged fifty-five and over) were approximately three times as numerous, as a proportion, in the farm labour force than among railway employees or coal miners. A more broadly-based comparison is made in Table 35.3.

Youths loomed large as a proportion only because of the shortage of men in their twenties and thirties, and by this time even they were sometimes hard to come by. Thus in south west Wales farmers had become reliant in part on the importation of lads from English reformatories, ragged schools, and industrial schools.[58] An Easingwold farmer remarked that they were 'quick in getting hold of machinery and interested in it, and in that respect better than the older men'; but, he added, they did not care to learn 'the old-fashioned arts'.[59] These were increasingly the province of the elderly, and the situation produced mixed effects. Often enough, and especially if they worked heavy land, men were 'very much bent' by their fifties.[60] Yet it was

Table 35.3   *Age composition of the male labour force aged 10 and upwards, England and Wales, 1891**

		Percentage aged					
		under 20	20–24	25–34	35–44	45–54	over 55
A. Agricultural labourers, farm servants, shepherds		28.0	11.9	16.8	12.7	11.9	18.6
B	Remainder of male occupied population	19.8	13.9	23.6	18.1	12.9	11.7
C	% by which A exceeds B	+41.4	−14.3	−28.8	−29.8	−7.7	+58.9

*Based on BPP 1893–4 CVI [C. 7058]. *1891 Census, England and Wales. Ages, etc., Abstract.* Table 5, pp. x–xxv.

claimed in the 1870s, 'go where you will, you find old servants retained . . . sometimes receiving full wages, sometimes treated as "three-quarters", or "half" men, but hardly ever earning the wages paid them'. One of Clifford's Suffolk correspondents remarked: 'Neither I nor any decent farmer would turn a man off simply because he was old.'[61] From the employer's point of view sentimental considerations would often coincide with his interest in handling the lighter work of the farm cheaply, if with only modest efficiency. Taking this into account, Charles Booth remarked that 'in one way or another, effective working life is ten years longer in the country than in the town, or . . . is as seventy to sixty', and in a study of 262 rural parishes he found that 55 per cent of persons aged sixty-five and over could exist by their own earnings or means.[62]

Matters of the kind so far discussed do not exhaust the list of factors detrimental to labour efficiency. A very lengthy walk to work might result in labourers resting the moment the master's back was turned, as Farmer Norgate of Sprowston (Norfolk) complained in 1867.[63] Moreover, for many years the condition of the labourer, especially in the south, bred what Jefferies described as 'an oriental absence of aspiration'.[64] A Suffolk farmer recalled that when he asked labourers who had finished their stint of piece work by 1 p.m. to continue, the response was, 'No, master, we don't want no more money. We've as much as we care about! We'd rather go home and smoke a pipe.' Likewise in the west country the reluctance of labourers to forgo their cider allowances in order to secure a higher wage was much remarked upon in the 1860s and 1870s, and indicatively a meeting of eight men (with a total of fifty-two children) at Newent agreed, with one exception, that they preferred their cider allowance to 1s. 6d. extra wages, its cash equivalent.[65] It may be that the ensuing years saw a greater responsiveness to cash incentives but the process has yet to be traced in detail.

Many of these features served to encourage a stereotyped image of the farm labourers' bearing and address. According to Flora Thompson they detested nothing as much as being hurried,[66] and their sedate pace appears to have communicated itself to the young. Youths who, unlike their urban counterparts, had not been trained 'to appreciate the value of time' were criticized in characteristic terms by a speaker at the Framlingham Farmer's Club in 1867; if asked to fetch a rake a boy would 'open his mouth, turn his eyes on you and wheel on his heels with the precipitate motion of a Polar Bear'.[67] An article in the *Girls' Own Paper* in 1885 described the country lads of Dorset moving 'as though they have a heavy weight tied to each leg, so that it can only be moved by a heave of the whole body in the opposite direction'.[68] Such witticisms were heard more frequently with the passage of time: society as a whole, perhaps particularly the working classes, were prone to judge their own social and economic progress, albeit unconsciously, by the extent that they distanced themselves from the farm labourer's style and standard of life. There was point in their doing so. For notwithstanding a perceptible improvement in the agricultural labourer's condition during the Victorian era, it was pointed out in 1913 that in only five northern counties did his income reach the level necessary to avoid primary poverty;[69] and also—it would seem correctly—that he received a much smaller proportion of the wealth he helped to create than did his urban counterpart.[70]

Notes

1 See, for example, Chambers, 1972, 97–106; Tranter, 1973, 90–3; Martin, 1976, 33–8.
2 Flinn, 1965, 151–2.
3 Greenhow, 1858, 162–4.
4 Ratcliffe, 1850, 50. No doubt these farm labourers able to afford membership of the Manchester Unity were better off than the average, but this would also apply to other occupations to some extent. The data appear to cover upwards of 17,000 rural labourers.
5 BPP 1912–13, XII [CD. 6578] xli, xliii, 73–87.
6 Anon., *Cornhill Magazine*, 1864, 179.
7 Anderson, 1976, 65, 76.
8 Flora Thompson, 1954, 112, 142, 143.
9 Innes, 1938, 47.
10 Deane and Cole, 1962, 108; R. Jones, 1968, 9–10; information on Ash from Mrs A. E. Newman.
11 Hunt, 1973, 237.
12 Clapham, I, 1930, 113–14.
13 These and the following statistics are drawn from BPP 1852–3 XXXVIII pts I and II. Census 1851, population tables, pt II, vols I and II. See especially pp. lxxviii–lxxxi, clxxv, cclxxxii.
14 BPP 1867–8 XVII. Appendix, Pt I, 77.
15 Heath, 1874, 35.
16 BPP 1867–8 XVII. Appendix, pt I, 9, and pt II, 31, 36, 61, 77; Flora Thompson, 1954, 49.
17 Dunbabin, 1974, 155; BPP 1893–4 XXXV [C. 6894–III] 104.

18 For examples see Morgan, 1975, 39–40.
19 Collins, 1976, 43–5.
20 *Ibid.*, 50–1.
21 Samuel, 1972; Samuel 1975b, 3–5.
22 BPP 1893–4 XXV [C. 6894–IV] 66; Land Enquiry Committee, 1913, I, 4.
23 See, for example, Wilson, 1851, III, 874.
24 Little, 1845, 177.
25 Howell, 1978, 93–4.
26 Digby, 1975, 79; Morton, 1868, 76.
27 Orwin and Felton, 1931, 233.
28 Dent, 1871, 348.
29 Horn, 1976b, 132; Orwin and Whetham, 1964, 234.
30 Hasbach, 1966, 284; BPP 1893–4 XXXVI [C. 6894—XIV] 48.
31 Dent, 1871, 346–7; E. L. Jones, 1964, 328–9.
32 BPP 1893–4 XXXV [C. 6894—IV) 84.
33 Clifford, 1875b, 117.
34 Horn, 1976b, 124.
35 Hasbach, 1966, 337, 411.
36 BPP 1893–4 XXXV [C. 6894—V] 8, 76.
37 Clifford, 1875b, 121.
38 Land Enquiry Committee, 1913, I, 21.
39 Heath, 1874, 165.
40 BPP 1893–4 XXXVII [C. 6894—XXV] 84.
41 Land Enquiry Committee, 1913, I, 4.
42 E. L. Jones, 1964, 331.
43 BPP 1893–4 XXXV [C. 6894—II] 45, 57, 83.
44 See, for example, BPP 1893–4 XXXVI [C. 6894—XIV] 172; Howell, 1978, 93; Dent, 1871, 361–3.
45 BPP 1893–4 XXXVII [C. 6894—XXV] 87.
46 Rowntree and Kendall, 1913, 33–4.
47 Caird, 1852, 511.
48 Hunt, 1973, 1, 58.
49 *Ibid.*, 121.
50 Hunt, 1967, 286.
51 Metcalf, 1969, 118; David, 1970, 504–5.
52 BPP 1867–8 XVII, Appendix, pt I, 138.
53 Aronson, 1914, 63, quoting evidence to the Select Committee on the Housing of the Working Classes Amendment Bill, 1906.
54 Flora Thompson, 1954, 3, 141; Heath, 1874, 71.
55 Thackrah, 1832, 14; Ratcliffe, 1850, 50, 116.
56 BPP 1893–4 XXXV [C. 6894—II] 92.
57 BPP 1893–4 XXXVII [C. 6894—XXV] 33; Hasbach, 1966, 341.
58 BPP 1893–4 XXXVI [C. 6894—XIV] 9.
59 BPP 1893–4 XXXV [C. 6894—VI] 68.
60 Heath, 1893, 224, quoting Dr Batt of Witney.
61 Clifford, 1875b, 120.

62 Booth, 1894, 321, 339. *N.B.* his figures exclude those in union workhouses.

63 BPP 1867–8 XVII, Appendix, pt, II, 29.

64 Jefferies, 1880, II, 78.

65 Clifford, 1875b, 106; Heath, 1874, 88; BPP 1867–8 XVII. Appendix, pt II, 133–4.

66 Flora Thompson, 1954, 46.

67 BPP 1867–8 XVII. Appendix, pt I, 14.

68 Kerr, 1968, 117.

69 Rowntree and Kendall, 1913, 31. Note, however, that they compared earnings in 1907 with prices current in 1912.

70 Aronson, 1914, 73. The statistics in Deane and Cole, 1962, 152, 166, confirm this impression. Thus in 1901 the share of wages and salaries in the total income generated in the agriculture, forestry, and fishing sector stood at 38.8 per cent against 48.1 in mining, manufacturing, and building, and 46.5 per cent in trade and transport.

36 In the Sweat of thy Face: The Labourer and Work

Alun Howkins

I think that the Tiller of the soil is the highest and oldest workman of all. No one can do without him and the product of his hands. The Gold miner cannot eat his gold, nor the Coal miner his coal, nor the Iron miner his Iron. All and every one is dependent upon the soil. He is the Father of all Workers.[1]

I

The farm workforce of the nineteenth century was far from being an undifferentiated mass of John Hodges. Although the national census of 1901 was the first to acknowledge the major divisions they certainly pre-date it, while even the divisions of 1901—shepherds, horsemen, cowmen and labourers—conceal the gradations of skill and prestige attached to these different jobs. On occasion these bland descriptions can be seriously misleading. Joseph Arch, for instance, was a champion thatcher and hedger and ditcher. At these crafts he earned enough to buy his own house and find employment throughout the south Midlands, although a known 'troublemaker'. Yet he would appear in the census as a labourer.[2] Similarly, oral evidence reveals an enormous variety of jobs and job descriptions. The father of one man I interviewed was by turns a labourer, thatcher and quarry man, while another was a builder's labourer, farm labourer, poacher, marl digger and fish hawker.[3] It would be sheer chance which of these jobs he was following on census day.

506

Further, there were regional distinctions. These produced a variety of localized categories of worker as a direct result of different types and patterns of farming. In Aberdeenshire the continued survival of the croft system, where married labourers held a small piece of land, created a peculiar intermediate stratum of labourer-farmers.[4] In south west Wales up to the 1900s the men of the farms went to the coalfield in the winter months, returning in the summer to help pay off the families' labour debts.[5] In large areas of Northumberland and Durham the bondager system, whereby a labourer had to provide a woman worker (the bondager) to work with him, created another local category.[6]

Even beyond these local categories there were variations, meaningless perhaps to the outsider, but important in the village community. In the south east, for example, it was usual for the horseman to be the 'superior' workman and, therefore, the older. When a boy went on a farm he went to 'learn a trade' which would stand him in good stead and increase his earning power as he grew older. Elsewhere, though, the situation was quite different. In Aberdeenshire, Cardiganshire and the East Riding of Yorkshire, among other areas, the process was reversed.[7] Here, because of the living-in system and hiring by the year, the young men looked after the horses and the older, usually married workers, did the less skilled work. As David Jenkins has written of south west Wales,

> A farm servant (*gwas*) was quite distinct from a farm labourer (*gweither*). Farm servants were unmarried and generally young men who were engaged to work with horses and lived in at the farm while labourers were usually married men who lived in their own houses. The general labouring work of the farm such as hedging, ditching and drainage was specifically the work of the farm labourer. . . . The care of cattle . . . was for men the work of the lowest standing and accepted only as a last resort when nothing else was available.[8]

However, through all the regions basic divisions remained. As Wilson Fox wrote in 1905:

> On farms of a sufficient size to admit of definite spheres of occupation being allotted, the work is organised, as far as possible under a system of sub-divided labour. With the exception of stewards, bailiffs, and foremen, the most responsible positions are those of the men in charge of the animals, and these are speaking generally, a higher paid class of farm servant than the 'ordinary labourer' and are usually on longer terms of engagement.[9]

In addition we can observe divisions within these categories. Firstly, within the category of men employed with animals it is important to divide them by the kind of animals they were working with. Secondly, it is necessary to divide the 'ordinary labourer' category into regular and casual. And, lastly, it is essential to note that the situation throughout the nineteenth century was not a static one.

The skills involved in farm work were many and various. Wilson Fox's division between those who worked with animals and those who did not seems to have been the primary one, yet quite how the division came about is difficult to determine. In most cases there seems to have been very little on-the-job training; as Jack Leeder said about the old horsemen he worked with, 'They weren't too good at [teaching] . . . you had to find out for yourself. They used to say, "Find out for yourself and you'll know how to do it." '[10] In many cases boys seem to have learnt from their fathers. A boy would go to work with his father from an early age to 'help out'. Arthur Amis, for instance, who was the cowman son of a cowman, did this,[11] as did Bert Hazell, whose father was a horseman.[12] Even this, though, could not guarantee that a boy would become a horseman or a cowman. There was always competition for jobs, and the individual's temperament was very important, particularly with horses. As Jack Leeder said, many boys were simply 'scared' of horses and had no control.[13]

The father–son situation, however, was almost universal in labourers' skills. A man who could thatch a rick, for instance, inevitably taught his son. Charles Leveridge started with his father when he was eleven years old: 'We used to have to go to pull the straw, before we left school, that was where I learnt my thatching.'[14] One suspects that this informal training in basic skills, and there were many, went right down the scale of farm work since all those interviewed spent a good deal of time, before and after school, in the holidays and playing truant, in the fields with their fathers.

II

The Victorian labourer, unless he or she was casually employed, was hired by the year. In most of north eastern Scotland, Northumberland, Durham, Cumberland, Westmorland, Yorkshire, north Lancashire and north Lincolnshire 'all classes' of workers were still hired and paid by the year in 1900.[15] In north Cambridgeshire and south Lincolnshire men hired by the year were mostly horsemen and shepherds. A similar situation existed in parts of the Midlands: mainly in Derbyshire, Shropshire, Staffordshire, Warwickshire, Leicestershire, Worcestershire, Oxfordshire, Berkshire and Buckinghamshire. By 1900, however, even the yearly hiring of 'skilled' men went on 'to a much smaller extent than formerly'.[16] In the south west the system 'was rapidly dying out', though it still continued in some parts of Monmouthshire and Herefordshire, and to a lesser extent in Hampshire, Dorset, Wiltshire and Gloucestershire.[17]

Where men were hired by the year, they were engaged at a hiring fair ('feein' fair' in Scotland; 'sittings' in Yorkshire; 'mop' or 'statty' in the south). Here the worker stood in the streets on the day of the fair with a badge of calling in the lapel of the coat. Indoor and semi-indoor female servants were also hired by the year. A description of Bridlington hirings in 1895 catches much of the flavour of the fairs:

Everyone tried to look smart; it is only right to say that. Many of the girls
were brightly dressed, and only their speech betrayed them; but the lads
still cling to the past in their sartorial get-up, which includes gaudy silk
neckties and pearlies. . . . The waggoner has a bit of fancifully twisted cord in
his cap, a bright flower . . . in his buttonhole, and his jacket not buttoned.
. . . The proper fastening is two or three inches of brass chain, the better to
display a capacious chest. Feathers on some of the bowler hats are
suggestive of the fold yards, while the occasional flashes of bright colour in
the feminine head-gear are suggestive of primitive Arcadia rather than the
latest Paris fashions.[18]

Men and women hired in this way worked for a fixed wage plus board and lodging.
This was the dominant pre-industrial pattern, though it had been gradually
disappearing since the mid-eighteenth century, especially in the economically most
advanced wheat-growing areas of the south and east. As early as 1804 Arthur Young
noted that the custom of living and feeding in the farmhouse was vanishing, while in
Suffolk by 1813 he noted that 'the great mass of work in this county is done by the *piece*'
[*sic*][19] which was the antithesis of yearly hiring. Where the system did continue the
men usually lived in 'bothies', separate rooms over the stables, and the women in the
house. On the smaller farms both sexes lived in the farmhouse itself.

The transitional form of employment between living-in and weekly labour was
hiring by the year, when a man lived off the farm but actually received his money
weekly or fortnightly. This usually applied to men who worked with animals. In 1905
Wilson Fox noted that shepherds were almost inevitably employed by the year, as
were stockmen, since 'it might put employers at great inconvenience if their shepherds
or stockmen left them at short notice'.[20] This kind of contract was often extended to
horsemen. The overwhelming weight of oral evidence suggests that horsemen (in
Norfolk team-men) were employed by the year, and this is borne out by prosecutions
under the Employer and Workmen's Act. Men employed to look after animals were
graded. Each farm had a head horseman (in Norfolk head team-man, in the north head
carter), who was the most skilled.[21] Similar grades existed for stockmen (in the south
east, cowmen) but not for shepherds, except on very large farms, as the shepherd
usually worked alone with his page (boy).[22] This group of labourers was often housed
in tied housing near the farm—the only substantial nineteenth-century group, other
than those on estate villages, to live under this system.

Finally there were those groups hired by the week. Even here there was a sense that
the contract of employment ran for a year. Wages books from Norfolk farms show
that by the 1870s there was a regular core workforce of labourers, employed all the
year round in many cases,[23] though often laid off in wet weather. This retention of the
notional year's contract was related to the domestic economy of the labourer,
especially the necessity of paying the rent once a year (usually at Michaelmas). In
addition to these more or less regular workers there were those who were truly
casual. The work of E. J. T. Collins and David Morgan has shown how the economic

and organizational changes in agriculture in the early years of the nineteenth century created an enormous seasonal demand for casual workers. In the late 1860s this could mean a temporary increase in the workforce of 30–100 per cent.[24] Until the mid-1870s this extra workforce came largely from travelling and migrant workers. The Irish, the Scots, town-dwellers, gipsies, all once tramped the roads, following the same routes year after year. In some areas these migrants formed bands of skilled men and women who would travel from one farm to another taking harvests in turn. Such were the men of Blaxall in Suffolk described by George Ewart Evans, the travelling harvesters of Leafield in Oxfordshire or, in a different context, the travelling sheep-shearing gangs of Sussex.[25] As well as those who travelled, there were local workers who could be drawn upon for casual work. Crucial among these, until the mid-1870s again, were women and children. The practice of using the wives and children of labourers was at its most developed under the gang system. This was a system of subcontracting work to a gang-master, who then provided labour for particular tasks; it was widely used in Norfolk, Suffolk, Cambridgeshire and north Lincolnshire between the mid-1820s and the 1870s.[26]

In the course of the nineteenth century all these regional variations in hiring, work and classification were in a state of flux. In the south and east the dominant trend was away from a regular living-in workforce employed by the year towards a casual workforce living away from the farm, with a reduced number of regular, and usually skilled, workers. Thus at the end of the 1840s there seem to have been in Norfolk three casual to every two regular workers.[27] After the late-nineteenth-century depression the pattern seems to have been reversed. As early as the 1860s there were complaints of labour shortage as rural depopulation bit and the supply of Irish casuals dried up after the Famine.[28] This really began to show at the end of the 1890s. By 1900 all observers were agreed that there was a serious labour shortage in rural areas, leading to much more regular employment. As Wilson Fox wrote in 1905: 'Generally speaking, since about the year 1896, ordinary farm labourers have been regularly employed. During this period farmers in all parts of the country have complained a scarcity of labour.'[29] The most eloquent testimony to this change is that by 1920 there were nationally five regular workers to every casual one.

The reasons for this are not far to seek. By the 1890s there had been a century-long drain on the over-populated rural areas, and even by the early 1870s some signs of crisis were apparent. However, the depression, coupled with some mechanization, softened the blow, and it was only with recovery in the 1890s that the full extent of the loss was clear. Additionally, in the south at least, women and children had been withdrawn effectively from regular involvement in the workforce by the gangs legislation of 1867 and the Education Acts. In the north the situation was different. The farms were smaller and had always competed with industry in terms of wages. This meant that a regular workforce, living-in, had been set as the pattern early in the nineteenth century: it was simply not possible to casualize the labourer when all could earn high regular wages nearby. Thus young men living-in, together with married men living out, but in regular work, was the northern pattern.

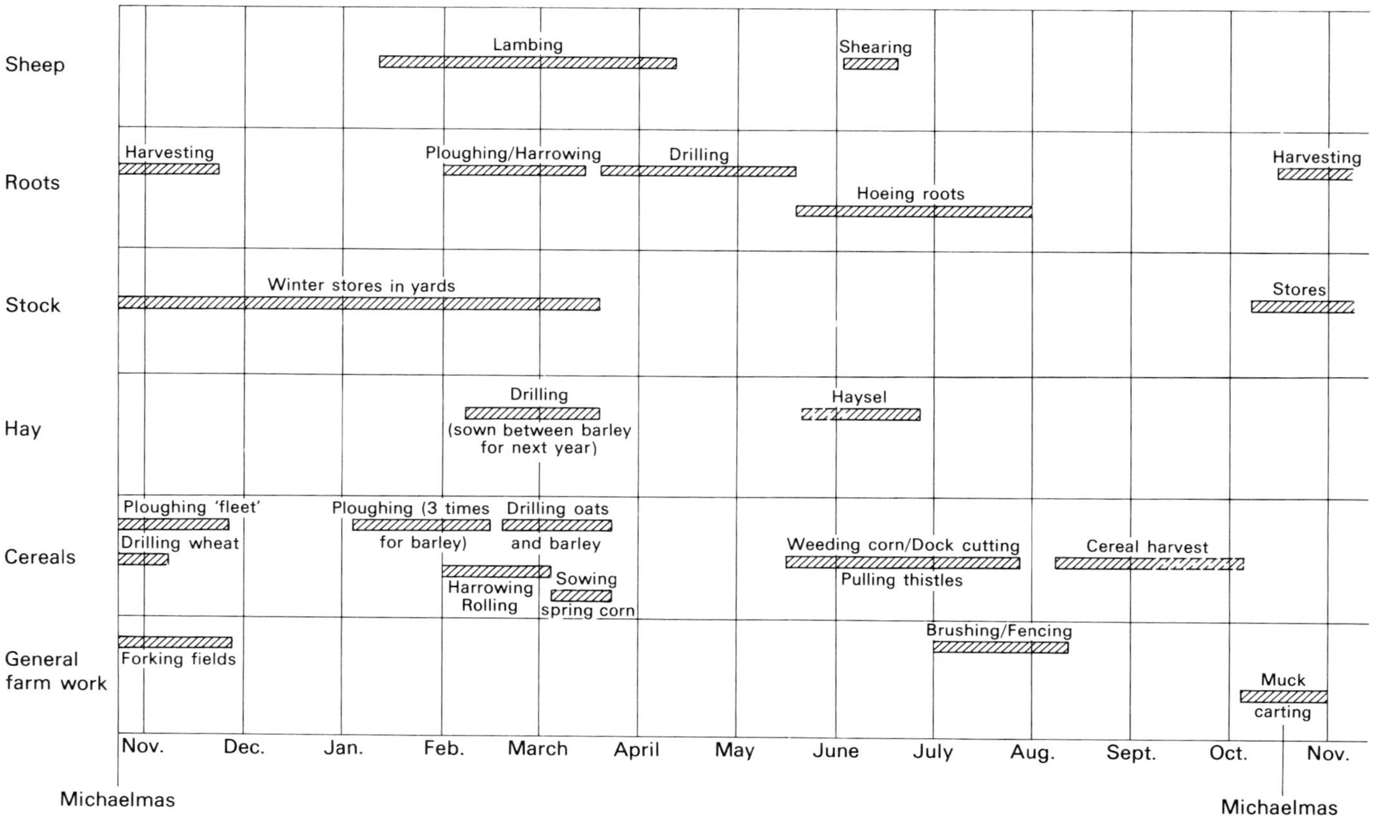

Figure 36.1 The seasonal cycle of farmwork, Norfolk 1900–20 — based on a four-course shift: hay/wheat/roots/oats

511

III

The actual work done by the farm worker varied according to skill and, crucially, season. This is best shown, in the first instance, diagrammatically. Figure 36.1 is based on the farming year in Norfolk at the turn of the nineteenth century, but with very little modification it could stand for the cereal-growing areas of the country for most of the century. The non-cereal modifications to this figure will be considered briefly at the end of this chapter.

The working year began and ended at Michaelmas or old Michaelmas. This was the end of harvest when the rent was paid and men changed jobs. As the daughter of a Norfolk team-man told me:

> In those days you see, farm workmen [at] Michaelmas, that was the 11th October in the country [old Michaelmas day], if they wanted another place they left the one they had and moved to another one . . . well then if they wanted to move again they just packed up and moved again. . . .[30]

Another respondent said the roads were 'thick' with 'dicky carts' at Michaelmas.[31] Even here there was considerable regional variation. Michaelmas or old Michaelmas seems to have been the predominant time of year for moving in the arable areas, but elsewhere, especially in the north and Scotland, old May Day, Martinmas or Whitsun were favoured.[32]

The horseman who came on the farm in the autumn faced a short period of intensive work, provided the weather was not hard:

> You'd start after harvest . . . what we called 'scaling', that's ploughing very fleet, which really cuts all the stubble and the weeds, harrow it . . . so it all pulls out, walk behind and lift the harrows . . . and of course that then all had to be shook about by hand, by fork, and then ploughed in.[33]

For the labourer, apart from forking behind the fleet ploughing, and muck carting, the main work of the winter was the root harvest. Early in the autumn the work, though hard, was pleasant enough:

> The method employed was this: you grasped the leaves of the mangold with the left hand. . . . You pulled the mangold out of the ground, swung it upwards, and at the right moment slipped your knife blade through the leaves where they joined the root. Then, if you had judged it correctly, the mangold flew into the cart and you were left with the leaves in your hand. You dropped them, and stooped to pull another. The whole process took the labourer one second.[34]

As the winter came on the process was less pleasant. Once the frost came the mangolds froze in the ground and getting them out became backbreaking work in which a misplaced swing of the knife could take a thumb or finger off. Along with the potato harvest, the root harvest in mid-winter was the most disliked of farm work. If

512

the weather held, ploughing fleet was followed quickly by ploughing for wheat and barley: 'they'd start and plough, plough as much as they could before Christmas'.[35] Ploughing for barley was a much longer process: 'they used to plough three times for barley ... that was a big job, with all horses, and of course you couldn't rush'.[36]

Ploughing was the most skilled work of the most skilled men—the team-men or horsemen.[37] Under horse culture even a relatively small farm of 100–150 acres employed two or three team-men. A man who started work on a farm near Wyndham in Norfolk in 1919 talked about the organization of this side of the farm:

> You had five horsemen, five adults and a boy ... [and] we all had six horse each, and then there would be another two or three looked after by someone else. They would be sub-divided so that we would run ten plough teams.[38]

The teams were rigidly organized. At the top was the head team-man: he was the most skilled, was paid more, and occasionally received a free cottage. He acted as a kind of foreman, 'keeping time and setting men off to work'.[39] This relationship was symbolized by the order of going out in the morning:

> When we were working in the plough teams [the head team-man] would take the lead, and nobody would dare to leave the yard until he'd got onto his horse and he'd got in front. He'd be followed by the second team-man and then subsequently down the line.[40]

Once in the fields he usually 'cut the field out'. Every forty yards across the field ('a forty-yard rig') the head team-man would cut one furrow, then turn it back. He was then followed by a less skilled man with a three-horse and double-furrow plough, who took his line from him. When the gap between the rigs narrowed the head team-man would finish the work.[41]

The skill required of a team-man was considerable and was surrounded by mystique. Even in the 1820s there were old horseman who believed in and practised magic, mainly connected with the bones of the 'running toad'.[42] The younger generation were more sceptical. Jack Leeder, who started work in 1915, knew about the 'toad's bone' but 'didn't believe in it'. Nevertheless he did know recipes for making horses eat, making their coats shine and dealing with cuts.[43] Team-men were very close about this kind of knowledge. All those I talked to, even the young ones, were extremely wary. Few learnt from their fathers: Jack Leeder's grandfather was 'a great horseman ... but most of the things that he knew died with him'.[44]

To return to the yearly cycle. As winter set in farm work gradually came to a stop. Starting at the bottom men were laid off, although this practice was dying out by the 1900s. Nevertheless, the *Labour Gazette* regularly noted that numbers of labourers were out of work in Norfolk parishes.[45] Team-men and cowmen were seldom laid off in winter—their skills were too valuable:

> some of the labourers was laid off, but see that's where you got the benefit of it if you was team-man or yardman you got your full time in. But if you got a

lot of bad weather, labouring chaps, they used to send them home.[46]

The period of laying off depended crucially on the state of the weather. In a really bad winter, for instance that of 1911–12, men could still be out of work at the end of March, having suffered three or even four months of unemployment. However, in most years farm work started up again soon after Christmas. Ploughing continued and drilling of spring wheat started as soon as possible. There was also threshing, although this was most usually done by travelling gangs hired by the threshing contractor. The men who worked the threshing tackle were a separate breed, men who for various reasons could not get or did not want a regular job. It was often the resort of a man dismissed for trade union activity, like Billy Dixon, who was sacked after leading a strike in a wood yard. He spent a year as 'second corn' on Bullimore's 'chining' crew from Bacton.[47] Another group who went threshing were fishermen. The enginemen often had experience of steam engines from the drifters, and many crew men 'did a couple of days threshing' in January and February when there was no fishing.[48] Threshing also provided work for the few true casuals as well as frozen-out farm workers.

In the middle of March, as the weather improved and the days grew longer, the workforce went on to summer time. The date of the change and the actual hours varied considerably. In Paston men went on to fifty-four hours on 1 March and wages went up by a shilling a week.[49] In Trunch they went on to sixty hours on 21 March for an extra shilling. Labourers worked all round the clock but team-men usually went two journeys, six in the morning until eleven, and one-thirty until six-thirty. The single journey was six until four.[50]

Also by March drilling was under way. This again was highly skilled work. If a man's ability could be judged by a straight furrow it could just as well be judged by the rows of green shoots as the corn came up. On a Sunday it was a favourite pastime of team-men and labourers alike to walk around the parish and those nearby, gaining 'traveller' status and thus able to drink, but also examining the ploughing of their peers. A phrase like 'it looks as though a lot of bloody old chicken have been in there' could easily lead to a fight in a strange pub.[51] Drilling was usually done with a three-horse team, harnessed in a row, and led by a boy to get the accuracy needed.[52] Drilling followed a strict pattern. In many areas wheat went in in October if the weather was fair, though this was by no means universal. Then in February the rest of the wheat went in, then oats, then barley; in April, May or even June the roots were drilled.

Between the end of drilling and the beginning of haysel (hay harvest) there was a period of slack:

> By the time you got your turnips and mangolds in there'd be quite a spell then, that'd be perhaps the slackest time on the farm. Then you'd do repairs and weeding of corn. There was a lot of dock digging them days and cutting thistles.[53]

At this time women and children appeared in the fields, weeding and picking stones. Stone-picking was paid by the piece—a penny a bushel[54]—as was weeding. As the

514

roots came up they were thinned and hoed. This was done by the piece, usually by men working in gangs, the price negotiated by the head labourer, still called the 'lord' in some areas.[55]

At the beginning of June, again depending on the weather, haysel began. The hay crop was vital to the horse economy, and because of weather its gathering was fraught with some of the tensions which were so much a part of the later cereal harvest. For much of the century hay was cut by scythe, but by the 1900s mechanical mowers were becoming common. The haysel was perhaps the hardest of all harvests. Once the hay was cut it lay in the fields to dry, as the stacking of green hay could easily lead to spontaneous combustion. While in the fields the hay had to be turned by hand every couple of days, then raked into cocks and eventually loaded and stacked. There was seldom any extra payment for haysel and the men very rarely worked in gangs or by the piece. All this produces very different memories of haysel than the pictures evoked by the idyllic writings of many contemporaries. To the labourer the turning, raking, cocking and loading in the heat of June, without the compensation of the extra money earned at harvest, was drudgery.[56]

Between haysel and cereal harvest there was another slight lull. In this hedges were cut, weeding of corn continued, and the fields were brushed. This was the laying of thorn bushes across the cut fields to stop poachers long-netting rabbits on them.[57] Then in mid-August cereal harvest began. As the corn yellowed the men would begin harvest bargaining. With the head team-man speaking for the horsemen, and the lord for the labourers, the rate for harvest was fixed on each farm. All watched their neighbours, as the first to agree usually set the price for the whole area, and even within a county there would be considerable variation.[58] When the price was fixed the men 'had a day hanging their scythes' at the blacksmiths. This involved sharpening and getting them set at the right angle in the shaft. Hanging was usually accompanied by drinking, with part of the cost borne by the farmer.[59]

The following day harvest began. Through the nineteenth century changes in technology can be observed—the change from the sickle to the bagging hook and scythe, and from the scythe to some form of mechanical reaper. Until well into the second half of the century the scythe predominated. Working in gangs of about twenty, the men cut in staggered line across the standing corn, taking their timing from the lord who stood at the head of the line: they stopped as he stopped and started as he started. Behind them a row of women scooped the corn into armfuls (sheaves or shooves) and tied them with bands of straw. In the stifling summer heat it was backbreaking work, but had a dignity and power about it that fixed this part of the labourers' work in the minds of those who saw it in its final years. One old man who had helped take the harvest with a scythe said: 'They were men in them days real men . . . they seemed more happy at work, they were continually whistling and singing. That's something I'm glad I've been able to be mixed up with, those old times. . . .'[60]

By the mid-1890s the sight of a gang of mowers strung out across a field was becoming rare. Although a man still 'mowed round the edges' to clear a path for the mechanical reaper, the gang was gone. In its place the windmill-like blades of the sail reaper, and then the less poetic drum of blades of the reaper-binder, cut their way through the corn.

In the weeks of the cereal harvest the men battled against the weather. While it held they worked fifteen or sixteen hours a day. Rain would not only ruin the crop but crucially delay work. Since harvest was paid by the piece this could be disastrous. As one labourer said: 'The season ruled all, if you got a wet time you'd be about eight weeks, and your harvest [wage] was five pounds . . . and they were in debt [and] they'd drawn all their money . . . before they'd got half the corn in. . . .'[61] But harvest did not end with the cutting of the corn. It was shooved, and when dry carted and stacked. Stacking was a skilled job. Wrong stacking or stacking too early could lead to rotting or burning. Crucially, it had to be thatched. Sometimes this was done by the head team-man, if he had the skill, more commonly by a local thatcher.[62]

When harvest ended there was a period of respite. The farmers would often go to sales while the men took their traditional harvest holiday. In the middle of the century, and up to the 1900s in some areas, they would 'cry largesse', visiting the market town and collecting pence from the tradesmen who dealt with their masters.[63] Later it was a trip by train to the county town or the sea to buy boots and clothes with the harvest earnings.[64] In some areas it was the start of the fair season. By the 1870s labourers flocked in their thousands by excursion train to fairs like Saint Giles in Oxford.[65] And then, after a brief glimpse of pleasure, the yearly round began again with moving place, ploughing fleet and the bitter cold of the root harvest.

IV

In sheep country, like Sussex, the pattern of seasonal work centred round the flock and took on a different rhythm, though few farms produced sheep alone and so the basic pattern of cereal production was still present. In the autumn in Hampshire sheep were turned out on to the stubble or folded with rape and turnips; in Sussex they went out on the downs.[66] Lambing, the shepherd's harvest, was between January and March, depending on the area and the mildness of the weather. During this time the shepherd lived out in the fields in a wheeled shepherd's hut, alone, except for his pages, for weeks on end. After lambing the shepherd had a period of ease: 'as a general rule, save for lambing and other busy times, a shepherd reckoned to finish his actual laborious work by dinner time. After that he studied your sheep.'[67] Dipping and shearing were in June: 'June was one of the busiest months in the sheep farmer's year. It brought none of the anxieties of lambing time, but in terms of sheer hard work, it stood out from all the other.'[68] A. G. Street summed it up well when he wrote:

> [Then] you will require swedes and kale for the flock. So your ploughs and harrows must follow them in May, June, and July as they feed on the rye, winter barley, and vetches, and then sow swedes and kale for winter. And so it went on, year after year, one continual hopeless striving to feed the

flock. . . . Your life was ruled by them the whole farm revolved round
them. . . . They were a kind of Moloch, to which we were all sacrificed.[69]

Cattle reared for beef were frequently grazed in the summer in the upland areas, or
even over in Ireland, and then taken south in the winter. In Norfolk cattle were
'stored' in yards and fed on roots throughout the winter, and sold in spring when
prices were high and the fodder ran out. On better upland pastures the beasts were
sold direct to the slaughterers. In dairying areas a more regular pattern of stock-
tending emerged, in which the cereal cycle had practically no part and which
produced a different hierarchy of workmen and workwomen. Where some cereals
were grown dairymen were as separate and aloof as shepherds, as were the yardmen
where beef cattle were reared. As Street said of the Hampshire dairymen, 'they ran
their job without outside assistance. Give them the cattle and food, and they would do
the rest.'[70]

Even where one system predominated there were almost endless variations of
payments and work patterns. In Suffolk, harvest was taken by travelling gangs which
were seldom seen in Norfolk, except in the south of the county. The huge variety of
ways of paying for harvest work has been charted by Morgan[71], but it extended to
other areas too. In Sussex muck was sometimes carted by the piece and hay harvest
taken by gangs,[72] while in south Oxfordshire no work was done by the piece at all,
except the women's work of dock-pulling, weeding and stone-picking, and the men
received an extra 50s. at Michaelmas.[73] Twenty miles north, harvest and a whole
range of other work were done by the piece.[74].

V

Nor were these processes constant, even within one area, although there was, in fact,
surprisingly slow technical innovation in much of nineteenth-century agriculture.
For decades the hay and cereal harvests were taken with bagging hook or scythe,
stooked and loaded by hand, carted by horse, and stacked by hand. It was the 1870s
before as much as two-thirds of all corn was cut and threshed by machine, and until
the 1930s the great bulk of ploughing, harrowing, rolling and carting was done by
horses.

But changes came, changes which ultimately transformed the labourers' lot
decisively, and for the better. The first was the steam- or horse-threshing machine.
Appearing in the south in the early years of the century (though earlier in the north),
it was well established by the 1850s.[75] The reaper and then the reaper-binder spread
more slowly. The reaper became available during the third quarter of the century and
the Appleby string reaper-binder from the early 1880s, but Rider Haggard did not buy
his first reaper until as late as 1898,[76] and the reaper-binder was by no means totally
established even in the 1920s.

It is common to attribute this slowness in adopting technical innovation to the conservatism of the farming community. Certainly many labourers were doubtful about change, preferring old ways. In the 1900s A. G. Street's 'improving' father came up against constant opposition, as did Henry Williamson in Norfolk in the 1930s. More recently many of the men interviewed by George Ewart Evans expressed grave misgivings about artificial fertilizers and the tractor.[77] Yet it is not that simple. The labourer was often mistrustful of change because he feared it might do him out of a job—as the threshing machine, the binder and the reaper-binder certainly did. The master saw that good profits had been made under the old system, and was loth to risk high capital investment. Even the depression of the 1870s and 1880s did little to shake the faith of many.[78] Yet in the long term, among the labourers at least, few regretted the change: even the last generation of horsemen, those who started work in the early 1920s, welcomed the tractor in the end.

'In the sweat of thy face shalt thou eat bread', says chapter 4 of Genesis, and to the poorest of Victoria's subjects this represented literal truth as well as a biblical punishment. Farm work was unremitting toil in all weathers, from the sleet that accompanied winter ploughing to the burning sun of August. Harvest took a terrible toll. Every year boys 'riding holdya' fell from the horses and were crushed under the wagon wheels, and a scythe or an unguarded binder could cause a terrible wound which often went untreated and led to death.[79] Old men and women, driven by poverty to work in the fields at the busiest time of the year died of heatstroke, and in the end many were turned off the farm crippled with rheumatism or arthritis.[80] These things were as much a part of Victorian life as the skill of the thatcher or the dignity and strength of the mower and they are remembered as such by those who lived at the end of the horse economy. As one old team-man said, 'They were having their own way, the farmers was, they were putting us just anywhere . . . they never cared whether you lived or died.'[81]

Notes

1   Haggard, 1935, 102–3.
2   Arch, 1898, 4, 57.
3   Interview with Herbert Neale, Paston, Norfolk; interview with Charles Leveridge, Carbrooke, Norfolk (tapes in author's possession).
4   Carter, 1976a, 93.
5   Jenkins, 1971, 251.
6   BPP 1900 LXIII 582–4.
7   Carter, 1976a; Jenkins, 1971; Caunce, 1975, 45–53.
8   Jenkins, 1971.
9   BPP 1905 XCVIII 357.
10   Interview with Jack Leeder, Happisburgh, Norfolk.
11   Interview with Arthur Amis, Trunch, Norfolk.
12   Interview with Bert Hazell, Wymondham, Norfolk.
13   Interview with Leeder.

14 Interview with Leveridge.
15 BPP 1900 LXIII 582.
16 *Ibid.*, 587.
17 *Ibid.*, 587–8.
18 *Bridlington Gazette*, 16 November 1895.
19 Young, 1804, 484; Young, 1813, 223.
20 BPP 1905 XCVIII 360.
21 For example, *Eastern Weekly Press*, 3 April 1903.
22 For example, Evans, 1956, 28–9; Copper, 1971, 65.
23 For example, Norfolk RO: Labour Book, Ditchingham–Hempnall area.
24 Collins, 1970; Morgan, 1975; Collins, 1976, 39.
25 Evans, 1956, 85; Morgan, 1975, 51; Copper, 1971, 116–17.
26 BPP 1867 XVII, *passim*.
27 Computed from censuses of 1831 and 1841 and other contemporary material.
28 Collins, 1976, 50.
29 BPP 1905 XCVIII 354.
30 Interview with Mrs Moy, Yaxham, Norfolk.
31 Interview with Hazell.
32 BPP 1900 LXIII 585–8.
33 Interview with Leeder.
34 Bell, 1930, 36.
35 Interview with Leeder.
36 Interview with Leeder; Street, 1932, 40, for cross-ploughing for barley.
37 Evans, 1960, *passim*.
38 Interview with Hazell.
39 Interview with Leeder.
40 Interview with Hazell.
41 Interview with Leeder.
42 Evans, 1960, 260–71.
43 Interview with Leeder.
44 *Ibid.*
45 *Labour Gazette*, February 1908, 55; November 1906, 340.
46 Interview with Charlie Barber, Great Fransham, Norfolk.
47 Interview with Billy Dixon, Trunch, Norfolk.
48 Interview with Sidney Watts, Happisburgh, Norfolk (tape at University of Essex); I am grateful to Trevor Lummis for this material.
49 Interview with Lee.
50 Interview with Dixon.
51 Interview with Amis.
52 Interview with Leeder.
53 *Ibid.*
54 Interview with 'Butcher' Rayner, Swanton Morely, Norfolk.
55 Interview with Jack Sadler, Tichwell, Norfolk.
56 Interviews with Lee and Leeder.
57 Interview with Dixon.
58 Morgan, 1975, 45–53.

59   Interviews with Amis, Lee, Leeder, Dixon and Neale.
60   Interview with Rayner.
61   *Ibid.*
62   Interview with Leveridge.
63   Interview with Dixon.
64   Interview with Leeder.
65   Alexander, 1970, 28.
66   Street, 1932, 40; Copper, 1971, 65–6.
67   Street, 1932, 35.
68   Copper, 1971, 107.
69   Street, 1932, 40–1.
70   *Ibid.*, 36.
71   Morgan, 1975, 38–45.
72   Copper, 1971, 174–5.
73   Moreau, 1968, 66.
74   Morgan, 1975, 50–2.
75   Collins, 1972.
76   Haggard, 1899, 274.
77   Street, 1932, 33; Williamson, 1941, 111; Evans, 1960, 17.
78   BPP 1895 XVII 407.
79   *Eastern Weekly Press* 28 August 1902; 12 September 1908; 29 September 1900.
80   *Eastern Weekly Press*, 14 September 1907; 26 August 1905.
81   Interview with Dixon.

37 Country Children

Pamela Horn

I

For most country children—the offspring of labourers, village craftsmen and small shopkeepers—life began in a small and overcrowded cottage, without any of the ceremonial which attended the arrival of children in the better-off sections of society. Normally a doctor would not be present at the confinement unless complications were feared. Instead, for the modest charge of a shilling or so the local midwife or perhaps a neighbour would preside, returning later to help nurse the mother and baby for a few days after the birth. Families were large, with four, five or six children common, and although perhaps not all of them slept at home—some of the older ones lodging with grandparents or friends whose own youngsters had grown up—most houses were sadly overcrowded. Thus, to take a typical example, in the small Oxfordshire village of Mapledurham (population 509 in 1851) about one quarter of the households had four or more children still living with their parents, the largest being a family of eight plus mother and father.[1] This excludes those households where grandchildren or lodgers might fill the customary two- or three-roomed cottages to overflowing. Where a large family shared a single bedroom there might be some attempt to obtain privacy by hanging counterpanes or old gowns, cut and sewn to form a curtain, across the room. But this had the disadvantage of preventing the circulation of air in what was already a close and uncomfortable atmosphere.

In such circumstances, furniture was kept to a minimum—a fact which family poverty was in any case likely to reinforce—while even cooking facilities and the supply of water were inadequate in many communities. In mid-century Norfolk water was sold at 1*d*. or 1½*d*. a pail in years of drought, and a woman from Shotesham in that county remembers fresh water being brought to her home and to neighbouring cottages in milk churns twice a week by horse and cart as late as 1900. It was stored in large earthenware pots in the pantry. 'Water for washing the clothes and linen was obtained from a large pit, and for bathing, rain water was stored in large tubs.'[2] Elsewhere a regular evening task for older children would be to take a pail to the nearest pump or well in order to collect water for the morning.

It was against this background that the Rev. James Fraser could report in 1867:

> The majority of the cottages that exist in rural parishes are deficient in almost every requisite that should constitute a home for a Christian family in a civilized community. They are deficient in bedroom accommodation, very few having three chambers, and in some parishes the larger proportion only one; they are deficient in drainage and sanitary arrangements; they are imperfectly supplied with water; . . . and in many instances are lamentably dilapidated and out of repair. . . . 'I only wonder,' writes one clergyman to me, 'that our agricultural poor are as moral as they are.'[3]

In most households the provision of food and clothing presented a perennial problem, particularly before the final quarter of the nineteenth century. Then, thanks to the growing importation of foreign wheat, meat and dairy produce, and the effects of mass-production in cutting the price of clothing and footwear, conditions began to ease a little. Nevertheless children often wore clothes that had been handed down from older members of the family. In the case of the boys these were usually made from serviceable corduroy, while the girls wore long pinafores over their dresses, black woollen stockings, and stout boots like those of their brothers. Although poorer children might run around cottage and village barefoot, especially during the summer months, they had to have suitable footwear to attend school, and buying the family's boots was, therefore, the first charge on a farm worker's harvest money. Due to the strong hard leather from which they were made they were extremely uncomfortable to wear when new, and during the winter months children's heels and toes would be rubbed raw with blisters and chilblains. As late as the 1890s there are frequent mentions in school log books of children being kept at home because of 'broken chilblains' or 'bad feet'.[4]

As regards diet, bread and weak tea formed the staple items of consumption for many families, supplemented by vegetables grown in the garden and a little bacon or cheese—though often these latter would be reserved for the father, the major breadwinner. Dr Edward Smith, in his survey of dietaries in 1863, concluded that children were normally given the cheaper foods, like bread smeared with dripping or treacle, while milk was in surprisingly short supply, as farmers preferred to feed their surpluses to the pigs rather than make them available in small quantities to labouring families. According to Dr Smith, tea was the only item of which women and children consumed more than men; and in many cases this was made from tea leaves which had been used more than once.[5] Four years later, a shepherd's wife from Blandford in Dorset confirmed the general picture:

> We don't have a bit of butcher's meat for half a year, not from Christmas to Christmas; we sometimes get a bit of mutton at 3*d.* the lb., when a giddy sheep is killed on the farm; . . . We have a pig; sometimes we kill, perhaps, two in the year. We live on potatoes, bread, and pig-meat, and are very thankful if we can get a bit of pig-meat; we often sit down to dry bread. . . . We never have a bit of milk.[6]

By the end of the Victorian era, however, increasing imports had enlivened the diet of many families so that fresh meat—beef or mutton—was now within the reach of all, at least once a week. Other articles of food like tinned meats, fish, jam, pickles, coffee, cocoa, currants and cake, which were virtually unknown in the 1850s and 1860s, were by the 1890s being brought round in carts to the labourer's door by grocers and butchers from nearby towns.[7]

II

Against this background of poverty it is not surprising that most children from labouring families were sent to work as early as possible in order that they might contribute to household income. Often this meant employment on a local farm. At the 1861 census about one in nine of all boys in England and Wales aged between ten and fourteen worked as agricultural labourers, while the number of those engaged on a part-time casual basis would push the proportion up still higher. Among the girls domestic service provided the principal outlet, although in some parts of the country this predominance might be challenged by the survival of cottage industries, at least to the 1870s. But in the busy seasons girls, too, worked on the land alongside the rest of the family.

In addition to poverty, a second reason for the widespread use of child labour in agriculture was the desire of farmers to have available a cheap and amenable workforce which could be used flexibly as the seasons dictated. In some counties, like Dorset, it was customary to require married male labourers to keep members of their family available for employment as needed. Even in the 1890s the *Dorset County Chronicle* contained advertisements, inserted by farmers, for labourers 'with a working Family', while others indicated a preference for men with large families. Similarly in Northumberland, under the bondager system, a male worker had to supply a female labourer as part of his contract of employment. Often she, too, would be a child, with ten as the usual minimum age. The London barrister, Arthur Munby, saw bondagers at work in the early 1860s and noted that Northumberland farmers liked to have their 'wenches under bondage, because then [they] can send them afield to hoe or dig in all weathers, and they can't shirk it'.[8] There was also a belief among

523

some agriculturalists that if the children were not set to work at an early age they would never become efficient labourers. One large farmer from Great Yeldham in Essex solemnly informed a Royal Commission on agricultural employment in the late 1860s 'that a boy taken to work at 5 would be worth twice as much when he [was] 12, as a boy not taken to work before 10'.[9] Others maintained that unless a boy began to work at six or seven, 'or at the latest 8, he [would] never grow into the man he ought to be'.

These remarks ignored both the educational weaknesses of such a policy and the physical effects which premature manual labour had on the young workers. A Dorset doctor claimed that when lads went out to help with ploughing at the age of eight or nine the work prevented

> proper muscular development, and very often [produced] . . . 'tuberculous diseases'. . . . The sameness and overhardness of toil mars the young yielding muscles . . . it is seen in their after life in a way . . . most clear; there is a want of physical energy . . . a deadening of mind and body force. . . . I see the effect of the early work in making the boys bow-legged.[10]

A colleague from Witney in Oxfordshire agreed: 'I think that children are employed too young in heavy ploughed land; it tells on them in after life; when they get to be about 50 they go at the knees and are very much bent.'

Only in parts of the north of England, where adult agricultural wage rates were higher and, more important, opportunities for child employment limited, was this early and extensive use of young labour not applicable. In Holderness in Yorkshire, for example, children were little employed except at haytime and harvest because with few root crops grown they were not required for weeding, while the draining, banking and hedging which formed much of the farm work in the area were unsuitable for children. Similarly in Northumberland, youngsters were rarely employed below the age of ten—though here parents' interest in education also played a role. As early as 1843 it was noted of the county that 'no greater stigma can attach to parents than that of leaving their children without the means of ordinary education, and every nerve is strained to procure it'.[11]

The jobs carried out by children naturally varied with the character of agricultural activity in a particular area. Normally they included scaring birds from the newly-sown crops, watching animals feeding in unfenced areas (usually called 'tenting'), weeding crops, stone-picking, bean-setting, hay-making, harvesting, fruit-gathering and potato-picking. In Herefordshire, indeed, one commentator noted in the 1860s that children were employed in at least seven different annual harvests. These comprised bark-peeling for the tanning trade, hay-making, corn harvest, hop-picking, potato-picking, apple-gathering and the collecting of acorns to feed to the pigs.[12] Hop-picking likewise employed many children in Hampshire and Kent.

Of all the tasks undertaken, however, bird-scaring was perhaps the loneliest, with the children setting off for the fields at daybreak and remaining there until it grew dusk. Usually they went armed with a wooden rattle or an old pail and stick which they would beat to drive the birds off. Only one boy per field was normally permitted, for farmers believed that 'two boys is half a boy and three boys no boy at all', since they would spend their time at play instead of at work. A Warwickshire Congregational minister, writing in the 1870s, stressed the generally unkempt appearance of the scarers, with heavy boots encasing their thin legs, battered hats on their heads, and over-large coats or sacks wrapped round their slight frames. He noted, too, their constant plaintive appeals to passers-by: 'Plase, Master, can ye tell us wot toime it is?', adding, 'if you pass them seven times a day, they will seven times urge their enquiry'.[13] The isolation in which the children worked was blamed by contemporaries for the slowness of speech and of comprehension which were considered characteristic of the country child.

III

During the cold weather many of these young workers, inadequately fed and clothed and sleeping in overcrowded homes, fell an easy prey to disease. For although mortality in the country was lower than in industrial areas—so that in 1897 only 28 per cent of all deaths in Dorset and Oxfordshire and 31 per cent of those in Norfolk were accounted for by children under five, as opposed to 46 per cent in Durham and Cheshire and 44 per cent in Lancashire in the same year—the number of child deaths was still relatively high. And earlier in the century it had been a good deal more serious, with about 33 per cent of Oxfordshire's deaths in 1865 involving children under five, and 3 per cent those aged between five and nine; in Dorset the respective figures were 35 per cent and 5 per cent, and in Norfolk, 37 per cent and 4 per cent.[14] Within the schools epidemic diseases like scarlet fever, diphtheria, measles and whooping cough took a regular toll, while contaminated water led to periodic outbreaks of typhoid. Tuberculosis, too, was an ever-present hazard.

When children became ill parents relied as far as possible on home remedies to effect a cure, with herbs widely used. As a last resort the poor law medical officer might be called in, though some of his prescriptions would appear surprising to modern eyes. Thus at Culworth in Northamptonshire during the early 1870s a twelve-year-old girl received wine for a 'chest affection', while a six-year-old boy was given meat and wine for measles. In other cases children as young as ten were prescribed half-a-pint of brandy a week when recovering from typhoid.[15]

But whatever might be the effects of the use of child labour during the spring, autumn and winter months, it was at the hay and corn harvests that the greatest demands arose and the largest gaps appeared in the school ranks. Often the exact timing of the pupils' summer or 'harvest' holiday would be determined by the ripeness of the corn. At Wasperton in Warwickshire in 1898, the vicar, who was also the school correspondent, wrote firmly in the log book: 'The . . . holidays of this School should in future be regulated by the commencement of Harvest.'[16] He was merely making explicit what was already common practice. Indeed, in many villages the return to school would also be delayed until the end of harvest. Typical is the entry at Sydenham National School, Oxfordshire, on 20 September 1886: 'School reopened, but closed again by order of the Vicar, the harvest being not quite finished.'[17]

Youngsters were engaged either in looking after younger brothers and sisters at home whilst their mother helped with the harvest, or they would themselves work in the fields, leading the horses, carrying food and drink to the harvesters, and helping to bind the corn into sheaves. So great was the pressure to bring in the crops speedily that the hours of work were desperately long, especially for the younger children. Arthur Wilkinson, who was born at Bladon, Oxfordshire, in 1884, recalled going into the harvest fields first when he

> was about 9 years old. I used to have to go with my Father and lay bands for
> him then I used to tie the Shaves [*sic*] up and then shock them up,
> and . . . rake up between the rows of shocks from 6 o'clock in the morning
> until 9 or 10 o'clock at night.

Arthur subsequently began full-time work on a farm three miles from home at the age of eleven for a wage of 2*s*. 6*d*. a week.[18]

Later, when the grain had been carried, a mother and her children would go out gleaning or leazing. The corn they secured would then be threshed and sent to the miller for grinding. With the flour thus obtained a family's bread supply was secure for a month or two.

The children of the smaller farmers were also much involved in helping on the land. Indeed, at the end of the 1860s it was reported of the rural south west that their offspring were

> in a worse position in the matter of education than those of the labourers,
> and more particularly in those parts of Devon where the holdings are
> small . . . the farmers . . . are obliged to keep their children at home to do the
> work of the farm as soon as they are able to endure the fatigue or are strong
> enough to undertake the labour.[19]

Similar comments were made concerning the farmers of south Durham, where the land was much subdivided, and also of the small proprietors (or 'statesmen' as they were called) in Westmorland and Cumberland. Indeed, one of these latter frankly admitted that he began to employ his children 'as soon as they [could] crawl'.

But if the need for child labour was accepted in almost all rural areas during the Victorian era, it probably reached its highest level of exploitation on the large arable holdings of the eastern counties during the 1850s and 1860s when the notorious public 'gang system' was in operation. The gangs seem to have appeared first at Castle Acre in Norfolk in the mid-1820s—in a village surrounded by large arable farms—though they soon increased, particularly following the passage of the 1834 Poor Law Amendment Act with its restrictions on the payment of out-relief.[20] During the next two decades they spread over the neighbouring area thanks to the sparse population of the region and the labour-intensive methods of cultivation then in vogue.

Numerous groups of children, youths and women were regularly recruited by a gang-master to carry out weeding, stone-picking, potato-setting and other tasks, first on one farm and then on another. About half the gang members were in the age-range of six to eighteen years, though in some the role of young children was proportionately greater. The Sixth Report of the Royal Commission on Children's Employment, which was solely concerned with agriculture, revealed that in 1866 one Northamptonshire gang of seventy-two included thirty-five boys and twenty-six girls, all aged between seven and twelve years, together with five boys under seven and one of five years of age, who had to be carried home from work! It was quite common for youngsters to have to walk five, six or even seven miles to their employment, and in winter the children often returned from the fields crying with the cold. According to witnesses: 'You see the big ones come dragging the little ones home, and sometimes taking them on their backs when they are overtired.'[21] Furthermore, since the overseer's remuneration usually depended on the amount of work he could extract from his gang, discipline was strict, with kicking, knocking down and beating the methods adopted to make the laggards or the youngest children keep up with the rest. Among the older girls and boys charges of immorality were common.

As a result of these findings, shocked public opinion—and Parliament—demanded action. On 2 April 1867, J. D. Dent, M.P. for Scarborough, declared that the 'horrors disclosed ... were greater than anything he could possibly have conceived, and worse than anything that had been brought before the notice of the House', while Henry Fawcett, M.P. for Brighton, referred scathingly to the 'sacrificing' of the minds and bodies of 'hundreds of children and bringing immense numbers of women to a state of perfect degradation', purely in the interests of agriculture.[22] Against this background the Gangs Act was passed in 1867. It prohibited the employment of any child below the age of eight in a public agricultural gang, laid down that all gang-masters must in future be licensed by local magistrates, and prohibited gangs of mixed sex. Although it eliminated some of the worst excesses of the system, it did not cover children engaged in other areas of agricultural employment, nor did it do much to protect children working in the gangs once they had reached the age of eight. It was left to the education legislation of the 1870s and beyond to seek to remedy this. And here the relevant measures were the Education Acts of 1870, 1876 and 1880, and the Agricultural Children Act of 1873.

The 1870 Education Act laid down that every child was to have an elementary school place, and in areas where the existing voluntary (usually church) schools could not provide sufficient accommodation the local ratepayers must form an elected school board, financed partly out of the rates, to remedy the deficiencies. School boards were authorized to make by-laws forbidding the employment of children below the age of ten and requiring attendance at school at least part-time to the age of thirteen, unless they could pass a leaving examination. Unfortunately the measure was only of limited importance in rural areas since voluntary schools continued to supply the bulk of school places, even in the 1890s. So in 1873 a Private Member's Bill was introduced by C. S. Read, M.P. for South Norfolk, seeking to prevent the employment of any child in agriculture below the age of eight and demanding a specified number of attendances at school for those between eight and twelve. The minimum age for workers in a public gang was raised to ten. Although the Act came into operation on 1 January 1875, its failure to nominate an enforcement agency soon led to widespread evasion. As one Somerset clergyman wrote to the Home Office on 12 February in that year:

> The Agricultural Children's Education Act . . . is, in this parish, being openly and deliberately set at naught. . . . Appeal to parents and masters is useless. The same may be said of other parishes in the neighbourhood. . . . Is the new law to be utterly ignored and are employers and employed to break it with impunity? Already it is very difficult among rural populations to induce a respect for law in general.[23]

Her Majesty's Inspectors of Schools likewise confirmed that the Act was a 'dead letter'.[24]

So it was following this earlier failure that the 1876 Education Act imposed full-time attendance for all children aged five to ten, and part-time attendance thereafter to fourteen, unless the child could pass an approved leaving examination in the three R's. Parents neglecting to send their children to school could now be fined, as could employers of illegal child labour. And despite the laxity of school attendance officers and magistrates, a number were. The need to enforce the regulations was further underlined in 1880, when a fresh Education Act made the adoption of attendance by-laws mandatory for all authorities; this was necessary because some had failed to act under the 1876 legislation. In 1891 attendance was made virtually free, as fees— usually of 1*d.* or 2*d.* per child per week—were abolished in most elementary schools. Two years later the minimum school-leaving age was raised from ten to eleven, and in 1899 it was further increased to twelve, though in most rural areas eleven still seems to have been accepted.[25]

Yet despite this legislative framework, it remained difficult for teachers and attendance officers to keep children within the walls of a school for the time laid down by the law. As one inspector reported of the Boston area of Lincolnshire in 1898:

> At one time the cereals were the only objects of cultivation which offered serious obstacles to regularity of attendance. But now potato and turnip setting, turnip thinning, and early and late potato picking have all to be reckoned with . . . there are areas in which little, or nothing, is done to check irregularity or illegal employment at any time of the year, and in which the local authorities and magistrates . . . combine to make Bye-Laws and Education Acts dead letters.[26]

The children, for their part, often felt guilty if they were *prevented* from working. A man from the Lotting Fen area of Huntingdon noted of the late 1870s:

> Arter I were about nine year old, I got real ashamed o' going to school when

other folks went to work. One morning some men were working in a field as I passed on my way to school, and I 'eard one on 'em say 'Look at that bloody grut ol' bor still a-gooing to school. Oughta be getting 'is own living.' After that I used to get into the dykes and slink along out o' sight in case anybody should see me and laugh at me.[27]

He eventually left school at the age of twelve. Not until the final years of the nineteenth century did the old attitude which saw the child as a small adult, who must play his part in the money-making process, begin to disappear for the offspring of rural labourers and small farmers, as it had already disappeared for the progeny of the better-off groups in society.

IV

But even for the labourer's child, life in Victorian England was not all gloom. At least he was surrounded by green fields and hedgerows rather than the grimy walls and streets of his urban fellows, while through Sunday school excursions, St Valentine's Day and May Day celebrations, fairs and other festivities he could forget for a time the serious business of earning a living. Even the Band of Hope, though founded in 1847 to wean children from the 'demon drink', had its lighter side with annual celebrations at which a plentiful tea and games would feature prominently. Skipping, hopscotch, marbles and bowling a hoop provided simpler pleasures. In the autumn there were the small hedgerow harvests to gather—blackberries, sloes for wine-making, mushrooms, walnuts and conkers. As one woman recalled:

Living where we did and how we did, we used to make the most of anything a bit out o' the ordinary, and we looked for'ard from one special day to the next. Looking back on it now, I'm surprised to see how many high days and holidays there were during the year that we kept.

Much of the fun, though, was made by the youngsters themselves:

We dug up tansy roots to eat, and filled our pockets with buckwheat whenever we could. We sucked the taste of honey from the tip ends of the white dead-nettle flowers, and suffered agonies peeling thistle buds down to get at the little white nut in the middle. Then off to gather different sorts of flowers again to dress ourselves up to play 'Kings and Queens' . . . Now and again we had the luck to find a reed-warbler's nest slung atween three rushes, and everywhere there'd be a mass o' beautiful butterflies.[28]

It was a welcome compensation for the harshness of the daily round, and as such the children valued it.

Notes

1   PRO HO 107.1691, 1851 Census Return for Mapledurham.
2   *Within Living Memory*, 1971, 22; Springall, 1936, 56.
3   BPP 1867–8 XVII 35.
4   Horn, 1974b, 23.
5   Barker, Oddy and Yudkin, 1970, 31–2.
6   BPP 1868–9 XIII, Evidence, 15.
7   Fox, 1903, 292.
8   Horn, 1976b, 257.
9   BPP 1867–8 XVII 13.
10 Horn, 1974b, 180.
11 BPP 1843 XII 302.
12 Horn, 1976b, 78.
13 Attenborough, 1872, 24.
14 BPP 1867 XVII 98–101; Horn, 1974b, 183.
15 Horn, 1974b, 176.
16 *Ibid.*, 76.
17 Oxford RO: T/SL/53/1.
18 Oxford RO: no ref.
19 BPP 1868–9 XIII 41.
20 BPP 1843 XII 274–7, 280; Pinchbeck, 1930, 87.
21 BPP 1867 XVI 71.
22 *Hansard*, 3rd ser. 1867, CLXXXVI, 1010, 1011.
23 PRO HO 45/9373/38913.
24 BPP 1876 XXIX, Appendix F, 195.
25 Simon, 1965, 141.
26 BPP 1899 XXI, Report on the Eastern Division, 5.
27 Marshall, 1967, 21.
28 Marshall, 1967, 195–6, 199.

38   Country Homes

Enid Gauldie

For Dr Johnson a cottage was 'a hut or mean habitation'. Between Dr Johnson and the present day a major revolution in ideas has affected the meaning of the word. The Romantic era of literature and painting brought with it a taste for the idyllic country scene, the sun-bonneted group of pretty, healthy children about the door of a rose-decked, white-washed dwelling, which has endured in the English national consciousness until the present day.

I

The first purpose of the cottage was to provide shelter. This could mean the building by a labourer of the most primitive of coverings, the raising of poles crossed at the top to hold a ridge-pole, and the covering of these poles by a framework of woven wattles, daubed with mud or draped by rough thatching. From this developed the cruck-form cottage, with wattle and daub walls known variously in different parts of the country as *stud and mud, wattle and daub, post and plaister*.[1] At the beginning of Victoria's reign the clay or *cob* cottage was a very common form of construction. At its best the thick walls provided good insulation and kept the interior of the cottage dry. At its worst its inevitably porous nature allowed the penetration of damp, and the crumbling clay required endless repairs.

These old places are built of a timber frame-work, studded outside with laths and daubed over with plaster or with a mixture of clay and chopped straw. Many of them have not been lined with lath and plaster inside and so are fearfully cold in winter. The walls may not be an inch in thickness and where the laths are decayed the fingers may easily be pushed through. . . . The roof is of thatch, which, if kept in good repair forms a good covering, warm in winter and cool in summer, though doubtless in many instances it served as harbour for vermin, for dirt, for the condensed exhalations from the bodies of the occupants of the bedrooms, and, where persons suffering from the various fevers are nursed therein, possibly also for the infectious material which propagates such diseases.[2]

Where the local stone was sound and easily worked a tradition of stone building developed. In the Cotswolds the mellow colour of the stone and its cutting quality produced fine workmanship and soundly built cottages of dressed masonry. On the Sussex downs and in Norfolk flint cottages were common, in the better houses the harsh quality of the flint softened by rough-casting outside and plastering with clay inside.[3] In the Lake District slate stone was used, undressed, or rough hewn and mortared either with clay, in the earlier examples, or with lime mortar.[4]

One of the best ways to study housing is to examine what remains on the ground. For this the comparatively recent interest taken by architects in vernacular buildings has provided a useful body of new evidence for historians, as well as a new set of criteria by which to judge those buildings about which we already know something. For instance, the division of architecture into 'polite' and 'vernacular' is an interesting indication for historians of the economic and cultural influences at work in any given region at any given time. Buildings falling into the polite category have been influenced by aesthetic as well as functional considerations, and by national rather than regional fashions in design. Their existence suggests a landowner of some financial and social standing, influenced at least as much by his own aesthetic sensitivity and the opinions and esteem of his social equals as by the functional demands of his tenantry. Vernacular architecture, on the other hand, has been influenced by the needs of its inhabitants, the skill of the local workmen, and the region's resources in building materials.

Unfortunately for students of the humbler style of cottage life, in large areas of England and Wales the *vernacular threshold* was not crossed until the nineteenth century.[5] This means that cottages of a type so flimsy as to have decayed without physical trace were not replaced in most parts of rural Britain until that time. For the most part what seem to be much older cottages were, in fact, small farmhouses or manor houses at the time of their building, falling to the labourer's use only after the building of a new house for the farmer.

Physical evidence gives a great deal of information about those cottages built during the Victorian period. It can be used to some extent to confound those who believe that only deterioration took place in the conditions of the rural labourer. To judge what social or economic pressures caused their building we must go back to the written records, but the evidence on the ground forces acknowledgment of the fact that many cottages were built in Victorian times. Their existence, of course, does not necessarily prove that those cottages which preceded them made less comfortable homes, but the extent of rebuilding in the nineteenth century, together with the dearth of earlier cottages in most parts of the country, suggests that the earlier buildings were by then crumbling into decay to an extent which became increasingly hard to ignore.

II

The largest part of the written evidence about cottage housing was collected early in Victoria's reign and again in the last quarter of the century by those zealous for 'moral and sanitary reform'. Their natural tendency to strengthen the case by stressing the horrors provides a wealth of descriptions of appalling living conditions. It is, however, for the most part counteracted by concern for truth, and the miserable hovels are balanced by the neat and commodious cottages wherever comparison is possible. The general impression of a rural people living in conditions of misery and squalor throughout Victoria's reign is, however, inescapable. It cannot easily be dismissed by the wishful thinking of the more romantic reporters of the period whose view of the idyllic conditions of the countryside was coloured chiefly by hatred of industrial towns.

William C. Little, reporting on the conditions of the agricultural labourer in 1893, wrote: 'the accommodation provided in respect of the number, size and comfort of the rooms, the sanitary condition and the water supply are lamentably deficient generally and require amendment'.[6] The Royal Commissioners on Housing in 1885 reported that rural conditions varied tremendously, from Wiltshire, where the bedrooms were not high enough to stand up in and the rotting thatch dropped filth on sleepers' heads, to Cheshire, where Lord Tollemache had recently built 300 excellent cottages. They stressed that 'evils were found everywhere'.[7] As late as 1917 the Royal Commission on the Housing of the Population also found lamentable conditions prevailing everywhere. And in 1907 Kaufman wrote that 'the agricultural labourer's home nowadays does no longer suggest itself to the fancy of the poet or the brush of the painter for ideal treatment'.[8]

In the last years of Victoria's reign, then, it was possible to find descriptions of rural slums which matched those of the early decades of the nineteenth century, when 'the dwellings of the poor are, in most counties, but mud cabbins, with holes that expose the inhabitants to the rigour of the climate'.[9] Edwin Chadwick had revealed in 1842 the prevalence of 'mere mud hovels', 'dwellings which, instead of being built of solid materials are complete shells of mud on a spot of waste land'.[10] Cobden wrote of country people who 'herd together in this beastly state in dwellings worse than the wigwams of the American Indians'.[11] Sir John Simon exposed

the cottage speculators [who] buy scraps of land which they throng as
densely as they can with the cheapest of all possible hovels. And into these
wretched habitations, (which, even if they adjoin the country, have some of
the worst features of the worst town residences) crowd the agricultural
labourers of England.[12]

The worst horrors of the early years could in every particular be matched by
instances from the end of the century. Dorset in 1842 had 'springs bursting through
the mud floor of some of the cottages and little channels cut from the centre under the
doorways to carry off the water'.[13] In 1893 there were still parts of the country where
floors are

> laid directly on the ground and are almost invariably damp, often indeed
> reeking with moisture. The bricks also get broken, the floor becomes uneven
> and the bare earth may be exposed. To obtain some slight degree of comfort
> bits of board are laid down and several thicknesses of sacking and mats are
> laid upon the floor.[14]

III

Throughout our period the worst cottages remained almost unbelievably bad, not
noticeably better at the turn of the century than they had been at the beginning. But
there is one important difference, and that is the proportion of houses to population.
John Simon was forced, even in the face of the evidence of deplorable lack of
sanitation and jerry-building, to say that 'even the general badness of the dwellings is
an evil infinitely less urgent than their mere numerical insufficiency'.[15] But William
Little, while deploring in 1893 the condition of a great many cottages, wrote that the
supply 'is not now generally defective in respect of numbers'.[16]

An increased provision of cottages for rent was motivated first by the farmers' new
wish for privacy in their homes. Traditionally, farm labourers had been accommodated by the farmer in his own house, just as town apprentices were in the homes of
their masters. The medieval habit of all sleeping together in the 'hall' of the house
gave way only slowly in rural areas to the removal of the owner's family to sleeping
chambers. The next stage, in which workers were accommodated on the farm but not
in the farmhouse, had in it the seeds of the tied cottage system.

Those rural workers not sheltered by their employers in these ways built for
themselves; that is, they built cottages with their own hands on such uncultivated
ground as they could acquire. The materials for construction were those which could
be obtained without money and handled by one man, with the assistance of friends
and family and only the most primitive of tools.

The eighteenth century had revived the ancient practice which allowed a man to
build on common land if he could raise the roof over his head and have a fire in his
grate between sunrise and sunset.[17] It is not hard to believe that a dwelling raised at

such speed would conform to Dr Johnson's definition of a 'hut or mean habitation'. In fact, permission to build in such a manner was granted because of the ease with which such dwellings could be removed should they become offensive. This practice was not entirely dead in the nineteenth century.[18] Cottage rows and semi-detached cottages date from the need on large farms to employ more men than could comfortably be accommodated. Only gradually throughout the eighteenth century (and only then in the more prosperous districts) did speculative builders come to recognize the profitability of letting to rural workers. The building of cottages to rent was very rare indeed before 1700, and as there seems to have been less new building between 1725 and 1760 than at any time since 1550 it must have been at best unusual until the last quarter of the eighteenth century. For the most part, the poorly constructed and decaying cottages so much criticized in the 1840s had been built in the period between 1780 and 1815.[19]

This period saw the publication of a number of cottage pattern books whose influence on the taste of the upper classes was perhaps greater than on the comfort of their dependants. The attitude of their writers was both condescending and unrealistic, and many of the resultant buildings were fanciful rather than comfortable.[20] The most influential of all was John Claudius Loudon, whose *Encyclopaedia of Cottage, Farm and Villa Architecture*[21] was to have a drastic effect upon the imagination of landowners, producing ornate Gothic cottages while hardly reducing the deficit in the housing of the rural poor.[22] Cottages of his kind were unlikely to be built cheaply enough for letting at rents agricultural labourers could afford.[23]

IV

Thus, at the beginning of Victoria's reign there were in existence the most primitive of one-roomed cabins, the most useless of architectural fancies, many examples of vernacular building in the forms most cheaply afforded in their own regions, some respectable cottages in areas where estate owners took a paternal interest in their tenants, but very few homes for rural workers which provided any real degree of comfort. There was, however, some interest in the need for change, an interest aroused by the noticeable growth in population.

Although a predominantly rural population changed in the years between 1780 and 1850 into a predominantly urban one, there was also an absolute rise in population. By 1861 the proportion of urban to rural was 5 to 4: by 1881 the urban figure was double the rural one. But, although the proportion of the nation's population living in the countryside declined, the actual numbers continued to increase, very fast between 1810 and 1820, slowly from the 1820s to the 1840s, faster during the 1850s, and only ceasing to grow in 1860.[24] The increase in the rural population was masked by the drastic effects which the faster rise in town population was having on urban living standards. Country people were aware of increased pressure on rural housing, even though they knew that large numbers were leaving the country for the towns.

The situation was made worse by the new and more severe interpretation of the Poor Law. Each district had a financial interest in the reduction of labourer families, to the extent of destroying existing cottages. 'Large proprietors have but to resolve that there shall be no labourers' dwellings on their estates and . . . be virtually free from half their responsibility for the poor.'[25] By the end of the Napoleonic wars the demand for housing greatly exceeded the supply of cottages but only a small proportion of landlord investment was directed to the building of cottages.[26] James Hole thought the landowner's agent 'the real despot of the soil', keeping the estates as far as possible free of cottages, and driving labourers into adjoining parishes.[27] The response of landlords to the surveys which revealed the true condition of those living on their estates was one of shock and horror. Their distress, however, was not always reflected in immediate orders to their agents to begin building cottages.

The publication for the first time in 1831 of census figures and mortality rates, the Registration Act of 1836, the reports of Poor Law commissioners, the interest of the new statistical societies in death and disease, the cholera epidemics of 1832 and 1848 and Chadwick's resultant reports all gave Victoria's subjects little chance to ignore the plight of the agricultural poor. Country people were living in homes no less appallingly inadequate than those of town dwellers. The absence of sanitary provision within the homes was not surprising. What shocked was the fact that so many houses were built upon ground so ill-drained that it could not absorb their waste. Privies drained into filthy channels between the houses, choked with refuse and flowing too sluggishly to clear themselves. Isolated cottages sat sometimes in a sea of their own sewage, the ground too waterlogged to bear it away. Only the low density of housing and the comparatively dispersed population prevented the spread of fatal infection. As long as the 'miasma' theory held sway among doctors, that is, as long as it was believed that infection was air-borne, it was possible to believe that clear country air dispersed the 'noxious exhalations' so much dreaded in the towns. But in 1848 Snow's discovery that cholera was water-borne demolished that comfortable belief.

If the total population of a parish was low compared with a town parish of comparable acreage, the population within doors was not less than in towns. The surveys commissioned by the Board of Agriculture in the early part of the nineteenth century reported overcrowding in most parts of England and Wales. The decrease in infant mortality meant that children who in earlier times would have died in infancy had to be accommodated, while the increased, if temporary, demand for agricultural workers encouraged parents to keep children at home who would earlier have been sent into service. The traditional one- and two-roomed cottages bulged with growing children. But after 1813, when the fall in agricultural prices reduced the number of jobs on the land, the habit of dispatching children early from the family home took hold again. Arthur Young and other reporters to the Board of Agriculture saw the evident overcrowding as a good reason for landowners' building on their estates, and until the end of the wars a number did; there was also a considerable amount of cottage construction by speculative builders who guessed that steadier agricultural wages would allow profit-making from rents. But the general post-war depression put a stop to this.

The discomfort of the rural population was not mitigated by contemporary methods of construction. Single-storey houses for the most part were open to their thatched roofs, the steadily deteriorating thatch dropping into the room below. Two-storey houses had the gaping floor of the bed chamber as ceiling to their living kitchen. Thatch was the usual roofing material everywhere until the nineteenth century. In the marshy Fens reeds would be used, but elsewhere farm labourers roofed and repaired their own cottages with long straw readily available in arable country until the introduction of the threshing machine, or with heather in highland districts.[28]

Floors were of earth or, in areas where local quarries provided stone, of flags. Boarded floors were still an occasion for congratulation as late as the 1880s. Nothing perhaps illustrates so well the country housekeeper's ability to make the best of bad conditions as the custom of sanding the floors. Begun merely as an aid to relative cleanliness it reached decorative heights with a tradition of casting the sand into complicated whorls and patterns, the whole thing to be regularly swept out and renewed.[29] In Silas Marner's cottage it was the undisturbed, freshly scattered sand over his secret hole, contrasting with the well-trodden scuffed sand over the rest of his brick floor, which betrayed his treasure hoard. Brick floors, however, became common only in the second half of the century. In the Midlands earth was mixed with fine ash and ox blood to produce a floor hard enough for polishing.[30] But these were the habits of country wives with extra energy. Trodden earth and its resultant damp and dirt were the lot of most country dwellers.

Despite the widespread distribution of pattern books with designs for cottages in brick and tile, and despite, too, the reformers' constant advocacy of brick,[31] the replacement of traditional and cheap vernacular materials was achieved only slowly. The brick walled, slate or tile roofed, wooden floored and partitioned cottage had to await the mechanization of production processes, the removal of the brick tax (1850) and the provision of cheap transport. Building in brick began to be common after 1850[32] but the pace of cottage building had by then slowed down, so that although thereafter new cottages were most often brick-built, their numbers were small in relation to the numerous old cottages still standing in the last quarter of the century.

V

Weber's index of house-building shows a very slight upswing in rural house-building from 1841 to 1871, with a downward movement for twenty years thereafter.[33] Throughout Victoria's reign agricultural wages never reached a point which would encourage speculators to believe that house-building on any scale could be profitable.[34] Rents which varied from as little as one shilling to, at the best, seven shillings a week were no inducement to cottage builders.[35] Nevertheless, the one difference, as we have seen, between the reports of the early part of the reign and those at its end is that the first speak everywhere of dereliction, bad building and an insufficient number of houses, while the later reports emphasize the continued existence of very poor, decaying cottages but allow that the number is not insufficient.

This closer approximation of demand to supply was facilitated partly by the declining rate of growth in the rural population after 1860, and partly by the response of those landowners most sensitive to criticisms in the published reports. In 1845 an 'Act to facilitate estate improvement' provided government loans for improvements, and travelling inspectors who insisted on reasonable standards of construction. In Nottinghamshire, for instance, they approved the building in 1860 of thirteen brick cottages to replace thatched huts of 10 feet square containing one room downstairs and one under the roof.[36]

There is little doubt that landed proprietors, especially those like Salisbury and the Bedfords—already in the public eye as propagandists for urban reform—were distressed at revelations of squalor existing even on their own estates. The natural result of moral pressure upon landowners and the near cessation of speculative cottage-building was the *close* village. Estate owners exhibiting some paternal care for their employees, and those who even in times of agricultural recession saw the advantage of a steady supply of well-disposed workers, were often much influenced by the fashion for romantic cottage-building and found it advisable to build superior cottages on their estates. In them they housed their permanent estate workers, the skilled artisans of the countryside—gamekeepers, horsemen, shepherds, gardeners— and they found the practice conducive to docility. 'These families', it was said, 'are placed in a situation productive of good morals.'[37]

It seems possible that the first step towards the creation of close villages was taken by the dukes of Norfolk. In East Anglia they had as landlords accepted responsibility for repairs to agricultural workers' cottages as early as the seventeenth century, and by the end of the eighteenth, had begun the housing of workers on their estates.[38] William Cobbett attributed its origin to the famous Coke of Holkham, and of course resented the undue control over the conduct of workers which this dual role of landlord and employer gave: 'Stupid and greedy Coke of Norfolk was the beginning of it; and ever since that system was begun, there has been war between the labourers of England and the owners and occupiers of the land.'[39] Simon disliked the close village for different reasons. He deplored the landowners' habit of building pretty villages of well-kept cottages for a few permanent workers while evicting from their land all the others. These were bound to the estate by employment but were refused permission to live within its bounds. They found homes in the nearest 'open' village, which might be either a group of very old and neglected cottages or a cottage speculator's piece of land 'thronged with the cheapest of all possible hovels'.[40]

By the end of Victoria's reign the most noticeable variation in cottage accommodation was caused not so much by regional as by social differences. The very oldest cottages had for the most part simply crumbled away. The mechanization of the cheap brick and tile industries, and the development of transport to distribute the products throughout the country, had caused the supplanting of regional vernacular traditions by standard cottages. But between the estate worker's cottage, with its wooden floors, well-made windows and ample proportions, and the labourer's cramped cot there was a wide gulf.

The pretty villages on the great estates were exceptional in every way. Much the more common form of provision for agricultural workers was the 'tied cottage', built by farmers on their own land for the use of their workers and available only during their employment on that farm. This system produced resentment even in the days of the labourers' most extreme poverty and dependence. The 1893 report found that although farms by then had usually two or three cottages, labourers rejected the advantages they offered, such as gardens and closeness to their work. They preferred to walk some miles at the end of a long working day to live in villages where the cottages might be worse and the rents higher, but where they had independence from their employer, schooling for their children and the society of their fellows.[41]

By the end of the century the vast weight of evidence about deplorable rural housing conditions had produced very little improvement. Nothing could change the fact that low agricultural wages did not allow rents which would reward investment in housing, and that it was in the interest of landowners to reduce the number of cottages to minimize the burden on the poor rates. 'It would be too much to expect', as Simon said, 'that land-owners as a class should be the voluntary bearers of a taxation which the law leaves them option to escape.'[42] The slackening in the rate of population growth after 1860 was more directly responsible for what improvement occurred. At least when the numbers seeking houses were reduced it was possible for tenants to choose from the best available rather than to accept any shelter afforded them. Thus the very worst cottages fell into disuse. At the same time the labourer's chance of building his own substandard cottage was reduced. Marginal land became less readily available as agriculture became more efficient. Supplies of traditional building materials dried up—timber was no longer there for the taking.

VI

The countryside was almost untouched by the succession of Acts of Parliament designed to improve the housing of the poor. The Nuisance Removal Acts, although intended to apply to rural areas, were for the most part ignored.[43] Their enforcement required the co-operation of a strong and articulate community, a condition not easily met in rural areas. Charles Dilke, writing in 1885, thought that the Public Health Act of 1875 had been useful in the west of England: 'enormous good seems to have been done by the working of the Public Health Act in these villages which undoubtedly were very bad indeed some years ago'.[44] And William Little thought that the 1875 Act and the 1890 Housing Act between them had been very effective in Surrey, Essex and Worcestershire: 'but in some districts the Board seems to be doing nothing'.[45] The rural sanitary authorities, although they had been given the power to do so, hardly ever built cottages. In answer to a question in the House of Commons in 1905, Gerald Balfour reported that the number of cottages for which loans had been sanctioned under the 1890 Act was only thirty-two for the whole of England.[46] The 'improvements' which had taken place involved most often the destruction of cottages, the removal of insanitary eye-sores, rather than the building of good, new cottages. Farm labourers remained too often dependent upon the goodwill of their employer for their homes. Country dwellers in general remained in houses without indoor sanitation or water supply, and most often in conditions of damp and discomfort.

In one sense the history of the cottage ends almost before it has begun. Hardly had the habit of building a substantial home for the rural labourer supplanted the earlier custom of leaving him to house himself in flimsy and primitive structures than the incentive to build cottages had dwindled with the fading profitability of the land. The great lords of Devonshire and Bedford were not, as they thought, setting an example which lesser proprietors might follow so much as creating a museum of the might-have-been.

Notes

1   Brunskill, 1970, 48, 52; Barley, 1961, 264–5; *Architects Journal*, 17 April 1977, 781–93; *Builder*, 16 January 1864, 6 February 1864.
2   BPP 1893–4, XXXV V, 1, 103.
3   Young, 1804, 24; Brunskill, 1970, 44.
4   Brunskill, 1974, 66–74.
5   *Ibid.*, 16.
6   BPP 1893–4 XXXV 123.
7   BPP 1884–5 XXX, 29.
8   Kaufman, 1975, 59.
9   Young, 1813, 22.
10 Chadwick, 1842, 82.
11 Cobden, 1908, I, 80–1.
12 Simon, 1887, 186.
13 Chadwick, 1842, 83.
14 BPP 1893–4 XXXV, 103.
15 Simon, 1887, 189.
16 BPP 1893–4 XXXV, 123.
17 Oliver, 1975, 7.
18 Chadwick, 1842, 86–7; Perkins, 1975b, 50; Harvey, 1944–5, 127–9.
19 Barley, 1961, 243.
20 Elsam, 1816; Robinson, 1822.
21 Loudon, 1833.
22 *Architectural Magazine*, November 1837, 506–7.

23 Gloag, 1970, 105–6.
24 Mitchell and Deane, 1962, 2–7.
25 Simon, 1887, 183; Brockington, 1965, 224.
26 Perkins, 1975b, 53.
27 Hole, 1866, 6.
28 Barley, 1961, 81–2; Brunskill, 1970, 56.
29 Hartley, 1962, 57.
30 Barley, 1961, 82.
31 Chadwick, 1867–8, 266–7.
32 Brunskill, 1970, 46.
33 Weber, 1955, 104–32.
34 BPP 1893–4 XXXV, 14–15.
35 Caird, 1852, 437–9; *Builder*, 1862, XX, 925; BPP 1884–5 XXX, Minutes of Evidence 16414–5.
36 Spring, 1963, 136–63.
37 Young, 1813, 22.
38 Barley, 1961, 249.
39 Cobbett, 1930, III, 868.
40 Simon, 1887, 186; BPP 1884–5 XXX, 43; Stevenson, 1971, 39–47.
41 BPP 1893–4 XXXV, 14; BPP 1884–5 XXX, 45.
42 Simon, 1887, 186.
43 Hole, 1866, 129; Simon, 1887, II, 190.
44 BPP 1884–5 XXX, App. 9, Sept. 1884.
45 BPP 1893–4 XXXV, 16.
46 Kaufman, 1975, 64.

39   The Country School

Roger Sellman

The Victorian Age coincided almost exactly with that during which the State became increasingly involved in the education of the 'poor', while each village (except the most minute) still remained individually responsible for providing and managing schools. For the first half of this period, until the 1870 Act, the government (acting from 1839 through the Committee of Council for Education) confined itself to aiding local funds and initiative. Only after 1870 did it require the provision of efficient schools for all children of the labouring classes, where these did not already exist. Consequently the quality of rural schooling—and until the sometimes belated operation of the 1870 Act its very existence—depended on various local factors.

I

At the beginning of Victoria's reign some villages had an endowment, which in a few cases was sufficient to support a free school with a full three Rs (reading, writing, arithmetic) curriculum, but in most was no more than a subsidy to a dame for teaching a few children to read. Some villages had parochial schools supported in part from parish lands or rates; a growing number possessed 'National' schools[1] maintained by a combination of fees, subscriptions, sermon collections, and in the last resort by the incumbent; and some had schools built and entirely maintained by a local landowning patron. Many, on the other hand, had none at all, or only a private dame school; and some did not boast even a Sunday school where, in default of a day school, local volunteers endeavoured to teach reading as an adjunct to religious instruction.

Provision depended on many things—for example, on whether there was a resident landowner or incumbent with some concern for education, or a surviving local tradition reaching back to the days of the schoolmaster licensed by the bishop. Some parishes had a nucleated core which favoured Church influence; and others were made up of scattered hamlets where Nonconformity typically flourished, but the chapel was seldom able to support its own school or ready to aid one attached to the local church. In many, the demand for early child labour effectively ruled out any length of school attendance.

Few villages had a school building, as such, at Victoria's accession, and most used a variety of makeshift premises: the vestry room or 'church house' where such existed, the church itself, or a room in the parsonage. Most frequently the school was to be found amongst domestic paraphernalia in a cottage kitchen. Once government building grants were offered, the number of purpose-built schools grew rapidly but often at first in an oddly haphazard fashion. As one witness informed the Newcastle Commission:[2]

> When first I was connected with the Committee of Council, we could scarcely get the applicants for grants to send up any plans . . . they did not build schools from plans; the village carpenter and the village bricklayer built them by rule of thumb; anything was thought good enough for a school . . . we sometimes got a little scrap of paper with a pen and ink or pencil sketch on it.

The few teachers who then had any sort of training were nearly all employed in large town schools which operated the 'monitorial' system of using older pupils to pass on lessons to small groups—a method of little use in villages where schools were too small and older pupils too few and irregular in attendance.

At the same time as the Education Department appeared, Diocesan Boards of Education were established to inspect and aid Church schools and encourage the provision of new ones; and from 1840 all schools receiving a government building grant were required to be open to the department's inspectors. The consequent reports give direct evidence on the poverty-stricken rural schools of the 1840s (though the worst still escaped inspection). 'It cannot be expected that persons so little educated as the present class of schoolmasters should be able to carry on a school by themselves', wrote one diocesan inspector in 1844,[3] 'although they may be made useful when acting under the direction, and with the assistance, of the clergyman'; and ten years later an H.M.I. in Devon reported:[4]

> With regard to many of the smaller schools, I regret that it is impossible to realise that any great work is going on, either in moral or religious training or in the simplest elements of school instruction. . . . In one school the leaves of a Book of Common Prayer were torn out and retorn into halves, to be

> given to the junior children that they might learn from these tattered
> portions their first school lessons. . . . These schools for the most part depend
> on local funds . . . drawn almost entirely from the clergy with a few small
> subscriptions, and for this reason inefficient teachers are allowed to hold
> their places, and the schoolroom remains unfit for the teaching and training
> of the children of the poor.

The Bible was commonly used as a reading primer, more for its subsidized cheapness than its religious significance.

The early initiatives of the Committee of Council were designed to improve schools capable of improvement with the introduction of teachers' certificate examinations and of pupil-teacher apprentices in 1846–7, and with the offer in 1853 of a capitation grant on average attendance, subject to H.M.I.'s approval, for adequately maintained schools with certificated teachers. The expansion of training colleges run by Diocesan Boards (as well as by the British[5] and other societies) also made a better-grounded type of teacher available to parishes able and willing to pay for them. But these developments only increased rural disparities, improving the better schools while leaving the majority untouched. For the fortunate few, nevertheless, the effect could be revolutionary, as is shown in H.M.I.'s report on Halberton in Devon in 1855,[6]

> where a few years ago the people had no desire for education, where local
> circumstances are wholly averse to education, yet where, through the zeal
> and energy of the clergy, backed up by an active missionary spirit in the
> master and mistress, the farmers and parishioners have been made to look
> favourably upon the work of education, and the attendance has become so
> good and regular that the capitation grant was made for 40 boys and 39 girls.

Good and regular attendance was indeed exceptional in the rural context, and remained so, despite legislation, to the end of the century. It remained vital for the children of country workers to supplement the family income, especially where there was no alternative industrial employment to force up agricultural wages.

Until the famous Revised Code of 1862 was introduced, the number of rural schools with certificated heads and pupil-teachers receiving capitation grant steadily grew. But the Revised Code for the time checked this development. The code abruptly cut off government salaries for pupil-teachers, augmentation for certificated teachers, and grants for books and apparatus, and confined State payment to a single grant based on average attendance and passes in the set examination. Some managers, in fact, were obliged to dismiss their qualified staff and repudiate the State connection. The code introduced a curriculum for schools under inspection, arranged in six 'standards' for those above infant level. In reading, for example, the standards ranged from 'narrative monosyllables' to a 'short introductory paragraph in a newspaper or other modern narrative'. Most nineteenth-century rural children, however, never stayed beyond Standard IV, which required only reading from a book in use in the school (with which they were already familiar), the writing of a sentence dictated

544

from a school book, and a sum in compound rules. On this basis, invariably reading and writing secured more passes than arithmetic: and the standard arrangement, devised for large town schools where each standard could form a separate class, lay heavy on a village school where several, and often all, standards must be taught together by one teacher. A seventh standard was introduced in 1882, but very few rural children ever reached it.

Grant-earning extras were gradually added in the form of 'specific subjects' taken by individuals, and 'class subjects'—mostly grammar, geography, history, and girls' needlework—taken by several standards together as one class. But these were less effective than intended in broadening the curriculum. Geography inclined to 'capes and bays' (though a few masters took their boys out surveying, or constructed sand-maps in the playground), and history to the rote use of 'wretched little manuals which are to be had by the dozen for a few pence, all professing to be short cuts to knowledge'[7] and 'too much a mere record of the doings of royal personages'.[8]

Not till the late 1890s, after the set examination had ceased, did the department recognize that rural schools might be something other than pale imitations of those in towns, and attempt more local relevance by allowing 'principles of agriculture' as a specific subject, cookery and laundry work for girls (if a village school could provide facilities), and cottage gardening for boys. Rather belatedly came the admission that:[9]

> Some of the reluctance shown in various agricultural neighbourhoods to raise the admittedly low level of many of our rural schools may be traced to a conviction that . . . country schools should do more to interest country children in country life. . . . A country school fails if it misses the opportunity of showing its scholars how much skill and knowledge underlie the operations familiar to them in their daily life, and of teaching them to feel pride in practical work well done . . . [a] mechanical form of bookish instruction [cannot achieve this but is] unfortunately the cheapest kind of teaching . . . consequently it tends to prevail in inferior schools, staffed by inferior teachers. . . . The aim should be not to produce multitudes of clerks but multitudes of good craftsmen.

The department had at last accepted that it was wrong to force on rural schools a curriculum divorced from the environment and designed to produce 'clerks', which the great majority of country children would never be; but its previous policy had conditioned many rural teachers to follow the book and the code rather than develop the initiatives towards local relevance, for which it was, by the end of the century, now asking.

II

Meanwhile, the Act of 1870 had introduced the entirely new element of compulsion on parishes to provide adequately for all their school-age children—though its operation in this respect was often much less immediate than is commonly assumed. Where existing voluntary schools could not be brought up to the size and 'efficiency' required, or where there was as yet no school at all and no adequate move to provide one on a voluntary basis, a School Board had to be formed to raise rates, borrow if necessary from the Public Works Loan Commission, and carry out the duty of building and maintenance.

Most rural School Boards were formed compulsorily four or five years after the Act, and they took two or three years more to build and open their school. Many were still not ready when the Act of 1876 purported to set up machinery for enforcing attendance. The Newcastle Commission had earlier taken the view that 'good elementary education cannot be obtained without considerable expense ... which parochial bodies would be reluctant to admit', and 'it scarcely requires to be confirmed that a body of ratepayers, or a board of farmers ... must be incompetent to select a proper master for a school'.[10] Yet this was precisely the course which the legislators of 1870 felt bound to adopt in the absence of any local government body in the countryside transcending the parish—apart from the Poor Law Unions whose nature and unpopularity did not commend them as education authorities. Their centralizing workhouse economies could not, moreover, apply to schools; nor could their remote impersonality provide the active local interest and management hoped for; and their later record as attendance authorities for parishes not under boards suggests that it was wise not to give them charge of schools.

The membership of parochial School Boards, and their consequent adequacy or otherwise in running a school, depended variously on the local influence on and attitude to education of the incumbent and major landowners, the relative voting strength of Nonconformity, and the extent of local concern—increasing with the onset of agricultural depression—to keep down the rates. The majority of such boards, at least two-thirds and perhaps three-quarters, were not elected by poll but chosen by show of hands at a parish or vestry meeting or by some other form of prior arrangement designed to avoid the cost of a contested election. Some, and often the worst, were indeed 'a board of farmers', much more concerned with economy than with the education of their future labourers.

The quality of rural schools in the last quarter of the century, though all were officially 'efficient' and working to the same code, thus continued to vary greatly with the adequacy or otherwise of their support. Some surviving voluntary schools enjoyed up to three times as much income as others of the same size, and board schools up to twice as much,[11] and this was inevitably reflected in the salaries offered and the quality of staff and adequacy of equipment. The better-supported village schools, providing a good house as well as a good salary, could attract and keep a headteacher of quality, or a married certificated couple able to run separate boys' and girls' or mixed and infants' departments. Meanwhile the poorer ones scraped by. Some had a rapid succession of young girls just out of pupil-teacher apprenticeship and boasting only provisional certificates, who moved on as soon as they had improved their market value by passing the external certificate examination. Others employed middle-aged failures who had been dismissed elsewhere for inefficiency and were to be so again. In the first case, under an effective long-service teacher (or teachers) the school was likely both to prosper and to gain public acceptance; in the latter, it could continue to be regarded as an irksome and ineffective imposition from without.

Well above half the rural schools in Devon, both board and voluntary, provided a house, often rate-free and sometimes with fuel in addition (besides 'furnished rooms' where only unmarried women were employed). Certificated headteachers' salaries varied with the size of school, and between schools of the same size, but in 1903 they averaged £105 for men and £75 for women (the national figures being respectively £150 and £96). The poorer voluntary school salaries had by then been raised by aid grant and were, if anything, better than those of rural boards; but in schools with average attendance under a hundred men heads were paid (including emoluments) from £55 to £176, and women from £40 to £100.[12]

Whether the school were voluntary or board, much depended on the degree to which the influence of prominent local personages was exerted in its support, and the hold which such influence had over parents and children. Much, too, depended on the capacity and personality of the headteacher—not only in the school but as affecting his prestige in the community—and on the apparent relevance or otherwise of the teaching. Where, for instance, a master could claim (with complete confirmation from his report record) that 'correspondence is now almost solely carried on by the children, between their parents and relatives, while the children who have left, some of them sons of mechanics, work out their fathers' measurements etc. by cross-multiplication',[13] the value of the school was amply demonstrated: in this case in a village which, until seven years before, had had no school at all.

On the other hand, the rural school at its worst could remain very bad indeed, saved from H.M.I.'s declaration of complete inefficiency only by his knowledge that to close it would serve no practical purpose. As one inspector reported in 1883:[14]

> Many of the small country Boards seem to consider that their paramount duty is to keep the school rate at the lowest possible figure. The buildings, sometimes shamefully scamped by some local 'jerry-builder', go from bad to worse; the teacher's salary is cut down to the lowest sum that some person who has failed elsewhere is willing to accept; the staff is kept at the minimum, and the inspector's requirements as regards staff, books, maps, etc. are resisted or evaded up to the last moment, and then complied with only to escape the threatened fine. When we consider that farmers as a class have no interest in or experience of the management of schools, that they commonly regard popular education as injurious to their interests, and that they have to bear a new burden in the school rate for an object with which they have no sympathy, we cannot wonder that the results of committing the charge of education to this class should prove so unsatisfactory.

In the smallest and poorest schools, those with only one teacher, the fate of the infants could be particularly depressing. A Hampshire H.M.I. saw them[15]

> in the hands of a dull monitor, frequently packed away in a dark corner of the main room or in a dingy classroom, where the luckless little creatures have only the opportunity of learning how, without crying, to sit still for hours together, with dangling legs and aching backs.

Rural infants' classrooms were usually minute and nearly filled with a gallery (rows of tiered desks) which inhibited movement, while the kindergarten methods currently being introduced in town schools required space, equipment, and a teacher with some special training to use them.

The department's inspectors were only too well aware of deficiencies, and anxious to correct them, but they were largely impotent while the poorer schools remained under parish administration. The Revised Code, moreover, had replaced their earlier benevolent advisory function with that of an itinerant reporting agent, able to do little more than conduct the annual examination. Until this ceased in 1891 the grant, and so in many cases the teacher's income, depended on H.M.I.'s subjective estimate of 'intelligibility' in reading and 'legibility' in writing, in conditions of haste and strain; and he could reduce the total earned by up to a half for defaults of teachers or managers. A testy inspector, one who framed his questions outside the vocabulary of the rural child and assumed a lack of response to mean ignorance or stupidity, could be an object of dread against whom the teacher had no defence. At the same time, reiterated reports to the department of widespread defective management and neglect to enforce attendance failed for many years to evoke any effective reaction. Not till the 1890s did teacher–inspector relationships improve. Then, the abolition of the 'annual parade day' and the substitution of two 'visits without notice' in a more relaxed atmosphere gave scope for a return to the inspectors' original function. As one teacher noted in 1897, 'HMI gave us teachers some valuable help, a thing so different from coming and taking the bare results in the old form of examination.'[16]

But the effects of the old régime took long to eradicate, and in 1900 it was still reported that 'the work of the inspector . . . has not been very fruitful: he has been expected to act as a sort of ambulant training college among teachers of mature years, of fixed habits of thought, and sometimes of insufficient knowledge of their own shortcomings'.[17] By the end of the century, rural teachers of intelligence and personality were at last being let off the leash: but others, and probably the majority, found the revolution in official attitudes bewildering.

The abolition of school fees in 1891, with the readily accepted offer of 10s. per annum 'fee grant' in lieu, also marked a change in official attitudes and led to a considerable easing of the lot of teachers and parents. Fees had long been defended on the assumption that free schooling would pauperize the parent, and that he would not value what he did not pay for; but it had been left to each village board or voluntary committee to set its own terms, sometimes with vicious results. One common practice, particularly of farmer-dominated boards, had been a massive increase of fees for any children who were entitled to leave, and whose continuance at school was therefore regarded as evasion of employment. As one master noted:[18]

> The Board say that if a labourer can afford to keep his children from work after that Standard, he can afford to pay treble. But many boys and girls pass Standard IV when 10 years old, and surely they are too young to be put out to work.

This was not, evidently, the view of many contemporary rural school authorities, or even some teachers, as the chief inspector for the South-West Division saw in 1888:[19]

> It is sometimes the interest of teachers in the small country schools to get rid of children from their upper classes. These children are often few in number, irregular in their attendance, and troublesome to teach. The fee for them is therefore made partially prohibitive, and the teachers will sometimes defend the practice by saying that after all they are only sacrificing the few to the many who will benefit by the more individual attention that can be given to them.

Parents, moreover, naturally resented paying a week's fee for less than a week's schooling, and a day's absence (for whatever reason) was often likely to mean a week's. The end of school pence removed these pressures, but also ended the reward for good attendance of a partial return of fees which some voluntary committees had long operated. The ending of fees undoubtedly eased the pockets of hard-pressed labouring parents, though not to the extent of making them forgo an income supplement from occasional child employment. Its effect on attendance was chiefly to encourage that of infants who could not earn, and for whom the rural school often made the least adequate provision; but no more was heard of 'pauperizing the labourer'.

Attendance, as already mentioned, remained markedly irregular in all but the most prestigious rural schools until the transfer to county administration in 1903. Acts of 1876 and 1880 had established means of enforcement and they compelled boards and unions to make approved by-laws; but to get these put into effect locally was quite another matter. As one H.M.I. commented in 1880:[20]

> visits from attendance officers, a few attendance orders issued, and an occasional fine inflicted, serve to keep alive the idea that there is machinery in existence by which attendance may be enforced, when those whose duty it is to put the machinery in motion shall see fit to do so.

Faced with the expense of prosecution and the reluctance of country magistrates to do more than make ineffective attendance orders, rural boards and unions were soon discouraged from taking action. Moreover, 'the illegal employment of children . . . practised even by persons who have undertaken, as members of School Boards or Attendance Committees, to enforce the law they violate'[21] was a commonplace of many logbooks.[22] Irregular absence, compelling the teacher to repeat lessons or leave some pupils to flounder, continued to the end of parish administration. It contrasted notably with the record in towns, and had the effect of reducing average attendance to three-quarters or two-thirds of roll number, except where local influence was purposefully exerted or the school was particularly well-regarded.

III

As Victorian England changed from a predominantly rural to a predominantly urban country it was perhaps natural that legislators and the department should view elementary education in an urban setting, at least until rural depopulation caused some rethinking at the end of the century. Until the middle of the century, at least, school provision in the countryside (with all its admitted defects and its motivation of religious proselytizing and social subordination) may not have been noticeably worse than that in industrial towns. But industrialization provided a market for literacy which agriculture did not; and after 1870 the large urban School Boards pioneered educational advance leading to higher grade schools with a technical basis, and were much better able to make full use of the expanding possibilities of the code. Attendance enforcement there was far more effective, and with the development of sophisticated machinery the demand for early child labour was less of an obstacle. In the countryside, on the other hand, openings for work other than on farms were relatively few and the relevance of an urban-based code consequently less. Small schools needed more income per head to function effectively, and for the most part received less; and isolation narrowed the horizons of the teacher as well as the pupil. As one perceptive village master confided to his logbook:[23]

> It is a very hard matter to cultivate the intelligence of our children. There is no foundation to work upon, they have seen nothing, the parents do not read nor in many cases attend worship. To talk of Railways, Manufactures, Telegraphs, or ordinary Arts of Civilisation, is to make sure of not being understood at the very commencement.

Rural assistant teachers (if provided at all) were mostly untrained 'Supplementaries', whose only qualification was to be over eighteen and annually passed by H.M.I. They were normally local women without external contacts or knowledge of what was happening in progressive schools. Pupil-teachers, nearly always ex-pupils of the same school, likewise lacked the stimulus of the training centres open to their urban counterparts. The majority of country headteachers had never been to a training college, having acquired certificates only by external examination; and by the 1890s the smallest schools were no longer required to employ a certificated teacher. While towns grew and prospered, the countryside suffered depression and depopulation; and in 1900 the gap between urban and rural standards was still widening. In general, the more urbanized an area the greater the popular demand for education as a route to better employment; the greater the financial backing of Dissent and consequently its capacity both to support its own schools and to stimulate Anglican counter-response; the greater the probability of active and forward-looking school administration; and the less the demand for school-age labour.

Rural schools of the later nineteenth century, in fact, suffered great disadvantages; and some, under unsympathetic and cheese-paring management, had no chance to provide more than the barest smattering of literacy, a literacy which was mechanically taught, and of doubtful duration when pupils left as soon as possible after grossly irregular attendance. Others, under teachers of quality and initiative, did far better; and the variation between the best and the worst remained great despite increasingly generous State aid offered in the 1890s. This included the fee grant already mentioned, a 'small population' grant, a grant for staffing on a new special small-school teacher/pupil ratio instead of that designed for town schools, and finally an aid grant for the poorer voluntary schools. By 1900, in fact, some rural voluntary schools were receiving as much as 90 per cent of their income from public funds,[24] a development which prepared the way for complete county maintenance.

Meanwhile, since 1888 rural areas had been given a new potential source of school administration in the county councils, which were already serving an apprenticeship as education authorities by aiding and inspecting evening classes established under the 1889 Technical Education Act. These classes were held in school premises, were generally under local teachers, and provided a variety of craft and commercial instruction for those who had left the day school. The eventual transfer of day schools to the county in 1903 (under the Act of 1902) was the essential preliminary to a levelling up of standards. The transfer provided for the first time a wider rating basis (including relatively flourishing towns) than the individual parish, professional advice for local managers and control of appointments, and the very necessary extinction of the worst type of village School Board. The county also made compulsory attendance a reality, and before long brought a ladder to secondary schools, an opportunity previously almost unknown.

Even so, much had been achieved under the old system, particularly in the last quarter-century. The combination of State aid and initiative with local effort (even if this was compelled) had revolutionized rural education by comparison with the standards of thirty (and particularly of sixty) years before. For the great majority of country children the result was probably little more than some grounding in social disciplines, the ability to read the less demanding newspapers, to write (if with a limited vocabulary), and to do simple sums: but this in itself was a great step forward. For the brighter few, in the better schools, pupil-teacher apprenticeship offered a route into teaching; but otherwise, even if a pupil stayed the course till thirteen, escape from low-paid rural work was probably dependent on the chance of craft apprenticeship or migration.

There was more opportunity in country towns, where there existed a wider variety of employment and less of the parental poverty which caused so many village children still to leave school as soon as possible. With greater educational motivation, towns sometimes also offered the chance of scholarships to further education in institutions reorganized by the Endowed Schools Commission. Educationally, as in other respects, the villager at the turn of the century was still the poor relation of the urban majority; but if his advance was slower than theirs, advance there had been, nevertheless. Its limitations and disparities had been at least partly due to the survival of the parish as a separate education authority, particularly while it remained under what Matthew Arnold was moved to describe as 'the feudal and ecclesiastical organisation of the Middle Ages, or of France before the Revolution'.[25]

Notes

1 Schools attached to the National Society for Promoting the Education of the Poor in the Principles of the Established Church, 1811.
2 *Report on the State of Popular Education*, BPP 1861 XXX (Newcastle Report), vi 93, Z. 670, evidence of H. Chester.
3 *Exeter Diocesan Board of Education Report*, 1845, 15.
4 *Committee of Council for Education Report*, 1853–4, ii, 239–40 (hereafter cited as CCER).
5 British and Foreign Schools Society (Undenominational/Nonconformist), 1808–11.
6 CCER 1855–6, 383–4.
7 CCER 1875–6, 309.
8 CCER 1889–9, 295.
9 CCER 1897–8, xii–xv.
10 BPP 1861 XXX i 302–3, 471.
11 Return for all public elementary schools, year ended 31 August 1889, BPP 1890 LVI, *passim*.
12 Devon RO: Devon Education Committee staffing and salary registers, showing situation at takeover in 1903.
13 Devon RO: Bradford (N. Devon) logbook, 1885.
14 CCER 1883–4, 279.
15 CCER 1884–5, 249.
16 Devon RO; Loddiswell National (S. Devon) logbook.
17 Board of Education Report 1900–1, ii, 136–7.
18 Buckland Brewer (N. Devon) logbook, 1890.
19 CCER 1888–9, 290.
20 CCER 1880–1, 284.
21 CCER 1883–4, 280.
22 Sellman, 1967, 118–20.
23 Devon RO: Holbeton (S. Devon) logbook, 1883.
24 Devon RO. See, for example, account books of Littlehempston and Clyst St Mary, Devon.

25 Arnold, 1868, 274. For detailed treatment of matters touched on in this chapter, and for other aspects of Victorian rural schooling, see R. R. Sellman, 'Public Elementary Education in Rural Devon, 1833–1903: The State and the Community', unpublished Ph.D. thesis, Exeter University, 1974.

40   Country Diet

John Burnett

I

The rural labourer's diet, like other aspects of his material life, was a direct reflection of his economic position and his ability, or inability, to command the essentials of subsistence—food, clothing and shelter. Over the course of the Victorian age that economic position changed and gradually improved, but more significant and critical were the differences in standards which divided one region of the country from another and divided one family from another even within the same region. Thus, the labourer's wage varied widely in different parts of the country, but also varied locally with his degree of skill and responsibility for the numerous branches of farm work: yearly men fared better than day labourers, stockmen better than field workers, men with exceptional skills, like expert hedgers and ditchers, best of all. But, more narrowly still, the amount and quality of the labourer's food depended on the size and age of his family, the ability of his wife and children to bring in extra earnings, the generosity of his employer in allowing him an allotment or potato-ground, the rent of his cottage, the produce of his garden, the availability of shops, of free fuel, and a score or more of other local and individual factors. The man who could subsist comfortably with two children might starve if they grew to six, and for most labourers there was a regular cycle of poverty from childhood to early married life, then to old age, with only brief periods of comparative comfort as a single man and when his children became earners. Such considerations indicate that overall generalizations about 'the labourer's standard of life' are of strictly limited usefulness.

554

With that caution in mind, the available evidence suggests that the standard was probably at its lowest point immediately before the opening of the Victorian age. The general prosperity of English agriculture during the Napoleonic Wars and the growth of intensive farming had had a detrimental effect on the labourer's diet by encouraging the practice of 'boarding-out'. Formerly, many labourers had lived in the farmhouse, boarded and lodged as part of their wage, and by most accounts boarded well, on much the same food as their employers—bread and cheese and pork for breakfast, joints of meat, pies or puddings for dinner, more cold meat and cheese for supper with small beer at every meal.[1] But with the concentration of farmers on production of food for the market during the war years, combined with what some contemporaries claimed was their growing preoccupation with 'gentrification', labourers were increasingly forced to live out on board-wages, almost always with adverse effects on their standard of diet. In the depression which followed the price fall of 1813 a reduced demand for labour brought lower wages which in many parts of the country had to be supplemented by parsimonious doles under the Speenhamland system: pauperized by his dependence on public charity, uneducated, unenfranchised and immobilized by his poverty, the labourer's position, especially in the south and east of England, often sank to that of chronic destitution.

In 1824 a survey of agricultural wages showed levels in some southern counties as low as 3s. a week for a single man and 4s. 6d. for a married man: astonishing variations occurred within small areas—in the district of Wingham in Kent, for example, from 6d. a day to 1s. 6d. a day. Generally, wages were lowest in the south, south west and east, where the 'allowance system' was widespread, higher in the border counties and in Wales, and highest in the north and north west where opportunities of industrial employment often pushed up the demand for labour. In Oldham, Lancashire, a labourer could earn 12s. a week, in Cumberland up to 15s.[2] This was the economic background to William Cobbett's *Rural Rides*, compiled between 1822 and 1830, and written in a tone of passionate indignation at the injustices of the labourer: 'dogs and hogs and horses are treated with more civility, and as to food and lodging, how gladly would the labourers change with them!'[3] For a family of five, he calculated, a man needed £62 6s. 8d. a year merely for bread, meat and beer, yet with a wage of 9s. a week supplemented by an allowance of 7s. 6d., he could at best afford only half the minimum necessary for basic foods. Cobbett was the arch-traditionalist, mourning the passing of the Englishman's beef, ale and household bread, and roundly condemning his new-fangled foods—white bakers' bread, tea and, worst of all, 'Ireland's lazy root', the cursed potato. Home baking and brewing, and probably cooking generally, were on the decline as supplies of free fuel for the oven dwindled before the advance of the plough, and by a curious inversion white bread and tea, the luxuries of the eighteenth century, became the hallmarks of a poverty-line diet in the nineteenth. The harsh fact was that white bread, without meat, bacon or cheese to go with it, was more palatable than the coarse household bread, and a cup of weak tea (2 oz per family per week was usual) converted a cold meal into something like a warm one. And despite Cobbett's strictures, a dish of potatoes, especially if eaten from their skins and with the addition of a little fat or bacon, was a cheap and nutritious meal; one of his chief complaints was that they were simply too easy to grow.

Dietary ignorance was not the main cause of the labourer's difficulties, as some contemporaries believed. 'The want and misery of many families arise more from want of discretion in managing their resources than from the real scantiness of their income', wrote Esther Copley, and recommended bread made from maize, barley and rye, 'tea' of rue and strawberry leaves, scrap pie, 'mutton chitterlings' and other cheap but unappetizing dishes.[4] The dietary pattern was generally better in the north than in the south, not primarily because northern labourers were more frugal, but because wages were higher, conditions of employment were different, and the range of locally produced foods more nutritious. The much praised oatmeal diet of the northern counties and of north Wales was made palatable by the addition of milk, which was not easily available to the southern labourer who had no cow-pasture and often found it difficult to persuade farmers to 'break bulk' by selling him a pint or two. Again, potatoes were more widely cultivated in the north, and the predominance of pastoral farming often meant that meat and animal fats were more plentiful than in the south. Equally important, yearly hiring of labour persisted longer in the north, and it was still customary for the labourer to be paid partly in grain or meal, irrespective of fluctuations in market prices, and to be granted cow-pasture, potato-ground, or accommodation for pigs and poultry. These allowances gave much greater stability to the family economy than in the south, where the day-labourer usually received only beer or cider in the harvest field, or an occasional meal in which his wife and children had no share. Where yearly hiring continued in some southern counties, as in Dorset, the lowness of wages was at least counteracted to some extent by free or cheap cottages, fuel, allotments and other real benefits.

II

Little change in the pattern is evident by the middle of the century. The 1840s were probably no 'hungrier' as a decade than the 1830s or the 1850s, and the contemporary accounts of hardship collected by T. Fisher Unwin span the years both before and after 1846. In bad times bread was sometimes made out of 'crammings' left after the flour and bran had been extracted, porridge out of bruised beans, and 'tea' from burnt crusts of bread, while pig pease, turnips and swedes were all unwillingly consumed; fresh meat was a rare luxury, and a family was lucky if it had salt pork or bacon more than once a week.[5] In 1843 a report on the employment of women and children in agriculture showed that the poorest counties were Wiltshire, Dorset and the south west, East Anglia was somewhat better, Yorkshire and Northumberland were best of all. Of Wiltshire it was reported:

> The food of the labourer and his family is wheaten bread, potatoes, a small

quantity of beer, but only as a luxury, and a little butter and tea. To this
may sometimes be added (but it is difficult to say how often or in what
quantities) cheese, bacon and . . . a portion of the entrails of the pig. Where
from poverty bacon cannot be obtained, a little fat is used to give a flavour
to the potatoes.[6]

This was the irreducible minimum. Wherever wages were least, or families of young
children largest, cereals and potatoes were the great staples, if possible made more
palatable by small amounts of butter, cheese, bacon and tea. In a budget from
Lavenham, Suffolk, bread took 9s. a week out of total family earnings of 13s. 9d.,
potatoes 1s., tea 2d., sugar $3\frac{1}{2}d.$, butter $4\frac{1}{2}d.$, and cheese 3d. Here there was no meat of
any kind, though the family had the reputation of being neat and clean, and the
children worked from the age of eight upwards.

Above this economic level there was scope for more home cooking, variety and
palatability in the diet. Meat was the invariable ambition, preferably fresh, but
failing that bacon or salt pork, and a Sunday joint with accompanying vegetables and
pudding was the sure indication of domestic comfort: if meat appeared in some form
once or twice more during the week the family was prosperous. The place of the pig in
the labourer's economy was crucial. If he could afford to buy and rear a piglet—even
if, as sometimes happened, he had to mortgage half of it for feed or salt—his family
would have pork and bacon, sausages, black puddings and other local specialities for
some months to come, and the monotony of bread and potatoes could be transformed
by a clever housewife into a range of appetizing dishes. A sheep's pluck, a cow's heel,
an ox-tail and other cheap cuts of meat were also important occasional additions to
the diet, as were the bloaters and red herrings which were now being transported
inland. Increased earnings were also evidenced by increased quantities of tea, sugar
and treacle in the diet, by the mention of fruit pies and puddings, dumplings and
broth, eggs, milk and green vegetables.

Of the eastern counties Lincolnshire stands out in 1843 as the best fed, with more
meat and milk than in Norfolk and Suffolk, and bacon every day for some labourers.
But still the pattern was of increasingly varied and nutritious food the further one
went northwards. In Yorkshire the labourer was often able to make a significant
contribution to his larder from his own garden or allotment, and some even had cow-
pasture; here home baking of bread persisted longer than in the south, and
housewives prided themselves on their pies, hasty puddings and oatmeal porridge. In
Northumberland, where the hinds frequently had a cottage and garden free, cow-
pasture, potato-ground and an allowance of wheat, oats, barley, rye and peas as part
of their 'yearly bond', the diet was probably the most nutritious in England and the
labourers described as 'a splendid race'. In this remote region the cash wage was only
a few pounds a year, and the labourer and his wife had little opportunity to squander
it in the town or the beershop.

III

Twenty years on, in the 1860s, the picture is largely unchanged. The labourer's standard of life apparently moved independently of the fortunes of the agricultural economy of which he was an essential part—or, rather, it often moved inversely with such fluctuations: while the farming industry remained highly profitable in the third quarter of the century the labourer's standard was generally most wretched, and only as the agricultural depression deepened in the 1880s were there indications of dawning improvement.

In 1863 the first national food inquiry in Britain was undertaken by Dr Edward Smith on behalf of the medical officer of the Privy Council, Sir John Simon: it covered the diets of 'the poorer labouring classes', which were taken to include farm labourers and certain low-paid indoor workers such as shoe-makers, silk-weavers and stocking- and glove-makers.[7] Smith examined the diets of 509 farm workers—377 from England, the rest from Scotland, Wales and Ireland—families being chosen who were regarded as representative 'in industry, thrift, intelligence, health and capability for labour'. From Smith's careful inquiries certain facts emerged clearly. The average English labourer's diet was less nutritious than that of Ireland, Wales or Scotland (the best); in England the north/south division in wages and conditions still existed, though now less sharply than formerly. Since James Caird's investigation of 1850–51, when the average agricultural wage for the country was 9s. 6d.,[8] wages had improved somewhat, particularly in some of the 'bad' counties like Devon (by 19 per cent) and Dorset (by 14 per cent). Table 40.1 shows the average quantities of foodstuffs consumed by Smith's two groups, the farm workers and the indoor domestic workers, and converts the quantities into nutritional equivalents: it will be seen that in every respect the outdoor workers had the advantage.

The great staple of the labourer's diet was still bread, eaten at the rate of approximately $1\frac{1}{2}$ lb per person per day, and providing approximately 40 per cent of total calories. Almost always in England it was now white wheaten bread made of 'seconds' flour; home baking was rapidly disappearing except in the more prosperous north, 30 per cent of all families always buying baker's bread and another 50 per cent using it as an adjunct. But it is clear that the next most important food of the labourer was not meat but potatoes. The average consumption of $4\frac{1}{2}$ lb per person per week was subject to very wide variation, and where a labourer was able to rent a potato-ground a family consumption of 56 lb a week was not uncommon. Smith approved of the general adoption of potatoes, which made a hot dinner or supper with the addition of a morsel of meat or bacon. Meat, eaten at the rate of a little over 2 oz a day, was clearly a luxury, and 30 per cent of all families reported that they never ate butcher's meat. In Dorset, Somerset and several eastern counties 'meat' meant pickled pork or bacon, which had the advantage that it could be cut up and used as flavouring for the potatoes. Where fresh meat was eaten it was generally reserved for the Sunday dinner, the only time in the week when the whole family dined together. The remains would then go into the husband's lunch-basket on following days and, if possible, into evening meals.

Table 40.1   *Diets of indoors and rural workers, 1863*

		Indoor workers	*Rural workers*
Bread	lb/week	9.1	11.6
Sugar	oz/week	7.9	6.6
Potatoes	lb/week	2.4	4.4
Milk	pt/week	0.75	1.6
Meat	oz/week	12.3	15.3
Fats	oz/week	4.7	5.2
Kilocalories	/day	2,190	2,760
Protein	g/day	55	70
Fat	g/day	53	54
Carboh.	g/day	370	460
Iron	mg/day	12.5	15.9
Calcium	g/day	0.36	0.48

Source: Barker, Oddy and Yudkin, 1970, 43.

Other purchased foods appeared only in very small quantities in Smith's budgets. The common assumption that cheese played an important part in the labourer's diet seems to be contradicted by the average consumption of little more than $\frac{1}{2}$ oz a day, though again regional variations were important, south Wales having a high cheese consumption.[9] Milk consumption was less than $\frac{1}{4}$ pint a day, and fat consumption (butter, lard, suet and dripping) at about $\frac{3}{4}$ oz a day was also low: the poorer families, reported Smith, 'for the most part had two days a week in which the children ate dry bread'. Partly for this reason, tea was now the all but universal drink, consumed (very weak) at the rate of $2\frac{1}{4}$ oz per family a week; sugar, at 1 oz per person daily, was also increasingly important, both as a sweetener for tea and, in the form of treacle, to spread on bread.

Although the survey of 1863 showed the farm labourer to be generally better fed than the indoor worker, wide regional variations still persisted. Labourers in North Wales, Scotland and Ireland all received more nutritious diets than the English and, Smith calculated, the best fed of all were those of Anglesey with 60,784 grains of carbonaceous food weekly. North Wales came next with 45,613 grains, then England with 40,673 and, finally, south Wales with 38,675 grains. Potatoes, barley bread and oatmeal in various forms were still the staple foods of Wales, and Smith believed that the high nutritional status of the north was due to the use of oatmeal and ample supplies of milk, with only moderate amounts of sugars and fats. He regretted that the use of tea and coffee was increasing in poor districts in south Wales 'where there is no room for spending money upon luxuries'.

Smith's calculations, though the most detailed so far, can hardly have been complete. Many labourers could grow some food, cabbages and root vegetables being important but unquantified additions to diet, and raw onions often eaten as a 'relish' to help down the bread. The man might expect an allowance of beer or cider at his work and, if careful, could bring a little home to his family. Apples might be given, blackberries picked, and a hare or rabbit poached, though the risks were great. Again, the possibility of fattening a pig every year, or of keeping a few chickens, could make a major difference to the labourer's diet. All this suggests that the quantities recorded by Smith generally represented the minimum, to which there were varying additions with degrees of prosperity. Another uncertain factor is the way in which the available food was distributed within the family group. Smith believed, probably rightly, that the lion's share of the meat and other 'best' food went to the man, as chief breadwinner: 'It is remarkable that this is not only acquiesced in by the wife, but felt by her to be right, and even necessary for the maintenance of the family.' The obvious consequence was that the other members of the family had proportionately less of the better foods than a straight division would indicate, and there are many references to the wife and children existing through the week essentially on bread, potatoes and tea. This is borne out by some of the actual menus of meals collected by Smith:

> WILTSHIRE (Case No. 211). *Breakfast*—water broth, bread and butter. *Dinner*—husband and children have bacon (sometimes), cabbage, bread and butter. Wife has tea. *Supper*—potatoes or rice.
> (Case No. 212). *Breakfast*—sop, bread, and sometimes butter. *Dinner*—bread and cheese. *Supper*—onions, bread, butter or cheese.
>
> LINCOLNSHIRE (Case No. 248). *Breakfast*—milk gruel, or bread and water, or tea and bread. *Dinner*—meat for husband only: others vegetables only. *Tea and supper*—bread or potatoes.
>
> YORKSHIRE (Case No. 471). *Breakfast*—husband—milk and bread: family—tea, bread and butter. *Dinner*—husband—bacon daily: others—three days weekly, potatoes or bread, tea. *Tea*—tea, bread and butter.

These may be compared with the more plentiful diets of the north:

> CUMBERLAND (Case No. 301). *Breakfast*—husband—oatmeal and milk porridge: the others—tea, bread, butter and cheese. *Dinner*—meat and potatoes daily, bread, cheese and milk. *Supper*—boiled milk, followed by tea, bread, butter and cheese.
>
> LANCASHIRE (Case No. 304). *Breakfast*—milk porridge, coffee, bread and butter. *Dinner*—meat and potatoes, or meat pie, rice pudding or a baked pudding; the husband takes ale, bread and cheese. *Supper*—tea, toasted cheese, and bacon instead of butter.

The uncertainties as to possible additional sources of food, and the distribution of total food within the family, make an assessment of the nutritional adequacy of the Smith diets difficult, if not impossible. Somehow or other the heads of families must have got enough to eat to sustain them in long hours of field labour, largely unaided as yet by machinery. By modern calculations 3,500–4,000 calories a day would be regarded as necessary for an adult male engaged in heavy manual labour, though in the 1860s body size was smaller and calorie requirements were somewhat less than today. Even so, the calorie intakes in Smith's diets would tend to suggest a restriction of physical output by workers—a low level of activity, severe exhaustion, or both— and sub-optimal growth by children. Children were almost certainly inadequately supplied with protein, as were pregnant and lactating women, though quantities for adult males were probably adequate. Supplies of iron in the diets of the 1860s seem adequate, though calcium was only about half that of today. What is more desirable from a nutritional viewpoint, sugar consumption was only about half that of today, and fat consumption 50 per cent less.

The 1860s were, perhaps, the last decade of widespread bad feeding. In the same year as Dr Smith's survey a Select Committee on Prison Discipline heard from the legal secretary to the Poor Law Board that there was little doubt that the workhouse dietary in rural districts was better than the average diet of the free labourer. Many workhouses, it was revealed, served cooked meat three times a week, which was far in excess of what most labourers could get.[10] Despite the intended operation of 'less eligibility' principles, most paupers and criminals were better fed than most farm workers—or, at least, than their wives and children. These were the real casualties of the labourer's poverty. In many families in the 1860s there was never any fresh milk, in many more only one or two pints a week, often of watery, skim milk, even in the dairying counties. An assistant commissioner reporting on the county of Somerset in 1867 wrote:

> A little girl in the vale of Taunton Deane, being asked what she had for breakfast, said 'bread and butter'. What for supper? 'Bread and butter and cheese'. It is a fair sample of what the agricultural labourer lives on, except that where no cheese or butter is produced, he has nothing but the bread dipped in cider; the wife drinks tea, and there is sometimes a bit of bacon for the husband after his work. There is besides a concoction, called tea kettle broth, given to the children; hot water flavoured with a few herbs or tag ends of bacon, sometimes little but the pure hot water.

IV

Slow but sustained improvement in the labourer's diet is first noticeable in the 1870s—paradoxically, the decade which witnessed the onset of agricultural depression. By this time 'the flight from the land' was in rapid progress and, aided by the early attempts at unionization, farm workers were at last beginning to experience the advantage of some bargaining power. In 1872 an official inquiry showed a range of day-labourer's wages from 10s. 4d. a week in Dorset to 20s. 6d. in Durham, the mean for England and Wales being 14s. 8d.[11] The most wretched living conditions were still in the south west, especially in Dorset, Somerset and Devon, where Canon Girdlestone portrayed the dismal progress from poverty to destitution:

> The labourer breakfasts on tea-kettle broth, hot water poured on bread and flavoured with onions; dines on bread and hard cheese at 2d. a pound, with cider very washy and sour, and sups on potatoes or cabbage greased with a tiny bit of fat bacon. He seldom more than sees or smells butcher's meat. He is long lived, but in the prime of life 'crippled up', i.e. disabled with rheumatism, the result of wet clothes with no fire to dry them by for use next morning, poor living and sour cider. Then he has to work for 4s. or 5s. per week, supplemented scantily from the rates, and, at last, to come for the rest of his life on the rates entirely. Such is, I will not call it the life, but the existence or vegetation of the Devon peasant.[12]

Further west, in Wales, wages were still low at 10s. to 14s. a week, but were described as 'satisfactory in view of the thrifty habits of the people'. They had risen between a third and a half since the 1840s, mainly as a result of railway developments. Diet, working power and resistance to disease had all improved compared with twenty-five years before, and the labourers of north Wales were described in 1870 as 'a muscular and robust race, capable of undergoing great labour'.[13] Probably the main advantage of the Welsh labourer compared with his counterpart in southern England was the availability of much more abundant supplies of milk and dairy products, a consequence mainly of the persistence of small farms and of part-payment in board and lodging.

By the late 1870s and, more certainly, during the 1880s, the labourer was beginning to be helped by falling prices as much as, or more than, by increasing wages. Large-scale imports of wheat and, later, frozen meat were at last forcing prices down to a level he could afford—the quartern loaf from 7d. or more to 4d. or $4\frac{1}{2}d$., beef and mutton from 1s. to 8d. or less, tea to 2s. a pound and sugar to 3d. a pound. By the mid-1880s the increasingly regular use of these former 'luxuries' was noticeable, and in particular some meat every day was becoming normal for all but the poorest. This dawning improvement was confirmed by the reports of the Royal Commission on Labour in the 1890s. The exodus from the land had continued in almost every county; employment was more regular and hours shorter; field work for women and children had greatly diminished; the provision of allotments was much more generous; wages had risen to an average of 13s. $5\frac{1}{2}d$. while prices of commodities had continued to fall.[14] Here, in the last decade of the century, the note was for the first time unmistakably optimistic. 'His standard of life is higher', it was reported; 'he dresses better, he eats more butcher's meat, he travels more, he reads more, and he drinks less. . . .'

An increased meat consumption was the first object of the labourer's choice. Frozen Australian mutton or Argentinian beef may not have had the flavour of prime English meat, but at half the price it was welcomed by those for whom 'meat' had usually meant bacon, salt pork or offal. But also, the 2 oz of tea per family a week of Dr Smith's budgets had grown to $\frac{1}{2}$ lb thirty years later, sugar to over 4 lb a week as well as $1\frac{1}{2}$ lb of treacle, syrup and jam; butter consumption at just over 1 lb a week, and the same quantity of lard, margarine and dripping, also indicated a strong trend towards greater fat consumption. Other 'new' foods like coffee and cocoa, canned meats, salmon and sardines, eggs, raisins and pickles now appeared regularly, making the diet both more palatable and nutritious than formerly.

In 1902 evidence as to the wages and expenditure of labourers was collected by the Board of Trade in a detailed survey by 114 investigators.[15] The average weekly wage, including all extra earnings, was now given as 18s. 6d., 73 per cent of which was spent on food, as shown in Table 40.2.

Table 40.2 *Labourers' average weekly expenditure on food*

Articles	Northern counties	Midland counties	Eastern counties	Southern and south western counties	General average for England
	lb oz	lb oz	lb oz	lb oz	lb oz
Beef or mutton	4 10	3 12	1 12	3 5	3 5¾
Pork	0 3	1 5	2 1	0 14	1 1¾
Bacon	3 7	3 0	2 0	2 6	2 11¼
Cheese	0 12	1 5	1 2	1 10	1 3¼
Bread	5 0	27 0	17 0	29 0	19 8
Flour	23 0	7 0	20 8	9 0	14 14
Oatmeal and rice	1 4	1 8	1 0	1 4	1 4
Potatoes	26 0	22 0	24 0	31 0	25 12
Tea	0 8	0 7	0 6½	0 9	0 7½
Coffee or cocoa	0 1	0 5	0 1	0 3½	0 2½
Butter	1 6	0 15	0 14½	0 15	1 0¾
Lard, margarine, or dripping	1 13	0 10	0 15	0 12	1 0½
Sugar	4 12	4 12	4 0	3 12	4 5
Syrup, treacle, or jam	1 12	1 8	1 0	2 4	1 10
Milk { new or skimmed	6½ pints	4 pints or 9 pints	3½ pints or 7¾ pints	4 pints or 9½ pints	4½ pints or 8¾ pints
Average total Value	14s. 10½d.	13s. 6½d.	12s. 4½d.	13s. 4¾d.	13s. 6½d.

NOTE: the average family was taken to be the labourer, his wife and four children.

Although the old north/south differences were still noticeable, they were less marked than formerly, and in particular the southern labourer had considerably increased his consumption of fresh meat. Especially significant was the fact that the national average now showed a greater expenditure on meat (4*s*. 2*d*. weekly) than on bread and flour (3*s*. 5*d*.), and even in the 'poor' southern and south-western counties the two figures were similar. Compared with the menus collected by Dr Smith forty years earlier the labourer's meals were now considerably more varied, palatable and nutritious; more cooked meals were eaten and the old dependence on bread and potatoes had diminished. Even in Dorset, still the worst fed county, the range of foods had expanded considerably:

> DORSETSHIRE. *Breakfast*—bread, butter, cheese, cold bacon, tea (Sundays, fried bacon). *Dinner*—boiled bacon, potatoes and other vegetables (Sundays, mutton or beef, with pudding); or salt pork, vegetables, dumplings (Sundays, a little fresh meat or pork). *Tea*—bread, butter or jam, cheese, tea (Sundays, cake). *Supper*—very rarely any, or if any, vegetables and salt pork.

And in Derbyshire, one of the best fed, the labourer's diet was now scarcely inferior to that of the farming class:

> DERBYSHIRE. Weekdays—*Breakfast*—bread, butter, bacon, cheese, tea. *Dinner*—beef, pork or bacon, potatoes, tea or beer. *Tea and supper*—bread, butter, syrup, jam, tea; perhaps fish (fresh or tinned). Sundays—*Breakfast*—bread, butter, bacon, tea. *Dinner*—beef or pork, occasionally a fowl, potatoes, tea, beer. *Tea*—bread, butter, jam, tinned fish, tea; perhaps some fancy bread. *Supper*—the same sort of diet as tea, perhaps some beer.

The farm labourer was the last of all fully employed workers to make substantial gains in his standard of life—this only towards the very end of the Victorian age. By then, he was beginning to be better paid, better housed, better educated and, perhaps most noticeably of all, better fed. In some parts of the country the increased provision of allotments was enabling him to make an important contribution towards the diet of his family—Seebohm Rowntree estimated that an average of one twelfth of food was self-produced, though the proportion varied greatly.[16] Village shops were better stocked than formerly, especially with the expanding range of groceries, some under the new proprietary names, and were supplemented by the travelling vans of local co-operative societies and itinerant purveyors of meat, fish and milk.[17] Now that the labourer had a little surplus purchasing power, and the ability to travel to a nearby market town for his weekly shopping, his custom was sought by an increasingly competitive retail trade, and he was no longer exploited by the monopoly of the village store. Equally important, his wife no longer regularly worked at field labour, and had more time and energy to give to cooking, baking, preserving and other domestic skills which made home life much more pleasant and comfortable than in the past. The appetizing dishes with which country life is often associated—the pies and puddings, stews and dumplings, hams, brawns and infinite local varieties of pasties, breads and cakes—were becoming available to the labourer as regular fare instead of as occasional treats only as the queen's reign ended.

Yet still there remained many whose poverty was as crushing as ever, who were too old or infirm to work, who had lost a breadwinner, or whose families were too young and numerous. In their survey of forty-two labourers' families Rowntree and Kendall found that only in five northern counties (Northumberland, Durham, Westmorland, Lancashire and Derbyshire) was the wage paid by farmers sufficient to maintain a family of average size in a state of 'merely physical efficiency': sixteen families had no fresh milk, twenty had no butter, and in many meat was still 'for the man only'.[18] If sheer hunger had diminished by 1900, many labourers and their families were still undernourished, especially in the protein foods, in calcium and in several vitamins. And what improvement there had been had come principally from agricultural developments overseas, from reduced duties on food and from the retailing revolution which was penetrating even the villages by the end of the century. In consequence of these changes the countryman's diet was becoming more standardized, regional differences were beginning to decline and local dishes to disappear. The labourer, who knew that his gains outweighed the losses, can have had little nostalgia for the past.

Notes

1   Marshall, 1817, 131.
2   BPP 1824 (392).
3   Cobbett, 1930, 390.
4   Copley, 1849, 92.
5   Unwin, 1904.
6   BPP 1843 XII 18–19.
7   BPP 1864 XXVIII 220 ff.
8   Caird, 1852, 512.
9   BPP 1864, 202.
10   BPP 1863 IX 355.
11   BPP 1873 LIII.
12   Quoted in Heath, 1874, 100.
13   BPP 1870 XIII 6–15.
14   BPP 1893 I–XIII pt 2.
15   BPP 1903 XVIII 209 ff.
16   Rowntree and Kendall, 1913.
17   Davies, 1909, 192 ff.
18   Rowntree and Kendall, 1913, 308–9.

41   Rural Crime and Protest

David Jones

I

For many years it was customary to ignore the protests of rural labourers which arose between 1830 and 1870, except to contrast their rarity with the frequency of those in town and city. The Chartist movement had little success in the countryside, and trade unionism never established a firm hold there. Crime, too, especially the rising tide of theft and juvenile delinquency in the second quarter of the century, was generally assumed to have been an urban problem. Only in the later decades of the twentieth century have scholars begun to look closely at this aspect of the rural scene. They have discovered that, in some areas at least, the spectacular exploits of 'Captain Swing' or 'Rebecca' were part of a continuous pattern of crime and protest. Dr Peacock tells us that the rural labourer in East Anglia 'protested *all* of the time, and most of the time very effectively indeed'.[1] Direct action was one of the few weapons in his armoury.

Contemporaries were not unaware of this situation. Although some landowners in Parliament praised the quiescence of the peasantry at critical moments, their private correspondence in the early Victorian years was often full of uncertainty and alarm. Other observers of rural society could be more detached, and did much to demolish the pleasant myth of the 'innocence and simplicity' of the peasantry. Some of them relished the task. Middle-class reformers like John Bright, Edwin Chadwick and Thomas Campbell Foster revealed the darker side of village life. So did Thomas Plint and other defenders of the new urban order.[2] Rural workmen, they claimed, were more ignorant, superstitious, immoral and criminal than their counterparts elsewhere. The last accusation proved highly controversial, partly because so much depended on the districts chosen for comparison. While it was true, for instance, that rural Wales and the north west had a low recorded level of serious crime in the middle years of the century, commitments for trial in East Anglia were well above the national average. John Glyde, who made a unique regional study of crime at this time, identified Suffolk villages in which violence and malicious damage to property were more common than in large neighbouring towns.[3] At certain periods, as in 1843–4 and 1849–51, such intimidation and destruction of property reached a massive scale, and indicated that paternalism and deference were vitally fractured.

II

It is difficult to measure the extent and movement of crime and protest during the Victorian years. Many petty session files no longer exist, contemporary opinion could be notoriously unreliable, and newspaper coverage was highly selective. Only after the administrative changes of the late 1850s are we able to calculate the number of crimes known to the police. Even so, all criminal statistics are of limited value. The dark figure of unrecorded crime was undoubtedly important in some rural areas. Judges in Wales in the second half of the century were suspicious of the empty calendars, and policemen there sometimes admitted that violence and petty theft were much greater than most people realized. Farmers were regularly criticized in the early Victorian period for not protecting their property and for not reporting depredations on it. Some of them budgeted for such losses, and in bad years even welcomed the insurance payments for arson. Accusations were also made at this time that farmers sympathized with certain criminals, especially poachers, sometimes letting them off with a warning or a beating. And, finally, many cases were not prosecuted because of the fear of reprisals in the shape of personal violence, animal maiming and incendiarism. In Cheshire and Suffolk this was one popular contemporary interpretation of the phrase, 'the tyranny of the countryside'.[4]

Changes in the character, numbers and efficiency of the police also had an effect on the incidence of crime in the countryside. The traditional form of policing was a mixture of community and private enterprise. Although some observers spoke highly of the work of the old village constables, they were a poor organ of social control and in many districts their impact on crime was very limited. They were essentially a part-time defensive force, owing loyalties to their communities, and unable to suppress major outbreaks of crime or disorder, as the events of 1830–44 cruelly demonstrated. The authorities preferred to rely in an emergency on a system of rewards, special constables and military help. Private policing, too, had long been popular in rural society, with farmers arming their families, employing watchmen to guard their estates, and forming protection societies. Many such associations were established in the south and east during the 1830s, and these paid for professional policemen and met the expenses of prosecuting poachers, sheep-stealers and the like.

Ironically, the cost of these ventures strengthened the widespread opposition to the establishment of a national police force. By the time the County and Borough Police Act was passed in 1856 only about half the counties had appointed paid policemen. From the beginning the country poor were suspicious of the new police, and their arrival caused protests and riots in many areas. Although there were considerable disputes over the impact of the 'blues' on village life, most seemed to agree that they quickly established themselves as an 'improving agency'. Much to the delight of the clergy, the paid policemen imposed new standards of order in the community. They attended fairs, festivals and public houses, and gave a new dimension to the term 'Sunday observance'. They also provided greater protection for persons and property. In Hampshire, Essex and Norfolk families and gangs of sheep-stealers and poachers were ruthlessly dispersed. Night patrols and constant harassment kept the 'idle and dissolute' on their guard, and the Poaching Prevention Act of 1862 legalized the hated practice of searching working people on the road. Again, in Dorset, Norfolk and some other counties the new police were used in a somewhat brutal fashion to remove vagrants or gipsies from the countryside. Finally, they helped to ensure the free and safe passage of goods from one region to another. Altogether, then, one can see why many property owners were quickly converted to the benefits of appointing officers, and why problem villages like Wymondham in Norfolk and Hindon near Bradford in Wiltshire were said to have been transformed by their presence. Even so, it is worth remembering that police numbers remained small in some villages, that criminals and vagrants moved to unpoliced areas, and that episodes such as the remarkable Rebecca poaching raids in mid-Wales could reduce them to helplessness.[5]

Another factor affecting the crime rate was changes in prosecution. In the early Victorian period new legislation and the coming of the new police made prosecutions cheaper, commitments more certain and punishments less severe. The result, much to the chagrin of some contemporaries, was that villagers, especially juveniles, were taken to court for petty theft and minor breaches of the peace that had once been ignored. Much, of course, depended on the initiative of the large property owners. For them, legal prosecutions were only one aspect of the wider question of control and discipline. Landowners who displayed ruthlessness in dealing with the 'Swing' rioters sometimes used mere cautions and confessions during the Game Law controversy of the 1840s and election disputes of the 1860s. In some areas, too, where work was scarce, social prosecution of criminals through loss of job, home and income could be just as effective as legal action.[6] Similarly, the wider village community had its own way of dealing with offenders without resort to law. In the more remote parts of Britain the mock trial and physical intimidation were regularly used in the 1830s and 1840s, and were not unknown two generations later.

It is impossible, therefore, to estimate the extent of crime and protest in the countryside. The labourers were a 'secret people' and all we can say with certainty is that the authorities reacted with alarm in the second quarter of the century and with growing confidence thereafter.

III

Contemporaries attributed much of the tension in rural society to the collapse of mutual respect between classes. The Rev. Henry Worsley of Easton in Suffolk argued in 1849 that crime and protest were the natural result of neglect in a paternalist society.[7] A contrast was drawn between those parts of northern, midland and western Britain where the concept of a one-class society was grounded in the reality of people working, living and playing together, and other districts where important proprietors had distanced themselves physically and culturally from the rest of the village community. Flora Thompson was to write later of the 'Romans' and 'Britons' of the countryside, and her metaphor is a useful one.[8] In parts of the south and east two separate worlds faced each other, the one trying to impose its view of the countryside, justice and history on the other. The Swing riots of 1830 revealed the gulf between rich and poor in the village, but in one sense the protests over the 1834 Poor Law Amendment Act were more significant. For many, this Act was the final confirmation that landowners, farmers and clergymen placed their own selfish economic interests before those of the wider community. And with alienation came sullenness and a desire for revenge:

> It was a matter of congratulation among the men as they talked at work they had succeeded in 'doing' a person in a better position, or even if they had 'sloped summat' from the well-to-do. . . . It is the idea of a legitimate prey, the right to make some folk disgorge, the suggestion of a just reprisal! It is often the same spirit, too, which initiates poaching rather than actual material gain.[9]

Significantly, the major outbreaks of discontent in the years before Arch's union were preceded by sharp increases in rural crime, especially poaching.

Complaints about the commercial and sectional approach of farming people usually revolved around the issues of employer–employee relationships, custom and charity. During the forty years following the conclusion of the Napoleonic Wars the insecurity of the labourers of the south and east took on new dimensions. Their contracts were shortened or cast aside, allowances or perks of fuel, produce and grazing were reduced, and wages were kept low by all manner of devices. Under-employment was widespread, not least amongst the young adults, and unemployment, too, was a permanent feature of villages, like Hawkhurst in Kent and Coombs in Suffolk. This situation bred frustration, especially in areas such as northern Essex and the Norfolk–Suffolk border where the population was very dependent on corn production and where alternative employment was scarce and declining. Various surveys of the 1830s and 1840s revealed that riotous protest and arson were most common in districts and periods of poor employment and low wages, that theft fluctuated with the cost of living index, and that poaching and animal stealing increased noticeably once the harvest money had been spent. Threatening letters and outbursts in court told the same story: 'farmers, we are starven, we will not stan this no longer'. The introduction of machinery and the employment of non-parish labour was often the final insult to families on seven shillings a week and memories.[10]

Such people were unusually sensitive to changes in customary rights and charity. Proprietors in the Victorian years continued to press their claims to Crown, common, waste and forest land, and their actions were sometimes bitterly resented by squatters and inhabitants of the 'open villages'.[11] In Oxfordshire, Norfolk and Caernarvonshire, for instance, there were between 1830 and 1870 long struggles over the loss of fuel, grazing and game.[12] In Wales, and some English districts, many of the crimes of theft, and some of the violence, occurred on disputed or newly enclosed land. What caused particular annoyance was the legislation defining ownership of wild produce, birds, fish and animals. Posters on some south midland farms in the middle of the century warned the poor not to take berries, mushrooms, cress, rabbits and birds. At the same time, attempts were made to limit customs of gleaning corn, root vegetables and fallen wood. Relays of old men, women and children appeared before early Victorian courts pleading their innocence before 'God and tradition'.[13]

Charity was another 'long-established right'. Most villages had received bequests of land, houses and money for the poor, and there were annual gifts of clothing and fuel. However, certain kinds of charity were being criticized at the very time when they were most needed. Donations were increasingly being given not as of right, but on conditions and in a manner that angered working people. Parish lands in East Anglia were sometimes divided into allotments for the 'better class of labourers' or let out cheaply to farmers, and the income used to finance unpopular poor law policies. The battle over charity land and rights has been much neglected by historians, but it was a recurring theme in the protests, threatening letters and reminiscences of village folk.[14]

At the heart of this conflict was the question of poor relief. This relief had long been regarded in some districts as a necessary allowance for the lowly paid and the unemployed. Changes in the administration and size of relief had often provoked an angry response, but the New Poor Law produced widespread disbelief.[15] The poor felt, with good reason, that a right had been replaced by a mechanism of control. Farmers who dominated the boards of guardians manipulated the new system to keep wages low, especially for the young, and to remove the 'idle and desperate' from their parishes. As new workhouses were built, stricter regimes introduced, and rates reduced during the late 1830s and early 1840s, labourers vented their anger on the person and property of poor law officials. 'Better go to gaol than starve or go to the union' became the standard excuse of a generation of rural criminals, and the immediate result in some of the southern and eastern counties was a sharp rise in offences both within and outside the workhouse.[16]

The economic or 'rational' approach to relationships in the countryside was accompanied by an assault on traditional village culture. Once again the targets were the 'idle', 'dissolute' and 'desperate', and the objectives were control, respectability and productivity. The attack, which came from both outside and inside

570

the village, was conducted through the church, the school and the law. The years from 1830 to 1870 saw the disappearance of many holidays, fairs and 'violent and sensual' amusements, and the emergence, in certain parts of Britain, of an alternative recreational pattern. Where popular protests were unavailing, many of the labourers signalled their indifference to the march of progress by their persistent attendance at the beerhouse. Beerhouses, which were legalized by an Act of 1830, were condemned by many observers as the home of rural crime; and there were indeed famous drinking places like the Chequers Inn, Thetford (Norfolk), and Higg's beerhouse in Charlton (Oxfordshire) in which poaching and protests were organized. Ministers, policemen and a new breed of temperance reformers launched several major onslaughts against the village pub and produced a series of waves in the crime statistics.[17]

Law, then, was used in the nineteenth century, as in the eighteenth, to push through radical changes in relation to property, custom, charity and behaviour. The peasantry reacted to these changes in various ways; in mid-Wales emigration was a traditional response; in parts of the south west there were reports of deep fatalism amongst the poorest labourers, but in East Anglia hostility remained near the surface. Certain villages, like the large open communities, seemed especially prone to crime and protest, though much depended on local circumstances. Paternalistic regimes and individual acts of kindness help to explain why places like Langley in Essex remained extraordinarily stable in a sea of discontent. After brief periods of resistance many villages settled down to enjoy a kind of peace in the mid-Victorian years, but others, such as Exning in Suffolk, had an inextinguishable militancy.[18]

IV

A study of crime statistics reveals that the countryside, like Britain generally, experienced a marked rise in the number of offences during the first half of the century, with the highest peak in the early 1840s.[19] The crime rate remained high until the early 1850s and then fell persistently, despite brief recoveries, as in the late 1860s and early 1880s. Within this overall trend, however, there were some interesting developments.[20] Crimes of violence, which formed between one tenth and one fifth of rural offences, continued to worry the authorities until the critical turning-point of the mid-1860s. Typical cases were family and neighbour disputes, drunken brawls and the Sunday pranks of young servants. In the early 1830s and early 1840s the incidence of serious assault reached record levels, and there were reports from East Anglia, Somerset and Cheshire of respectable people being unable to leave their homes after dark for fear of being attacked and robbed.[21] The people who suffered most were farmers, agents, gamekeepers, poor law officials and policemen. At least twenty keepers were murdered in the years 1843 and 1844, and in Staffordshire alone double that number were injured in fights during the sixteen months, September 1860 to January 1862.[22] The new police were also frequently assaulted on their first appearance in the countryside, as the statistics of the late

1850s, and early 1860s indicate. Some of these victims were shot and maimed in the most brutal fashion.

The major crime in the countryside was undoubtedly theft, though one notes a significant decline in reported cases during the second half of Victoria's reign. Earlier, incidents of stealing were very common in difficult years like 1837, 1842 and 1868, and many of them occurred in the winter months. The most notorious form of theft was of farm produce and livestock. Wood, corn, vegetables, fruit and cheese were taken from sheds, barns, fields, allotments and gardens, usually by labourers and their families. The loss of poultry, sheep, cattle and horses was a more serious affair, and was at its height in the late 1830s and early 1840s, although in the south west it was still a prime concern ten years later, and in Cumberland forty years later. In the less policed parts of Lincolnshire, Norfolk and Essex the daily losses were so enormous that weary farmers guarded their herds day and night.[23] Finally, the theft of rabbits, hares, game birds and fish sometimes reached astonishing proportions. In 1843, for instance, one in four convictions in Suffolk was against the Game Laws, whilst in Norfolk over two thousand poachers were fined or imprisoned in the years 1863–71.[24] Many of the poachers were young labourers who took a few rabbits at weekends, but there were also—as in the case of sheep-stealing—gangs based in villages and towns. These gangs, often armed and disguised, virtually controlled isolated parts of the countryside until the time of the Poaching Prevention Act of 1862.[25]

Crimes of trespass and malicious damage formed a small but persistent element in the statistics of rural crime. Unfortunately, it is difficult to distinguish between ordinary criminal offences and those which are regarded as acts of protest. The removal of gates and fences, which so annoyed East Anglian farmers in the first half of the century, was both a common youthful prank and a recognized form of intimidation and revenge. Similarly, prosecutions for trespass and for the destruction of weirs, walls, trees and produce could indicate battles over disputed property and rights of way. The bitter conflict between Welsh landowners and squatters in the later years of Victoria's reign has not yet been researched.[26] The most serious of this category of crimes was arson, and we know that most cases were the result of pique and protest. Rural incendiarism reached unprecedented levels in the period between the Swing riots and the emergence of Arch's union. During the outbreaks of 1843–4, 1849–52, 1862–4 and 1868–9, burning ricks and outhouses were often a daily fact of life for farmers south of a line from the Wash to the Severn, and fires continued to flare in Hampshire, Dorset and certain other counties during later years of tension.[27] In the 1860s, however, there was a change in the character of this crime: an increasing number of these offences were carried out by vagrants. In north Wales during this decade at least forty-nine of the eighty-two people charged with arson at the assizes can be identified as tramps.[28]

Other important groups of rural crime included poor law and vagrancy offences. These were committed by the 'lowest' members of society and reflected economic influences and the initiatives of government and local authorities. A small but

572

constant stream of labourers appeared before the courts charged with deserting or neglecting to support their families, and a more irregular number were found guilty of misconduct in the workhouse. The latter crime, which involved tearing clothes, smashing windows, refusal to work, arson and riot, was especially prominent in the 1830s and 1840s, and again in the late 1860s and early 1870s. During these times, south-west Wales, Norfolk and Suffolk, and parts of the western and home counties, witnessed something of an institutional revolt.[29] Vagrancy offences were also a matter of deep anxiety in these years. In counties such as Cumberland, Merioneth, Kent and Shropshire tramps and gipsies were blamed for almost all petty crime in the countryside. The problem of vagrants was never solved but rather, as the statistics and conferences at the turn of the century demonstrated, it was often simply pushed from one district to the next.[30]

Although vagrancy and certain other offences remained a permanent source of concern in the second half of the nineteenth century, there were, nevertheless, important changes in the composition of rural crime during this period. Cases of assault and stealing, which had once constituted about a half of all petty session proceedings, lost much of their prominence in the criminal statistics. Their place was partly taken by newer categories of crime. In the 1880s and 1890s as many as a quarter of all offences involved cruelty to animals and breaches of the Education and Highways Acts. Villagers still continued to be arrested in large numbers for drunkenness and disorderly conduct, but the high figures of the 1870s and 1880s may well indicate changes in prosecution policy as much as a frightening outburst of debauchery.[31]

By the close of the Victorian era there can be little doubt that the alarming violence which had characterized the 1830s and 1840s had largely evaporated. Reports and reminiscences of the turn of the century tell of village constables who spent much of their time on routine matters, keeping an eye out for vagrants and poachers, and grumbling when called upon to apprehend mere night revellers. Like so many other hamlets, 'Candleford Green' was essentially 'law-abiding'.[32]

V

The relationship between crime and protest in the years before the establishment of a permanent trade union is a particularly difficult matter. Inevitably there is a danger of romanticizing men and gangs who were regarded by working men themselves as private adventurers, willing to exploit the poor and their grievances.[33] Certain offences, however, especially arson, sometimes reflected community anger, and there were others which were overwhelmingly crimes of protest. The sending of threatening letters fall into this category, and the early 1840s saw perhaps the last major outbreak of this form of intimidation. Where this attempt to enforce better conditions failed, labourers resorted, much more than we realize, to the killing and maiming of birds and animals.[34] In years of tension, such as 1837, 1842 and 1849, hundreds of pheasants were poisoned and cattle injured in East Anglia and the counties of the south west. The periodic attacks on farm machinery formed another reminder of workmen's willingness to break the law in their fight for work and better wages. Between 1815 and the 1860s two generations of East Anglian farmers bought threshing machines, ploughs and hoes only to see them destroyed by hammer and fire.[35]

Occasionally the frustration of labourers erupted in major explosions of unrest which covered a large area of the British countryside. Such outbursts occurred in the 1790s, 1816–19, 1822–3 and 1830–1, and their epicentre was usually East Anglia and the counties of the south east. The events of 1830–1, the so-called 'Last Labourers' Revolt', have been well documented by Professors Hobsbawm and Rudé, though subsequent research suggests that the rising was even more widespread and complex than they described. Most counties south of the Scottish border had their share of threatening letters and incendiarism. At their meetings the labourers voiced complaints about many secondary issues from tithes and new machinery to the influx of Irish workers, and on these matters they found certain farmers unexpectedly sympathetic; but the heart of their message was 'more work and higher wages'. The fear which the Swing mobs engendered was reflected in the terrible judicial revenge taken by the authorities: 19 people executed, 481 transported and some 700 imprisoned.[36]

A few years later another series of protests greeted the Poor Law Amendment Act and its implementation in East Anglia and various counties of the south and south west. When the Rev. Maberley of Bourn in Cambridgeshire, and a few other respectable leaders, took the initiative in calling public meetings against the Act the labourers attended in good numbers, but generally violence was their instinctive response. Between 1834 and 1844 riots, arson and attacks on the person and property of guardians were common occurrences in the affected counties. Sometimes labourers tore down half-built workhouses with their bare hands. The climaxes in this particular contest included the bloody 'Battle of Bossenden Wood' in Kent (1838), the attack on Carmarthen workhouse (1843), and the Great Bircham affair in Norfolk (1835), when 800 men confronted soldiers and policemen drafted in to enforce the new government policy.[37]

Between 1839 and 1844 the poor law question merged with more pressing problems of low farm prices, unemployment and wage-cuts. The consequent discontent has been hardly studied by historians, except in two areas. In south-west Wales the accumulated anger of tenant-farmers and labourers exploded in the savage Rebecca riots. These riots, famous for the destruction of toll gates and the burning of farm property, were the occasion for a community rebellion.[38] In many other parts of the country, too, there were angry meetings of labourers, violent demonstrations and a quite extraordinary wave of incendiarism. I discovered evidence of a minimum of 250 fires on the property of farmers, clergymen and poor law guardians in Norfolk and Suffolk during the period October 1843 – December 1844.[39] Villages in Bedfordshire and Cambridgeshire were literally put to the torch. In later years, notably 1849–52,

1862–4 and 1868–9, unrest was again common in the south and east and arson remained a popular form of intimidation; but of greater interest to historians was the slow growth of rural trade unionism.

All these protests were characterized by their localized nature. They were often well organized and supported by the village community, but links between districts were tenuous. The demonstrations and disturbances were also non-political in a formal sense. Political reformers had an influence on the Swing and Rebecca mobs, but generally the rioters were inspired by a sense of natural justice and feelings of revenge.[40] The crime and protest of the first half of the nineteenth century were those of a depressed people, although there were interesting lines of development and shifts in consciousness. If by the 1860s some of the ferocity and vision of lost rights had gone, many labourers entered the trade union era with a greater sense of purpose and independence.

VI

There are at least four important questions to be asked about crime and protest in this period. First, who committed the offences? The myth of the criminal outsider was strong, and had some basis in fact in villages close to large urban centres. The Swing and Rebecca riots were said to have been organized by 'suspicious strangers', and rural crime was attributed to vagrants, gipsies and navvies. One recent analysis of criminal records, however, indicated that theft and violence in the countryside were usually committed by residents.[41] Some of these were members of criminal families and gangs, but the concept of a criminal class with its own sub-culture is hardly relevant to the rural scene. Many rural criminals, including thousands of poachers, were ordinary working men.[42] Arsonists, too, were often young farm labourers with no criminal past. Mobs could be a cross-section of the village population, with its more independent members to the fore. And, finally, there is overwhelming evidence that certain offenders operated with the support of most of the community; people protected wanted men, cheered outside courtrooms, and refused to act as special constables or fire-fighters.[43]

The second question is more complex. What did direct action achieve? We know, for instance, that jobs were saved by it, wage-cuts reversed, mechanization halted and poor law allowances increased.[44] In some areas these successes added to the self-respect and confidence of workmen, but the reverse also seems to have been true. Villages decimated by the transportations and emigrations of the 1830s and 1840s, or stifled by the tight control of the gentry, sometimes developed that bleak fatalism, religious and otherwise, which George Sturt and others discovered many years later.[45] All protests, however, had one common result: they drew public attention to the plight of the labourer: and produced a variety of economic, educational and social initiatives. In the aftermath of each major explosion, new charitable and recreational enterprises were begun, designed to bring classes closer together. Allotments were undoubtedly the most fruitful economic response, though migration and emigration schemes were popular in years such as the late 1840s and early 1850s.[46]

The third question is one which intrigued contemporaries—why did crime and rioting decline in the second half of the nineteenth century? It is a difficult question because this movement in the crime rates was apparently a phenomenon of the western world, and must have been linked to major economic developments, processes of social change and new policing methods.[47] As we saw earlier, the last factor had a considerable impact on life in the countryside. So did the improved employment and wage situation in the mid-Victorian years and the greater ease of mobility consequent upon railways. Perhaps the most complex influences were changes in habits and attitudes. Joseph Arch and others claimed that people had become more law-abiding and less tolerant of those who got their living 'on the side'.[48] If this were so, it had long been an objective of the gentry. Allotments, enclosures and poor law schemes were both economic and moral experiments, and we still know very little of the efforts made to denigrate and remove the independent elements in the village.[49] There is evidence, too, that in the 1840s and 1850s the rioter, the poacher and the machine-breaker were losing much of the crucial support that tenant farmers had once given them.[50] Even so, it may well be that changes in attitude and action by working people were the result not of external pressures but of internal ones.

This brings us to the final question of the relationship between direct action and peaceful methods of protest in the Victorian countryside. It is worth emphasizing that workers' anger took many forms, both before and after the critical years of the 1860s and 1870s. The village meetings, petitions and union activities of Arch's early campaigns had their precursors in most of the southern and eastern counties a generation earlier. Between 1838 and 1846 political meetings and local unions were more common in the country than historians have hitherto realized. Similarly, in the Great Depression illegal acts of intimidation enjoyed a revival in the south. Yet the connections between criminal and peaceful forms of protest do not appear to have been strong, even during some of the Swing troubles. Although the poacher, the arsonist and the union activist often had similar grievances and worked a close regional furrow, there were differences in support, organization and method. The first union leaders were older men and had developed their values, priorities and organizational skills in the militant Nonconformist chapels which had spread like a rash over the countryside during their lifetime. The climate of political and social change and the labourers' improved bargaining position gave these men the advantage, and the underground terrorism of the earlier years gradually faded away.

Notes

1 Dunbabin, 1974, 27.
2 Plint, 1851. Note the biased account of country life in publications like the *League*, and in the evidence of Chadwick and Bright in BPP 1839 XIX; 1846 IX.

3 *Journal of Royal Statistical Society*, XIX, i.

4 For this paragraph, see *Morning Chronicle*, 29 December 1849, Jones and Bainbridge, 1975, and especially the evidence in BPP 1839 XIX, and 1852–3 XXXVI.

5 BPP 1839 XIX; 1852–3, XXXVI. See also Horn, 1976b, 219–21.

6 Glyde, 1856a, 133; Jones and Bainbridge, 1975.

7 Worsley, 1849, ch. 2. Compare Glyde, 1856a, 147.

8 Flora Thompson, 1973, 291.

9 Holdenby, 1913, 26–7.

10 Hobsbawm and Rudé, 1969, chs 2, 4; Amos, 1971, 41–5, 165; *Social History*, I, i, 27–32; *Morning Chronicle*, 8 and 22 December 1849.

11 *Journal of Social History*, VII; E. P. Thompson, 1975; David Jones, 1973; Hay, *et al.*, 1975.

12 For example, Reaney, 1970; *Llafur*, I, iii, 7.

13 Henslow, 1844, 18; Dunbabin, 1974, 46; Samuel, 1975b, 53–61.

14 Some conception of the importance of charity rights and land can be gained from the reminiscences of Ashby, 1961, and Haggard, 1935.

15 For popular opposition to changes in the administration of poor relief prior to 1834, see Amos, 1971, 82–3; Digby, 1972, 168–70; Peacock, 1965, 31–42; Hobsbawm and Rudé, 1969, 69.

16 It is difficult, as Thomas Campbell Foster found, to establish a precise connection between anger over fear of the workhouse and the readiness to commit crimes, but the evidence of prison chaplains and the prisoners themselves leaves little room for doubt. See, for instance, the evidence of F. Gowing in BPP 1846 IX pt I, 629, and prison reports for Suffolk and Norfolk in BPP 1844 XXIX, and 1846 XXI. See also Glyde, 1856a, 185–7.

17 For remarks about the decline of traditional forms of amusement, the boredom of young workmen and their capacity for drink and crime see Henslow, 1844, 25–6; Kay-Shuttleworth, 1971, I, 604–5, 612–13; Howkins, 1973.

18 See Amos, 1971, 167–70; *Social History*, I, i, 14; Hobsbawm and Rudé, 1969, 59, 81–2.

19 See Wrigley, 1972, ch. 8.

20 The following paragraphs are based on a study of the criminal statistics in BPP 1835–92.

21 See, for instance, BPP 1839 XIX 38–42.

22 *Morning Chronicle*, 19 August 1844; BPP 1849 XLIV 448–50; 1862 XLV 222–8. The Staffordshire figure is based on a study of the *Staffordshire Advertizer* for the period. Such violence occurred on a somewhat lesser scale at a later date. See Horn, 1976b, 233, and the story of assaults on, and murders of, water bailiffs in BPP 1872 X 45, 57–8, 62–3, and in the *Carlisle Journal*, 17 January 1862, 21 January and 22 February 1870.

23 See BPP 1839 XIX, and 1852–3 XXXVI; Dunbabin, 1974, ch. 3; Horn, 1976b, ch. 11.

24 BPP 1846 IX pt I, 784; 1872 X, app. 4. Between 1845 and 1871, two fairly average years, the number of people in England and Wales committed under the Game Laws doubled to some 10,000 (excluding 929 under the new Poaching Prevention Act).

25 The later nineteenth century saw some final and brutal confrontations between poaching gangs, keepers and the police: Horn, 1976b, 233; *Llafur*, II, i. For new evidence on poaching and assaults in a previous era, see Hay *et al.*, 1975, ch. 5; Cockburn, 1977, ch. 9.

26 See BPP 1839 XIX 38, 131, 134. The best starting-point for the Welsh conflict is the

extensive report in BPP 1896 XXXIV.

27 Dunbabin, 1974, 30–6, 52–3, 56–69, 62–70; Caird, 1968, 420, 467–8; Olney, 1975, 26; *Morning Chronicle*, letters of December 1849 – January 1850.

28 *Welsh History Review*, VIII, iii, 335.

29 As far as I know, little research has been done on this form of protest. John Glyde said that 807 people were moved from seven workhouses to Ipswich gaol between 1844 and 1852; Glyde, 1856a, 187.

30 *Welsh History Review*, VIII, iii. See the many references to vagrancy in BPP 1852–3 XXXVI. Ribton-Turner, 1887, is still useful.

31 The battle against alcohol was particularly interesting in Wales and the south west, but one wonders just how much could have been drunk: Glyde, 1856a, 359; Flora Thompson, 1973, 65. For the verdict on the sobriety or otherwise of the labourer at the end of the century see BPP 1893–4 XXXV.

32 Flora Thompson, 1971, 479–84; Horn, 1976b, 237–8.

33 A good deal was made of the anger of working people at certain criminal activity, and of their willingness to use the new police and the law for their protection. See, for instance, BPP 1852–3 XXXVI 21, 68, 127. The former was certainly true, but one should not underestimate the suspicion both of the legitimacy of the property law and of the new police in the countryside. Compare Philips, 1977, 285.

34 The only published account of this is in Dunbabin, 1974, ch. 3. Hobsbawm and Rudé, 1969, 80, underestimated the popularity of this crime.

35 The men attacked machinery for a variety of reasons. See Samuel, 1975b, 61–6; Amos, 1971, 21–4; Peacock, 1965, 70.

36 Hobsbawm and Rudé, 1969; Amos, 1971; *International Review of Social History*, XIX.

37 Digby, 1972, 170–5; Amos, 1971, 82–3, 91–2, 172–3, ch. VIII; Dunbabin, 1974, 36–9; Springall, 1936, 27–31. Some of the East Anglian story can be followed in the *Norwich Mercury*, 1834–6, and PRO: HO 52/26, 73/6–7.

38 Williams, 1955.

39 *Social History*, I, i.

40 Amos, 1971, 118; Hobsbawm and Rudé, 1969, 65–6, 89–90.

41 Jones and Bainbridge, 1975, chs VI, X; *Welsh History Review*, VIII, iii, 324–8.

42 See BPP 1845 XXIV 174, 186, and 1846 IX pt I, 630, pt II, 313. On the other hand, there were gangs in the countryside around Stoke-on-Trent, Nottingham, Chester and Norwich, which seen to have existed almost exclusively by well-organized poaching and stealing. See, for instance, BPP 1839 XIX 113.

43 *Social History*, I, i, 16–17; Dunbabin, 1974, 34–5, 52–3; Amos, 1971, 91, 108–12, 161. Sometimes workmen seemed keen to help the authorities, but the reasons for this varied: Amos, 1971, 65, 91.

44 E. P. Thompson, 1974, 228; Hobsbawm and Rudé, 1969, 281.

45 Hobsbawm and Rudé, 1969, 288–91.

46 *Social History*, I, i, 35–6. The subject of allotments deserves a major study; their introduction was said to have brought about a great reduction in crime: *Morning Chronicle*, 26 December 1849.

47 Zehr, 1976; Gurr, Grabovsky and Hula, 1977.

48 For this, see BPP 1872 X: evidence of Donne and Arch; Ashby, 1961, 3–4.

49 *Longman's Magazine*, July 1883. The question of social control in the village is a

difficult subject. Social activities and behaviour were transformed in places, but observers suspected that the mind and solidarity of villagers remained untouched. Howkins, 1973, 44; BPP 1893–4 XXXV pt I, 13, pt II, 19, and many other entries. On the other hand, there had always been subtle differences within villages.

50 Williams, 1955, 243; Reaney, 1970, 68. Where, as in Wales and Hertfordshire, poaching activities threatened to turn into a wider attack on property rights, the limitations of non-working-class help were obvious: BPP 1846 IX: evidence of Robertson and Pearce. Significantly, many landowners allowed tenant farmers to kill a greater share of the ground game in mid-Victorian years.

42 Labour Organizations

Pamela Horn

I

Labour organizations in the Victorian countryside fell into two broad categories. First of all, there were the friendly societies, which had as their principal aim the provision of financial and medical help to members during sickness and old age as well as benefits to cover funeral expenses at death. Secondly, there were the trade unions, whose objective was the far more dynamic one of raising general living standards by improving wage rates and reducing the hours of work. Each had its own particular role to play in the lives of country workers.

The history of friendly societies is a long one, dating back in the view of some writers to the craft gilds and religious fraternities which protected skilled workers in the Middle Ages. Certainly, by the late seventeenth century there are accounts of friendly societies which would have been recognizable as such to a nineteenth-century club member.[1] But it was from the middle of the eighteenth century that their numbers began to rise sharply—as with the Beaminster society in Dorset which was formed in May 1762 for 'Parishioners under 30 years of age'. Members were to pay a 3s. entrance fee and a contribution of 2d. per week towards a sick benefit scheme, while meetings were to be held every six weeks on a Monday evening at a local public house. Fines were imposed on those who disrupted proceedings by swearing, coming into the club-room intoxicated with liquor, causing a quarrel and similar offences. In return, benefits ranging from 4s. to 6s. per week were to be paid during sickness, together with a funeral benefit of £3 and a pension of 2s. per week for members aged between sixty-three and seventy, increasing to 2*s*. 6*d*. per week for those aged seventy and above. An annual dinner or feast was also to be held, preceded by a procession of members walking 'two by two' to Beaminster church, where a 'sermon [was to] be preached by the Vicar or Curate of the parish'. Any members who failed to take part in the procession 'regularly in their proper places' would be fined the substantial sum of sixpence. In aims and organization this society was similar to countless fellows in other rural communities during the eighteenth and nineteenth centuries. Indeed, the Beaminster society itself survived in substantially unchanged form until its dissolution in 1892.[2]

But it was following the passage of the 1834 Poor Law Amendment Act that the friendly societies became most popular, as small craftsmen and labourers, anxious to avoid the harshness and stigma of poor relief, made what provision they could to help one another in times of sickness, accident or death. One of the poor expressed a widespread attitude in declaring: 'We must look out for ourselves, and provide for a day of sickness and old age, now that there is no parish to look to.'[3] And the club banner at Bledington in Gloucestershire expressed the common sentiment with its device of clasped hands and its slogan: 'Bear ye one another's burdens.'[4]

In the early days many of these clubs, like the Beaminster and Bledington societies, were purely local affairs, based upon a single village or town, and often with little financial stability since scant attention was paid to actuarial principles when their rules were formulated. Membership was generally too limited to permit them to meet any unexpectedly heavy drain upon resources, so that 'an epidemic or the bankruptcy of a farmer' might ruin some of the smaller bodies. Other critics felt that rather than being instruments for the encouragement of prudence and thrift, they were often merely an excuse for convivial meetings and for the holding of an annual feast— which might in itself almost exhaust their reserves when it was a substantial dinner washed down by large quantities of beer. In fact, as one witness to the Royal Commission on Friendly Societies sourly remarked in the early 1870s, a number of men merely joined a club because 'it had the best feast and the pleasantest meetings every month'.[5] Its financial strength and stability were little considered.

A further weakness was that in the earlier years many of the smaller organizations were established on the 'dividing' principle, so that every five or seven years there was a share-out of funds, and then the whole process would start again. Under this arrangement a man 'might find that he was not eligible for re-election because of age or health, and so found himself without assistance when he most needed it'.[6] However, by the middle of the nineteenth century some of these problems were being overcome as the larger and more secure national societies, like the Oddfellows and the Foresters, became increasingly common in country districts. In Dorset, for example, the number of lodges attached to the Manchester Unity of Oddfellows had increased from three in 1845 to thirty-one by 1875, and in Norfolk from forty-eight to ninety-six over the same period.[7] In addition, the Friendly Societies Act of 1875, by encouraging the registration of the smaller societies and by tightening up their financial administration, helped to foster a more responsible attitude to management in the final quarter of the nineteenth century.

Certainly both landowners and farmers encouraged their workers to join benefit clubs by offering prizes at the annual agricultural shows to those men who had been members longest. In some villages, indeed, the local gentry would subscribe towards a society's working expenses—as they did to the clothing and coal clubs which likewise flourished in many communities. (A survey of south Warwickshire parishes in 1893 revealed between twenty and thirty clothing and coal clubs, together with twenty-four pig insurance societies and, in one village, a cow insurance society.)[8] It was felt that the thrifty man would be a more careful worker—and also one less likely to be a burden on the poor rates. Typical of the provision made, therefore, was that of the Loughborough Agricultural Association, which in September 1871 gave a prize of two pounds to Joseph Bramley of Kingston, who had been a friendly society member for fifty-six years.[9]

Friendly societies were one way in which men could learn to work together and run their own affairs, while on club nights they had the opportunity to discuss topics of common interest. Both of these aspects were to be of importance when the time came for the formation of agricultural trade unions. Unlike workers in many other industries, farm labourers came relatively late to the idea of unionism. Admittedly the first unsuccessful attempts at combination had been made in the 1830s—with the 'Tolpuddle Martyrs' of Dorset in 1833–4 one obvious example that springs to mind. But their impact was both restricted in scale and short-lived. It was not until the later 1860s, at a time of rising prices and of agitation among urban workers for the 1867 Reform Bill to extend the parliamentary franchise, that sustained interest in unionism began to appear in the rural areas. Among the counties affected at this time was Buckinghamshire, where a Buckingham Farm Labourers' Union was formed in the small parish of Gawcott in the spring of 1867. In a handbill issued in March of that year the men appealed for a wage of 12s. per week, so that they might live 'not as paupers, but by our own industry'.[10] In their efforts to secure higher wages they had a measure of success. But in terms of leadership and in area of recruitment the union was too limited to make any lasting impression.

II

Other attempts at combination were also made at around this time, so that in 1866 an ephemeral Agricultural Labourers' Protection Association was established in Kent, with a similar body set up in the following year in the vicinity of Leicester. However, it was not until 1871 that a more permanent organization was at last established, centred upon the counties of Shropshire and Herefordshire and operating under the name of the North Herefordshire and South Shropshire Agricultural Labourers' Improvement Society. It was an essentially peaceful organization, with the slogan 'Emigration, Migration, but not Strikes'. At its peak it claimed a membership of about 30,000 in six different counties, and one of its main achievements was the dispatching of 'surplus' labour from low-wage Herefordshire to better-paid employment in Yorkshire, Lancashire and Staffordshire.

In the months that followed, similar organizations appeared in Leicestershire and Lincolnshire, the latter under the leadership of a local republican agitator named William Banks.[11] Each had as its principal objective the improvement of wage rates at a time of sharply increasing prices and of general trade boom. Yet, despite these pioneering ventures, it was from agitation among the labourers of south Warwickshire that the prime inspiration of the rural union movement was to derive. The Warwickshire men began to combine in February 1872 under the leadership of Joseph Arch, a forty-five-year-old hedgecutter from the village of Barford and a Primitive Methodist local preacher. Arch was a man of great determination, and as he stumped the countryside addressing meetings during the wet spring of 1872 he was able to instil some of his steely qualities into his listeners. For, as he subsequently wrote: 'All that stirring time I felt as if there was a living fire in me. It seemed to me that I was fulfilling a mission; that I had been raised up for the work. . . . The people responded nobly to the call.'[12] Many of the union songs of those days paid tribute to his role—as in the chorus of 'We'll All Be Union Men':

> Joe Arch he raised his voice,
>   'Twas for the working men,
> Then let us all rejoice and say,
>   We'll all be Union men.[13]

The timing of this upsurge of militancy is significant, for it came at the end of a period of prosperity for English agriculture—albeit a prosperity in which the farm worker had shared to but a limited degree. At the same time the passage of the 1871 Trade Union Act had drawn attention to the legal and financial benefits which unions could now enjoy, while the success of a contemporary movement for a nine-hour working day among engineers and builders further underlined the possible benefits of combination. It is notable that one of the early demands of the agricultural unions was for a nine-hour day, though this was later dropped when the main attention of the men turned to securing higher wages and an end to the truck system in wage payments.[14] By the early 1870s the isolation and ignorance of rural labourers were gradually being eroded. Thanks to the availability of railway excursions, increased elementary school provision, cheaper newspapers and the activities of emigration agents, their knowledge of the outside world and its prospects was steadily increasing.

III

Once the Warwickshire men had formed their union they were anxious to achieve positive benefits from it as quickly as possible. So, early in March 1872, they put forward demands for an increase in wages to 2*s*. 8*d*. a day and a reduction in the hours

583

of work. These proposals were incorporated in a circular letter which was sent to local farmers in the Wellesbourne area. The latter ignored the missive, believing that the new organization would prove too weak to support effective industrial action. But on 11 March their complacency was rudely shattered when the men came out on strike.[15]

Press publicity followed rapidly, and from an early stage money began to flow into the union's coffers, sent by a sympathetic general public anxious to help provide strike benefit—for most of the men were too poor to have resources of their own to fall back upon. A number moved to better-paid employment elsewhere in England, while a few emigrated to New Zealand and, less happily, to Brazil. But most stayed in their home community and were eventually rewarded with an increase in pay. The dispute was finally wound up in the middle of April, but its effect in rousing rural workers in other parts of the country was a good deal more permanent. As the *Eastern Morning News and Hull Advertiser* of 8 April 1872 put it:

> Two years ago a strike of agricultural labourers would have been deemed impossible. It was believed that our clod hoppers were incapable of combination. Yet, now that a combination has been effected, that a strike has been struck, the movement is spreading over the country with marvellous rapidity.[16]

In the meantime, on 29 March at a large demonstration held at Leamington, the new Warwickshire Agricultural Labourers' Union was formally established under the leadership of Joseph Arch. Two months later this body was to form the nucleus of the National Agricultural Labourers' Union, the first national society ever to cater for farm workers. By now Arch's fame had spread throughout the countryside, and although not all of the local unions which sprang up in these hectic weeks joined the N.A.L.U.—the Lincolnshire Labour League and the Kent and Sussex Union were two which stayed out—there were representatives from most of the counties in southern and central England among the sixty or so delegates who attended its inauguration at Leamington. Their speeches were punctuated with 'devout utterances of "Amen", and "Praise Him"'. For many of the most active leaders of the new organization were, like Arch himself, local Methodist preachers. Indeed, in the three counties of Lincolnshire, Norfolk and Suffolk alone, 95 per cent of the leaders whose religious affiliations can be traced were Methodists of one kind or another.[17] And in many respects the forms of meeting adopted by the union were adaptations of Primitive Methodist practice: 'Social, missionary and fund-raising elements were characteristic of the tea meetings held by both organisations. Premises and equipment were lent between the two.'[18]

There was more than a hint of millenarianism, too, in some of the speeches made at this first gathering. As one delegate declared: 'Sir, this be a blessed day: this 'ere Union be the Moses to lead us poor men up out o' Egypt.' While another man, deliberating on the ways of Divine Providence, declared that 'he were remoinded o' many things in th' Scripters, more perticler o' th' ram's horns what blew down th' walls o' Jericho, and frightened Pharaoh, King of Egypt'.[19]

Once the preliminary arrangements had been completed, Arch was unanimously elected president of the National Union. In the following month a sympathetic Leamington newspaper owner and journalist, J. E. Matthew Vincent, who had agreed to act as union treasurer, also helped it to launch a newspaper, the *Labourers' Union Chronicle*. This latter was to provide a valuable link for the movement, since in its pages could be found reports of branch and district assemblies from all over the country, as well as general discussions of union policy. Within two years it could boast a circulation of over 50,000, and it is significant that both the Kent and Sussex Union and the Lincolnshire Labour League also had newspapers of their own from an early stage.

In the months that followed the formation of the N.A.L.U. the pressure for higher wages continued. But one of the major weaknesses of the movement was that it never managed to recruit a majority of farm workers. Even at its peak in the spring of 1874, when there were around 86,200 N.A.L.U. members, plus perhaps a further 49,000 belonging to other independent organizations like the Lincolnshire Labour League, this was still a small minority of the one million or so male and female agricultural labourers, shepherds and farm servants employed in England and Wales.[20] Even in the best unionized counties the N.A.L.U. was unable to recruit more than about one in three or one in four of the men. In part this was due to the nature of agricultural employment itself, with small groups of workers in isolated units having little opportunity to meet together to discuss their grievances. Then, too, many of them lived in tied cottages and faced the possibility not only of dismissal but of eviction from their homes if they offended their employers by being over-active in the wrong cause.[21] Nonetheless, despite these difficulties considerable progress was made. In many areas, indeed, pay advances were won without resort to strike action.[22] But farmers and landowners much resented this intervention by 'outsiders' in rural labour relations—and it was a development they were determined to resist. The Earl of Denbigh, for example, warned his workers against 'paid agitators, who are going about deceiving the people as to their true and highest interests', and he threatened to evict from their cottages any who refused to work when 'fair wages and conditions' were offered to them by the farmers; Joseph Arch himself was denounced as an 'agitator, an apostle of arson, who was setting class against class'.[23]

It was against this background that in the spring of 1874 the N.A.L.U. faced its stiffest challenge in the eastern counties—one of the best organized areas in the country—from agriculturalists determined to end once and for all the 'dictatorship' of its officials in wage matters. The immediate cause of the dispute was a demand during February 1874 by labourers in the small Suffolk village of Exning for a rise of 1s. a week. Their employers, who had joined together in the Newmarket Farmers' Defence Association, responded by locking out all union men on their books. In this unplanned, almost casual, fashion, therefore, the dispute began. In the months that followed it spread to many of the surrounding counties, with nineteen different union districts eventually involved.[24] Ultimately about 6,000 men were drawn into the conflict, and the National Union executive committee was involved in paying strike benefits amounting to over £24,000. Once the dispute was under way one of the major tasks for Arch and his fellow leaders was to try to raise funds to support the men locked out. But the scale of operation proved too great for them and on 27 July it was decided to recommend those men still out to return to work. In the event some found difficulty in doing so, and although a number emigrated, others were re-employed only on the understanding that they left the union.[25]

Although the outcome was probably inevitable, given the financial fragility of the N.A.L.U. and the scale of expenditure required to support the men in dispute, there is no doubt that the July surrender led to disillusion among many members. From this there developed conflicts among the union leaders themselves, so that in the spring of 1875 J. E. Matthew Vincent, the N.A.L.U. treasurer, broke away to form a new, though short-lived, body called the National Farm Labourers' Union. This had as its main objectives the provision of allotments and smallholdings, and the avoidance of strikes. In the months that followed its leaders and those of the N.A.L.U. indulged in bitter recriminations, in which the small independent unions which had survived also joined. Naturally this did little to encourage their supporters, especially at a time when the movement was already under pressure from a serious decline in arable farming following bad harvests at home and growing imports of cheap grain from abroad. N.A.L.U. membership slumped to a mere 20,000 by 1880, as the union proved unable to withstand 'the economic pressure from without, and the fierce dissensions from within'.[26] Three years earlier, in a desperate attempt to strengthen the loyalty of members, it had embarked on a sick benefit scheme; but sadly, as with many similar bodies outside its ranks, this had served rather to weaken its financial structure than to strengthen it, as withdrawals soon began to exceed payments. In that respect the Kent and Sussex Union had a rather more successful career, with the arrangement of voluntary 'good feeling' collections from an early stage to cover sickness, bereavement, emigration expenses and similar matters. Eventually, in the autumn of 1874, the union decided to establish a permanent sick fund of its own.[27]

IV

By the early 1880s, then, due to the general economic difficulties, wage rates were beginning to fall back from the peaks achieved in the upsurge of 1872–4 as employers reacted to the drop in food prices by cutting labour bills. Paradoxically, the cheapening of foodstuffs did mean that, despite their smaller cash earnings, the real incomes of most labourers rose in the 1880s. Even cash payments did not fall to pre-1872 levels. Nevertheless, the fact that unions could give so little protection in the vital matter of wages served to add to the disillusion of their members.

By this time a number of the remaining unionists were turning away from purely economic concerns to the political field, pressing for a widening of the franchise to rural workers to match the rights given to townsmen in 1867. Even in the early days franchise reform had been a feature of N.A.L.U. policy, with the *Labourers' Union Chronicle* putting the acquisition of the vote second only to higher wages as a union objective as early as June 1873. Although in the final pressure for reform in 1884 the union's influence was weakened by losses of membership—with support for the N.A.L.U. down to a mere 15,000 by the end of 1883—Arch, at any rate, did not allow himself to be downcast. During the exciting months as the Bill passed through Parliament he addressed many village meetings on the issue, speaking from a Liberal standpoint—he had long been a strong supporter of the Radical wing of that party.

Rural householders were admitted to full political rights in December 1884, and at the general election held in the following year Arch was elected Liberal member for the North-West Norfolk constituency. His success was indicative of results in other rural areas where Liberal gains were also recorded. Unfortunately from his point of view, the shadow of Irish Home Rule hung over the new Parliament from the beginning, and when the Liberal Party split over the issue in the early summer of 1886 Arch was among the pro-Home Rule supporters of Gladstone who lost their seats at the general election held shortly after. For him and for the union the next years were bleak ones. In the face of agricultural depression and dwindling support there was little that could be achieved, and by 1889 N.A.L.U. membership had slumped to a mere 4,254, while that of the Lincolnshire Labour League had dropped to only ninety, as compared with the 18,000 or so it had claimed in 1873.[28] The Kent and Sussex Union had by this time become involved with the recruitment of general labourers rather than solely with those working on the farms, and in 1892 it changed its name to the London and Counties Labour League and moved its headquarters to London.

However, just as the demise of the whole movement seemed imminent, an upsurge of trade, coupled with the successful outcome of a strike by London dockers, gave a brief reprieve. Poorly paid workers in a whole variety of industries—including agriculture—were inspired to combine once more. The N.A.L.U. shared in this revival, particularly in Norfolk, where it had to thank the tireless efforts of the local organizer, Zacharias Walker, also an active Primitive Methodist lay preacher. Here a membership of over 12,000 was recorded in 1891, and in the general election held in the following year Arch recovered his seat as Liberal member for North-West Norfolk—a position he continued to occupy until his retirement from public life in 1900.[29]

The N.A.L.U. was not the only body to benefit from this change of fortune. Even the Lincolnshire Labour League pushed up its membership to almost 300 by 1890. But, more significantly, a Radical organization called the English Land Restoration League, set up in 1884 to promote land tax reform, now sought to win farm labourers to its cause by supporting a number of county agricultural unions. It also aimed to improve wages and housing conditions in rural areas. Even the London Dockers' Union, concerned at the ability of farm workers to migrate to the capital and undercut the wages of its members, recruited briefly among rural labourers in Oxfordshire and Lincolnshire in the early 1890s.[30] But it was the Land Restoration League which was the more effective of these two bodies. Its first 'missionary' tour was organized in 1891 in Suffolk, where its representatives worked alongside the newly established Eastern Counties Labour Federation, whose headquarters were at Ipswich. The campaign was a success and was quickly followed by others, with county unions springing up in Norfolk, Wiltshire, Berkshire, Hertfordshire, Herefordshire and Warwickshire. But apart from the Eastern Counties Labour Federation, which in 1892 claimed a membership of almost 17,000, the new organizations had little success. In some cases their Radical leadership, and the fact that farm labourers were not prominent on their executives, may have contributed to this failure. Thus the Berkshire Union was financed largely by two middle-class Socialist sisters from the small town of Wokingham.[31] Perhaps not surprisingly in view of its financial weakness the rule book of this latter society carefully stated in 1892: 'Our members are requested to observe that they must not go on strike without the written authority of the Executive Committee, as we are anxious to avoid strikes in all cases if possible. Arbitration is more efficient than strikes.'[32] At that stage the union had a membership of about 570 out of a total agricultural work force in Berkshire at this time of over 17,000, including both male and female labourers.

Everywhere, in fact, the rural revival proved short-lived, for the early 1890s saw a fresh onset of general economic recession and, in rural areas, the serious effects of drought upon crop yields. Arable farmers were hit by the continuing importation of cheap foreign grain—in 1894 wheat prices reached their lowest level for the century—and meat and dairy producers were facing increased competition from abroad. Inevitably the bargaining position of the unions weakened, and one by one they collapsed. The N.A.L.U. itself was wound up in 1896, and in the following year the English Land Restoration League abandoned its rural campaigns. The remnants of the Kent and Sussex Union disappeared in 1895, and although the Lincolnshire Labour League claimed a membership of twenty-one in 1900, it was to all intents and purposes moribund.

V

Yet, despite this decline, there were some gains to show for this second brief spurt of agitation. Wage rates had been raised for many labourers in the initial upswing, and these gains were largely retained in the years that followed. In addition, when the first parish councils came into being at the end of 1894 labourers in villages where branches of trade unions still survived stood a greater chance of being elected to the new bodies. Thus, of the Norfolk parish elections a contemporary declared: 'The success of the Norfolk labourers [placed] them in the van of the army of labour; they have without doubt achieved a signal victory.' In Warwickshire, ninety-one 'labourers' candidates' were elected with the support of the county agricultural labourers' union, fifty-four of them being farm workers and the remainder artisans and tradesmen adopted and run by the local branches of the union.[33] Elsewhere labourers were often too diffident to put themselves forward for election against more influential members of village society. And even the limited progress registered in 1894 was not maintained at subsequent contests. None the less, despite their weaknesses, without these union ventures of the 1890s 'a whole generation of labourers would have grown up without experience of combination'.[34]

Perhaps the fairest assessment of the role of agricultural unions in the later nineteenth century has, in fact, been made by Ernest Selley:

> Though the Unions did not succeed in permanently improving the labourer's economic position, they gave him a taste of power. He was no longer a submissive, inarticulate beast of burden. His back had been straightened; he stood erect and took his own measure. The Unions had given him knowledge; they had given him a voice. . . . In villages where formerly there had been practically no communal life, the Unions had succeeded in drawing the labourers together in social intercourse.[35]

However, not all contemporaries would have agreed with his favourable comments. In particular, the Nonconformist-led unions were accused by many village clergymen of undermining relationships between themselves and their parishioners—as at Chearsley, Buckinghamshire, where the incumbent complained in 1875:

> Lately the agents of the N.A.L.U. have been in the parish, & held meetings, often on Sundays, & they have disquieted the people, & said much against Landowners & the Clergy . . . there can be no doubt that the congregation diminished, & the people became irregular in their attendance, & careless about their public religious duties.[36]

Even when the union movement had faded away, some of the parish clergy's residual suspicion survived to poison relations between the incumbent and his flock over such matters as distribution of village charities and allocation of allotment land. In this regard it is worth noting that when Arch died in February 1919, the *Church Times* declared in an obituary:

> It is regrettable, when we look back to the early days of the agitation he led, to recall the loss of a great opportunity by the country clergy. They might have won the labourers to the Church, but, largely ranging themselves on the side of the squirearchy, they alienated, in too many instances, their struggling parishioners. Since then a more enlightened spirit has prevailed but there remains much leeway to be made up.

Meanwhile, as the days of Arch and the N.A.L.U. faded, men who were dissatisfied with village life left the land for good, creating fears of 'rural depopulation' in the last years of the nineteenth century.[37] In fostering the spirit of independence which made that migration possible the rural unions undoubtedly played an important role.

Notes

1 Gosden, 1961, 1–2.
2 Hine, 1928, 115–20.
3 Russell, 1975, 3.
4 Ashby, 1974, 376.
5 BPP 1872 XXVI Q 26, 357.
6 Springall, 1936, 60.
7 Gosden, 1961, 31.
8 Ashby and King, 1893, 203.
9 *Loughborough Advertiser*, 5 October 1871.
10 Bucks. RO: Gawcott labourers' handbill; Horn, 1973, 298–301.
11 Dunbabin, 1974, 74.
12 Arch, 1898, 78.
13 Sage, 1951, 20.
14 Horn, 1971, 19, 47.
15 *Ibid.*, 49.
16 Russell, n.d., 18; Horn, 1972, 89–92.
17 Scotland, 1977, 4.
18 Gurden, 1976, 5.
19 'Labourers in Council', *Congregationalist*, 1872, 421.
20 Horn, 1971, 24, 73.
21 *Ibid.*, 52.
22 Horn, 1976b, 132.
23 Sage, 1951, 14; Horn, 1974c, 134.
24 Green, 1920, 56.
25 Horn, 1971, 109–10.
26 Green, 1920, 69.
27 Arnold, 1974b, 84–5.
28 Dunbabin, 1974, 80–1.
29 Horn, 1971, 206–10.
30 Horn, 1974a, 19–20.
31 *Reading Observer*, 2 July 1892, 30 June 1894.
32 Rule 30 of the Rules of the Berkshire Agricultural and General Workers' Union: PRO FS 7.18.817.
33 Horn, 1976b, 142–3.
34 Peacock, 1962, 177.
35 Selley, 1919, 80, 82.
36 Bodleian Library, Oxford: MS Oxf. Dioc. Pp. c. 340.
37 Orwin and Whetham, 1964, 332–3.

43   The Rural Poor

Anne Digby

I

'A sentimental journey in search of the horrible' was one reaction to the *Morning Chronicle*'s reports on the condition of the rural poor during 1849–50.[1] The bucolic idyll was revealed as a convenient sentimentalism, and life for many labourers and their families only a lingering, dragging existence. The alleged rigours of the pauper inside the country workhouse were exposed as luxuries when compared with the deprivations of independent labouring life. Moreover, the rural labourer— sustaining an autonomous existence on low wages—resented being assessed for poor rates which were used to maintain the superior life-style of the indoor pauper.[2]

This investigation into the social conditions of the early Victorian countryside gave a uniquely detailed picture of rural poverty, though enquiries which followed it tended to focus on the menacingly urgent problems of deprivation in the towns. The more dispersed poverty of the countryside remained substantially hidden, and even in its more obvious manifestations it bore a quaint rusticity which induced nostalgia in observers rather than remedial activity. In any case, those who, like Thomas Hardy, knew the Victorian countryside intimately felt that the condition of the agricultural labourer had improved markedly during the second half of the nineteenth century.[3] Subjective impressions were substantiated to some extent by objective data which revealed that during this period agricultural wage rates had risen from under 10s. to 15s. a week. Yet in comparison with the industrial worker, whose wages had also risen, the farm worker remained very poorly paid. The ratio between agricultural and industrial wage rates was almost static in this period: the agricultural labourer continued to receive only half the wage of his industrial counterpart.[4]

In the early twentieth century, scientific investigations into rural poverty followed the pioneering urban studies of Booth and Rowntree. But like the earlier reporters on the *Morning Chronicle* researchers were as puzzled at the way in which the agricultural labourer eked out an existence as was the labourer's wife herself. How the household budget was balanced remained something of a mystery; clearly, economic survival involved continued struggle and a fair measure of good fortune.[5] A study of the agricultural village of Ridgmount in Bedfordshire during 1903 concluded that 34 per cent of the population was in a state of primary poverty such that their income was insufficient to keep them in physical health. This figure was even worse than the comparable urban statistics of 30 per cent of the population living in primary poverty in London and 28 per cent in York, which had been recorded by Booth and Rowntree. As in these studies, a poverty cycle was discernible in Ridgmount. The worst deprivation occurred during childhood, recurred after several years of marriage when there were a number of dependent children, and it was experienced again during old age. Only during the intervening stages of early adulthood, and again when the children were old enough to earn wages, might the agricultural labourer hope to rise above the poverty line. Common reasons for Ridgmount families sinking into primary poverty were the death, desertion, ill-health or old age of the wage-earner, and the presence of a large number of children. What accounted for half the families sinking below the poverty line, however, were the effects of irregular work and low wages.[6]

The low wages of the agricultural labourer in the southern counties (which included Bedfordshire) had been described by James Caird in 1851. He discerned two rural nations in one kingdom, and diagnosed the cause in the over-stocked labour market of southern England. Here average weekly wage rates were only 8s. 5d., whereas in the northern counties the proximity of mining and manufacture forced farmers to pay average wages of 11s. 6d. if they were to retain labour in the countryside.[7] In the mid-nineteenth century the labour surplus of the south, with its accompaniment of low wages and high poor rates, was often wrongly blamed on the settlement provisions of the poor law. Rural labourers were likened to serfs shackled to the soil by provisions which restricted the right of relief to the parish of settlement or, after 1865, to the union of parishes. In reality the settlement laws did little to check labour mobility, as was shown by substantial migration from village to town in the Victorian period.[8] The disparity between the standard of living of rural and urban inhabitant was sufficiently great to break the psychological fetters of inertia which had been forged by the abject poverty of the rural labourer. For many, the benefits of social paternalism in the village community, and the better health enjoyed by the rural inhabitant, were not sufficient to offset his low, precarious earnings and his poor cottage accommodation.

By the end of the Victorian era the migration of the rising generation from the land had led to widespread complaints by farmers about scarcity of labour, its indifferent calibre, and the increasing average age of the farm worker.[9] These demographic changes altered the nature of rural poverty and pauperism; whereas the Royal Commission on the Poor Law of 1832–4 had focused on the needs of the able-bodied labourer in the countryside, the later investigation of 1905–9 emphasized those of the aged and infirm.[10] By this time the plight of the old rural labourer aroused widespread sympathy, since it was recognized that a lifetime of meagre earnings had made it all but impossible for him to subscribe to a benefit club or friendly society. His usual recourse was to apply for poor relief at a meeting of the board of guardians at the union workhouse:

> Hodge, who, Atlas-like, supported on his shoulders the agricultural world, comes in his old age under the dominion of his last masters at the workhouse. There, indeed, he finds almost the whole array of his rulers assembled. Tenant farmers sit as the guardians of the poor for their respective parishes; the clergyman and the squire by virtue of their office as magistrates; and the tradesman as guardian for the market town.[11]

II

This commonplace example of an old agricultural labourer—a deserving case needing help because of poverty rather than destitution—serves to uncover some of the deficiencies in the Victorian philosophy of social welfare. The main responsibility of local guardians of the poor was to relieve destitution, a duty of which the central Poor Law Board periodically reminded them in its attempt to keep alive the spirit of the Poor Law Amendment Act of 1834. Yet in the countryside of southern England the line of demarcation between poverty and destitution was imperceptible during the mid-nineteenth century. Even the central board admitted that the destitute pauper in the workhouse enjoyed a better material standard of living than the independent poor.[12] Equally problematical for administrators of both poor relief and charity were the ethical distinctions necessary, because poverty was often seen as arising from individual moral failure, and because it was thought desirable to assist the deserving poor on better terms than the non-deserving. The way to achieve this, according to the Charity Organization Society (founded in 1869), was for charitable agencies and guardians to operate in separate but co-ordinated spheres, with official relief reserved for destitute and non-deserving cases. This parallelism was accepted in the celebrated Goschen Minute of 1869, written for the metropolitan area by the president of the Poor Law Board, and highly influential in central poor law policy in the late Victorian era. It was approved by the authors of the majority report of the Royal Commission of 1905–9 in their recommendation of voluntary aid and public assistance committees. But this blueprint of social welfare was not implemented administratively in the Victorian countryside: the Charity Organization Society remained almost entirely urban in its organization, and liaison between rural boards of guardians and charitable trustees or benefactors was minimal. A fundamental weakness in the scheme was the economic inadequacy of charitable resources to sustain their designated role of assisting the large numbers of deserving poor. In practice, the concept of sheep and goats within the village community served not so much to separate the spheres of charity and poor relief as to determine policy within the poor law. The non-deserving poor (including the mother with illegitimate children, the poacher, the drunkard, and the vagrant whose immorality or laziness was held to have led to penury) were offered indoor relief in the workhouse. Deserving cases (including the widowed, sick, unemployed or aged who had fallen on hard times through adverse circumstances beyond their control) were given outdoor relief in their own homes. In these circumstances private charity to the deserving formed a supplement, rather than an alternative, to poor relief.[13]

Rural philanthropy consisted both of endowed charity (mainly the product of past generosity in the form of bequests) and voluntary charity (involving contemporary, private benevolence). Endowed charity in the form of almshouses or pensions for the aged reduced the numbers on the poor rate but in its commonest form of doles it was held to have done little to reduce pauperism. In spite of the efforts of the charity commissioners to put these endowments to more constructive educational uses, Christmas doles of coal, clothing, blankets, bread, meat, or money continued to be made to the poor of many parishes. Contemporaries criticized the indiscriminate distribution of these alms and rightly suggested that they pauperized as much as did outdoor relief.[14] In contrast to the defects of much endowed charity, private benevolence was supposed to elevate the moral character of the recipient; it increased his self-respect and therefore helped him towards the desirable goal of self-help. The charitable donor also allegedly benefited by the exercise of moral discipline; he chose the object and amount of his charitable contribution instead of participating only in the passive routine of paying poor rates. In practice, private almsgiving did show more social sensitivity to individual need than the bureaucratic mechanism of the poor law, although the latter avoided the capriciousness of some personal charitable endeavour.[15]

Both the charitable help of individuals and the relief administered by poor law guardians increased personal contact between members of different social classes. In the early Victorian period particularly, charity was seen as an individualistic, and the poor law as a collectivist, exercise in social control within a disturbed society.[16] Yet the fragmentary character of private charity and the localism of poor law administration meant that their social impact was neither uniform nor comprehensive. The poorest and most populous villages might have few charitable resources to supplement or provide an alternative to the statutory poor law. There might be a striking contrast between the close parish or estate village, with a wealthy paternal proprietor to care for a few residents, and an open parish having several small proprietors, little charity, and many penniless inhabitants.[17] As in the locally financed poor law, where the most poverty-stricken parish (or poor law union after 1865) was rated for the relief of the greatest burden of pauperism, so with voluntary charitable assistance: resources might be least where need was most urgent. Where private charity was available it was valuable in helping the able-bodied labourer who had a large family of children too young to earn. This was an important social category within the rural community which was often neglected by endowed charity with its concentration on the aged or widowed, and was also one for which guardians had to bend the rules in order to assist with outdoor relief.

The precise extent of voluntary charity is unknown, although the cumulative amount was probably considerable. In the mid-nineteenth century the aristocracy, it is estimated, devoted 4–7 per cent of their gross income to charitable purposes, and gentry families applied 1 or 2 per cent.[18] The charitable account book kept by the Le Strange family, who owned some 8,000 acres in west Norfolk, gives an interesting insight into help given by one gentry family for the years 1868–93. About £5 was spent each year on gifts made during personal visits to cottages. Each month a dozen or so presents were made: widows, infirm old people and mothers during confinements received bottles of porter, mutton, or tea; those who were sick were sustained by basins of broth or rice pudding; and the budgets of those with large families were eased by presents of broth, meat, or tea.[19]

Complementing this kind of individual help were the collaborative schemes for helping the village poor which most commonly took the form of coal or clothing clubs. The labourer made regular payments to the club and his thrift was rewarded at the end of a year by a supplement provided by voluntary subscription. The paternal character of these clubs is indicated by their frequent practice of paying out by tickets rather than money at the end of the year—because tickets could be redeemed only at specified retailers whilst money might be squandered on drink. In some purely rural areas all the subscribers' cards for these clubs might be given to local farmers on behalf of those they employed, as occurred in the Cambridgeshire village of Oakington.[20] In these circumstances, where the charitable bond was fastened tightly between master and man, the dividing line between charity and perquisites or payments in kind becomes difficult to draw. Victorian farmers frequently supplemented low money wages by payments in kind, which included cider or beer allowances, coal, wood, potatoes or skim milk, while the provision of potato plots, allotments, or low-rented cottages was not uncommon.[21] One informed observer described these benefits as 'perquisites and privileges'.[22] This emphasizes both the instrumental quality and the unpredictable quantity of many payments in kind, while a modern historian has uncovered the self-interested nature of much Victorian philanthropy in relation to the psychological or social advantages which it conferred on the benefactor.[23] The experience of rural areas suggests that an economic dimension needs to be added to the analysis—the financial benefits which 'charity' conferred on the donor by facilitating the payment of low wages. This aspect of perquisites indicates why the National Agricultural Labourers' Union emphasized that a purely cash nexus between labourer and employer was essential.[24] The success of trade union pressure in achieving this, together with the more limited financial resources of farmers and landlords during the agricultural depression, helps to explain why the river of private charity had diminished to a stream by the end of the Victorian period.

Charity was usually held by Victorian commentators to possess one crucial advantage over the poor law in that it enhanced the independence of the labourer whereas relief had a demoralizing effect. But it is arguable that what was crucial to the rural labourer was the retention of respectability, a state which could be threatened by the wrong kind of charitable assistance and yet survive the acceptance of certain types of relief. Deferential gratitude under a socially paternalistic regime was customary in an estate village, but in less favoured villages where altruism by farmer, squire, or clergyman was infrequent the rural labourer might resent or even reject such charity as was offered. Labourers at Winfrith, in the Wareham district of Dorset, refused during the winter of 1849–50 to collect the prizes given by local farmers to the Labourers' Friend Society and stated that 'they were no longer to be gammoned by such professions'. Occasional acts of generosity in the form of coats with brass buttons, given as prizes by the society, were felt to be no compensation for day-to-day miserliness by farmers who provided squalid cottage accommodation, and paid beggarly wages of 8s. a week in summer and 7s. in winter.[25] Increasingly, charity was felt by more independent individuals in the village community to be less than disinterested humanitarianism but assistance which bore an oppressive cost in social obligation. This feeling was reinforced by the inquiries made by the charity commissioners, which revealed cases of mal-administration by trustees of endowed charities during the mid-nineteenth century.[26] In the Warwickshire village of Tysoe the villagers insisted that what was patronizingly managed by the vicar as the Charity Estate was in fact the Town Lands and, as such, their own property. In a celebrated event, red flannel distributed by the vicar's wife as part of the proceeds of the Charity Estate was washed free of charity and ostentatiously hung out to dry. Another non-deferential village woman insisted on receiving money from the Tysoe Town lands rather than the usual flannel, and explained that in her view such doles pauperized the recipient.[27]

This assertion that charity led to pauperization is significant when set beside contemporary rural attitudes to outdoor relief which was not so regarded. Outdoor relief when sick, temporarily unemployed, widowed, or old was accepted by the Victorian villager in the low-wage sector of southern England as pretty well inevitable, and assistance from the poor law in these circumstances did not lead necessarily either to loss of one's own self-respect or that of one's neighbours. To the rural labourer the distinction between charity and relief tended to be obscured when the same persons—clergyman, squire, or farmer—administered both kinds of assistance. Respectability was lost irrevocably only when social excommunication— indoor relief in the workhouse—was exacted as the price of help.[28] A Suffolk woman expressed this vividly when she commented: 'I'd work the flesh off my bones afore I'd be parted and locked up like a felon' in the workhouse.'[29]

596

III

'As regards shelter and food, an industrious man is much better off if he pauperizes himself. . . . To him independence is privation, whereas pauperism would be comfort.'[30] This comment was representative of those made by informed observers in southern England during the first quarter-century of the union workhouses' operation. The indoor pauper's superior material standard of living was most obvious in diet: the workhouse inmate usually ate meat twice a week whereas the staple fare of the southern labourer was bread and potatoes.[31] 'Lor, bless you, we shouldn't know ourselves if we got meat', observed an East Anglian in 1849.[32] However, there were no queues at the workhouse gates: relative material comfort was more than offset by the psychological discipline enforced. The individual became lost in the inmate, an anonymous unit with cropped hair and shapeless pauper uniform, whose day was regulated by the workhouse bell from the hour of rising at five in summer or seven in winter, to that of going to bed at eight. The tasks of work and the separation of members of families were the most publicized of the deterrent features of the workhouse, but equal weight should be given to the tedious purposelessness, social isolation, and lack of specialist facilities. Rural boards of guardians were notoriously inefficient at organizing such punitive workhouse tasks as oakum picking, so that for much of the time male inmates were either unemployed or engaged in household tasks like chopping wood or pumping water, while the women were more fully occupied in such familiar work as cleaning, cooking, and laundering. The harshness of the classification scheme which separated members of a family into different parts of the workhouse did not affect many of the inmates of country workhouses. Few families were offered indoor relief, since guardians were only too well aware that the cost of keeping a farm labourer with a wife and several children in the workhouse was double that of maintaining them in their own home either by wages or outdoor relief.[33] Only small numbers of able-bodied were indoor paupers, and these often consisted of mothers with illegitimate children, unemployed single men, and vagrants. Increasingly, the occupants of country workhouses were therefore not the able-bodied for whom the regime had been designed but children (usually deserted, illegitimate, or orphans), old people too infirm to look after themselves in their own homes, and the chronically sick.[34]

The durable fabric of the workhouse was increasingly unsuited to the real requirements for social welfare of the Victorian rural community. As such it represented a monumental testimony to the superficial analyses of the 1832 Royal Commission and the resulting inadequacy of the Poor Law Amendment Act of 1834. This Act had aimed to revolutionize the existing system of parochial outdoor allowances by offering poor relief to the able-bodied labourer only in a workhouse. Parishes were grouped into unions in order to provide the resources to build and staff the new workhouses. Four-fifths of the unions of the New Poor Law were of a rural or semi-rural nature, although the proportion of the pauper population which lived in them declined from more than a half in 1841 to fewer than a quarter by 1901. Rural guardians built workhouses either in the centre of the union in a purely country setting or, for administrative convenience, on the edge of a market town.[35] Usually the buildings were erected on a cruciform or rectangular plan, the front entrance and windows embellished with neo-classical or Tudor ornamentation, and the surrounding land made into gardens or employed as farm land.[36] Typically, buildings were designed to accommodate from 100 to 300 paupers, and cost from £2,000 to £6,000.[37] The anger of local ratepayers against the ambitious scale of these institutions was averted by long-term loans obtained from private bankers or Exchequer Loan Commissioners. Nevertheless, the magnitude of the enterprise remains puzzling in the context both of widespread farming depression in the years after 1834 and of the groundswell of discontent over high poor rates in preceding years. Presumably the guardians—many of whom were poorly educated farmers—were indoctrinated by the propaganda of the central board into thinking that immediate capital expenditure on the workhouse would produce long-term savings on the relief bill. In the enthusiasm, or perhaps confusion, of implementing a radical new system the inescapable burden of permanent running costs of a large institution was overlooked.

In the late nineteenth century the cost of workhouse administration was highlighted by the declining numbers of pauper inmates. Prolonged agricultural depression had emptied the pockets of rural ratepayers, while lack of resources made it impossible to improve standards for the old and sick inmates by modifying antiquated buildings designed for quite other purposes. Whereas at the beginning of Victoria's reign the newly built workhouses in country areas had compared favourably with old institutions in large towns, by the end of the reign their lack of specialist facilities contrasted strikingly with those of the urban workhouses and infirmaries which had been built in the second half of the nineteenth century. On the other hand, many country workhouses avoided the barrack-like appearance of the town institution and might have the advantage of a more relaxed atmosphere. However, generalizations are problematical since variety rather than uniformity characterized the country workhouse. For example, visitors to one exceptional country workhouse in the early twentieth century found infants playing in a hay field, old men contentedly gardening, and the convalescent sick sunning themselves in an airy courtyard. Not all workhouses had the benefit of enterprising officials as did this one, and bad officers (tolerated by guardians because of nepotism in the making of appointments) might do little to combat the dirt and squalor which continually threatened to engulf an ageing building.[38]

IV

A comparatively small proportion of able-bodied paupers was relieved in a rural workhouse in spite of the policy directives of the central board. The model of Benthamite centralization embodied in the New Poor Law was more successful in theory than in practice; its main success was in stimulating local guardians to submit, punctiliously, satisfying orthodox returns on pauperism to their London masters. Behind this paper façade, many rural boards learnt to manipulate their returns so that sickness appeared to be the reason for giving outdoor relief to the temporarily unemployed or low-paid able-bodied labourer. This was an exception to the general prohibition of such relief promulgated by the central board in its strict Outdoor Relief Prohibitory Order of 1844 and, as such, was permissible. These local initiatives by rural guardians were tolerated by an ineffectual central administration and its over-worked inspectorate. Outdoor relief was preferred by local administrators because it could be justified to the ratepayers as economical while it was humane to the poor.

Relief in aid of wages was the device chosen during the mid-nineteenth century in many unions in eastern and southern England to harmonize the requirements of ratepayer, labourer, and employer. The farmers who were the main group of ratepayers and employers in the countryside also dominated the composition of rural boards of guardians. As a consequence social policy and public money tended to be subordinated to private economic interests in reaching decisions on relief.[39] However, it must be remembered that the settlement laws might operate to the farmers' disadvantage in that they gave a right to relief to those having a settlement in a given parish before 1865, or a poor law union thereafter. Farmers could be forced into employing men with settlements, since if as employers they did not keep a man with wages, then as ratepayers they would have to finance his relief. A small Dorset proprietor commented

> that the farmer was often placed in a difficult position, when he had to take incompetent labourers as well as efficient ones . . . it was well worth consideration that if the farmer were neither to keep the sick nor employ the inefficient labourers rather than let them go on the parish, he might be able to give higher wages to the men who were really competent.[40]

This dilemma was most acute in arable farming areas where the demand for labour during harvest time was far greater than during the rest of the year. In 1890 an urban guardian condemned the practice of farmer guardians in giving 'lavish out-relief during the winter in order to keep the labourers there for the summer'.[41]

The New Poor Law principle of minimizing outdoor relief to the able-bodied was not entirely lost sight of in rural administration. In the pastoral and mixed farming areas of western and midland counties the demand for farm labour was generally more continuous and wages were higher. Here rural guardians found little necessity to grant outdoor relief to the unemployed labourer. And in a few exceptional unions in rural England the policies of the central board were carried out to the letter. The Atcham Union in Shropshire was guided under the firm hand of its chairman, Sir Baldwin Leighton, into maintaining orthodox policies right through the middle of the nineteenth century. Powerful personalities on the boards of other rural unions were activated from the 1870s by the spirit of the Charity Organization Society and systematically reduced outdoor relief to *all* categories of poor. The most notable of these were the Northamptonshire Union of Brixworth under Albert Pell and Canon Bury, and the Berkshire Union of Bradfield under Mr Bland Garland. The latter wrote a book whose title, *From Pauperism to Manliness*, captured the ethos of this movement. The restriction of outdoor relief caused some poor people to migrate, while others were assisted by charity and the remainder suffered hardship. Although the central board was delighted by such rare examples of devotion to the truths of the 1834 Act, local ratepayers gave them no permanent support, and all such experiments eventually foundered.[42]

V

The countryside was not the most dynamic sector of the New Poor Law, except during the workhouse building phase immediately after the 1834 Act. A speaker at the Central Poor Law Conference in 1900 felt that rural concerns were seldom discussed at these annual gatherings. She lamented that guardians from country areas returned home 'with a depressing sense of the impossibility of carrying out the different, admirable reforms they have heard so ably advocated' because the low yield from rural rates made the public hostile to improvements in the institutions.[43] The Poor Law Conference Movement had begun in 1868 with a meeting of those interested in poor law affairs in the west Midlands; this had led to a central conference in 1869, and to the organization of district conferences in all other regions by 1877. In this context it is revealing that the two most rural districts—those of eastern and south-western England—were the most apathetic, and held conferences least often. Evidence given by rural guardians to the Royal Commission of 1905–9 suggests that there was a widespread complacency which was informed by a greater regard for economic pragmatism than for social principle.[44] A comment in a report to the Royal Commission on relief administration in the eastern counties had wider geographical application than this, and provided a fair verdict on the operation of the poor law in country areas at the end of the Victorian period:

> The common aims are to keep down the rates and to assist the poor,
> especially the old people. The workhouse is looked upon as a nursing home
> or infirmary. It is rarely offered as a test of destitution, as the guardians
> believe outdoor relief to be more humane and less costly than indoor.[45]

The farmer-guardians' habitual preoccupation with economy had not been removed even by the Agricultural Rates Act of 1896, which had relieved farm land of half its rating burden.

A study of rural poverty in 1913 found that only in five northern counties did the agricultural labourer earn wages sufficient for him to maintain physical efficiency if he also had to keep a wife and three or more children. An earlier analysis of a Wiltshire village in 1905–7 suggested that two-thirds of the children were living in either primary or secondary poverty.[46] In a situation where poverty was so widespread rural guardians did not so much relieve destitution among the able-bodied as supplement low incomes, while charity might provide an additional increment.[47] Adequate provision for an independent old age was recognized as being virtually impossible for the low-paid farm labourer. Before the provision of old age pensions in 1908 those who were rich in years, but poor in every other possession, received an assortment of assistance. In its piecemeal inadequacy this typified the plight of other categories of rural poor in the Victorian period:

> It is hard to say with any precision how the aged pauper spends the weekly florin or half-crown. Rent, coal, bread, butter, tea, sugar, oil and the burial insurance are the recurring items. The garden supplied vegetables. Neighbours are kind. There are small charities at Christmas from the church. Perhaps a married son pays the rent and a daughter in service sends a few shillings every month or half-yearly. The clergyman leaves something when he calls.... It is a lonely and precarious existence sustained by faith in Providence and the Poor Law. The latter can always be relied on for two shillings a week and the former for something in addition.[48]

Notes

1   *Morning Chronicle*, 30 March 1850.
2   *Morning Chronicle*, 26 January 1850, 14 November 1849, 5 December 1849.
3   Letter quoted in Rider Haggard, 1902, I, 282.
4   Bellerby, 1968, II, 271.
5   *Morning Chronicle*, 26 January 1850; Rowntree and Kendall, 1913, 54.
6   Mann, 1904, 176–8, 192.
7   Caird, 1968, 510–16.
8   Rose, 1976, 32–6. *Transactions of National Association for Promotion of Social Science*, 1869, 560.
9   Rider Haggard, 1902, II, 539, 565–6.
10 R.C. Poor Laws, 1834, 5th ed. 1905 [Cd. 2728] 14; R.C. Poor Laws 1905–9 [Cd. 4499] I, 174, 228.
11 Jefferies, 1880, II, 295.
12 BPP 1836 XXIX pts 1, 6.
13 Webb, 1963, pt 2, I, 457–9; Mackay, 1967, 501–4; Owen, 1965, 211–12; BPP 1909 XLII 737, 739. R.C. Poor Laws, 1905–9, II, 42, 83–4, 223.
14 BPP 1909 XLII 743–4; R.C. Poor Laws 1905–9, I, 292; II, 43–7. Lascelles, 1934, II, 340–4.
15 Burn, 1964, 115, 118; Woodroofe, 1962, 37–8, 51. *Poor Law Conference Reports, 1895*, 1896, 581.
16 Woodroofe, 1962, 48–50; R.C Poor Laws 1834, 5th ed. 1905, 262–4.
17 Havinden, 1966, 113–19; Clifford, 1875a, 185–90, 206–7.
18 F. M. L. Thompson, 1963, 210.
19 Norfolk RO: Le Strange Account Book of Charities, 1868–93.
20 Cambs. RO: P126/1/3.

21 BM Add. MS 40587, ff. 168–70; PRO: MH 32/49 Report October 1837.
22 Clifford, 1875b, 117–20.
23 Harrison, 1966, 357–65, 368, 371.
24 Countess of Warwick, ed., 1898, 87–8, 107; Horn, 1971, 28–9.
25 *Morning Chronicle*, 8 December 1850.
26 Owen, 1965, 204–7, 305–11.
27 Ashby, 1974, 46–9.
28 Davies, 1909, 187–9; BPP 1895 XIV Qs 6725–8.
29 *Morning Chronicle*, 5 December 1849.
30 *Morning Chronicle*, 10 November 1849.
31 BPP 1836 XXIX pt I, 56–9; BM Add. MS 40587 ff. 169, 172, 187 191–4, 217; *Morning Chronicle*, 10 November 1849, 26 January 1850.
32 *Morning Chronicle*, 5 December 1849.
33 BPP 1835 XXXV 169–70, 175; Chadwick, 1842, II, 37; Digby, 1976, 156–62.
34 BPP 1892 XXXVIII 157; BPP 1895 L 21; R.C. Poor Laws 1905–9, I, 53–6, 174.
35 Digby, 1976, 149–58.
36 Longmate, 1974, 286–91.
37 BPP 1836 XXIX pt I, 567–8; 1837 XXXI 253–4; 1837–8 XXVIII 343–5.
38 BPP 1910 LIV 233; *Transactions of National Association for Promotion of Social Science*, 1869, 552.
39 Digby, 1975, 69–83; *Transactions of National Association for Promotion of Social Science*, 1872, 394; *Morning Chronicle*, 8 December 1850.
40 *Transactions of National Association for Promotion of Social Science*, 1872, 409.
41 *Poor Law Conference Reports, 1890*, 1891, 236.
42 Webb, 1963, pt 2, I, 459–62; Mackay, 1967, 533, 539 40, 587 80; *Poor Law Conference Reports, 1889*, 1890, 317–20; *1899–1900*, 1900, 195–203; *1907–8*, 1908, 489–92.
43 *Poor Law Conference Reports, 1890*, 1891, 236.
44 BPP 1910 XLVII.
45 BPP 1909 XLIII 628.
46 Rowntree and Kendal, 1913, 31; Davies, 1909, 287.
47 R.C. Poor Laws 1905–9, II, 48; BPP 1881 XLVI 21.
48 BPP 1909 XLIII 631.

44   Leisure

Robert W. Malcolmson

I

Forms of recreation deserve more attention from social historians than they have usually been accorded. For a culture is fashioned not only through the processes of work and the meanings attached to labour, but also through those occasions of play and festivity which punctuate, and are sometimes intimately a part of, the cycles and routines of manual labour. Recreation was an important component of plebeian culture, complementing the necessities of labour and offering distinctive satisfactions which were highly valued by working people. Festive occasions were very much times of freedom: they temporarily liberated men and women from normal cares and constraints, helped to alleviate the monotony and drabness of everyday life, allowed opportunities for personal indulgence and provided moments of excitement, gaiety, and spectacle—moments to enjoy, to look forward to, to be remembered. They were times of social suspension when the necessities of life could be subjectively transcended. Play and festivity offered, in a sense, an alternative reality to the reality of ongoing labour. A feast, a fair, a communal celebration, a major sporting event— indeed, most recognized holiday occasions—gave a labouring person, as one writer has aptly put it, 'the opportunity to be something other than what work made one'.[1]

During much of the eighteenth century these occasions of play and festivity were widely established and broadly accepted. The long-established holiday calendar, the character of which was determined largely by the seasonal rhythms of agriculture and the celebrations of the ecclesiastical calendar, offered an essential framework for the annual cycle of public festivities. Christmas, Shrovetide, Easter, May Day, Whitsuntide, the harvest: all these festive occasions were widely observed, and each one was marked by its own special customs, rituals, and recreational attractions. In addition, annual parish feasts (or wakes) were held almost everywhere, generally in late spring or in late summer or early autumn. In the early eighteenth century an annual feast was celebrated in at least two-thirds of the parishes of Northampton-shire; around 1730 Thomas Hearne recorded a feast day for 132 places in Oxfordshire or on its borders; and around 1750 at least 122 places in Devon were reported to have a feast.[2] Country fairs were also prevalent—in the 1750s there were some three hundred fairs in the three counties of Essex, Suffolk, and Norfolk—and some of them functioned at least partly as occasions for festivity, entertainment and sociability. There was also a considerable variety of sports and pastimes available to the common people: some were closely associated with a particular holiday, others were practised at various times of the year. Football was very common, cricket rather less so; wrestling and cudgelling (or backswords) were popular in some regions, and quoits, skittles, and bell-ringing were probably widely enjoyed. Bull-baiting and cock-fighting were the most common of the animal sports. And in many places some distinctive annual event was observed, a holiday featuring certain peculiar practices which were rooted in local custom and tradition: Bishop Blaze festivities among the woolcombers (on 3 February), the bull-running at Stamford (13 November), the 'Whipping Toms' at Leicester (Shrove Tuesday), the Haxey Hood customs in the Isle of Axholme (Twelfth Day). The evidence available suggests very strongly that in the mid-eighteenth century traditional forms of recreation in England were thriving, deeply rooted, and widely practised.[3]

From the later eighteenth century, however, many of these recreational traditions were seriously undermined. There are numerous reasons for this, but clearly one of the principal explanations is that men of property were becoming increasingly hostile towards their practice. Previously most gentlemen had tolerated the common people's recreational customs; indeed, some gentlemen patronized, even sponsored, certain festivities and sporting events. But with time these attitudes changed: customs which had once been accepted came to be questioned and often vigorously condemned. Popular recreations were subjected to an exacting 'moral' scrutiny, and their many deficiencies came to be widely publicized. The movement of evangelicalism was of central importance to these cultural changes: it grew from strength to strength from the later eighteenth century, and it offered a determined and powerfully backed critique of the people's pastimes. Some practices, such as those involving cruelty to animals, were especially vulnerable to the reformers' attacks, though the movement for moral improvement did not confine its attention to blood sports: it was concerned with a broad range of popular behaviour, including Sabbath observance, the enjoyment of pleasure fairs, and many specific manifestations of 'worldly' pleasure-seeking. During this period most men of substance were coming to regard the traditional patterns of recreation as wasteful of time and money, as threats to property and public order, and as remnants of a primitive past. Popular recreations were seen to be incompatible with proper labour discipline and with the 'march of progress'; they were intolerable to men of an enlightened age. If men of reforming disposition conceded the value of recreation at all, they now spoke of 'respectability', and respectability was usually in direct opposition to all that was involved in popular recreations: their boisterousness, their 'vulgarity' and 'crudity', their 'disorderliness', their sometimes revelrous licence. Alfred Williams, an authority on the region of the upper Thames, was not an impartial assessor of these changes, but his general representation of the heightened hostility to traditional forms of recreation is, in most respects, firmly supported by a large body of evidence from other sources. He spoke of the rise of respectability and reforming fervour:

> The village fair and club festival were condemned because simple people assembled together to indulge in simple amusements. The sight of so many 'poor foolish' peasant folk thronging the streets: the Henries, and Thomases, and Georges, the Emmas and Mary Anns, laughing immoderately at the antics of a fifth-rate clown, or gaping at the Punch and Judy show, or dancing together around the old fiddler sitting on the ground, or throwing at the 'knock 'em downs', or bowling at the 'milky cocoa-nuts', was an offence to those who affected a superiority of taste and were possessed with means of indulging it. They did not like the noise of the crowd; they said it was hateful and abominable, pure barbarism; it was time it was put a stop to; they could see all manner of evil in it, it was nothing but a 'drunken, rowdy show', a public pest, and a nuisance. So, in time, from one cause and another, the old sports fell away; this was prohibited, and that was prohibited; a standing was refused here, and something else objected to there; at any rate, extinction was aimed at, and almost effected; a great many of the villages are silent all the year through together at this time; though I cannot for the life of me see that any good has been done by it. . . . The old sports and festivals used to brighten up the year for farm-people, and if they were rude and simple, noisy and boisterous, they served their purpose very well, and were always hailed with unfeigned joy and delight.[1]

II

Williams, writing in the early twentieth century, was a late observer of the undermining of rural recreations, but evidence of a similar character may be found in the testimonies of many earlier writers. Indeed, there is little doubt that the recreational culture of the countryside during the middle of Victoria's reign was considerably more constricted than it had been in the mid-eighteenth century. Between about 1780 and 1850 numerous sports and festivities had passed from the scene or were obviously on the wane; and contemporaries, whether they applauded or regretted these changes, were virtually unanimous in speaking of the decline, or even disappearance, of many traditional recreations. They spoke of the demise of such animal sports as cock-fighting and bull-baiting, of the decay of village feasts and festivals and holiday celebrations, of the declining support for many athletic sports.[5] By the second half of the nineteenth century most informed observers were acknowledging the very limited range of recreational opportunities which were available to the labouring people. It was said of the farm labourers in Darrington, Yorkshire, for instance, that about 1870

> their amusements were few. . . . The labourer's life . . . was work and rest; of honest, healthy, whole-hearted play he had none. . . . his only amusements were the drinking of a pint of beer at the inn, and the enlivenments of the village feast, which was celebrated once a year. Nothing was known of bank holidays; even on Good Friday and Christmas Day the labourer had to do certain work about the farm.[6]

Recognized holidays were rare: as one villager (born in 1871) said of the annual feast in his parish, its popularity 'may be partly explained by the scarcity of holidays—my father frequently said that at the time of his youth two holidays only each year were recognized—Christmas Day and the Feast.'[7] This was a common situation. Moreover, while certain older forms of recreation had died out, few new ones were emerging. It was reported that in Canewdon, Essex, in the 1860s 'although tradition speaks of a public play ground, few recreations either bodily or mental are now provided for the people, except those enjoyments afforded by the public houses',[8] and many other villages must have been in much the same position. 'There are scores—perhaps hundreds—of villages', wrote Augustus Jessopp in 1881, 'where the inhabitants have absolutely no amusements of any kind outside the public-house.'[9] 'In most agricultural districts', thought one observer in 1859, 'it is wonderful how little play there is in the life of the labouring class. Well may the agricultural labourer be called a "working-man", for truly he does little else than work.'[10]

III

However, limited as plebeian forms of recreation may have become, they had not disappeared. The erosion of rural culture was a long-term and often gradual process, extending over several generations, and some of the traditional enjoyments survived through the second half of the nineteenth century, though often in a rather attenuated form. Many country fairs continued to flourish, and they offered, as in the past, important occasions for excitement, spectacle, sociability, and contacts with a wider world. In the East Riding of Yorkshire, for instance, the Martinmas hiring fairs remained major festive occasions for thousands of farm servants during the mid-Victorian period.[11] For many villagers throughout the country the local fair was the principal holiday of the year. 'Everyone, young and old alike, looked forward to the local fairs for weeks before they arrived', recalled one writer of the Norfolk fenland around 1900

> because these events were not simply the only holiday that many men had, but they gave the women a chance to escape for a few hours from the hard work of running a house and family, the children a few hours of fun and everyone a chance of meeting old friends and making new ones.[12]

A few of the largest fairs in the country, such as the Nottingham Goose Fair and St Giles's Fair in Oxford, may have been more popular than ever before.[13] On a more intimate level, parish feasts or wakes were still fairly common after 1850, though certainly much less so than they had been in the previous century, and in those places where they persisted their character, texture, and purposes remained remarkably traditional, much like those of the feasts which we know of from eighteenth-century sources. In Darrington, Yorkshire, the parish feast was the one occasion of the year when 'everybody, young and old, made merry. . . . During the feast everybody kept open house; friends and relations who had left the village came back to it, sometimes from far distances, and there was a great reunion of families'.[14] It was said that during the later nineteenth century in Haddenham, Buckinghamshire

> No institution was more popular, or more deeply rooted in village sentiment, than our annual Feast, which fell on the first Sunday after the nineteenth of September, and was always celebrated on the following day. . . . the village always honoured the Feast with a zest that it brought to no other event. . . . it should be remembered that as lack of plenty to eat was the normal experience of the poor a century ago, so a day given to fill the belly with good food was a delight. . . . the ancient celebration was really of that character, a literal feast of good food and drink, with the mirth that goes with these things. Long rows of stalls were put up, where every kind of delicacy to tempt the appetite was displayed, sausages, cakes and sweets, baked pears and nuts, and all for sale. . . . It was a whole day of festivity, when, from outlying farms, lads and lasses, hired for the year, were given a day's leave and arrived early, buxom and smiling. Each cottage home was ready for them; the gleaned corn had been ground, the pie of pears had been made from its flour, and a joint of fresh meat had been cooked. . . . I have heard of ploughmen not able to afford to lose the day's labour, who would rise extra early and be out on the fields when it was barely possible to see the furrows, so that they might knock off for the Feast before noon. For the thrill of anticipation was in every heart; it seemed to all to be the violation of deep-rooted sentiment, to work on the day of the Feast.[15]

A few other major holidays were also observed. In many places the annual 'club day'—the feast day (often around Whitsuntide) of the local friendly society—served as a special occasion for village festivities. For although some of the customary rituals and feastings were solely for the club's own members, the day itself had often come to be regarded as a festive occasion for the whole community and it was celebrated in a manner much like that of any parish feast or small pleasure fair. Indeed, in villages where an actual parish feast no longer existed, Club Day frequently came to function as the community's principal holiday of the year. These festive occasions, which were still very widespread in the mid-Victorian period, are well known and have often been described.[16] The only other holiday of the first importance was Christmas, perhaps the most resilient and universally celebrated of the traditional times of popular festivity. It was one of the few 'official' holidays in rural England, and it was commemorated in ways which had been long acknowledged as customary. In some parishes diversions were still provided by mummers, bell-ringers, carollers, or wassailers. But most of all Christmas was a time for domestic conviviality and hearty eating and drinking. The distinctive foods and drinks of the season included plum puddings, Christmas cakes, pumpkin pies, frumenty, mincemeat pies, spiced ale, and home-made elderberry wine. The Christmas celebrations among the labouring people in Harpenden, Hertfordshire, as remembered by Edwin Grey (born in 1859), must have been typical of those which would have been found throughout the countryside in the later nineteenth century:

> every household ... endeavoured to provide something extra, and also if possible different from the ordinary, for the Christmas season, especially in the way of meat. Those men working on the various estates and farms just round about brought home from thence their Christmas boxes, generally a piece of beef. ... Most of the farmers, too, saw to it that their hired hands had extra and choicer food provided for Christmas day dinner. I have heard these men say that they had what they called 'A good blow out', at the Christmas dinner at their place.[17]

No other holidays were so widely observed. Harvest feasts were still found here and there, but they were meagre remnants of what had once existed. And May Day, a major spring holiday for earlier generations, had now been reduced for the most part (when it survived at all) to the status of an occasion solely for the games and processions of children.

IV

But popular recreation was not confined to these few annual holidays: much of it was of a less remarkable character, and it was fitted into those intervals of 'free time' which punctuated the processes of labour. In some regions, at appropriate seasons, men would find time for angling, catching birds, and hunting small animals. Collecting nuts or berries provided social outings for women and children. Many cottagers raised a pig or maintained a garden allotment, and a few kept bees, and these activities were also a source of both pleasure and material sustenance. In the west of England, according to one observer:

> It may fairly be said that amongst the greatest of the few 'pleasures' of our English peasantry are the keeping of pigs, and the tilling of allotments or 'potato ground'. Indeed, 'potato ground' is a kind of farm labourer's Arcadia—that is to say when it is his own, and either given or let at a moderate and fair rental. All the odd half hours he can spare from his toilsome work 'for the master' he spends delightedly in turning and dressing, planting and hoeing his potato ground. We give it this one designation, because the familiar, wholesome and nutritious tuber is the staple article which the peasant cultivates. But other vegetables frequently share the tiny space which is allotted or let to the small cultivator, whose happiness is probably at its maximum when, on Sundays, he wanders across, with his hands in his pockets, to see 'how things are growing' in his little bit of ground.[18]

A similar personal attentiveness was commonly associated with the tending of the family pig, an animal which, for many cottagers, was an object of considerable interest and affection. Flora Thompson remembered that

> during its lifetime the pig was an important member of the family, and its health and condition were regularly reported in letters to children away from home, together with news of their brothers and sisters. Men callers on Sunday afternoons came, not to see the family, but the pig, and would lounge with its owner against the pigsty door for an hour, scratching piggy's back and praising his points or turning up their own noses in criticism.[19]

Pleasure and business might also be joined on market day, for the market place was a centre for social as well as economic transactions. It was a forum where news and gossip were exchanged, where showmen might be seen and pedlars' wares inspected, where contacts could be made with a wider world. As Walter Rose recalled:

> Going to market always brought with it a spirit of hilarity, as well it might, for a good deal of real drudgery belonged to village life. To put on clean clothes and lighter boots was itself an aid and inspiration to the spirit. Besides, however much one loved the village and enjoyed its life, to get away from it once a week for a few hours made it seem all the pleasanter on the return. And so the weekly market, though it was fundamentally a business matter, had a character beyond mere buying and selling; it was also a good-humoured gathering and meeting together, everybody expected this and responded to it heartily.[20]

Other diversions were completely recreational in character. Quoits might be played on summer evenings; some men belonged to a company of bell-ringers; brass bands were formed in rural areas during the later nineteenth century; some cottage gardeners entered their best flowers and vegetables in local shows; and many traditional ballads and songs continued to be sung during pauses from work (or even while actually working), at various public assemblies, and in numerous village alehouses.

The inns and alehouses of rural England were central to everyday leisure activities. A public house was the social centre of its community: men (women only infrequently) repaired to it for companionship, warmth, games and entertainment, and the exchange of news. It offered a refuge from the harshness of labour and the drabness and confinement of domestic life. It provided something of a sanctuary from the intrusions of genteel tastes, and thus its cultural character could be very much of the people's own making and fashioned to accord with their own desires and traditions. The village inn, said one observer,

> is a club where the labourer can feel at home and can talk over those matters which affect him closely. In summer, he sits on the benches in the open, in winter, in the settle round the blazing fire, the workaday world shut out by the red curtains drawn across the windows.[21]

An Essex villager recalled how the public house 'was our community centre and social club, and a most companionable place'; its patrons enjoyed being 'in communion with their fellows, with a warm fire, good company, no children under their feet or wives to nag them'.[22] Work and politics were probably the main topics of conversation. As well as being an everyday centre for conviviality, a public house often made special provisions for the diversion of its guests: these might include quoits, skittles, nine-pins, dominoes, cribbage boards, or pitch-and-toss. It was said that in the Magdalen region of Norfolk 'nearly every public house had a quoit bed and one public house used to play against another'.[23] By the later nineteenth century many village inns were subscribing to newspapers and sporting journals. The gregarious atmosphere in these public houses encouraged singers to perform: as Alfred Williams claimed, 'the inns had more to do than anything besides with perpetuation of . . . folk-songs. A few men never sang anywhere else. Their souls only expanded in society.'[24] Drink, moreover, was regarded as a social lubricant—a reinforcement of friendship, a necessary accompaniment to joviality and sociability. Drink brought people together and provided a vital underpinning to their recreational culture. And good ale was the social currency of public house life. For the agricultural labourer, said Richard Jeffries, the alehouse

> is at once his stock exchange, his reading-room, his club, and his assembly rooms. It is here that his benefit society holds its annual dinner. . . . Here he learns the news of the day; the local papers are always to be found at the public-house, and if he cannot read himself he hears the news from those who can. . . . As a rule the beerhouse is the only place of amusement to

135　A downland shepherd with his boy and dog (Museum of English Rural Life)

136 *above*   The staff of Home
Farm, Newcastle on Tyne. The
majority of farm servants were
young: the elderly man standing on
the right was George Summers, the
farm steward (Museum of English
Rural Life)

137 *above right*   Sheep-shearing at
Nookton, County Durham, in 1896
(Museum of English Rural Life)

138 *right*   A small sheep-shearing
gang at work near Caistor,
Lincolnshire (Hallgarth Collection)

139 *above* Cutting turnips for winter feed: a common farmyard scene (Hallgarth Collection)

140 *right* Jack Balding of Swaby in Lincolnshire. He was an expert hedger and ditcher, and thus one of the aristocrats of the rural labour force (Hallgarth Collection)

141 *opposite page above* Harvesting scene in the fens at Holbeach St John's, a few miles south of the Wash. The farmer and his lady watch the gang at work with a horsedrawn reaper (Hallgarth Collection)

142 *opposite page below left* Tree-felling in South Ormsby Park, Lincolnshire, late nineteenth century. Tom Dodds, the woodman, stands on the left (Hallgarth Collection)

143 *below right* A man stooking corn in the Spalding district of Lincolnshire (Hallgarth Collection)

144 *above* Hop-picking at Alton,
Hampshire, in 1880. Note the formal
dress and preponderance of women
and children (Hampshire County
Museum Service)

145 *left* Jenny Andrew of
Willoughton, Lincolnshire, poses with
her heavily loaded three-wheeled
hand-barrow (Hallgarth Collection)

146 A rare photograph of a young labourer posing with smock, pot, and lordly hat. He was from Dartford in Kent, and the picture was taken in 1862 (Munby Collection)

147 Children at Malmesbury, Wiltshire, pose for the camera in 1896—in their Sunday best? (Sir Benjamin Stone Collection, Birmingham Reference Library)

148   A scene at Hill Wootton, Warwickshire, 1890. These actually are boys wearing their sisters' cast-off clothing (Birmingham Reference Library)

149 *above* A country drama: children working in a
field gang in the 1860s. Concern about the children's
conditions led in 1867 to a regulatory Act (Cassell's
History of England, VI)

150 *right* A village street scene: thatched cottages, a
dealer making a call, and children at play (Museum of
English Rural Life)

FRONT ELEVATION

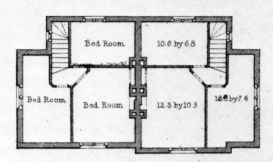

Bed Room.

10.6 by 6.8

Bed Room.

Bed Room.

12.3 by 10.3

10.0 by 7.6

UPPER FLOOR PLAN.

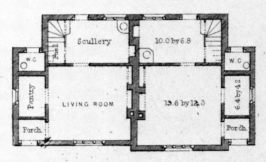

Scullery

10.0 by 6.8

W.C

W.C

Fuel

Pantry

LIVING ROOM

13.6 by 12.3

6.4 by 4.2

Porch.

Porch.

GROUND FLOOR PLAN

10   5   0   10   20   30 Feet

Day & Son, Lith to the

151 *left* Model cottage plan. One of several plans
designed by Henry Roberts, the architect to the
Society for Improving the Condition of the Labouring
Classes, and included in the 1867 edition of his book,
The Dwellings of the Labouring Classes. The provision
of three bedrooms and indoor sanitation was quite
generous for the period (RIBA)

152 *above* Shaldon Board School, Devon, an example
of Board school architecture of the 1870s. This school
replaced an entirely inadequate voluntary building
(Courtesy R. R. Sellman)

RULES OF THE
PEHEMBURY NATIONAL SCHOOL.

ADMISSION.

Children may be admitted any Monday morning, at a quarter before Nine o'Clock, under the following conditions, viz.— that the parents or guardians undertake to observe the following Rules.

ATTENDANCE.

On Sunday, children to assemble in the morning at half-past 9, afternoon at quarter to 2 o'Clock.

On Week-days, children to assemble quarter before 9 o'Clock, and in the afternoon at quarter to 2 o'Clock.

A child who comes late will have a mark on the Register.

School hours from 9 to 12, and from 2 to 4.

Children must be sent clean and neat in person and dress, or will have to be sent home

Children will be required to learn lessons at home in winter.

PAYMENTS, to be made in advance.

Labourers to pay 1s a quarter for each child ; Tradesmen 1s 6d. Double the above rates for such as write in copy books.

Parents who do not send their children to School when they can do so, will lose the privileges of the **Clothing Club,** and other Charities for themselves.

If three children of the same family, a small reduction will be made in the payments.

The school treat and prizes will depend on regular attendance.

All children above six years of age, residing in the Parish and attending the Day School, will be expected to be present on Sundays.

G. SWEETMAN, BOOKSELLER, WINCANTON.

153 *left* Rules of the Pehembury National School, Devon. The school was opened in 1881. Note the double fee charged for the use of paper in lieu of slates, and the pressures exerted by the incumbent for attendance (Courtesy Devonshire County Council)

154 *above* A country arrest: a very much posed picture taken at Laceby, near Great Grimsby (Hallgarth Collection)

155 *right* Violence in the woods by moonlight: the war between gamekeepers and organized gangs of poachers was constantly fought over much of the Victorian countryside (*Illustrated London News*)

WATCHING

DEATH OF THE LURCHER

156 *above* The armed poacher: a
photograph taken about 1890, probably in
Herefordshire (Hereford City Library)

157 *left* A meeting at Whitnash during
the Warwickshire farm labourers' strike
of 1872 (Cassell's *History of England*, VII)

UNITED

WE STAND

DIVIDED

WE FALL

WE DEMAND SOCIAL LIBERTY,
POLITICAL & RELIGIOUS EQUALITY,
& THE COMPLETE RIGHTS OF MAN.

58   The banner of the National Agricultural Labourers' Union (Nuffield College, Oxford)

159 Delegates of Joseph Arch's Agricultural Labourers' Union signing a petition for electoral reform at a conference held at the Memorial Hall, Farringdon Street, in 1876 (*Illustrated London News*)

160 *above*   In the 1890s the vans of the political parties quartered the countryside, drawing the attention of newly enfranchized labourers. Here a red van of the English Land Restoration League attracts a group into discussion of the land question (Courtesy Pamela Horn)

161 *right*   Joseph Arch in 1886, shortly after his election as MP for the first time (Courtesy Pamela Horn)

162 *above left* Cottage women ranged the lanes for firewood to carry home. Here is Mrs Clay of Swaby, Lincolnshire, with a load of kids or faggots (Hallgarth Collection)

163 *above right* Excitement for the folk of the fenland: a troupe of elephants leads the circus caravans into Spalding (Hallgarth Collection)

164 *left* A group of aged inmates of the Arrington Almshouse, Cambridgeshire, about 1900 (Cambridge and Country Folk Museum Collection)

165 *right*   Itinerant Italian musicians with a barrel-organ and tambourine, a photograph taken about the turn of the century at Fiskerton, on the Trent near Newark (Hallgarth Collection)

166 *below*   The King's Head, Horncastle, an old building overshadowed by more recent neighbours. This scene is little changed today (Hallgarth Collection)

COWBIT, LINCS.

eft A village band at Waltham on the Wolds, ...stershire, about 1860. One might think the ...bers were unusual in their instruments and in ... ability to read music (Leicestershire ...ums, Art Galleries and Records Service)

bove Rules of the Louth Cricket Club, ...ished in 1822. Among the club's honorary ...ers were such aristocratic patrons as the Earl ...ckinghamshire and the Hon. G. A. Pelham. ...rary members were exempt from fines levied ...n-attendance at the matches, riding upon the ...d during a match, and the leaving of bats at ...cket (Hallgarth Collection)

ntre Football, considered less gentlemanly ...cricket, grew in popularity and drew ...derable crowds in the later nineteenth ...ry. Here is a Gainsborough team of the 1890s ...garth Collection)

low Charlie Scholes crouches in his punt ...waits the moment to pounce: a photograph ... at Cowbit in the fens near Spalding ...garth Collection)

171 *left* Cowbit Wash in the fens south of Spalding was renowned for its ice-skating (Hallgarth Collection)

172 *below* Queen Victoria's Diamond Jubilee, 1897, was celebrated up and down the land: here is the lively scene outside the Hart Hotel, Spilsby, in Lincolnshire. Note the bicycles, very popular by this time (Hallgarth Collection)

which he can resort: it is his theatre, his music-hall, picture-gallery, and Crystal Palace.[25]

The public house, however, was not the only centre for social life: in many localities an alternative recreational culture was provided by organized religion, usually in the form of a nonconformist chapel. For chapel society offered more than salvation and spiritual nourishment: it was also a source of many secular satisfactions—novelty and excitement, companionship and conviviality, special outings and festivals—all of which were provided within a controlled context of godliness and respectability. Sermons, as one historian has said, 'were regarded as a superior form of entertainment',[26] and when preachers changed from week to week, as they did in many Methodist chapels, and when the preaching was intense and sometimes eloquent and the hymn-singing vigorous and compelling, a chapel service could be an event of some moment—even of exhilaration—to a labouring man or woman. 'Wesleyan acts of worship', it has been said,

> provided chapel-goers not only with the means of grace but also with the means of entertainment. In a society lacking public forms of diversion, Wesleyan Methodism offered a respectable counter-attraction to the beerhouse and village feast on the one hand and a more enjoyable alternative to the parish church on the other.[27]

The various bodies of dissenters devised a whole complex of their own special recreational events: Sunday School fêtes, tea meetings, 'love-feasts', camp meetings among the Primitive Methodists, chapel anniversaries, temperance festivals: these were often of considerable importance to the social life of a whole community. In Binbrook. Lincolnshire, for instance, 'the Methodists provided a good part of the social life ... as well as two-thirds of its religious activity. Their chapel anniversaries, love feasts and tea meetings were important dates in the village calendar.'[28] 'A lot of people used to come from nearby villages for the [Chapel] Anniversary,' recalled Arthur Randell of his childhood years in a Norfolk fenland village, 'for in those days there was little other entertainment beyond going for a walk or to church or chapel'; and many outsiders, he said, used to attend the camp meetings of the Primitive Methodists, 'for such events were exciting affairs in days when few people had much to entertain them'.[29] Much of the appeal of these special services was decidedly secular in character: friends would visit one another at the various local anniversaries, there were games and food, and people would take pleasure in cutting a fine figure. At Harpenden in Hertfordshire '"Anniversary day" was also the occasion when many of the young women and girls donned their new summer dresses and hats for the first time, for if funds permitted, it was almost imperative that something new should be worn in honour of the event.'[30] (In the second half of the nineteenth century a reinvigorated Church of England was exhibiting a similar interest in the provision of recreational occasions, though its efforts, on the whole, seem to have made less impact on the labouring people than those of its dissenting competitors.)

These religious services, then, derived much of their appeal and significance from their involvement with worldly pleasures. As James Obelkevich has suggested in a stimulating study of religious practice in Lincolnshire, a chapel anniversary tended to take on 'the character of a popular social festival, with respectable concourse and temperate conviviality as prime attractions. These were very real attractions to villagers whose traditional fairs and feasts had come under attack from parsons and magistrates.' The Primitive Methodists, he says—and much the same could be said of other nonconformists—offered to their members a distinctive festive calendar which served as 'an alternative to the unrespectable leisure activities of the rural populace: hymns, Sunday school, and tea meetings competed with folksongs, beer drinking and village feasts'.[31]

Here, in fact, in contrasting the cultures of chapel and alehouse and the conflicting ideals which they represented, we confront one of the principal tensions in Victorian popular culture—the tension between the 'rough' and 'respectable' traditions of plebeian conduct—and recreational practices were very much at the heart of this conflict of values and outlook. The rough tradition was the tradition of the past— fairs and feasts, folk customs, rough sports (backswords, wrestling), occasions of revelry and authorized licence (as at the harvest-home)—and its character was vitally conditioned by the customs of drinking and the sociability of the public house. In contrast, the tradition of respectability was concerned with moral reform and with 'rational recreation', and it was from this tradition that a whole range of recreational 'improvements' arose in the later nineteenth century: brass bands, public recitations and lectures, lantern shows, tea festivals, railway excursions, reading clubs, temperance halls, Bands of Hope, concerts and plays. These rational recreations, all of them deemed to be morally progressive and socially useful, were usually based on either the chapel or the church, and many of them were closely associated with (or totally dependent upon) the temperance movement and its vigorous efforts to wean people from the evils of drink by providing recreational alternatives to the public house. Nonconformists were particularly active in promoting an alternative culture of leisure based on the principles of temperance, or even total abstinence.

Some of this movement towards respectability, involving a rejection of most traditional practices, arose from the labouring people's own experiences as chapel members and 'saved souls'—in Tysoe, for instance, some of the men thought that 'Methodism had killed the [old] sports because the best sportsmen had been converted'; and indeed in all parts of the country the Methodists were intent on getting men to break with the rough habits of former years.[32] But many of these changes were also promoted from above as part of an effort to transform the character of popular leisure in the interest of greater orderliness, propriety, and individual self-discipline. Parsons and gentry, for instance, were particularly interested in patronizing village friendly societies, whose principles of self-help and well-regulated behaviour they found safe and congenial, and some of these clubs were actually founded by them and managed under their surveillance.[33] Respectability and the values of self-improvement which it embodied were not universally triumphant—Headington Quarry in Oxfordshire, for example, preserved a rich traditional culture and successfully resisted most of the forces of 'improvement'[34]—but there is no doubt that respectability was becoming the dominant cultural orientation for a growing proportion of country people through most of the Victorian period. Labouring people readily accepted some of these new forms of discipline themselves, others were forced upon them. As one historian has put it,

> the labourers' 'roughness' was subjected to a multiple assault: from working people themselves, seeking self-control; from moralizing 'reformers', largely Evangelical; from a remote élite anxious to curb popular 'disturbances'; from the churches, in rare unanimity; and from the psychological impact of capitalist civilization, which was no less powerful in the countryside than in the towns.[35]

V

By the early twentieth century there was little left of the traditional culture of rural recreations. Most parish feasts had disappeared, country fairs had dwindled in importance, and folk customs and festivities were much less often preserved than neglected and forgotten. Many recreations and festive occasions had succumbed to the realities of moral reform and the repressive intervention of clergymen, magistrates, and the newly formed rural constabulary. But some of these recreations had been the victims, not only of direct repression, but also of those larger processes of change which were radically transforming the character of rural society. From the 1850s the cultural continuities of rural life were seriously disrupted by the rapid depopulation of the countryside. As labourers became more disposed to migrate, and as villages contracted in size, the processes by which customary local practices had been passed on from generation to generation were no longer sustainable. The sense of separate 'community identities' was gradually disintegrating. As one student of folk customs, writing in the 1860s, said of the north of England: 'Now whole families uproot themselves and move into other districts; and it has been found that when people are wrenched away from local associations, though they may carry their traditions with them, they fail to transmit them to their descendants.'[36] Thomas Hardy wrote in the same vein of a culturally debilitating 'break of continuity in local history'.[37] The disruptive consequences of these changes were later exacerbated by the impact of the First World War, for many of the men who might have preserved village traditions never returned home.

But most important, perhaps, was the fact that the culture of the countryside was increasingly infiltrated by the manners, tastes, and recreational pastimes of the towns and cities. With the growth of communications between city and countryside (fostered first by railways, and later by bicycles and buses), and the consequent breakdown of rural insularity, country labourers had much more contact with urban life; and as urban culture became more accessible to them, the attractiveness of rural traditions was correspondingly weakened. A wider world was now open to them. It was said in the early twentieth century that in the parish of Corsley, Wiltshire, although traditionalism remained strong,

> the youth of Corsley as it grows up tends more and more to assimilate to the modes of thought and habit of the dweller in towns, and the more energetic, unless withheld by the prospect of becoming the master of a small farm or gardening business, continue to migrate to districts where their urbanised tastes may be gratified.

At the same time, moreover, there were 'ever increasing facilities for bringing the more varied, more exciting, or more intellectual life of the towns into the country districts'.[38] This triumph of an increasingly ascendant urban culture—in the form of football clubs, music-hall songs, railway excursions, popular newspapers—was occurring almost everywhere. And the result was that leisure in the countryside became little more than a modified offshoot (often in a paler form) of the recreational culture of the cities. A distinctive rural recreational culture, readily identifiable and central to the life of the country labourers, had been largely extinguished.

Notes

1   Mott, 1973, 94–5.
2   Malcolmson, 1973, 17–18; E. P. Thompson, 1974, 392; Bodl. MSS Top. Devon b. 1–2.
3   Malcolmson, 1973, chs 2–3.
4   Williams, 1912, 233–4; cf. Jessopp, 1887, 231–6; Obelkevich, 1976, 57–8, 84–5.
5   Malcolmson, 1973, chs 6–8.
6   Fletcher, 1910, 55–6.
7   Rose, 1942, 129; cf. Horn, 1976b, 159; Obelkevich, 1976, 70.
8   Benton, 1867, 128.
9   Jessopp, 1887, 21.
10   Boyd, 1859, 151; cf. Heath, 1880, 340–5.
11   See Morris, 1922, 176–7; 1928, 52–4; cf. Eddowes, 1854, 20–3; Obelkevich, 1976, 82–3.
12   Randell, 1969, 108; cf. Marshall, 1967, 211–15.
13   Church, 1966a, 213–14; Thomis, 1968, 134–40; Alexander, 1970.
14   Fletcher, 1910, 143–4.
15   Rose, 1942, 129–30; cf. Wright, 1913, 305; Hartley and Ingilby, 1956, 203, 235; Moreau, 1968, 89–91; Kebbel, 1891, 183–5; Flora Thompson, 1945, 227–9, 458–61.
16   Fuller, 1964, ch. 5; Gosden, 1961, 115, 119–20, 127, 217–8; Brill, 1973, 165–7; Williams, 1912, 234–6; Nicholson, 1890, 10–11; Horn, 1976b, 150–2; Howkins, 1973, 28–43; Ashby, 1961, 68–9; 1974, 375–6.
17   Grey, 1935, 185–6; cf. Fletcher, 1910, 149–58; Blakeborough, 1898, 66–7; Flora Thompson, 1945, 226–7.

18 Heath, 1880, 289–90.
19 Flora Thompson, 1945, 10; cf. Obelkevich, 1976, 63, and Ashby, 1961, 115.
20 Rose, 1942, 82–3; cf. Pulbrook, 1922, 163.
21 Pulbrook, 1922, 174.
22 Mays, 1969, 106, 109; cf. Flora Thompson, 1945, 53–4.
23 Randell, 1969, 76; cf. Moreau, 1968, 84–5; Evans, 1975, 141–2.
24 Williams, 1923, 20.
25 Jefferies, 1898, 100–1.
26 Obelkevich, 1976, 118.
27 Obelkevich, 1976, 212; see Ashby, 1961, 220–1; Marshall, 1967, 93–100.
28 Olney, 1975, 24.
29 Randell, 1969, 90–2, 94.
30 Grey, 1934, 205–6; cf. Marshall, 1967, 162–3, 205–6.
31 Obelkevich, 1976, 213, 230.
32 Ashby, 1961, 36; Williams, 1913, 158–9; Obelkevich, 1976, 247; Malcolmson, 1973, 106–7.
33 Howkins, 1973, 23–7; Jefferies, 1898, 227.
34 Samuel, 1975b, 162–3, 185.
35 Obelkevich, 1976, 80–1.
36 Henderson, 1866, Preface.
37 Hardy, *Madding Crowd*, preface; cf. Orel, 1966, 179–82, 188–9.
38 Davies, 1909, 95–6.

45   Rural Culture

Charles Phythian-Adams

I

The year of the Great Exhibition, when Britain celebrated its primacy as the most advanced technological nation in the world, also marked the numerical supremacy of town populations over those of the countryside. Yet even in the industrialized Leicester of 1851, there lived a 'wise woman', who was being consulted for her magical prowess from as far afield as Rutland.[1] Nor was she unique. 'Wise men' or 'cunning men' were still at work in or near other urban centres: Black Jock of Newcastle; Oakley of Tunbridge Wells in the 1860s; Snow and Tuckett at Exeter during the 1880s.[2] One of the more celebrated was 'Au'd' Wrightson of Stokesley in Yorkshire (*fl. c.* 1820) who had at least one successor; another was the wise man who lived between Hereford and Bromyard in the 1860s.[3] It is likely that market towns in many of the traditional areas of the country were the homes of such figures during at least the early decades of Victoria's reign.

These people were not simply the primitive vets of their age. Their powers were widely seen to be semi-magical: they charmed away the ills of both ailing farm animals and human beings and used spells and rituals in so doing. Above all, their aid might still be invoked when misfortunes were otherwise so inexplicable in normal terms that bewitching was suspected.

For the fear of witchcraft was not yet dead. Cecil Torr's father noted in 1844: 'Witchcraft a common belief to this day at Lustleigh (Devon), and prevalent even among the better informed classes.'[4] Writing from his own long and deep knowledge

616

of the north York moors, the Rev. J. C. Atkinson stated categorically in 1891:

> Fifty years ago the whole atmosphere of the folklore firmament in this
> district was so surcharged with the being and the works of the witch, that
> one seemed able to trace her presence and her activity in almost every nook
> and corner of the neighbourhood.[5]

In 1871, the affliction of the so-called woman-frog of Presteigne, who only ventured
out of the house to hop to and from the Primitive Methodist chapel, was solemnly
explained to Francis Kilvert as the outcome of a curse laid on the wretched woman's
mother when she was pregnant.[6] As late as the 1880s, a Hastings man was
recommended to singe the wrists of his bewitched wife with a poker before the hearth
'to make the evil spirit fly up the chimney'.[7] Writing about the same decade, Miss
M. A. Courtney claimed that 'belief in witchcraft in West Cornwall is much more
general than most people imagine'.[8] Long after witches were publicly exposed and
punished, the fear of them lived on in conservative areas. Even in 1939 Christina Hole

> was told of several witches who live in a village near Ilminster; one woman
> there takes the precaution of placing crossed knives on her stairs whenever
> the moon is full to defeat the spells of one of them whom she particularly
> fears.[9]

If, as a result, a whole range of protective devices against evil—from horse-shoes to
rowan twigs—was still widely employed in some regions during part of Victoria's
reign, no less bewildering to the modern mind are many of the popular cures which
similarly continued to be used. From the Lake District come newspaper reports in 1866
and 1876 (and from Cornwall in 1865) of ritual remedies against contagious abortion
or brucellosis amongst calving cows, which involved either the burial alive or roasting
alive of young calves.[10] Elsewhere popular cures for whooping cough were still, for
example, at best taking the sufferer into the mouth of a cave or through the arch of a re-
rooted bramble; at worst, either the consumption of a roasted mouse by the afflicted
child or the placing of the head of a live trout or frog inside his mouth.[11] As late as
1902–3, a Devon farmer claimed that his malformed baby was as likely to be cured by
being passed three times through a split ash tree at sunrise as by 'sloppin' water over'n
in church', and added significantly that 'all folk do it'.[12]

The survival, well into Victoria's reign, of what has been usefully dubbed 'the prior
culture' is thus hardly in doubt.[13] Its ritual expression was also more widespread than
is sometimes supposed. A remarkable survey of what are often regarded as mummers'
plays still extant in the nineteenth century, for example, associates them with
roughly 800 places in England alone.[14] Their distribution indicates that such
observances were not necessarily immediately vulnerable to the progress of either
commercial farming or urbanization. These plays were acted far beyond the confines
of Hardy's Wessex and were often performed by clusters of villages in close proximity
to cathedral towns like Lichfield or even near an industrialized centre like Leeds.

Above all it looks as though seasonal drama of this kind was a surviving cultural feature of the nucleated rural community in whatever region it might be found.

If vernacular culture was not yet moribund, neither was it monolithic. Different types of play, for instance, might be regionally restricted: to Lincolnshire and Nottinghamshire in one case; or to the North Riding, Durham and Northumberland in another. There were even significant calendrical differences with regard to the performance of the same type of play. To judge from those places where the timing is established, the so-called Hero-Combat type was usually performed in Cheshire around All Souls, but at Easter north of the county boundary—in Lancashire, an adjacent part of Yorkshire, Furness and southern Westmorland. In other parts of the country, by contrast, it was played between Christmas and Plough Monday. Still other areas—Wales on the one hand, and Bedfordshire, East Anglia, Essex and Hertfordshire on the other—appear to have been largely innocent of any such activity.

A study of the distribution of an identifiable form of popular drama shows that it would be premature to assert that in the earlier nineteenth century traditional activities and beliefs were restricted only to the remoter parts of the highland zone (the extent and significance of which is apt to be depreciated by the average lowland-based historian). Work done on the subject as a whole is geographically so scattered that it is impossible to map the incidence of survival in our present state of knowledge. What is clear is that even counties like Suffolk and Sussex contained pockets of traditional culture down to the Great War at least.[15] *Jackson's Oxford Journal* of 1837 was able to claim: 'In no other part of the united kingdom, we believe, are these old English revels [i.e. Whit Ales] celebrated with such spirit, so much original character, as in the midland county of Oxford.'[16]

If the 'prior culture' was still widely entertained, so too, were the springs of its inspiration. For all its faults, A. J. Ellis's great dialect survey, the rough outlines of which still seem to stand the test of time, indicated six major dialect divisions of the country in the 1870s (southern, western, midland, eastern, northern, and lowland Scottish), and no fewer than forty-two subdivisions or districts, each with 'a sensible similarity of pronunciation'.[17] Even within counties, linguistic diversity might be remarkable. In Somerset alone, no fewer than twenty-three—often very different— names are recorded for the scarlet pimpernel; and no fewer than thirty-three for the birdsfoot trefoil.[18] It can hardly be doubted that within the countryside problems of linguistic communication, together with short-range marriage patterns, still helped to conserve localized attitudes beyond the middle of the century.

Across the nation, indeed, local loyalties were expressed in such rhyming jibes as:

> Tring, Wing and Ivinghoe
> Three dirty villages all in a row,
> And never without a rogue or two:
> Would you know the reason why?
> Leighton Buzzard is hard by.[19]

A recently discovered notebook recording life in Cornwall at the turn of the century claims that in that county there were probably a rude nickname for the residents of every parish, ranging from 'Morvah chitchats' through 'Madron squerts' to 'Sennen hoars'.[20]

In these circumstances it is hardly surprising that certain basic popular beliefs were also variously expressed in contrasted regions. The wood or foliage of specific trees, in particular, were held to be peculiarly efficacious in protecting against witchcraft, for example. In different parts of the country, therefore, primacy in this respect might be accorded to the oak or the ash, hazel or holly, rowan or hawthorn. All were associated with lightning in one way or another; all appear to have been used for ritual fires at Christmas or other times. Similar differences in expressing the same attitudes may be detected with regard to 'sacred' birds. In much of England and Scotland, for example, the robin and the wren were widely termed 'God Almighty's cock and hen', the latter being described as the 'Lady of Heaven's hen' over the border. In both areas some people still held that it was taboo to kill these birds or to destroy their eggs or nests. In Essex, Sussex, the Isle of Man, Wales and (even today) southern Ireland, by contrast, the wren was deemed to be male not female, and was ritually hunted and killed around Christmas-time; where it was not, the outline of the custom often survived. The bird was still held to be sacred, however. One was particularly fortunate to possess one of its feathers, and a frequently found song on such occasions began

> The Wren, the Wren, the king of the birds
> S. Stephen's day was killed in the furze.[21]

Ancient cultural traditions of this kind—and many more—thus helped to perpetuate those invisible barriers between one locality and another which together still contributed to the colour and diversity of the more custom-bound countryside in early Victorian England.

II

Even as late as 1837, therefore, it may be claimed that established conventions still dictated mental attitudes, however variously across the country. That said, a balance must be struck. It is an undeniable fact that many popular superstitions and observances had been whittled away already in the more agriculturally developed localities over the preceding centuries. In so far as there had ever been something approaching a framework of beliefs before the Reformation, much of this had been eroded subsequently by Protestant activity in its many forms; by state intervention in such a basic matter as the alteration of the calendar in 1752; by the impact of enclosure on communal farming rituals; by the anti-blood sports campaign; and perhaps even by the Napoleonic wars, which may have been a cultural watershed comparable to that of the Great War a century later.[22]

Nevertheless, while certain observances had long been discontinued in many areas, and with them some or all of their attendant ritual detail, many of the mental *attitudes* on which such practices were founded do appear often to have survived. Only thus can we explain the fact that, despite the gloomy statements of the late Victorian folklorists (who anyway rarely interviewed their few informants systematically) on the imminent disappearance of their cherished subject-matter, a sensitive modern investigator like George Ewart Evans is able to elicit from old folk even today a truly remarkable amount of evidence for the survival of many old beliefs down to the Great War.[23] Moreover, while public rituals clearly disappeared long before some of the superstitions and culinary customs related to them, the memories of *private* ritual observance (particularly with respect to the defeat of witches or placating of fairies) were sturdily perpetuated in numerous folk-tales and songs. In these the traditional basic attitudes and beliefs continued to be interrelated in marked contrast to the confusing mass of separate superstitions collected by the early folklorists. It is worth noting that many of these tightly constructed tales have been recorded for the first time only in this century.[24]

If the essential medium of popular culture was oral, this in itself underlines the unchanging *circumstances* in which the old beliefs were perpetuated. Even by Victoria's reign the education of ordinary country folk had not progressed far. Such advances as had been achieved in medical and veterinary practice were far from always available to them. Above all, large numbers of small farmers, labourers and rural industrial workers continued to live in primitive conditions on the very edge of nature and in close relation to their farm animals. For such people the vagaries of the climate, of the environment, and of disease in both human being and animal were ever-present realities. In times of misfortune, especially, it is difficult to see how they could have fallen back on anything except what they took to be the conventional wisdom. Christian faith in itself would not cure the ailing family pig.

The major facets of this conventional wisdom, despite the local diversity of its expression, may be readily identified. Popular attitudes during much of the first half of the nineteenth century were still concerned with three matters. The first was the correct observance of established practices, whether these involved the customary prosecution of annual or day-to-day activities like planting or cleaning the house, the performance of private rituals, or obedience to certain taboos. Second, tradition taught that it was possible to anticipate the future in certain ways, and having done so either to take avoiding action where that was possible or, more often, to accept one's fate. Third, if dire and unanticipated misfortune did strike, however, even though the customary procedures had been observed, society could yet turn to the doings of the witch as the ultimate explanation. At root the mental attitudes involved were thus understandably obsessed with accounting for and meeting the omnipresent threats of destitution or dearth, disease and death.

For those who still clung to these beliefs (and it is impossible to measure precisely how strongly they held them by this period), all these preoccupations emanated from a world-view that was essentially medieval in its conception. Its central assumption was the existence of supernatural forces in the human body, in nature and in the heavens. This said, it is necessary to emphasize that there is no convincing evidence known to the writer— either from this or the preceding three centuries—which might suggest that even conservative country people thought in terms of pagan deities or tutelary spirits. Phoebus, Luna, Ceres and Pomona were figments of the classically educated imagination. Where not superimposed on the evidence by contemporary commentators, the unique cases sometimes quoted are highly suspect as rustic borrowings, as even a glance at the more primitive Anglo-Saxon evidence indicates.[25] That both the sun and the moon were still respected as ultimate sources of power, and particularly growth, is not to be denied. They might be feared, or even propitiated, but neither was worshipped. Both had long been assimilated into Christian lore or the church calendar. Indeed, perhaps the most marked feature of the folkloric evidence at this period is the absence of direct information conclusively linking, for example, the sun with the beneficial qualities of fire. If there was such a link in people's minds it has now to be *inferred* from the timing of ritual fires at Christmas (after the winter solstice), from the associations connected with the wood used, or from the prevalence of red or gold as colour symbols on certain occasions. It may thus be suspected that in many such rituals an element of convention had long been present.

There can be no doubt that a belief in the existence of forces abroad in the terrestrial world, however it originated, lay behind a mass of superstitions, rituals and popular cures. However we term them, such forces were deemed to be neither good nor bad, neither necessarily dominant nor invariably submissive to more powerful agents. All depended on the use to which they were put. Thus, to take but one example, a widespread superstition associated unusual hares with the physical transformation of witches; yet a hare's paw hung around the neck of a sufferer, or kept in his pocket, might be used as a specific against rheumatism or cramp. The connection was presumably that both afflictions impeded swift bodily movement.[26]

It was clearly because of this *potential* ambivalence that so much emphasis was placed on the correct observance of custom. In Herefordshire, for instance, the last sheaf cut at harvest appears to have been thought potentially so dangerous that the men threw their sickles at it from a distance—even over their shoulders—until by chance the stalks were cut.[27] The significance of the ubiquitous corn 'dolly' made out of this last sheaf thus probably lay not in its form, which anyway varied, but in the fact that it was plaited before being brought into the house. The same was true of other types of vegetation used for ritualistic purposes: the ashen faggot or the hawthorn bush at Christmas, even witch-sticks of rowan.[28] All were wrought, bound or knotted. It is relevant to note that superstitions frequently prohibited either the picking or the bringing into the house of wild or even garden flowers, except for culinary or medicinal purposes.[29]

The essence of popular attitudes, in fact, lay in a medieval desire for balance and harmony. There was a proper place for everything. When due order was disturbed in one sphere a disturbance might occur in another, as in the common jingle:

> A Saturday's moon with Sunday full,
> Was never good and never wull.[30]

Moon-day should properly follow Sun-day, which therefore ought to be given primacy. After all, the Man in the Moon was banished there for working on Sunday.[31] Troubled times for society would follow for the whole month if a new moon appeared not on the third, but on the fourth day.[32] Two moons in the already dangerous month of May meant rain throughout the entire growing season, for by definition a month should contain only one new moon.[33] An abnormality in nature thus implied a disharmony elsewhere which had to be interpreted. A snake on the doorstep, a bird tapping at the window—or, even worse, flying into the house—was so unnatural a trespass by a wild creature that death, illness or at least misfortune in society would be portended.[34]

Consequently, the future, not the past, was what mattered. History was usually relevant only in so far as legend might account for an unusual hillock, a prehistoric barrow or stone circle in terms which perpetuated the structure of superstition.[35] What did concern traditional country people was how to anticipate the future from signs provided in the present, whether they were indications of the arrival of a stranger, love divinations, weather omens (of the 'red sky at night' variety) or the portents of misfortune. Apparitions of persons about to die (even one's own neighbours) might be watched for in the yard or porch of the church on St Mark's eve (25 April) or All Saints.[36] Only in some cases was avoiding action possible. On different parts of the coast, for instance, fishermen would refuse to put to sea if they saw a hare, a rabbit, a pig or a priest while going to their boats.[37] For the rest, a degree of fatalism was implicit in such attitudes and it complemented the wretched living and working conditions in which these people usually existed.

Even if unanticipated, there were thus many ways in which current misfortune could be explained retrospectively. A palsied hand might be accounted for by the fact that it had been instrumental in breaking a taboo, such as killing a robin.[38] Similarly, a repeated moral of numerous folk-tales was that bad luck fell on those who failed to observe correct rituals like propitiating the fairies with a dish of cream, or committed ritual sacrilege by felling particular trees, for example.[39] When explanations of this kind were exhausted there was still an ultimate scapegoat available in the person of the witch and hence, hopefully, remedies to be found on the advice of a cunning man.[40]

The country-dweller thus sought to relate the fortunes of society to the signs and manifestations of the supernatural. Above all he evaluated nature not simply in terms of practical needs like food or fuel, but also in its living relation to culture. Within nature a tension was seen to exist between those forces that might be used on behalf of society and those that could be used against it. On the one hand were those aspects of nature which were most usually endowed with a supernatural quality of a non-malevolent kind: certain trees whose height and/or age separated them from mankind, and whose wood or foliage furnished a protection against witches; certain plants like the house-leek which when planted on the roof preserved a house from

622

lightning; certain winged creatures, whether especially sacred birds like robins or wrens or various groups of birds (like magpies or rooks) whose number or behaviour might indicate death (but not cause it), and even bees; and, finally, certain subterranean mineral substances such as running spring water, iron and silver—even coal—all of which could be employed in emergency as antidotes to the most threatening manifestations of the witch. On the other hand were those creatures—often nocturnal—which occupied much the same terrestrial plane as society and which were associated with the physical transformation of witches when secretly attempting to milk the cows: hares, hedgehogs, bats and even nightjars which nest on the ground.

In the contemporary folklore of creatures and plants, indeed, there were few living things that were not connected in one way or another (if only as popular cures) with the supernatural forces with which nature was held to be imbued. Though the evidence on these specific matters is embarrassingly rich, it must be emphasized that we cannot now tell, and perhaps never may, how far such beliefs dominated the day-to-day thoughts of the country-dweller in early Victorian England. It seems possible that increasingly he or she turned to such expedients only *in extremis* or when convention dictated.

III

The decline of the pre-scientific attitudes of mind which have been broadly outlined here is extraordinarily difficult to chart precisely. Not only has the subject as a whole been pointedly ignored by most historians, but the evidence is such that it is hard to disentangle an unambiguous general trend from the equally unambiguous indications of pockets of local resistance. Even the pace and timing of the change is in doubt. There are no censuses of mental attitudes to help us. In this context, and in the space available, it is thus only possible to propose three imprecise measures with which to assess the process.

The most intangible is that which relates to the altered structure of beliefs. It has already been suggested that convention may well have marked at least certain calendrical rituals early in the century. It may now be added that different superstitions relating to the same natural objects frequently range over such a spectrum of different significances that it may well be wondered how far any coherence behind such beliefs (if indeed that ever existed) was still perceived. When all allowances are made for local diversity, the implication must be that attitudes were increasingly fragmented. One family may have passed on one belief; another a quite different superstition relating to the same object. It is worth emphasizing, none the less, that even one such superstition, sincerely believed, could still have meant a passing attachment to that wider framework of attitudes which had once existed.

A second factor to be considered in assessing cultural decay during the later nineteenth century is more concrete. What is most probably at issue is the decline in the numbers and influence of the people available to hold these attitudes in common rather than the rapid dissolution of the beliefs themselves. For this situation, and important as it no doubt was, rural depopulation provides only part of the explanation. There was also a marked shift in the class, sex and age-groups of those who perpetuated the old attitudes. Where it had not occurred already, labouring families, and especially the women and children (who everywhere now dominated May Day, for example), were rapidly becoming the sole repositories of local customs.[41]

The third approach to the problem of decline has consequently to concentrate on the circumstances in which all these beliefs were both fragmented and perpetuated by fewer people. No single factor can be held responsible. The probable causes range from the increased activities of church and chapel through to the educational advances of the last decades of the century; from the incarceration of impoverished old women—potential witches—in the workhouses of the New Poor Law, to the increased experience of town life; from the growing mechanization of arable agriculture to the advent of cooking stoves in areas like the Lake District, where the old significance of the open hearth was consequently diminished; from the spread of friendly societies, and their attendant ceremonies, to the development of agricultural shows with their emphasis on more scientific farming. These and many other reasons may be advanced. What is more certain is that following the geographical and social intermixing engendered by the Great War, the year 1918—unlike 1851 with which this survey began—finally and symbolically clanged shut, like a blood-stained cast-iron gate, on an already dwindling cultural tradition that had evolved in one form or another over more than a thousand years.[42]

Notes

1   Henderson, 1879, 244–5.
2   *Ibid.*, 1879, 221–2; Simpson, 1973, 73–4; Briggs, 1971, II, 685.
3   Atkinson, 1891, 110–25; Leather, 1970, 53.
4   Torr, 1918, 8.
5   Atkinson, 1891, 73.
6   Plomer, 1964, 137.
7   Simpson, 1973, 75.
8   Courtney, 1890, 142.
9   Hole, 1944–5, 120.
10   Rollinson, 1974, 78; Courtney, 1890, 141; cf. Evans, 1966, 160.
11   E.g. Henderson, 1879, 264, 140–4; Gurdon, 1893, 20–1; Leather, 1970, 82–3.
12   Torr, 1918, 7.
13   Evans, 1970, 17.
14   Cawte, Helm and Peacock, 1967, *passim*.
15   Evans, 1966, 18–19 *et passim*; Simpson, 1973, 77–8.
16   Howkins, n.d., 5.

17 Ellis, 1889, *passim*; Wakelin, 1972, 48–51, 102.

18 Grigson, 1975, 290–1, 146–7.

19 Northall, 1892, 8.

20 H. H. (mine-engine driver, 1871–1908), 'Reminiscence of Old Times', dated 1930, 12. Transcript kindly provided by K. C. Phillips.

21 Henderson, 1879, 123–5; Billson, 1895, 35; Simpson, 1973, 148; Killip, 1975, 184–6; Jenkins, 1976, 141; Opie and Opie, 1959, 288–9.

22 Phythian-Adams, 1975, 10–30; Malcolmson, 1973, 118–38.

23 Evans, 1966, *passim*.

24 Briggs, 1970, I, 135 *et passim*; Briggs, 1971, II, 620 *et passim*.

25 Phythian-Adams, 1975, 9–10; Baker, 1974, 23–4; cf. Leather, 1970, 88.

26 E.g. Briggs, 1971, II, 642–4, 664–7, 699–700, 704, 736–7; Evans and Thomson, 1972, 160–77, 234; Henderson, 1879, 201.

27 Leather, 1970, 104; cf. Jones-Baker, 1977, 156–7.

28 Minchinton, 1975, 71; Leather, 1970, 91–3 and plate; Hole, 1944–5, 90–1, figs.

29 Baker, 1974, 62–3, 84.

30 Northall, 1892, 462; Baker, 1974, 23; cf. Henderson, 1879, 114; Courtney, 1890, 136; Billson, 1895, 146.

31 Briggs, 1970, I, 123; cf. e.g., Simpson, 1973, 30.

32 Dack, 1911, n.p., 'Folk Lore (3)'.

33 Briggs, 1970, I, 543–5.

34 Leather, 1970, 119; Baker, 1974, 64; Henderson, 1879, 49; Dack, 1911, n.p., 'Birds'.

35 Jefferies, 1880, II, 204. Grinsell, 1976, *passim*; Briggs, 1971, II, 151–400.

36 Gurdon, 1893, 32; Henderson, 1879, 51–3; cf. Billson, 1895, 61.

37 Courtney, 1890, 135; Evans and Thomson, 1972, 234; Simpson, 1973, 153; Killip, 1975, 122–3; Jenkins, 1976, 182.

38 Gurdon, 1893, 7; Courtney, 1890, 163.

39 Briggs, 1970, I, 240–5, 439–40.

40 Courtney, 1890, 139.

41 E.g. Howkins, n.d., 13, 14; Flora Thompson, 1968, ch. XIII; Ruddock, 1964–5, 69; Opie and Opie, 1959, 1–5, 232–92.

42 Evans, 1970, 103–5; Evans, 1966, 17–19; Howkins, n.d., 64.

46 Voices from the Past: Rural Kent at the Close of an Era

Michael Winstanley

I

One point of view is seriously under-represented in the tomes of evidence bequeathed to us by our Victorian predecessors—that of the humble labourer and his family. We are generally obliged to evaluate their way of life through the eyes of others: employers, officials, their 'betters'. The reason for this dearth of information is not hard to find. Even those men and women who had the ability to leave us their impressions rarely considered their simple lives worthy of recording for posterity. 'I feel that I have not done much that is worthy to be left on record,' commented one Kentish labourer who did try to write his autobiography in 1912.[1] Consequently he concentrates on the exceptional rather than the everyday occurrences, on detailed descriptions of places he remembers and on the personalities of local gentry with whom he came into contact. Many questions we would like to ask are left unanswered.

Fortunately, within the last few decades we have developed both the facility and desire to tap these reservoirs of experience. 'Oral history', the ungainly title given to the process of tape recording recollections, has arrived just in time to allow the last generation of Victorians to leave a more permanent record. The idea of turning to the older generation for knowledge is, of course, far from novel, but the technology which enables us to record it verbatim is. Had George Sturt had access to a tape recorder in the 1900s his attempts to reconstruct 'the old rustic economy of the English peasantry' as it had existed in the mid-nineteenth century would have been made

626

much easier and the results more vivid.

> Here at my door people were living in many respects by primitive codes
> which have now all but disappeared from England. . . . The perception came
> to me only just in time, for today the opportunities for further observation
> occur but rarely. The old life is being swiftly obliterated, . . . in another ten
> years' time there will be not much left of the traditional life whose
> crumbling away I have been witnessing during the twenty years that are
> gone.[2]

Not until the 1950s did George Ewart Evans, using the new technology of the tape
recorder, re-examine the 'traditional life' in the same way. Today the passage of time
has reduced our period of study still further. We can only just stretch back to the turn
of the century and the survivors are few.

The countryman's memories are not concerned with nationally significant events.
Queen Victoria's Jubilees, the Boer War, the activities of Lloyd George—these
excepted, there are few references to happenings which made the newspaper
headlines. Absent, too, are precise dates. The calendar he refers to is that of his own
life. His recollections tend to be parochial and personal, dealing with his family, his
work, his village, his daily life; but this in no way detracts from their significance, as
some sceptics would maintain. Through such details we are better able to understand
the values and outlook of our predecessors. These minutiae are interspersed with
shrewd comments based on personal observation and experience, which are capable
of opening doors of understanding which would otherwise remain locked. Once
convinced of the utility of their memories there is nothing most old folk would rather
do than talk about them, a trait noticed by many earlier writers. 'Country people have
tenacious memories, and the older ones delight in finding a listener to whom they can
relate things which they experienced when they were young or which they were told
by their parents or grandparents.'[3]

II

The outline of labouring life which follows relies almost exclusively on memories
collected from elderly people in Kent, a county usually referred to as a prosperous
area reliant on hops and fruit.[4] Most contemporaries tended to assume that the
labourers were correspondingly richer. 'It is a well nurtured land, and the people are
a well nurtured people', wrote Richard Heath.[5] 'The Kentish labourer is decidedly
better off as a rule than agricultural labourers generally are in other counties I have
visited', remarked Aubrey Spencer in agreement in 1893.[6] Even Alfred Simmons[7]
admitted that the labourers were 'favourably situated', and most farmers echoed his
sentiments, some arguing vehemently that 'he has got too big a share of the cake'.[8]
Wages, however, varied considerably from district to district and even between
farms, and it would be wrong to assume that all farmworkers were comfortably

situated. Investigations tended to concentrate on the hop and fruit districts where there were opportunities for piecework and plenty of seasonal jobs for women and children. Elsewhere, however, especially in the Weald (affectionately referred to as 'Yellow Belly Country'), wages were lower, and on the chalk downs—sheep and corn country—work for the rest of the family was 'irregular and uncertain'.[9] A labourer's age and health could also influence his income. Those then just beginning their working life remember their youth as a time of plenty. 'I was single then. Like the song says, when I was single my pockets they jingled, I wish I was single again.'[10] Married men had less opportunity to save: 'Not a gay living for a large family, 16s 6d per week, 2s for rent, 2s for fuel, 10d for school, myself and wife and 7 children to live . . . I must leave you to judge my condition.'[11] Even for the relatively secure yearly workers, as old age crept on 'every farm lane led to the distant workhouse'.[12]

Throughout the county, therefore, some degree of self-sufficiency was still vital for the labourer if he was to be able to maintain his family. Some non-labourers envied the labourer's apparent ability to supply himself with ample food:

> They lived like fighting cocks. It's true! No question about it at all. They had more than they wanted to eat, at practically no cost at all to them theirselves. . . . Now each of those cottages had, I should think . . . the best part of an acre of ground. Anyway sufficient for each of them to have a little bit of orchard in the bottom. Apples, pears, plums, plus two or three dozen gooseberry bushes, plus plenty of ground to grow all the vegetables they could ever want. They had free milk. No rent to pay.[13]

The labourers and their families are less ecstatic in their views. 'Half the time they [the parents] hadn't got the money to buy seeds to plant with. Might have been out to work and come home and hadn't had nothing to eat. And nothing to eat when they got home. No dinner. No nothing.'[14] Nor did many of them view gardening as a pleasant pastime. Labourers relied on easily cultivated plants which required little attention—cabbages, onions and especially potatoes, enough 'to last till taters come again'. The uncommon fondness for vegetables, especially soggy cabbage, which Richard Jefferies noted, was the result of necessity not choice. Whenever possible children were 'encouraged' to help in the garden:

> They didn't exactly *make* us, but they encouraged us. If we didn't do so much, well, we'd get a clip round the ear'ole. . . . If we see there was some weeds in the garden, did it voluntary, we might get a penny or a ha'penny at the end of the week.[15]

Despite the abundance of fruit in the county labourers had to rely almost exclusively on their own supplies:

> You could never buy any. They didn't sell them in the village. They all went up to the London markets. Unless you'd got a tree in your garden, then you never had any of those fruits. That's why the children used to pinch fruit.

628

> Apples you could buy, but only the drops. All the picked ones were sent to London. They say Kent is the garden of England, but in those days there wasn't a lot of fruit about. I always remember that.[16]

Even more of a problem was meat. Butchers' meat, although relatively cheap after frozen imports had begun to arrive, still remained a luxury. 'Mother never let us go hungry. We always had something to eat. The only thing is, we never used to get much meat.'[17] If anyone in the family regularly ate butchers' meat it was father. The main sources of meat, however, came from outside the market economy. Cottagers either reared their own or found 'other ways' of supplementing their supply. Pork featured prominently in many diets:

> That was the principal living, pork, in them days, you know. When I was as I say, in plough service, I lived on fat pork for twelve month. That's all we had. Bar Sundays. Used to have a beef pudding. But that's all I had for breakfast, dinner and tea. Fat pork. Fairly near done me in you know. Going straight from home too. . . . I don't know if I could stick it now. Cor blimey! And sometimes it wasn't done properly. When the knife went through you could hear it sort of crunch.[18]

So heavily did some cottagers rely on pigs for meat that many of the children were put off it for the rest of their lives, and now refuse to eat it. 'But you can understand that we got sick of pork . . . for years I've never touched a piece of pork. I don't even look at a piece.'[19] A Christmas gift from a local farmer in later years remained uncooked. None of the family could face it.

Not every cottage, however, kept a pig. As well as an agreeable farmer or landlord, it required a certain amount of capital, or a friendly working relationship with the local butcher and miller. In one village the butcher's practice was to donate two weaners to a labourer and supply him with sufficient food to fatten them up, then to repossess one to be sold in the shop and allow the labourer to keep the other. Practices varied considerably:

> My old gran'dad used to say, 'It's no good a man trying to keep one pig. You want three. When they're all fed, one to kill for the house, one to sell to pay the miller, and one to buy three more pigs.' And that's the way they went on and made a do of it.[20]

Most men tried to do it as cheaply as possible, buying the smallest pig in a litter (known variously throughout Kent as the darling, Dannull pig or Anthony pig) from a local farmer for a few shillings, relying on scraps from the kitchen and from neighbours, only filling him out with barley meal in the final stages. Fear of grain stealing, however, meant that some farmers refused to allow their tied men to keep pigs, and the men lost a valuable source of food as well as a certain peace of mind. As Cobbett had astutely pointed out, the sight of a couple of flitches of bacon upon the rack 'tends more to keep a man from poaching and stealing than whole volumes of

629

penal statutes. . . . They are great softeners of the temper and promoters of domestic harmony.'[21] With salted sides of bacon hung around the living room what need had the home of artificial decorations: 'You've got pictures!'[22]

Apart from pigs, the labourers frequently resorted to breeding chickens or even rabbits, an additional recommendation in favour of the latter being that their skins could be sold to travelling pedlars. Rabbit stew with swimmers (dumplings) is remembered as a common meal. A few enterprising men even kept the odd goat tethered on the roadside to utilize the free grazing on the verges. In almost every instance the feeding of domestic animals was entrusted to the wife or, even more likely, to one of the children.

These legitimate meat supplies were added to in a variety of ways. Most people from labouring backgrounds recall that much of it was either 'pinched or poached'.[23] 'You could earn a bit other ways. Only you've got to be dumb and simple like the others. But mum's the word. That was the only way you could get through.' Some farmers allowed their men to catch rabbits on their land, but if a pheasant was stupid enough to 'fall out of a tree' and get entangled in the snares then 'we carried him home— never said nothing to nobody—and picked him and burnt the feathers and ate the pheasant. Nobody knew anything about it. We had to be a bit dishonest to keep ourselves going.'[24]

Sparrow catching, on the other hand, was welcomed by farmers; they frequently made generous donations to the rat and sparrow clubs which flourished in many villages, usually with the pub as their base. The sparrow, this 'Avian Rat', was viewed as an unmitigated evil. 'Indeed I do not understand', wrote Rider Haggard in 1898, 'how it comes about that we are not entirely eaten up with these mischievous birds.'[25] For the patient labourer sparrows provided a source of food and, through the local club, a potential, if small, income. Most of them were caught with nets of some description, once again by the younger members of the family:

> We used to go round of a night with a net on two long poles. They used to beat the hedge and we'd be round the other side to slap the net together and put it on the ground. Round the eaves of some of the old buildings you used to have a long stick. The net was on eight-foot woodwork. Used to hold it up and touch the tiles and out would come two or three starlings or sparrows. Down with the net and we'd have them. They used to squawk. . . . Used to get round some of the laurels too, round the houses. Toffs' houses and that. . . . Cor, it used to be a game. We used to enjoy it.[26]

Even blackbirds, recognized as useful garden birds, were eaten:

> She [mother] used to pick them like a chicken, truss them all up, and fasten a bit of thread to their legs, stick a fork under the mantelpiece and hang them in front of the old kitchener. Put a plate down the bottom to catch the mess. The heat used to kind of turn these birds, and when it came near to the time they was done, they wasn't half lovely you know.[27]

A thrush was too bitter to eat, but rooks, pigeons and even moorhens were assiduously caught, prepared and eaten, either in pies or as table birds. A few families were even known to catch and eat hedgehogs. By rolling them in clay and baking them they were able to pull off the spines and skin. 'They used to say they were beautiful you know. But I should never fancy one. Would you?' 'I liked it. It was only the one time I ever did taste it but I liked it then. Of course, we were young, well you'd eat anything in them days, because you didn't get a lot of meat.'[28] Whatever the meat, it was often encased in a pudding or a pie to make it go further. 'You lived on puddin's. Flour and everything would be cheap wouldn't it?'[29]

III

Self-help born of necessity, not moral indoctrination, carried itself over into other areas of life. Children's clothes were invariably home-made, usually cut down from their parents' or some generous donor's cast-offs. Nor was there anything shameful about patches on clothes, although these sometimes symbolized the division between labourers' children and those from wealthier backgrounds:

> You take the butcher's sons and the grocer's sons, publican's sons, that I went to school with, they would all be better off and better dressed than me. . . . Of course the schoolmaster always favoured them people what had got the best clothes on. Us ragged ones always thought they got best treatment.[30]

The skill of a labourer's wife with a needle was all-important to the family economy. Few clothes, except the man's and the footwear, were bought. Boots were rarely taken to the 'snob' or cobbler to be mended. Father did them at home. For fuel wood was preferred since it could often be collected by the children. Coal, an expensive luxury, was sparingly used. Monday's washing was done in water heated by wood fires. In almost every aspect of material welfare the labourer's family sought to maintain themselves without recourse to spending their meagre income.

Nothing was wasted. No one was allowed to leave food uneaten. No part of a pig was useless: the 'chidlings' or intestines were scrubbed and used for sausage skins; 'fleed cakes' were made from the fat;[31] trotters, tail and head were boiled down for brawn and stews; even the bladder found a use as a football or a storage container for lard. Water, a valuable commodity in many villages when it had to be laboriously carried from the pump, was carefully rationed, and sometimes thrown on the garden after it had served its domestic purpose. Tea, despite its dramatic fall in price from the 1880s, remained relatively expensive and was treated as a luxury:

> The teapot was always kept on the hob and the boiling water was always poured into that teapot until there was no more tea came out of it. What came out was water, then that was thrown away. The tea was made in the

> morning and lasted all day until teatime, and they made fresh tea. I think
> tea must have been very expensive. You didn't buy a quarter or anything
> like you do now. It was a pennyworth or twopennyworth, so it had to last a
> long time.[32]

Paraffin and candles were conserved by the family's going to bed early. 'Nine o'clock
all the street was in darkness. You wouldn't see a light anywhere. People used to go to
bed very early. I do now. I always have done.'[33] Old clothes were cut up for rag mats
and even rabbit skins were stretched, treated with liquid alum 'till the skin was nice
and cured', and then sewn together to make a rug. 'They was quite warm to put your
feet on when you got out of bed in the morning.'[34] Old calendars from the village shop
were cut up and the pictures used to decorate the walls. What was not eaten or
recycled was burnt or buried. There was little need for a refuse disposal service.

Possibly the best-fed labourers, but the worst-paid in monetary terms, were the men
who boarded with their employer, a practice which lingered on in Kent, especially
outside the hop-growing areas, right up to 1914. Mates who lodged with the wagoner
were less likely to fare so well. The allowance from the farmer, about 9s. by the turn of
the century, which the wagoner had for feeding his lodger was all too often devoted to
improving his own family's diet. Several men, however, have fond memories of eating
at their employer's table, even if their diet did seem monotonous:

> When we lived in with the farmer, he always had a barrel of beer in, and we
> used to have small beer for breakfast, ale for dinner and small beer for
> tea. . . . The only time we had hot tea was on Sunday. For breakfast in the
> morning, living with the farmer, was a darn great lump of fat pork, half a
> loaf of bread and, if they'd got plenty of milk, a jolly great bowl of bread and
> milk. That was something to go to work on. We lived jolly well in them days.
> After I left that last farm, when I joined the service at nineteen, I weighed
> 12 stone, 4 pounds. I hadn't been in the service three months and I went
> down to less than 10 stone.[35]

IV

The disadvantage of living-in, however, was that it tended to destroy a man's self-
respect; and the achievement of self-respect was just as important as maintaining
physical welfare. As a lodger 'you was tied down like a prisoner more or less. A
prisoner free. Got it that way then.'[36] How a labourer maintained himself was just as
important to him as the standard of living he achieved.

Charity, as an aid to individual efforts, was welcomed and carried no sense of
disgrace or degradation, but to turn to the parish was to lose all hope, all sense of
decency, all self-respect. It was the source, not the content or level of relief, which
mattered. Although 'thousands of our poor village folk seem unable to conceive any
greater virtue in their superiors than open-handedness, and nothing but satisfaction

is felt on either side',[37] the Poor Law had successfully ingrained in them a dread of parish relief. 'I suppose they thought that's a gift [charity]. That's free. But they wouldn't apply, if it was to do with the workhouse. They'd got that in their heads—the workhouse was a disgrace.'[38] The legacy lingers on even today:

> I grew up with that dread. It was planted in us—save something. You must save so that you don't, in your old age, have to go to the workhouse. . . . Well it's so ingrained in me, that if I was starving, I wouldn't ask for public assistance, because with that it seems the same to me. I know they say it isn't, but anyway I've managed to save enough to do without it.[39]

Respectability also required the keeping of the Sabbath, but here an ambivalent attitude had developed. On the one hand, most forms of work were to be avoided on Sunday. Those who flouted this rule were widely condemned:

> Men out in the country wouldn't dig their gardens on a Sunday. . . . I can remember when I was a boy, there was a man come up to help on the farm and he went out in his garden digging and they talked—I heard my father and them say—they was all alike, the men round that way, 'I don't know who he is!' And they shunned that man because he worked on a Sunday.[40]

Church attendance, on the other hand, was far from obligatory in this moral code. There was no joy in being denounced from the pulpit (personally in some cases), in squeezing into the cold, draughty pews at the rear of the church, in being inspected by employers on the one day off. Not to mouth acceptance of religious mores was looked down on, but church attendance was not, at least among the labouring class, much to the dismay of the parsons. 'If people didn't go to church he'd [the vicar] go round to their houses and give them a dressing down. I don't know whether it made much difference or not.'[41] Although children attended Sunday School, many of them were astute enough to realize their parents had ulterior motives in sending them. 'It was just to get rid of us. But all the kids liked going,' even though they were taught by '"old toffs"' daughters'.[42]

Status, acceptance by their own kind, was of supreme importance to most families, and their quest for it detracted from any serious questioning of the structure of rural society. Although perpetually conscious of their class, even cynically critical of their social superiors, few labourers seem to have translated this into open hostility. They did not seek to better themselves by attacking their employers' privileged positions, and they brought their children up in the same way of thinking.

> There were certain people who were our superiors and we were supposed to adopt a courteous attitude to them. Nothing really terrible about it. We looked up to them and we expected them to be better than we were, and it gave us some standard.[43]

'You didn't know anything about the haves and have-nots. . . . We wasn't educated to that extent. Them was the days when you lifted your cap when you met anyone.'[44]

Social superiors who failed to live up to the standards set for them were criticized for their personal flaws, not as typical specimens of the employing class. Generally, even these failings were overlooked because 'they give us a living didn't they, you see?'[45] As Sturt observed:

> This village looks up to those who control wealth as if they were the sources of it: and if there is a little dislike of some of them personally, there has so far appeared but little bitterness of feeling against them as a class. . . . Being born to poverty and the labouring life, they accept the position as if it were entirely natural. . . . They suppose that it takes all sorts to make a world and since they are of the labouring sort, they must make the best of it.[46]

The survivors of the period agree. They accepted their position 'as a matter of course'.

It was within their own class, therefore, that labourers and their families strove to attain social acceptability and esteem. Poverty itself was no disgrace if brought about by misfortune, but if the cause was considered to be flaws of character then the family were outcasts. 'That class of people', as they were labelled, who refused to fend for themselves, to show themselves willing to 'make do and mend', were given little sympathy. They were frequently considered to be beyond reform, defective in personality not unfortunate in circumstances. 'The more they had the more they wanted.' Quite unconsciously the labourers assumed an individualist philosophy, accrediting everyone with the ability, but not always the will, to maintain himself independently.

Slovenliness or squalor were similarly degrading. To be clean was to be respectable. Dirty people 'sort of got looked down on, because you can keep clean even if you're poor can't you? It doesn't cost much to, although it was a lot more difficult in those days when every drop of water had to be heated for washing and baths.'[47] The contrast with townspeople, especially Londoners, struck one lady who, from 1900, spent several years working for some sisters of mercy at Rotherhithe:

> You could always depend on country people being clean couldn't you? You couldn't town people. If you went into their houses, when you went back home, you knew you'd got to strip and have a bath, and put all clean clothes on because you never knew what you picked up in their houses. I think country people would have died rather than not be clean. I know when we were children, we played in the dirt, we got filthy dirty, but we never went to bed dirty. We were always washed and clean before we went to bed. And that was clean dirt to what I got used to in London. . . . I can't describe the smell. It was terrible. . . . This smell in London would stick. Their houses used to stink and they couldn't smell it. They were so used to it. It was a dreadful smell. . . . Very different from country people. The difference was dreadful to me because I had always seen my mother cooking and cleaning and making, but not these people. They would sit for hours outside their doors talking and gossiping, but not to do any cleaning. Very few people

were clean. . . . I don't think you would understand what the dirt meant to me. I used to shudder.[48]

Many Kentish people had no need to travel to London to compare themselves with their city counterparts. The city came to them for hop picking each year, invading their privacy, overrunning their pubs, pilfering from their shops, and displaying their filthy habits for all to see. Country-dwellers, almost without exception, received a huge stimulus to their self-respect. The hoppers might be 'not too bad', 'tremendously good hop pickers', 'sociable people' and 'all right as a rule', but they were widely regarded as an inferior class of beings. Their women went into pubs and could be seen smoking, both criminal acts in the rural code. Above all they were dirty. 'After they went back we always used to pray for good rain.'[49] The greatest disgrace for a local child was to return to school with his or her head shaved, a victim of the lice which the seasonal migrants brought with them. Disinfectant, diarrhoea mixture, changes of clothes, the burning of straw and bedding left behind by the visitors, all were employed by the labourers to keep themselves free from infection. Everything about the Londoners indicated that they were a class apart. This self-righteous indignation persisted right down to the end of the 1950s when the Londoners, by now much altered in their habits and enjoying more hygienic lodgings, ceased to migrate in such numbers. Until that time, however, the labourer in the hop areas of the county was reminded annually that he was far from being a member of the lowest stratum in society.

V

Physical welfare and status—but what of that elusive quality of life? Were people actually happier in those days? There is a great temptation today to view the slow, peaceful ways of the horse-powered rural economy as part of a lost golden age. This is not a new phenomenon. Writers have always been at pains to point out that the idyllic days of the old organic community, traditional England, have just, and only just, departed. For Cobbett the golden age had already gone by 1820; for Sturt it was dying only from the 1890s. For the present generation of writers it was alive up to 1914, possibly even up to the 1930s. No doubt future writers will view the present decade with similar affection. Few of those old enough to remember the turn of the century would concur with the golden-age image. Although they bemoan their lost youth and hanker after their 'good young days', they reject out of hand any suggestion that their way of life then was intrinsically better than the one they now enjoy. 'They weren't about then, some of them what talk about it [the good old days]. Not when I was.' As for wishing to see them return: 'Oh God, no! No! Where there was a big family, pretty well starved out we was.' 'We was more or less convicts. You didn't dare smoke or anything like that at work.'[50] At best the labourer lived under a benevolent despotism, at worst a tyranny.

Yet elderly folk would agree that something has been lost in the changes of the past eighty years: a certain contentment. Lacking an ideal, living their lives 'in grooves', as Jefferies astutely called it, they merely desired to make ends meet, an aspiration pitched low enough for the majority of them to achieve it most of the time. If this was attained they were satisfied, they were content and relatively indifferent to all else around them, a trait which commentators like Heath attributed to their 'unceasing, protracted labour' which robbed them of any chance to aspire to higher things. As many recent social investigators have pointed out, perceptions and expectations play a significant role, possibly a more significant role than actual physical welfare, in determining an individual's level of satisfaction with his position in life. Most labourers recognize these two aspects and deliberately choose the words 'contented' or 'satisfied' to describe their outlook, in preference to the emotive, subjective 'happy'. 'They was hard old days but as I say they were peaceful. People knew that was their lot and they wasn't going to get no more. But nobody's satisfied today. The more money they got, the more money they seem to want.' 'Oh, things have improved in ever so many ways. Don't think I want to go back to my day—I don't. . . . Yet we was happy you know. We was contented, because we didn't know any different. We didn't expect anything, because if you did you didn't get it.'[51] Comments like these are not exceptional. They are typical of the majority of people who chose to remain on the land, and, surprisingly enough, many town-dwellers express similar opinions. As children and young adults they were subjected to social forces which made it only too plain to them what their lot in life ought to be.

Today we tend to consider that Victorian labouring families lived in what we would call poverty, but only with hindsight and a greater social awareness have many of those brought up in such conditions come to perceive their position as having been in any way unnatural, unsatisfactory, or resembling poverty:

> We never thought we were poor then, but we were. . . . I mean you never thought about it, but afterwards when you think how you've been exploited and have been exploited over the years, that's when you think about it. But not then. It never entered your head. It was just right that it should be so. . . . You never thought you had a *right* to have anything.[52] We were all poor. Well, I consider we were very poor, but it's only late years I've thought we were poor. . . . There was enough to eat, and just enough . . . I don't think you can realize how very poor people were, and yet to me they were always quite happy. There was no grumbling—I never heard anybody grumble. We could always manage to get something to eat.[53]

This 'self contained oblivion' or 'Oriental absence of aspiration'[54] which Jefferies found so depressing is the key to understanding the labourer's 'contented indifference', an attitude rudely disturbed by four years of war from 1914 and challenged over the years by the development of media and advertising.

What remains today? Agricultural methods have undergone another revolution. Farm cottages are now second homes or occupied by town workers eager to 'get away from it all'. The world, as the survivors of the Victorian age remember it, has vanished. Yet these survivors remain virtually unchanged, firmly embedded in the past, still sitting in the rear pews of the church where they were taught to sit as children, wary of drawing social security, the modern parish relief, avoiding pork, the staple of so many of their earlier meals. They are reminders that customs and values linger on long after they have ceased to be meaningful. Sturt had looked forward to 'a renaissance of the English countryside', but those who had little or nothing to look forward to then now have even less. They have only the past. Their memories are their only real possessions.

Notes

1 T. J. Pointer, 'An Agricultural Labourer's Autobiography' (1837–1912), MS Broadstairs Public Library.
2 Sturt, 1912, 8, 17.
3 Cornish, 1939, 117.
4 Extracts are from a few of the interviews collected between 1974 and 1977 for the SSRC project, 'Life in Kent before 1914'. Page references are to transcripts of interviews. All the respondents were born in the last two decades of the nineteenth century and come from labouring families unless otherwise stated. They make no distinction in their recollections between the late Victorian and Edwardian eras: the First World War is the watershed for them.
5 Heath, 1893, 160.
6 BPP 1893–4 XXXV 665.
7 Secretary of the Kent and Sussex Labourers' Union, BPP 1882 XIV 170.
8 Charles Hoare, Staplehurst farmer, BPP 1894 XVI pt 2, 503.
9 BPP 1868–9, XIII 81.
10 Albert Patterson (born 1892), 18.
11 BPP 1882 XV 165.
12 Green, 1920, 108.
13 P. C. Robinson (born 1892), bailiff's son, 12.
14 Freddie Moon (born 1887), 14.
15 Jack Larkin (born 1889), 15.
16 Bernice Baker (born 1884), 39–40. See also Harrison, 1928, 253.
17 William Darby (born 1892), 16.
18 J. H. Barwick (born 1886), 14–15.
19 Baker, 24–5.
20 Larkin, 18–19.
21 Cobbett, 1821, para. 139.
22 Steve Prebble (born 1891), fisherman/farmer, 27.
23 Patterson, 28.
24 Percy Barnes (born 1889), 21, 36.
25 Haggard, 1906a, 90.
26 Harry Gambrill (born *c*. 1890), traction engine contractor, 42.

27   Gambrill, 44.
28   Barwick, 47; Frank Kemsley (born 1889), horse dealer/higgler/farmer, 20.
29   James Styles (born 1887), country building labourer, 6.
30   Styles, 14, 28.
31   Fleed: the internal fat of a pig from which lard is made.
32   Baker, 75.
33   Baker, 28.
34   Barnes, 20.
35   Larkin, 4, 9.
36   Patterson, 7.
37   Bennett, 1914, 42.
38   Baker, 53.
39   Baker, 6.
40   Frederick Atkins (born 1883), labourer/thatcher, 4–5.
41   Barnes, 108.
42   Larkin, 46–7.
43   Harold Pilcher (born 1897), smallholder, 35–6.
44   George Post (born 1896), tailor, 18.
45   Winifred Beech (born 1894), 19.
46   Sturt, 1912, 103, 106.
47   Dora Fenney (born 1892), publican/carter/labourer, 51.
48   Baker, 18–20.
49   Laura Bryant (born 1892), 9.
50   Moon, 22; Barnes, 60.
51   Barnes, 35; Styles, 9 10.
52   A. Fordred (born 1896), 28.
53   Baker, 2, 32.
54   Jefferies, 1880, II, 78.

Bibliography

Bibliography

The place of publication is London, unless otherwise stated.

Acland, Lady Anne, 1976, *Holnicote Estate, Somerset*, National Trust.
Acland, John E., 1914, 'Dorset "Buttony"', *Proceedings, Dorset Natural History & Antiquarian Field Club*, XXXV.
Aflalo, F. G. (ed.), 1899, *The Cost of Sport*, John Murray.
'Agricola' (ed.), 1842, *Letters on the Rules and Regulations of Agricultural Societies.*
Agricultural Co-operative Association, 1954, *Farmers' Co-operatives in England.*
Agricultural Co-operative Association, 1966, *Agricultural Co-operation in England, Beginnings and Growth.*
'Agricultural Statistics of Scotland', 1875, *Transactions of the Highland and Agricultural Society of Scotland*, 4th ser., VIII.
Aiton, William, 1811, *General View of the Agriculture of the County of Ayr*, Glasgow.
Albery, W., 1927, *A Parliamentary History of the Ancient Borough of Horsham 1295–1885*, Longman.
Albion, R. G., 1926, *Forests and Sea Power*, Harvard University Press, Cambridge, Mass.
Alexander, D., 1970, *Retailing in England during the Industrial Revolution*, Athlone Press.
Alexander, Sally, 1970, *St. Giles's Fair 1830–1914: Popular Culture and the Industrial Revolution in Nineteenth-Century Oxford*, Ruskin College History Workshop pamphlet, Oxford.
Alison, Archibald, 1834, 'Hints to the Aristocracy', *Blackwood's Edinburgh Magazine*, XXXV.

Bibliography

Allen, C. W., 1914, 'The Housing of the Agricultural Labourer', *Journal of the Royal Agricultural Society*, LXXV.

Allen, William, 1846, *Life of William Allen, with selections from his correspondence*, Charles Gilpin.

Ambrose, P., 1974, *The Quiet Revolution: Social Change in a Sussex Village 1871–1971*, Chatto & Windus.

Amos, S. W., 1971, 'Social Discontent and Agrarian Disturbances in Essex, 1795–1850', unpublished M.A. thesis, University of Durham.

Anderson, M., 1971a, *Family Structure in Nineteenth Century Lancashire*, Cambridge University Press, Cambridge.

Anderson, M., 1971b, 'Urban Migration in Nineteenth Century Lancashire: Some Insights into Two Competing Hypotheses', *Annales de demographie historique*, VIII.

Anderson, M., 1976, 'Marriage Patterns in Victorian Britain: An Analysis Based on Registration District Data for England and Wales, 1861', *Journal of Family History*, I.

Andrews, G. H., 1853, *Modern Husbandry*, Nathanial Cooke.

Andrews, William, 1888–9, *North Country Poets*, Marshall.

Anon., 1864, 'The Life of a Farm Labourer', *Cornhill Magazine*, IX.

Arch, Joseph, 1898, new edn 1966, *Joseph Arch: The Story of his Life, Told by Himself*, Hutchinson.

Argyll, Duke of, 1876, 'The Agricultural Holdings Act of 1875', *Contemporary Review*, XXVII.

Arnold, Arthur, 1877, 'The Abuses of a Landed Gentry', *The Nineteenth Century*, I.

Arnold, M., 1868, *Schools and Universities on the Continent*, Macmillan.

Arnold, M. (ed.), 1879, *The Poems of Wordsworth*, Macmillan.

Arnold, M., 1888, *Essays in Criticism*, Macmillan.

Arnold, M., 1895, *Letters of Matthew Arnold 1848–1888*, ed. G. W. E. Russell, Macmillan.

Arnold, R., 1974a, 'A Kentish Exodus of 1879', *Cantium*, VI.

Arnold, R., 1974b, 'The "Revolt of the Field" in Kent, 1872–92', *Past and Present*, LXIV.

Aronson, H., 1914, *The Land and the Labourer*, Melrose.

Ashby, J., and King, B., 1893, 'Statistics of Some Midland Villages', *Economic Journal*, III.

Ashby, M. K., 1961, *Joseph Ashby of Tysoe 1859–1919*, Cambridge University Press, Cambridge.

Ashby, M. K., 1974, *The Changing English Village 1066–1914*, Roundwood Press, Kineton, War.

Ashford, L. J., 1960, *The History of the Borough of High Wycombe from its Origins to 1880*, High Wycombe Public Library.

Ashworth, W., 1966, *An Economic History of England 1870–1939*, Methuen.

Atkinson, F., 1966, *The Great Northern Coalfield 1700–1900*, Durham County Local History Society, Durham.

Atkinson, J. C., 1891, *Forty Years in a Moorland Parish*, Macmillan.

Attenborough, Rev. F. S., 1872, *Joseph Arch*, J. Matthew Vincent, Leamington.

Ausubel, H., 1960, *In Hard Times: Reformers among the Late Victorians*, Columbia University Press, New York.

Aydelotte, W. O., 1962, 'The Business Interests of the Gentry in the Parliament of 1841–47'. In G. Kitson Clark, *The Making of Victorian England*, Methuen.

Badeau, Adam, 1886, *Aristocracy in England*, Harper, New York.

Bagehot, Walter, 1859, 'Parliamentary Reform', *National Review*, VIII.

Bagshawe, T. W., 1972, 'Bedfordshire Basket Makers', *Bedfordshire Magazine*, XIII, 100.

Bailey, J., and Culley, G., 1805, *General View of the Agriculture of Northumberland, Cumberland and Westmorland*, Board of Agriculture, Newcastle.

Baines, D., 1972, 'The Use of Published Census Data in Migration Studies'. In E. A. Wrigley (ed.), *Nineteenth Century Society: Essays in the Use of Quantitative Methods for the Study of Social Data*, Cambridge University Press, Cambridge.

Baines, E., 1823, *History, Directory, and Gazetteer of the County of York*, II, Leeds.

Baker, M., 1974, *Folklore and Customs of Rural England*, David & Charles, Newton Abbot.

Barker, T. C., Oddy, D. J., and Yudkin, John, 1970, *The Dietary Surveys of Dr Edward Smith 1862–3*, Queen Elizabeth College Department of Nutrition, Occasional Paper 1.

Barker, T. C., and Robbins, Michael, 1963, *A History of London Transport*, I, Allen & Unwin.

Barley, M. W., 1961, *The English Farmhouse and Cottage*, Routledge & Kegan Paul.

Barnes, F. A., 1958, 'The Evolution of the Salient Patterns of Milk Production and Distribution in England and Wales', *Transactions and Papers, Institute of British Geographers*, XXV.

Barnett, D. C., 1967, 'Allotments and the Problem of Rural Poverty, 1780–1840'. In E. L. Jones and G. E. Mingay (eds), *Land, Labour and Population in the Industrial Revolution*, Arnold.

Barry, Alfred, 1867, *The Life and Works of Sir Charles Barry*, John Murray.

Barton, D. B., 1966, *The Cornish Beam Engine: its history and development*, privately published by the author, Truro.

Barty-King, H., 1977, *The Baltic Exchange: The History of a Unique Market*, Hutchinson/Benham.

Bateman, John, 1883, *The Great Landowners of Great Britain and Ireland*, 4th edn, Harrison.

Bateman, John, 1971, *The Great Landowners of Great Britain and Ireland*, new edn, Leicester University Press, Leicester.

Bear, W. E., 1897, 'The Food Supply of Manchester', *Journal of the Royal Agricultural Society*, 3rd ser., VIII.

Bear, W. E., 1898, 1899, 'Fruit and Flower Farming in England', *Journal of the Royal Agricultural Society*, 3rd ser., IX, X.

Beastall, T. W., 1954, 'The History of the Yorkshire Estates of the Ninth and Tenth Earls of Scarborough 1860–1900', unpublished M.A. thesis, University of Manchester, Manchester.

Beastall, T. W., 1973, *Collection for the History of Tickhill II*, University of Sheffield, Department of Extra-mural Studies, Sheffield.

Beastall, T. W., 1975, *A North Country Estate*, Phillimore, Chichester.

Beavington, F., 1963, 'The Change to More Extensive Methods in Market Gardening in Bedfordshire', *Transactions and Papers of the Institute of British Geographers*, XXXIII.

Bedford, Duke of, 1897, *A Great Agricultural Estate*, John Murray.

Belcher, C., 1863, 'On the Reclaiming of Waste Land as Instanced in Wichwood Forest', *Journal of the Royal Agricultural Society*, XXIV.

Bell, Adrian, 1930, *Corduroy*, Cobden-Sanderson.

Bell, Thomas, 1871, *History of Improved Shorthorn Cattle*, Newcastle.

Bellerby, J. R., 1953, 'Distribution of Farm Income in the U.K., 1867–1938', *Proceedings of the Agricultural Economics Society*, X.

Bellerby, J. R., 1959, 'National and Agricultural Income, 1851', *Economic Journal*, LXIX.

Bellerby, J. R., 1968, 'The Distribution of Farm Income in the U.K., 1867–1938'. In W. E. Minchinton (ed.), *Essays in Agrarian History*, II, David & Charles, Newton Abbot.

Bellerby, J. R., *et al.*, n.d., 'Agriculture and Industry Enquiry Research Papers', University of

Bibliography

Oxford Agricultural Economics Research Institute, Oxford (typescript).

Bennett, A., 1935, *The Old Wives' Tale*, Everyman ed., Dent.

Bennett, E. N., 1914, *Problems of Village Life*, Williams & Norgate.

Bentley, R., 1885, *New Book of Sports*.

Benton, Philip, 1867, *The History of Rochford Hundred*, A. Harrington, Rochford.

Beresford, J. T., 1959, 'Thoughts on the Agricultural Revolution', *National Provincial Bank Review*, XLVIII.

Best, G., 1971, *Mid-Victorian Britain 1851–75*, Weidenfeld & Nicolson.

Best, G. F. A., 1964, *Temporal Pillars: Queen Anne's Bounty, the Ecclesiastical Commissioners, and the Church of England*, Cambridge University Press, Cambridge.

Best, R., 1970, *Poorstock in Wessex*, Dorset Publishing Company, Bournemouth.

Bibby, J. B. and C. L., 1978, *A Miller's Tale*, Liverpool.

Bienefeld, M. A., 1972, *Working Hours in British Industry*, Weidenfeld & Nicolson.

Billson, C. J., 1895, *County Folk-lore. Printed Extracts, No. 3, Leicestershire and Rutland*, Folklore Society.

Blackmore, R. D., 1876, *Cripps, the Carrier*, Sampson Low.

Blake, S., 1974, 'An Historical Geography of the British Agricultural Engineering Industry 1780–1940', University of Reading Institute of Agricultural History, Reading (typescript).

Blakeborough, Richard, 1898, *Wit, Character, Folklore and Customs of the North Riding of Yorkshire*, Henry Frowde.

Blew, W. C. A., 1901, *A History of Steeplechasing*, J. C. Nimmo.

Blomfield, Reginald, 1940, *Richard Norman Shaw, R.A.*, Batsford.

Blomfield, Reginald, and Thomas, F. Inigo, 1892, *The Formal Garden*, Macmillan.

Bloomfield, R., 1803, *The Farmer's Boy*, 7th ed. Vernor & Hood.

Bloomfield, R., 1813, *The Banks of Wye*, 2nd ed., B. & R. Crosby.

Blythe, R., 1972, *Akenfield*, Penguin, Harmondsworth, Middx.

Bonham-Carter, V., 1952, *The English Village*, Penguin, Harmondsworth, Middx.

Bonnett, H., 1972, *Saga of the Steam Plough*, David & Charles, Newton Abbot.

Booker, J., 1974, *Essex and the Industrial Revolution*, Essex County Council, Chelmsford.

Booth, Charles, 1894, *The Aged Poor in England and Wales*, Macmillan.

Booth, M. R., 1972, 'The Metropolis on Stage'. In H. J. Dyos and M. Wolff (eds), *The Victorian City*, Routledge & Kegan Paul.

Borrow, George, 1903, *Lavengro*, Murray.

Boucher, C. T. G., 1963, *John Rennie 1761–1821*, Manchester University Press, Manchester.

Bourne, George (George Sturt), 1955, *Change in the Village*, Duckworth.

Boutflour, R., 1938, 'The Royal Agricultural College', *Agricultural Progress*, XV.

Bovill, E. W., 1962, *English Country Life, 1780–1830*, Oxford University Press, Oxford.

Bowick, T., 1862, 'On the Management of a Home Farm', *Journal of the Royal Agricultural Society*, XXIII.

Boyd, Andrew K. H., 1859, 'The Recreations of a Country Parson', Fraser's Magazine.

Boyd, J. (ed.), 1934, *Trollope. Hunting Sketches*, Hutchinson.

Boyson, Rhodes, 1970, *The Ashworth Cotton Enterprise: The Rise and Fall of a Family Firm, 1818–1880*, Clarendon Press, Oxford.

BPP (British Parliamentary Papers):

    1806 III Committee to Consider State of the Woollen Manufacture, Minutes of Evidence.

    1824 VI S.C. Agricultural Wages.

1835 XXXV First Report of Poor Law Commission.

1835 XXXII R.C. Condition of the Poor in Ireland.

1836 VIII S.C. on Agriculture.

1836 XXIX, pt I Second Report of Poor Law Commission.

1836 XXX–XXXIV R.C. Condition of the Poor in Ireland.

1837 XXXI Third Report of Poor Law Commission.

1837 XXXVIII, LI R.C. Condition of the Poor in Ireland.

1837–8 XXVIII Fourth Report of Poor Law Commission.

1839 XIX R.C. Constabulary Force.

1840 XXII–XXIV R.C. Handloom Weavers: Reports of Assistant Commissioners.

1842 XV R.C. Condition of Children in Mines and Manufactories.

1843 XII R.C. Employment of Women and Children in Agriculture: Reports of Special Assistant Poor Law Commissioners.

1843 XIV R.C. Children's Employment, Second Report (Trades and Manufactures).

1844 XXIX Inspectors' Reports on Prisons.

1845 XIX–XXII R.C. Occupation of Land (Ireland).

1845 XXIV Inspectors' Reports on Prisons.

1846 IX S.C. Game Laws.

1846 XXI Inspectors' Reports on Prisons.

1848 VII S.C. Agricultural Customs, Report.

1849 XLIV Returns of Persons killed and injured in Poaching Affrays.

1851 XLVII Return of Numbers of Justices.

1852–3 XXXVI S.C. Police.

1852–3 XXXVIII, pts I and II 1851 Census. Population Tables, II, vols I and II.

1852–3 LXVIII Return of Number of Justices.

1852–3 LXXXIX Census of Religious Worship, 1851.

1856 L Number of Justices qualified to act.

1856 LXVIII Abstract of Returns of Parishes in England and Wales, in which (during the last Fifteen Years, church Rates have been refused).

1861 II, XXI, XXX R.C. State of Popular Education in England (Newcastle Commission).

1862 XLV Memorial from Chief Constables and Return of Murderous assaults on gamekeepers in 1859.

1863 IX S.C. Prison Discipline.

1863 XVIII R.C. Children's Employment, First Report.

1864 XXIV Conditions in Mines to which Act 23 & 24 Vict. c. 151 does not apply.

1864 XXVIII Sixth Report of Medical Officer to Committee of Council on Health (report by Dr Edward Smith).

1867 XVI R.C. Children's Employment, Sixth Report.

1867 XVII Registrar General of Births, Deaths and Marriages in England, 28th Annual Report.

1867–8 XVII R.C. Employment of Children, Young Persons and Women in Agriculture, First Report.

1868–9 VIII S.C. on Parliamentary and Municipal Elections.

1868–9 XIII R.C. Employment of Children, Young Persons and Women in Agriculture, Second Report.

1870 XIII R.C. Employment of Children, Young Persons and Women in Agriculture, third and fourth reports.

1870 LXVIII Agricultural Returns.

1871 XIV Reports of Inspectors of Factories for Half-Year Ending 30 April 1871.

1872 X S.C. Game Laws.

1872 XXVI R.C. Friendly Societies, Minutes of Evidence.

1873 XIII S.C. Game Laws.

1873 XVI S.C. Improvement of Land.

1873 LIII Returns of Earnings of Agricultural Labourers.

1874 LXXII, pt III Return of Owners of Land and Heritages for 1872–3.

1876 XXIX Report of Commissioners Appointed to Inquire into Working of Factory and Workshop Acts.

1881 XLVI Tenth Report of Local Government Board.

1882 XIV, XV R.C. Depressed Condition of Agricultural Interests.

1884 XXXIII R.C. Condition of Crofters and Cottars in Highlands of Scotland.

1884–5 XXII Twenty-eighth Report of Commissioners of Inland Revenue.

1884–5 XXX R.C. Housing of the Working Classes, vol. II, Minutes of Evidence.

1886 C. 4848 Return of Number of Allotments and Agricultural Holdings in Great Britain.

1887 XXXVIII Inquiry as to Disturbances Connected with Levying of Tithe Rent Charge in Wales.

1888 LIII, LIV, LV and LVII R.C. Market Rights and Tolls, Asst. Commissioners' Reports.

1889 LIX Return of School Boards and Attendance Committees, 1889.

1890 LVI Return for Public Elementary Schools, 1889.

1890 C. 6144 Return of Number of Allotments and Smallholdings.

1892 XXXVIII Twenty-first report of Local Government Board.

1893–4 I–XIII, XXXV R.C. Labour: the Agricultural Labourer (England).

1893–4 XXXVI R.C. Labour: the Agricultural Labourer (Wales).

1893–4 XXXVII, pt II R.C. Labour: the Agricultural Labourer. General Report.

1893–4 CVI 1891 Census, England and Wales. Abstract.

1894 XVI R.C. Agricultural Depression.

1895 XIV R.C. Aged Poor, Report.

1895 XVII R.C. Agricultural Depression.

1895 XL R.C. Land in Wales and Monmouthshire, Evidence.

1895 L Twenty-fourth Report of Local Government Board.

1896 XVI R.C. Agricultural Depression: Particulars of Expenditure and Outgoings on Certain Estates.

1896 XVII R.C. Agricultural Depression.

1896 XXXIV R.C. Land in Wales and Monmouthshire, Report.

1896 XLIX Accounts and Papers.

1899 XXI Committee of Council on Education (England and Wales), Report for 1898–9.

1900 LXIII Report by Wilson Fox on Wages and Earnings of Agricultural Labourers in U.K.

1900 CI Agricultural Returns.

1901 LXXXVIII Irish Agricultural Statistics.

1903 XCIII Memoranda to Board of Trade on British and Foreign Trade and Industry.

1905 XX Departmental Committee upon the Fruit Industry of Great Britain.

1905 XCVIII Second Report of Wilson Fox on Wages and Earnings of Agricultural Labourers.

1906 XCVI Board of Agriculture Report on Decline of Agricultural Population of Great Britain 1881–1906.

1908 Cd. 6277 Census of Production for 1907.

1909 XLII, XLIII R.C. Poor Laws, Effect of Outdoor Relief, Endowed and Voluntary Charities.

1910 XLVII R.C. Poor Laws, Evidence from Rural Centres.

1910 XLIX R.C. Poor Laws, vol. IX. Evidence Relating to Unemployment.

1910 LIV R.C. Poor Laws, Report on Visits to Poor Law and Charitable Institutions.

1910 LXVIII Judgment and Minutes of Evidence, East Dorset Election Petition.

1912 Cd. 6277 Agricultural Output of Great Britain, 1908.

1912–13 XIII Registrar-General of Births, Deaths and Marriages, Seventy-fourth Annual Report (for 1911).

1917–18 Cd. 8881 Final Report Forestry Sub-Committee, Committee on Reconstruction.

1919 I, IX S.C. Wages and Conditions of Employment in Agriculture in Wales.

1920 VIII Report of Departmental Committee on Agricultural Machinery and Implements.

1922 VII Report of Departmental Committee on Lands in Scotland used as Deer Forests.

Brace, H. W., 1960, *A History of Seed Crushing in Great Britain*, Land Books.

Bradley, S. G., 1907, *Round about Wiltshire*, Methuen.

Brady, J., 1958, *The Big Sycamore*, Gill, Dublin.

Bravendar, J., 1850, 'The Farming of Gloucestershire', *Journal of the Royal Agricultural Society*, XI.

Brewster, D. M. M., 1970, 'Tadcaster in 1851: The Population of a Market Town', *Annual Report and Bulletin of the West Riding (Northern Section) Committee of the National Register of Archives*, National Register of Archives, Wakefield.

Bridges, J. A., 1906, *Reminiscences of a Country Politician*, T. Werner Laurie.

Briggs, K. M., 1970, *A Dictionary of British Folk-tales in the English Language, Incorporating the F. J. Norton Collection: Part A, Folk Narratives*; Routledge & Kegan Paul.

Briggs, K. M., 1971, *A Dictionary of British Folk-Tales in the English Language, Part B, Folk Legends*, Routledge & Kegan Paul.

Bright, J., and Rogers, J. E. Thorold (eds), 1870, *Speeches on Questions of Public Policy by Richard Cobden*, Macmillan.

Brightfield, M. F., 1968, *Victorian England in its Novels, 1840–1870*, University of California Library, Los Angeles.

Brill, Edith, 1973, *Life and Tradition on the Cotswolds*, Dent.

British Year Book of Agriculture and Agricultural Who's Who, 1908, Vinton.

Brockington, C. Fraser, 1965, *Public Health in the Nineteenth Century*, Churchill Livingstone, Edinburgh.

Brodrick, the Hon. G. C., 1881, *English Land and English Landlords*, Cassell, Petter, Galpin & Co.

Brodrick, the Hon. G. C., 1900, *Memories and Impressions*, Nisbet.

Brown, A. F. J., 1972, *Essex People, 1750–1900*, Essex Record Office, Chelmsford.

Brown, J. H., 1978, 'Agriculture in Lincolnshire during the Great Depression 1873–96', unpublished Ph.D. thesis, University of Manchester, Manchester.

Brundage, A., 1978, *The Making of the New Poor Law: The Politics of Inquiry, Enactment and Implementation 1832–39*, Hutchinson.

Bibliography

Brunskill, R. W., 1970, *Illustrated Handbook of Vernacular Architecture*, Faber.

Brunskill, R. W., 1974, *Vernacular Architecture of the Lake Counties*, Faber.

Buckinghamshire Federation of Women's Institutes, 1975, *A Pattern of Hundreds*, Richard Sadler, Chalfont St Giles.

Budd, William, 1873, *Typhoid Fever*, Longman.

Bull, L., 1926, *History of the Smithfield Club*, Smithfield Club.

Bulwer, Edward Lytton, 1970, *England and the English*, ed. Standish Meacham, University of Chicago Press, Chicago.

Burke, Bernard, 1894, *A Genealogical and Heraldic History of the Landed Gentry of Great Britain and Ireland*, 8th edn, Harrison.

Burke, Bernard, 1914, *A Genealogical and Heraldic History of the Landed Gentry of Great Britain*, 12th edn, Harrison.

Burke, John, 1836–8, *A Genealogical and Heraldic History of the Commoners of Great Britain and Ireland, Enjoying Territorial Possessions or High Official Rank; but Uninvested with Heritable Honours*, H. Colburn.

Burn, W. L., 1964, *The Age of Equipoise*, Allen & Unwin.

Burnett, John, 1966, *Plenty and Want: A Social History of Diet from 1815 to the Present Day*, Nelson.

Burnett, John, 1978, *A Social History of Housing, 1815–1970*, David & Charles, Newton Abbot.

Burnett, R. G., 1945, *Through the Mill. the Life of Joseph Rank*, Epworth Press.

Burritt, Elihu, 1865, *A Walk from London to Land's End and Back*, Sampson Low, Son, & Marston.

Butler, J. E., 1869, *Memoir of John Grey of Dilston*, Edmonston & Douglas, Edinburgh.

Butler, J. R. M., 1914, *The Passing of the Great Reform Bill*, Longman, Green.

Byerly, T. C., 1976, 'Changes in Agricultural Science', *Agricultural History*, L.

Bythell, D., 1969, *The Handloom Weavers*, Cambridge University Press, Cambridge.

Caird, Alex M'Neel, 1878, 'Land, Ownership and Tenure'. In *Report of the Present State of the Agriculture of Scotland Arranged under the auspices of the Highland and Agricultural Society*, William Blackwood & Sons, Edinburgh.

Caird, James, 1852, *English Agriculture in 1850–51*, Longman.

Caird, James, 1878a, 'General View of British Agriculture', *Journal of the Royal Agricultural Society,* 2nd ser., XIV.

Caird, James, 1878b, *The Landed Interest and the Supply of Food*, Cassell, Petter & Galpin.

Caird, James, 1968, *English Agriculture in 1850–51*, new edn, Frank Cass.

Cairncross, A. J., 1953, *Home and Foreign Investment, 1870–1913*, Cambridge University Press, Cambridge.

Cambrian Railways, 1904, *Time Tables* (reprinted 1977, Oxford Publishing Company, Oxford).

Cambridge, W., 1845, 'On the Advantage of Reducing the Size and Number of Hedges', *Journal of the Royal Agricultural Society*, VI.

Cannadine, David, 1977, 'The Landowner as Millionaire: The Finances of the Dukes of Devonshire c. 1800–c. 1926', *Agricultural History Review*, XXV, 2.

Carr, Raymond, 1976, *English Foxhunting: A History*, Weidenfeld & Nicolson.

Carslaw, R. McG., and Culpin, C., 1936, 'Labour, Power and Equipment in Arable Farming', *Journal of the Royal Agricultural Society*, XCVII.

Carter, Ian, 1976a, 'Class and Culture among Farm Servants in the North-east'. In A. A.

Maclaren (ed.), *Social Class in Scotland*, John Donald, Edinburgh.

Carter, Ian, 1976b, 'The Peasantry of North-East Scotland', *Journal of Peasant Studies*, III, 2.

Caunce, Stephen, 1975, 'East Riding Hiring Fairs', *Oral History*, III, 2.

Cavendish, Lady Frederick, 1927, *Diary*, ed. John Bailey, Batsford.

Cawte, E. C., Helm, A., & Peacock, N., 1967, *English Ritual Drama: A Geographical Index*, Folklore Society.

Census 1851, BPP 1852–3 LXXXVIII, pts I, II.

Census of 1851, 1854, Ages, Civil Condition and Occupations of the People.

Census 1861, BPP 1862 L, II.

Census 1871, BPP 1873 LXXI, pt I.

Census 1881, BPP 1883 LXXX.

Census 1891, BPP 1893–4 CVI.

Census 1901, BPP 1903 LXXXIV; 1904 CVIII, I.

Census of Woodland, 1928, Forestry Commission, HMSO.

Chadwick, Edwin, 1842, *Report on the Sanitary Condition of the Labouring Population of Great Britain* (new edn 1965, Edinburgh University Press, Edinburgh).

Chadwick, Edwin, 1867–8, *Report to Parliament on the Paris Exhibition.*

Chadwick, Mary E. J., 1976, 'The Role of Redistribution in the Making of the Third Reform Act', *Historical Journal*, XIX.

Chadwick, Owen, 1960, *Victorian Miniature*, Hodder & Stoughton.

Chadwick, Owen, 1966, 1970, *The Victorian Church*, I, II, Adam & Charles Black.

Chalklin, C. W. (ed.), 1975, *Early Victorian Tonbridge*, Kent County Library, Maidstone.

Chambers, J. D., 1972, *Population, Economy and Society in Pre-Industrial England*, Oxford University Press, Oxford.

Chambers, J. D., and Mingay, G. E., 1966, *The Agricultural Revolution, 1750–1880*, Batsford.

Chapman, S. D., 1967, *The Early Factory Masters*, David & Charles, Newton Abbot.

Chapman, S. D., 1971, *The History of Working-Class Housing: A Symposium*, David & Charles, Newton Abbot.

Charlton, Barbara, 1949, *Recollections of a Northumbrian Lady 1815–1866*, ed. L. E. O. Charlton, Jonathan Cape.

Charnock, J. H., 1848, 'On the Farming of the West Riding of Yorkshire', *Journal of the Royal Agricultural Society*, IX.

Chenevix-Trench, C., 1967, *The Poacher and the Squire*, Longman.

Cheshire Federation of Women's Institutes, 1961, *Cheshire Village Memories*, Cheshire W.I., Chester.

Chitty, S., 1974, *The Beast and the Monk: Life of Charles Kingsley*, Hodder & Stoughton.

Cholmondeley, Mary, 1897, *Red Pottage* (new edn 1968, Anthony Blond).

Christian, G. (ed.), 1961, *A Victorian Poacher: James Hawkers' Journal*, Oxford University Press, Oxford.

Church, Roy A., 1966a, *Economic and Social Change in a Midland Town: Victorian Nottingham*, Frank Cass.

Church, Roy A., 1966b, 'Messrs. Gotch and Sons and the Rise of the Kettering Footwear Industry', *Business History*, VIII.

Clapham, J. H., 1926–51, *An Economic History of Modern Britain*, 3 vols, Cambridge, University Press, Cambridge.

Clare, John, 1827, *The Shepherd's Calendar*, James Duncan.

Bibliography

Clark, Colin, 1973, *The Value of Agricultural Land*, Pergamon, Oxford.

Clark, G. Kitson, 1962, *The Making of Victorian England*, Methuen.

Clark, G. Kitson, 1973, *Churchmen and the Condition of England, 1832–1885*, Methuen.

Clark, Roger, 1975, *Somerset Anthology*, William Sessions, York.

Clarke, E., 1890, 'The Foundation of the Royal Agricultural Society', *Journal of the Royal Agricultural Society*, 3rd ser., I.

Clarke, E., 1898, 'The Board of Agriculture 1793–1822', *Journal of the Royal Agricultural Society*, 3rd ser., IX.

Clarke, J. A., 1847, 'On the Great Level of the Fens, Including the Fens of South Lincolnshire', *Journal of the Royal Agricultural Society*, VIII.

Clay, Christopher, 1968, 'Marriage, Inheritance, and the Rise of Large Estates, 1660–1815', *Economic History Review*, 2nd ser., XXI.

Clifford, Derek, 1962, *A History of Garden Design*, Faber.

Clifford, F., 1875a, *The Agricultural Lock-Out of 1874*, Blackwood & Sons, Edinburgh.

Clifford, F., 1875b, 'The Labour Bill in Farming', *Journal of the Royal Agricultural Society*, 2nd ser., XI.

Clow, A. and N.L., 1952, *The Chemical Revolution*, Batchworth Press.

Clutterbuck, J., 1869, 'On the Farming of Middlesex', *Journal of the Royal Agricultural Society*, 2nd ser., X.

Cobbett, William, 1821, *Cottage Economy*, P. Davies.

Cobbett, William, 1912, *Rural Rides*, Everyman ed., Dent.

Cobbett, William, 1930, *Rural Rides*, ed. G. D. H. and Margaret Cole, Peter Davies.

Cobbett, William, 1967, *Rural Rides*, ed. G. Woodcock, Penguin, Harmondsworth, Middx.

Cobbold, R., 1860, *Features of Wortham* (ed. R. Fletcher as *The Biography of a Victorian Village*, 1972, Batsford).

Cobden, Richard, 1878, *Speeches on Questions of Public Policy*, ed. J. Bright and J. E. Thorold Rogers, Macmillan.

Cobden, Richard, 1908, *Speeches on Questions of Public Policy*, 3rd ed., T. Fisher Unwin.

Cockburn, J. S. (ed.), 1977, *Crime in England, 1550–1800*, Methuen.

Coleman, J., 1871, 'English Cheese Factories', *Country Gentleman's Magazine*, VI.

Collings, J., 1908, *Land Reform: Occupying Ownership, Peasant Proprietary and Rural Education*.

Collins, E. J. T., 1969a, 'Harvest Technology and Labour Supply in Britain, 1790–1870', *Economic History Review*, 2nd ser., XXII.

Collins, E. J. T., 1969b, *Sickle to Combine*, The University, Reading.

Collins, E. J. T., 1970, 'Harvest Technology and Labour Supply 1790–1870', unpublished Ph.D. thesis, University of Nottingham, Nottingham.

Collins, E. J. T., 1972, 'The Diffusion of the Threshing Machine in Britain 1780–1880', *Tools and Tillage*, II, 1.

Collins, E. J. T., 1974, 'The British Agricultural Engineering Industry and its Records', *Social Science Research Council Newsletter*, XXIV.

Collins, E. J. T., 1975, 'Dietary Change and Cereal Consumption in Britain in the Nineteenth Century', *Agricultural History Review*, XXIII.

Collins, E. J. T., 1976, 'Migrant Labour in British Agriculture in the Nineteenth Century', *Economic History Review*, 2nd ser., XXIX, 1.

Collins, E. J. T., and Jones, E. L., 1967, 'Sectoral Advance in English Agriculture 1850–80',

Agricultural History Review, XV.

Collins, G. E., n.d. (1935), *Farming and Foxhunting*, Sampson Low.

Colvin, H. M., 1963, *A History of Deddington, Oxfordshire*, S.P.C.K.

Colyer, R. J., 1973, '"No Foot, No Ox"; Cattle Shoeing in Nineteenth-Century Wales', *Country Life*, CLIV, no. 3980.

Colyer, R. J., 1975, 'The Use of Estate Home Farm Accounts as Sources for Nineteenth-Century Agricultural History', *Local Historian*, XI.

Colyer, R. J., 1976, *The Welsh Cattle Drovers*, University of Wales Press, Cardiff.

Colyer, R. J., 1977, 'The Land Agent in Nineteenth-Century Wales', *Welsh History Review*, VIII.

Cook, E. T., and Wedderburn, Alexander (eds), 1903–12, *The Complete Works of John Ruskin*, George Allen.

Cooper, A., 1971, 'Victorian Newark', *Transactions of the Thoroton Society*, LXXV.

Cooper, Nicholas, 1967a, 'Housing the Victorian Poor', *Country Life*, 8 June, 1454–7.

Cooper, Nicholas, 1967b, 'The Myth of Cottage Life', *Country Life*, 25 May, 1290–3.

Cooper, T. Sidney, R. A., 1890, *My Life*, Richard Bentley & Son.

Copley, Esther, 1849, *Cottage Cookery*.

Copper, B., 1971, *A Song for Every Season*, Heinemann.

Coppock, J. T., 1956, 'The Statistical Assessment of British Agriculture', *Agricultural History Review*, IV.

Coppock, J. T., 1973, 'The Changing Face of England 1850–c. 1900'. In H. C. Darby (ed.), *A New Historical Geography of England*, Cambridge University Press, Cambridge.

Cormack, A. and A., 1971, *Days of Orkney Steam*, Kirkwall Press, Kirkwall.

Cornford, James, 1963, 'The Transformation of Conservatism in the Late Nineteenth Century', *Victorian Studies*, VII.

Cornish, J. G., 1939, *Reminiscences of Country Life*, Country Life.

Corran, H., 1975, *A History of Brewing*, David & Charles, Newton Abbot.

Corringham, R. W., 1845, 'Agriculture of Nottinghamshire', *Journal of the Royal Agricultural Society*, VI.

Country Life, 1904, 'The Duke of Bedford's Cottages', *Country Life*, 10 December.

Courtney, M. A., 1890, *Cornish Feasts and Folk-lore*, Penzance.

Cousens, S. H., 1961, 'Emigration and Demographic Change in Ireland, 1851–61', *Economic History Review*, 2nd ser., XIV, 2.

Cousens, S. H., 1964, 'The Regional Variations in Population Change in Ireland, 1861–81', *Economic History Review*, 2nd ser., XVII, 2.

Craigie, P. G., 1887, 'Size and Distribution of Agricultural Holdings in England and Abroad', *Journal of the Royal Statistical Society*, L.

Creyke, R., 1844, 'Some Account of the Process of Warping', *Journal of the Royal Agricultural Society*, V.

Crosby, T. L., 1977, *English Farmers and the Politics of Protection*, Harvester Press, Hassocks.

Crump, W. B., and Ghorbal, G., 1935, *History of the Huddersfield Woollen Industry*, Tolson Memorial Museum, Huddersfield.

Cullen, L. M., 1968, *Life in Ireland*, Batsford.

Cullen, L. M., 1972, *An Economic History of Ireland since 1660*, Batsford.

Cullen, L. M., 1975, 'Income, Foreign Trade and Economic Development: Ireland as a Case Study', unpublished paper read at New Orleans seminar on exports and economic development.

Cullen, L. M., forthcoming a, 'Economic Trends, 1691–1800'. In F. J. Byrne, T. W. Moody and F. X. Martin (eds), *A New History of Ireland*, IV, Clarendon Press, Oxford.

Cullen, L. M., forthcoming b, 'Castle, Countryside and Social Change'. In M. J. Craig (ed.), *Anglo-Irish Civilisation*, Collins.

Cullen, L. M., and Smout, T. C., 1977, 'Economic Growth in Scotland and Ireland'. In L. M. Cullen and T. C. Smout (eds), *Comparative Aspects of Scottish and Irish Economic and Social History 1600–1900*, Donald, Edinburgh.

Currie, B. W., 1901, *Recollections, Letters and Journals 1827–96*, Manresa Press.

Currie, R., Gilbert, A. D., and Horsley, L., 1978, *Churches and Churchgoers: Patterns of Church Growth in the British Isles since 1750*, Clarendon Press, Oxford.

Dack, C., 1911, *Weather and Folklore of Peterborough and District* (reprinted (n.d.) from original edition of the Peterborough Natural History and Archaeological Society).

Dale, H. E., 1956, *Daniel Hall—Pioneer in Scientific Agriculture*, John Murray.

Dale, T. F., 1899, *The History of the Belvoir Hunt*, Archibald Constable.

Dana, R. H., 1921, *Hospitable England in the 1870's*, John Murray.

Darby, H. C., 1940, *The Draining of the Fens*, Cambridge University Press, Cambridge.

Darby, H. C., 1964, 'The Draining of the English Claylands', *Geographische Zeitschrift*, LII.

Darby, J., 1898–9, 'The Evolution of Farm Implements and Machinery in the Past Sixty Years', *Journal of the Bath & West of England Society*, 4th ser., IX.

Darby, J., 1902, 'Reminiscences of Royal Shows', *Mark Lane Express, Carlisle Supplement*, 7 July.

Darley, Gillian, 1975, *Villages of Vision*, Architectural Press.

Darling, F. Fraser, 1955, *West Highland Survey*, Oxford University Press, Oxford.

Daubeny, C., 1842, 'The Application of Science to Agriculture', *Journal of the Royal Agricultural Society*, III.

David, P. A., 1970, 'Labour Productivity in English Agriculture, 1850–1914: Some Quantitative Evidence on Regional Differences', *Economic History Review*, 2nd ser., XXIII.

David, P. A., 1971, 'The Landscape and the Machine'. In D. N. McCloskey (ed.), *Essays on a Mature Economy: Britain after 1840*, Methuen.

Davies, C. S., 1960, *The Agricultural History of Cheshire, 1750–1850*, Cheetham Society, Manchester.

Davies, H., 1967, 'The Social Structure of South-West Wales in the Late Nineteenth Century', unpublished M.A. thesis, University of Wales.

Davies, M. F., 1909, *Life in an English Village*, T. Fisher Unwin.

Davies, V. L., and Hyde, H., 1970, *Dudley and the Black Country 1760 to 1860*, Dudley Public Libraries Transcript no. 16, Dudley.

Davies-Shiel, M., and Marshall, J. D., 1969, *Industrial Archaeology of the Lake Counties*, David & Charles, Newton Abbot.

Davis, D., 1966, *A History of Shopping*, Routledge and Kegan Paul.

Davis, R. W., 1972, *Political Change and Continuity 1760–1885*, David & Charles, Newton Abbot.

Day, W., 1857, *Mechanical Science and the Prize System in Relation to Agriculture*, Harrison.

Deane, P., and Cole, W. A., 1962, 2nd edn 1967, *British Economic Growth, 1688–1959*, Cambridge University Press, Cambridge.

Delgado, A., 1977, *The Annual Outing and Other Excursions*, Allen & Unwin.

Dent, J. D., 1871, 'The Present Condition of the English Agricultural Labourer', *Journal of the Royal Agricultural Society*, 2nd ser., VII.

Denton, J. B., 1864, *The Farm Homesteads of England*.

Dewey, P. E., 1975, 'Agricultural Labour Supply during the First World War', *Economic History Review*, 2nd ser., XXVIII.

Dibben, A. A. (ed.), 1960, *The Cowdray Archives*, West Sussex County Archives, Chichester.

Dickson, D. J., 1977, '*An Economic History of the Cork Region in the Eighteenth Century*', unpublished Ph.D. thesis, University of Dublin.

Dickson, John, 1867, 'On the Agriculture of Perthshire', *Transactions of the Highland and Agricultural Society of Scotland*, 4th ser., II.

Digby, A., 1972, 'The Operation of the Poor Law in the Social and Economic Life of Nineteenth-Century Norfolk', unpublished Ph.D. thesis, University of East Anglia.

Digby, A., 1975, 'The Labour Market and the Continuity of Social Policy after 1834: The Case of the Eastern Counties', *Economic History Review*, 2nd ser., XXVIII.

Digby, A., 1976, 'The Rural Poor Law'. In D. Fraser (ed.), *The New Poor Law in the Nineteenth Century*, Macmillan.

Digby, M., and Gorst, S., 1957, *Agricultural Cooperation in the United Kingdom*, Blackwell, Oxford.

Disraeli, Benjamin, 1845, *Sybil* (World's Classics edn, 1925, Oxford University Press, Oxford).

Disraeli, Benjamin, 1938, *Letters to Frances Anne, Marchioness of Londonderry, 1836–61*, ed. Marchioness of Londonderry, Macmillan.

Donnelly, J. S., jnr, 1975, *The Land and People of Nineteenth-Century Cork*, Routledge & Kegan Paul.

Dony, John G., 1942, *A History of the Straw Hat Industry*, Gibbs, Bamforth, Luton.

Douglas, R., 1976, *Land, People and Politics*, Allison & Busby.

Drennan, James, 1878, 'Farming of the West and South-Western Districts'. In *Report of the Present State of the Agriculture of Scotland Arranged under the Auspices of the Highland and Agricultural Society*, William Blackwood & Sons, Edinburgh.

Duckworth, A. M., 1971, *The Improvement of the Estate: A Study of Jane Austen's Novels*, Johns Hopkins University Press, Baltimore.

Dunbabin, J. P. D., 1965, 'Expectations of the New County Councils, and their Realization', *Historical Journal*, VIII.

Dunbabin, J. P. D., 1974, *Rural Discontent in Nineteenth-Century Britain*, Faber & Faber.

Duncan, R., 1963, 'Case Studies in Emigration: Cornwall, Gloucestershire and New South Wales, 1877–1886', *Economic History Review*, 2nd ser., XVI.

Dyos, H. J., and Reader, D. A., 1972, 'Slums and Suburbs'. In H. J. Dyos and M. Wolff (eds), *The Victorian City. Images and Realities*, Routledge & Kegan Paul.

Dyos, H. J., and Wolff, M. (eds), 1972, *The Victorian City. Images and Realities*, Routledge & Kegan Paul.

Eastlake, C. L., 1872, *A History of the Gothic Revival* (new edn 1970, ed. J. M. Crook, Leicester University Press, Leicester).

Eddowes, John, 1854, *The Agricultural Labourer as he Really is; Or, Village Morals in 1854*, Driffield.

Ede, R., 1838, 'The School of Agriculture, Cambridge University', *Agricultural Progress*, XVI.

Bibliography

Edlin, H. L., 1956, *Trees, Woods and Man*, Collins.

Edwards, George, 1922, *From Crow-Scaring to Westminster*, Labour Publishing Company.

Edwards, W., 1850, 'On Dry Warping at Hatfield Chase', *Journal of the Royal Agricultural Society*, XI.

Egan, Pierce, 1836, *Book of Sports and Mirror of Life*, Thomas Fagg.

Eliot, George, 1876, *Daniel Deronda*, Blackwood.

Elliott, D.J., 1975, *Buckingham: The Loyal and Ancient Borough*, Phillimore, Chichester.

Elliott, E., 1829, *The Village Patriarch*.

Ellis, A. J., 1889, *On Early English Pronunciation, Part V: The Existing Phonology of English Dialects Compared with that of West Saxon Speech*, Early English Text Society.

Elsam, Richard, 1816, *Hints for Improving the Condition of the Peasantry*.

Emerson, P. H., 1887, *Pictures from Life in Field and Fen*, G. Bell.

Emery, F., 1974, *The Oxfordshire Landscape*, Hodder & Stoughton.

Engels, F., 1950 (new edn), *The Condition of the Working Class in England in 1844*, Blackwell, Oxford.

Erickson, C., 1972, 'Who were the English and Scots Emigrants to the United States in the Late Nineteenth Century?' In D. V. Glass and R. Revelle (eds), *Population and Social Change*, Arnold.

Erickson, C., 1976, *Emigration from Europe, 1815–1914*, Black.

Ernle, Lord (Rowland Prothero), 1912, *English Farming Past and Present*, Longman Green.

Ernle, Lord (Rowland Prothero), 1938, *Whippingham to Westminster. The Reminiscences of Lord Ernle*, John Murray.

Ernle, Lord (Rowland Prothero), 1961, *English Farming Past and Present*, 6th edn, Heinemann; Frank Cass.

Escott, T. H. S., 1885, *England: Its People, Polity and Pursuits* (new edn, Chapman & Hall).

Evans, E. J., 1976, *The Contentious Tithe*, Routledge & Kegan Paul.

Evans, George Ewart, 1956, *Ask the Fellows who Cut the Hay*, Faber.

Evans, George Ewart, 1960, 1967, *The Horse in the Furrow*, Faber.

Evans, George Ewart, 1966, *The Pattern under the Plough: Aspects of the Folk-life of East Anglia*, Faber.

Evans, George Ewart, 1969, *The Farm and the Village*, Faber.

Evans, George Ewart, 1970, *Where Beards Wag All: The Relevance of the Oral Tradition*, Faber.

Evans, George Ewart, 1975, *The Days that We have Seen*, Faber.

Evans, George Ewart, and Thomson, D., 1972, *The Leaping Hare*, Faber.

Evans, H. T., 1948, *The Gorse Glen*, Hugh Evans & Sons, Liverpool.

Everitt, A. M., 1972, *The Pattern of Rural Dissent*, Leicester University Press, Leicester.

Everitt, A. M. (ed.), 1973, *Perspectives in Urban History*, Macmillan.

Everitt, A. M., 1976, 'Country Carriers in the Nineteenth Century', *Journal of Transport History*, n.s., III, 3.

Evershed, H., 1871, 'Market Gardening', *Journal of the Royal Agricultural Society*, 2nd ser., VII.

Eversley, Lord (G. S. Lefevre), 1894, *English Commons and Forests*, Cassell.

Eversley, Lord (G. S. Lefevre), 1907, 'The Decline in the Number of Agricultural Labourers in Great Britain', *Journal of the Royal Statistical Society*, LXX.

Fairfax-Blakeborough, J., 1936, 'Centenary of the Yorkshire Agricultural Society', *Trans-*

actions of the Yorkshire Agricultural Society, XCIV.

Fairlie, S., 1969, 'The Corn Laws and British Wheat Production 1829–1876', *Economic History Review*, 2nd ser., XXII, 1.

Farrell, T., 1974, 'Report on the Agriculture of Cumberland', *Journal of the Royal Agricultural Society*, 2nd ser., X.

Fawcett, Henry, 1865, *The Economic Position of the English Labourer*, Macmillan.

Felkin, W., 1867, *A History of the Machine-Wrought Hosiery and Lace Manufactures*.

Finlay, T. A., 1913, 'The Significance of Some Recent Irish Statistics', *Journal of the Statistical and Social Inquiry Society of Ireland*, XIII, pt XCIII.

Finney, S. G., 1860, *Hints to Landlords, Tenants and Labourers*, Ridgway.

Fischer, W., 1973, 'Rural Industrialization and Population Change', *Comparative Studies in Society and History*, XV.

Fisher, W. R., 1887, *The Forest of Essex: Its History, Laws, Administration and Ancient Customs*, Butterworth.

Fitzgerald, K., 1968, *Ahead of their Time: A Short History of the Farmers' Club*, Heinemann.

Fletcher, A. J., 1971, 'The Hope Valley in 1851', *Derbyshire Archaeological Journal*, XCI.

Fletcher, H. R., 1969, *The Story of the Royal Horticultural Society 1804–1968*, Oxford University Press, Oxford.

Fletcher, J. S., 1910, *Recollections of a Yorkshire Village*, Digby, Long.

Fletcher, T. W., 1961a, 'The Great Depression of English Agriculture, 1873–96', *Economic History Review*, 2nd ser., XIII.

Fletcher, T. W., 1961b, 'Lancashire Livestock Farming during the Great Depression', *Agricultural History Review*, IX.

Flinn, M. W. (ed.), 1965, *Report on the Sanitary Condition of the Labouring Population of Great Britain, 1842*, by Edwin Chadwick, Edinburgh University Press, Edinburgh.

Flux, A. W., 1930, 'Our Food Supply before and after the War', *Journal of the Royal Statistical Society*, XCIV.

Forbes, Christopher, 1975, *The Royal Academy (1837–1901) Revisited*, Art Museum, Princeton University, Princeton.

Forster, E. M., 1974, *Howards End*, Penguin, Harmondsworth, Middx.

Foster, John, 1883, *The Peerage, Baronetage and Knightage of the British Empire*, Nichols & Sons.

Fowler, J., 1894, *Recollections of Old Country Life*, Longman.

Fox, A. Wilson, 1903, 'Agricultural Wages in England and Wales during the Last Half Century', *Journal of the Royal Statistical Society*, LXVI.

Fox, H. S. A., 1979, 'Local Farmers' Associations and the Circulation of Agricultural Information in Nineteenth Century England'. In H. S. A. Fox and R. A. Butlin (eds), *Change in the Countryside: Essays on Rural England 1500–1900*, Institute of British Geographers.

Franklin, Jill, 1973, 'The Planning of the Victorian Country House', unpublished thesis, University of London.

Franklin, Jill, 1975, 'Troops of Servants: Labour and Planning in the Country House 1840–1914', *Victorian Studies*, XIX, 2.

Freeman, Edward A., 1877, 'Pedigrees and Pedigree-Makers', *Contemporary Review*, XXX.

Freeman, M. D., 1976, 'A History of Corn Milling, c. 1750–1914, with Special Reference to South Central and South Eastern England', unpublished Ph.D. thesis, University of Reading.

Freeman, M. J., 1977, 'The Carrier System of South Hampshire 1775–1851', *Journal of Transport History*, n.s., IV, 2.

Freese, S., 1957, *Windmills and Millwrighting*, Cambridge University Press, Cambridge.

Froude, J. A., 1872–4, *The English in Ireland in the Eighteenth Century*, Longman, Green.

Froude, J.A., 1876, 'On the Uses of a Landed Gentry', *Fraser's Magazine*, n.s., XIV.

Fuller, Margaret D., 1964, *West Country Friendly Societies*, University of Reading, Reading, Berks.

Fullerton, Lady Georgiana, 1847, *Grantley Manor*.

Fussell, G. E., 1929, 'The Rev. Dr John Trusler', *Notes and Queries*, CLVI.

Fussell, G. E., 1947, 'The Farming Writers of Eighteenth-Century England', *Agricultural History*, XXI, 1.

Fussell, G. E., 1948, 'The Dawn of High Farming in England', *Agricultural History*, XXII.

Fussell, G. E., 1952, *The Farmer's Tools 1500–1900: The History of British Farm Implements, Tools and Machinery before the Tractor Came*, Melrose.

Fussell, G. E., 1962, 'The Early Days of Chemical Fertilisers', *Nature*, 25 August.

Fussell, G. E., 1966, *The English Dairy Farmer 1500–1900*, Frank Cass.

Fyfe, N. W., 1862, 'Notes on the Application of Farm Implements in Dorset and Somerset', *Journal of the Bath and West of England Society*, n.s., X.

Gale, F., 1885, *Modern English Sports: Their Use and Abuse*, Sampson Low.

Galloway, R. L., 1898, *Annals of Coal Mining and the Coal Trade*, Colliery Guardian Company.

Gardner, R., 1852, *History, Gazetteer and Directory of the County of Oxford*, Peterborough, Cambs.

Garnett, W., 1849, 'Farming of Lancashire', *Journal of the Royal Agricultural Society*, X.

Gash, Norman, 1953, *Politics in the Age of Peel: A Study in the Technique of Parliamentary Representation 1830–1850*, Longman (2nd edn 1977, Harvester Press, Hassocks).

Gaskell, E., 1857, *The Life of Charlotte Brontë*, Smith Elder.

Gatty, A., 1884, *A Life at One Living*, privately published, Sheffield.

Gavin, Sir William, 1967, *Ninety Years of Family Farming*, Hutchinson.

Gibson, J., 1879, *Agriculture in Wales*, Hodder & Stoughton.

Gilbert, A. D., 1976, *Religion and Society in Industrial England: Church, Chapel and Social Change, 1740–1914*, Longman.

Gilbert, Heather, 1973, 'Mount Stephen: A Study in Environments', *Northern Scotland*, I, 2.

Gillispie, G. C., 1951, *Genesis and Geology: A study in the Relations of Scientific Thought, Natural Theology and Social Opinion in Great Britain, 1790–1950*, Harvard University Press, Cambridge, Mass.

Gilpin, M. C., 1960, 'Population Changes Round the Shores of Milford Haven from 1800 to the Present Day', *Field Studies*, I.

Gilpin, William, 1768, *An Essay upon Prints; Containing Remarks upon the Principles of Picturesque Beauty*, J. Robson.

Gilpin, William, 1782, *Observations on the River Wye*.

Gilpin, William, 1786, *Observations . . . Made in the Year 1772*.

Gilpin, William, 1798, *Observations on the Western Parts of England*.

Girouard, Mark, 1971, *The Victorian Country House*, Clarendon Press, Oxford.

Girouard, Mark, 1977, *Sweetness and Light: The Queen Anne Movement 1860–1900*, Clarendon Press, Oxford.

Girouard, Mark, 1978, *Life in the English Country House: A Social and Architectural History*, Yale University Press, New Haven, Conn.

Gladwyn, D. D., 1976, *The Waterways of Britain: A Social Panorama*, Batsford.

Gloag, John, 1970, *Mr Loudon's England: John Claudius Loudon 1783–1843*, Oriel Press, Newcastle.

Gloucestershire Community Council, 1950, *I Remember—Travel and Transport in Gloucestershire Villages 1850–1950*, Gloucester.

Glyde, J., 1856a, 'Localities of Crime in Suffolk', *Journal of the Statistical Society of London*, XIX, 1.

Glyde, J., 1856b, *Suffolk in the Nineteenth Century*, J. M. Burton.

Goddard, N., 1974, 'Kentish Farmers' Clubs in the Mid-Nineteenth Century', *Cantium*, VI.

Golding, S., 1975, The Importance of Fairs in Essex, 1750–1850', *Essex Journal*, X, 3.

Gore, Mrs, 1849, *The Diamond and the Pearl*, Colburn.

Gosden, P. H. J. H., 1961, *The Friendly Societies in England 1815–1875*, Manchester University Press, Manchester.

Gosse, Edmund, 1890, *Life of Philip Henry Gosse F. R. S.*, Kegan Paul.

Grace, D. R., and Phillips, D. C., 1975, *Ransomes of Ipswich: A History of the Firm and Guide to its Records*, University of Reading Institute of Agricultural History, Reading, Berks.

Graham, P. Anderson, 1892, *The Rural Exodus: The Problem of the Village and the Town*, Methuen.

Grant, J., 1844, ' A Few Remarks on the Large Hedges and Small Enclosures of Devonshire and Adjoining Counties', *Journal of the Royal Agricultural Society*, V.

Grantham, R. B., 1864, 'A Description of the Works for Reclaiming and Marling Parts of the Late Forest of Delamere in the County of Cheshire', *Journal of the Royal Agricultural Society*, XXV.

Granville, A. B., 1841, *The Spas of England*, Henry Colburn.

Gray, John Hamilton, 1862, 'An Essay on the Position of the British Gentry'. In Bernard Burke, *A Genealogical and Heraldic Dictionary of the Landed Gentry of Great Britain and Ireland*, 4th ed., Harrison.

Gray, Malcolm, 1957, *The Highland Economy, 1750–1850*, Oliver & Boyd, Edinburgh.

Gray, Malcolm, 1973, 'Scottish Emigration: The Social Impact of Agrarian Change in the Rural Lowlands, 1775–1875', *Perspectives in American History*, VII.

Great Victorian Pictures, 1978, Arts Council of Great Britain.

Green, F. E., 1913, *The Tyranny of the Countryside*, T. Fisher Unwin.

Green, F. E., 1920, *A History of the English Agricultural Labourer, 1870–1920*, P. S. King.

Green, John L., n.d. (*c.* 1895), *The Rural Industries of England*, E. Marlborough.

Green, John L., 1915, *Village Industries: A National Obligation*, Rural World Publishing Company.

Greenhow, E.H., 1858, *Papers Relating to the Sanitary State of the People of England* (reprinted 1973, Gregg International).

Greening, A., 1971, 'Nineteenth Century Country Carriers in North Wiltshire', *Wiltshire Archaeological and Natural History Magazine*, LXVI.

Greenslade, M. W., and Jenkins, J. G. (eds), 1967, *Victoria County History, Staffordshire*, II, Oxford University Press, Oxford.

Grey, E., 1935, *Cottage Life in a Hertfordshire Village*, Fisher, Knight, St Albans.

Griffin, C. P., 1977, 'Three Generations of Miners' Housing at Moira, Leicestershire,

1811–1934', *Industrial Archaeology Review*, I, 3.

Grigg, D.B., 1963, 'A Note on Agricultural Rent in Nineteenth Century England', *Agricultural History*, XXXVII.

Grigor, J., 1845, 'On Fences', *Journal of the Royal Agricultural Society*, VI.

Grigson, G., 1975, *The Englishman's Flora*, Paladin, St Albans.

Grimble, A., 1886, *Deer Stalking*, Chapman & Hall.

Grimshaw, T. W., 1884, 'Notes on the Statistics of Waste Lands in Ireland', *Journal of the Statistical and Social Inquiry Society of Ireland*, VIII, pt LXII.

Grinsell, L. V., 1976, *Folklore of Prehistoric Sites in Britain*, David & Charles, Newton Abbot.

Groves, R., 1949, *Sharpen the Sickle*, Porcupine Press.

Gurden, Helen, 1976, 'Primitive Methodism and Agricultural Trade Unionism in Warwickshire 1872–75', *Bulletin of the Society for the Study of Labour History*, XXXIII.

Gurdon, Lady E. C., 1893, *County Folklore. Printed Extracts No. 2 Suffolk*, Folklore Society.

Gurr, T. R., Grabovsky, P. N., and Hula, R. C., 1977, *The Politics of Crime and Conflict*, Sage Publishing, Beverly Hills, Calif.

Habakkuk, H. J., 1953, 'Economic Functions of English Landowners in the Seventeenth and Eighteenth Centuries', *Explorations in Entrepreneurial History*, VI, 2.

Hadfield, Alice M., 1970, *The Chartist Land Company*, David & Charles, Newton Abbot.

Hadfield, E. C. R., 1970, *British Canals*, David & Charles, Newton Abbot.

Hadfield, Miles, 1960, *Gardening in Britain*, Hutchinson.

Haggard, H. Rider, 1899, *A Farmer's Year*, Longman.

Haggard, H. Rider, 1902, *Rural England*, Longman.

Haggard, H. Rider, 1906a, *A Farmer's Year*, 2nd ed., Longman.

Haggard, H. Rider, 1906b, *Rural England*, 2nd ed., Longman.

Haggard, L. (ed.), 1935, *I Walked by Night*, Nicholson & Watson.

Hair, P. E. H., 1968, 'Mortality from Violence in British Coalfields 1800–1890', *Economic History Review*, 2nd ser., XXI.

Hall, A. D., 1905, *The Book of the Rothamsted Experiments*, John Murray.

Hall, A. D., 1913, *A Pilgrimage of British Farming*, John Murray.

Hall, A. D., 1939, 'The South-Eastern Agricultural College', *Agricultural Progress*, XVI.

Hall, P., 1973, 'England circa 1900'. In H. C. Darby (ed.), *A New Historical Geography of England*, Cambridge University Press, Cambridge.

Hammond, J. L. and B., 1913, *The Village Labourer*, Longman, Green.

Handley, H., 1838, *A Letter to Earl Spencer (President of the Smithfield Club) on the Formation of a National Agricultural Institution*, Ridgway.

Hanham, J. J., 1959, *Elections and Party Management: Politics in the Time of Disraeli and Gladstone*, Longman.

Hanscomb, C. E., 1967, *Common Blood*, Queen Anne Press.

Hanson, H., 1975, *The Canal Boatmen*, Manchester University Press, Manchester.

Hardie, Martin, 1968, *Water-Colour Painting in Britain: III, The Victorian Period*, Batsford.

Hardy, Thomas, 1883, 'The Dorsetshire Labourer', *Longman's Magazine*, July.

Hardy, Thomas, 1926, *The Mayor of Casterbridge*, Macmillan.

Hardy, Thomas, 1974, *The Return of the Native*, Macmillan.

Harleston Farmers' Club, 1850 *Reports of the Harleston Farmers' Club, 1838–1849*, Jarrold & Sons.

Harley, J. B., 1973, 'England circa 1850'. In H. C. Darby (ed.), *A New Historical Geography of England*, Cambridge University Press, Cambridge.

Harris, A., 1973, 'Changes in the Early Railway Age: 1800–1850'. In H. C. Darby (ed.), *A New Historical Geography of England*, Cambridge University Press, Cambridge.

Harrison, B., 1966, 'Philanthropy and the Victorians', *Victorian Studies*, IX.

Harrison, E., 1928, *Harrison of Ightham*, Oxford University Press, Oxford.

Hart, C., 1971, *The Industrial History of Dean*, David & Charles, Newton Abbot.

Hartley, Dorothy, 1962, *Food in England*, Macdonald.

Hartley, M., and Ingilby, J., 1953, *Yorkshire Village*, Dent.

Hartley, M., and Ingilby, J., 1956, *The Yorkshire Dales*, Dent.

Harvey, D. W., 1963, 'Locational Change in the Kentish Hop Industry and the Analysis of Land Use Patterns', *Transactions and Papers of the Institute of British Geographers*, XXXIII.

Harvey, J. H., 1944–5, 'Mudtown, Walton-on-Thames', *Surrey Archaeological Collections*, XLIX.

Harvey, Nigel, 1970, *A History of Farm Buildings in England and Wales*, David & Charles, Newton Abbot.

Hasbach, W., 1966, *A History of the English Agricultural Labourer*, Frank Cass.

Hatley, V. A. and Rajczonek, J., 1972, *Shoemakers in Northamptonshire, 1762–1911*, Northampton Historical Series, no. 6, Northampton.

Havinden, M. A., 1966, *Estate Villages, A Study of the Berkshire Villages of Ardington and Lockinge*, Lund Humphreys.

Hawke, G. R., 1970, *Railways and Economic Growth in England and Wales 1840–1870*, Clarendon Press, Oxford.

Hay, D., *et al.*, 1975, *Albion's Fatal Tree: Crime and Society in Eighteenth Century England*, Allen Lane.

Heath, F. G., 1874, *The English Peasantry*.

Heath, F. G., 1880, *Peasant Life in the West of England*, 2nd ed., Sampson Low.

Heath, R., 1893, *The English Peasant*, Unwin.

Heeney, B., 1973, 'On being a Mid-Victorian Clergyman', *Journal of Religious History*, VII, 3.

Henderson, J., 1853, 'Report upon the Rye and Derwent Drainage', *Journal of the Royal Agricultural Society*, XIV.

Henderson, William, 1866 (2nd edn 1879), *Notes on the Folk-lore of the Northern Counties of England and the Borders*, Folklore Society.

Henkin, L. J., 1963, *Darwinism in the English Novel, 1860–1950*, Russell & Russell, New York.

Hennell, T., 1934, *Change in the Farm*, Cambridge University Press, Cambridge.

Henslow, J. S., 1844, *Suggestions towards an Enquiry into the Present Condition of the Labouring Population of Suffolk*, Hadleigh, Suffolk.

Hey, David, 1968, *The Village of Ecclesfield*, Advertiser Press, Huddersfield.

Hey, David, 1972, *The Rural Metalworkers of the Sheffield Region: A Study of Rural Industry before the Industrial Revolution*, Leicester University Press, Leicester.

Higgins, J., 1830, '1830. The Turvey Abbey Scrap Book', MS in the possession of Professor M. S. Longuet-Higgins.

Hill, Francis, 1974, *Victorian Lincoln*, Cambridge University Press, Cambridge.

Hincks, T. C., 1845, *Hints for Increasing the Practical Usefulness of Agricultural Shows*, Ridgway.

Hincks, T. C., 1847, *Some Remarks on the Principles which should Regulate Public*

Encouragement, Thirsk, Yorks.

Hine, Richard, 1928, 'Friendly Societies and their Emblems', *Proceedings of the Dorset Natural History and Antiquarian Field Club*, XLIX.

H.M.S.O., 1911, *The Post Office: An Historical Summary*, H.M.S.O.

Hobsbawm, E. J., 1968, *Industry and Empire*, Weidenfeld & Nicolson.

Hobsbawm, E. J., and Rudé, G., 1969, *Captain Swing*, Lawrence & Wishart.

Hodder, E., 1887, *The Life and Work of the Seventh Earl of Shaftesbury*, Cassell.

Hogg, Thomas, 1824, *Concise and Practical Treatise on the Growth and Culture of the Carnation*, G. & W. B. Whittaker.

Holdenby, C., 1913, *Folk of the Furrow*, Smith, Elder.

Holderness, B. A., 1972a, 'Landlord's Capital Formation in East Anglia 1750–1870', *Economic History Review*, 2nd ser., XXV, 3.

Holderness, B. A., 1972b, 'Open and Close Parishes in England in the Eighteenth and Nineteenth centuries', *Agricultural History Review*, XX, 2.

Hole, C., 1944–5, *English Folklore*, 2nd ed., Batsford.

Hole, James, 1866, *The Homes of the Working Classes*.

Hollander, Samuel, 1973, *The Economics of Adam Smith*, Heinemann.

Hollingsworth, T. H., 1965, 'The Demography of the British Peerage', *Population Studies*, XVIII, 2, supplement.

Holroyd, Abraham, 1871, *Saltaire and its Founder, Sir T. Salt, Bart.*, Saltaire, Yorks.

Hooper, W. A. C., 1963, *Brief Record of the Founding and Progress of the Incorporated Oil Seed Association*.

Hope, Charlotte, 1881, *George Hope of Fenton Barns, A Sketch of his Life Compiled by his Daughter*, David Douglas, Edinburgh.

Hope, W., 1875, *Food Manufacture versus Pollution*, Edward Stanford.

Hopkins, E., 1976, 'Changes in the Scale of the Industrial Unit in Stourbridge and District 1815–1914', *West Midlands Studies*, VIII (Wolverhampton Polytechnic).

Hoppen, K. Theodore, 1977, 'Landlords, Society and Electoral Power in Mid-Nineteenth Century Ireland', *Past and Present*, LXXV.

Horn, Pamela, 1971, *Joseph Arch (1826–1919), The Farm Workers' Leader*, Roundwood Press, Kineton, War.

Horn, Pamela, 1972, 'Agricultural Trade Unionism and Emigration, 1872–1881', *Historical Journal*, XV, 1.

Horn, Pamela, 1973, 'The Gawcott Revolt of 1867', *Records of Buckinghamshire*, XIX, 3.

Horn, Pamela (ed.), 1974a, *Agricultural Trade Unionism in Oxfordshire 1872–81*, Oxfordshire Record Society, XLVIII.

Horn, Pamela, 1974b, 'Child Workers in the Pillow Lace and Straw Plait Trades of Victorian Buckinghamshire and Bedfordshire', *Historical Journal*, XVII, 4.

Horn, Pamela, 1974c, 'Landowners and the Agricultural Trade Union Movement of the 1870s', *Local Historian*, II, 3.

Horn, Pamela, 1976a, 'Agricultural Unionism and Emigration', *Historical Journal*, XVII.

Horn, Pamela, 1976b, *Labouring Life in the Victorian Countryside*, Gill & Macmillan, Dublin.

Horne, Eric, 1930, *What the Butler Winked at*, T. W. Laurie.

Hoskins, W. G., 1957, *The Midland Peasant*, Macmillan.

Howard, J., 1977, 'Thomas Hardy's Mellstock and the Registrar-General's Stinsford', *Literature and History*, no. 6 (Thames Polytechnic).

Howell, D. W., 1978, *Land and People in Nineteenth-Century Wales*, Routledge & Kegan Paul.

Howell-Thomas, D. (ed.), 1976, *Goodwood Letters from Below Stairs*, Goodwood Estate Company, Goodwood, Sussex.

Howitt, W., 1838, *The Rural Life of England*, Longman.

Howitt, W., 1840, *The Rural Life of England*, 2nd ed., Longman.

Howitt, W., 1971, *The Rural Life of England*, 3rd ed., Irish University Press, Dublin.

Howkins, Alun, 1973, *Whitsun in Nineteenth Century Oxfordshire*, History Workshop Pamphlets, no. 8, Ruskin College, Oxford.

Hudson, D., and Luckhurst, K. W., 1954, *The Royal Society of Arts 1754–1954*, John Murray.

Hudson, Kenneth, n.d. (1969), *The History of English China Clays*, David and Charles, Newton Abbot.

Hudson, Kenneth, 1972, *Patriotism with Profit*, Hugh Evelyn.

Hudson, Kenneth, 1976, *The Bath and West*, Moonraker Press, Bradford-on-Avon.

Hughes, Edward, 1949, 'The Eighteenth Century Estate Agent'. In H. A. Cronne *et al.* (eds), *Essays in British and Irish History*, Muller.

Hughes, T. J. (Adfyfr), 1887, *Landlordism in Wales*, South Wales Liberal Federation Offices, Cardiff.

Hunt, C. J., 1970, *The Lead Miners of the Northern Pennines in the Eighteenth and Nineteenth Centuries*, Manchester University Press, Manchester.

Hunt, E. H., 1967, 'Labour Productivity in English Agriculture, 1850–1914', *Economic History Review*, 2nd ser., XX.

Hunt, E. H., 1973, *Regional Wage Variations in Britain, 1850–1914*, Clarendon Press, Oxford.

Hunt, W. H., 1886, 'The Pre-Raphaelite Brotherhood: A Fight for Art', *Contemporary Review*, XLIX.

Hunter, James, 1973, 'Sheep and Deer: Highland Sheep Farming, 1850–1900', *Northern Scotland*, I, 2.

Hunter, James, 1976, *The Making of the Crofter Community*, John Donald, Edinburgh.

Hurt, J., 1961, 'The Role of the Hertfordshire Gentry and the Education Committee of the Privy Council in Providing Education in Hertfordshire in the Nineteenth Century', unpublished Ph.D. thesis, London University.

Hurt, J., 1968, 'Landowners, Farmers and Clergy in the Financing of Rural Education before 1870', *Journal of Education Administration and History*, I, 1.

Hurt, J., 1971, *Education in Evolution*, Paladin.

Hussey, Christopher, 1958, *English Country Houses: Late Georgian*, Country Life.

Hussey, S. M., 1904, *The Reminiscences of an Irish Land Agent*, Duckworth.

Hutchinson, G. T., 1935, *The Heythrop Hunt*, John Murray.

Huxley, Gervas, 1967, *Victorian Duke. The Life of Hugh Lupus Grosvenor, First Duke of Westminster*, Oxford University Press, Oxford.

Idstone (Rev. Thomas Pearce), 1874, *The Idstone Papers*, 2nd ed., The *Field* Office.

Innes, J. W., 1938, *Class Fertility Trends in England and Wales, 1876–1934*, Princeton University Press, Princeton, N.J.

Itzkowitz, D. C., 1977, *Peculiar Privilege. A Social History of English Foxhunting 1753–1885*, Harvester Press, Hassocks.

Janes, H., 1955, *The Master Millers: The History of the House of Rank 1875–1955*, Harley.

Bibliography

Jeaffreson, J. C., 1867, *A Book about Lawyers*, 2nd ed., Hunt & Blackett.

Jefferies, Richard, 1880, *Hodge and his Masters*, Smith, Elder.

Jefferies, Richard, 1898, *The Toilers of the Field*, Longman.

Jefferies, Richard, 1966, *Hodge and his Masters*, new edn, McGibbon & Kee.

Jefferys, J. B., 1954, *Retail Trading in Britain 1850–1950*, Cambridge University Press, Cambridge.

Jekyll, Gertrude, 1899, *Wood and Garden*, Longman.

Jekyll, Gertrude, 1900, *Home and Garden*, Longman.

Jekyll, Gertrude, and Weaver, Lawrence, 1912, *Gardens for Small Country Houses*, Country Life.

Jenkins, D., 1971, *The Agricultural Community in South-West Wales at the Turn of the Twentieth Century*, University of Wales Press, Cardiff.

Jenkins, G., 1972, *The Craft Industries*, Longman.

Jenkins, J. G., 1962, *Agricultural Transport in Wales*, National Museum of Wales, Cardiff.

Jenkins, J. G., 1970, 'Rural Industry in Brecknock', *Brycheiniog*, XIV.

Jenkins, J. G., 1976, *Life and Tradition in Rural Wales*, Dent.

Jenks, Edward, 1899, *Modern Land Law*, Clarendon Press, Oxford.

Jessopp, Augustus, 1887, *Arcady, for Better, for Worse*, T. Fisher Unwin.

Jewitt, L., 1850, *Handbook of Exeter and Visitor's Guide to the Show*, Royal Agricultural Society.

Johnston, H. J. M., 1972, *British Emigration Policy, 1815–1830: Shovelling out Paupers*, Clarendon Press, Oxford.

Johnston, W., 1851, *England as it is . . . in the Middle of the Nineteenth Century*.

Jonas, S., 1846, 'On the Farming of Cambridgeshire', *Journal of the Royal Agricultural Society*, VII.

Jones, Bernard (ed.), 1962, *William Barnes, The Poems*, Southern Illinois University Press, Carbondale, Ill.

Jones, David, 1973, *Before Rebecca: Popular Protests in Wales, 1793–1835*, Allen Lane.

Jones, David, 1974, 'Crime, Protest and Community in Nineteenth-Century Wales', *Llafur*, I, 3.

Jones, David, 1976a, 'The Second Rebecca Riots', *Llafur*, II, 1.

Jones, David, 1976b, 'Thomas Campbell Foster and the Rural Labourers: Incendiarism in East Anglia in the 1840s', *Social History*, I, 1.

Jones, David, 1977, 'The Criminal Vagrant in Mid-Nineteenth Century Wales', *Welsh History Review*, VIII, 3.

Jones, D. J. V., and Bainbridge, A., 1975, *Crime in Ninenteenth-Century Wales*, Social Science Research Council Report, Swansea.

Jones, E. L., 1964, 'The Agricultural Labour Market in England, 1793–1872', *Economic History Review*, 2nd ser., XVII.

Jones, E. L., 1968, 'The Agricultural Origins of Industry', *Past and Present*, XL.

Jones, E. L., 1975, *Agriculture and the Industrial Revolution*, Blackwell, Oxford.

Jones, G. P., 1962, 'The Decline of the Yeomanry in the Lake Counties', *Transactions of the Cumberland and Westmorland Antiquarian Society*, LXII.

Jones, I. G., 1961, 'The Liberation Society and Welsh Politics, 1844 to 1868', *Welsh History Review*, I, 2.

Jones, M., 1977, 'Y chwarelwyr: The Slate Quarrymen of North Wales'. In R. Samuel (ed.), *Miners, Quarrymen and Saltworkers*, Routledge & Kegan Paul.

660

Jones, R. E., 1968, 'Population and Agrarian Change in an Eighteenth-Century Shropshire Parish', *Local Population Studies*, I.

Jones-Baker, D., 1977, *The Folklore of Hertfordshire*, Batsford.

Jones-Evans, P., 1968, 'Evan Pan Jones—Land Reformer', *Welsh History Review*, IV, 2.

Journal of the Royal Agricultural Society of England, 1840 onwards.

Joyce, Patrick, 1975, 'The Factory Politics of Lancashire in the Later Nineteenth Century', *Historical Journal*, XVIII, 3.

Kain, R. J. P., 1975, 'Tithe Surveys and Landownership', *Journal of Historical Geography*, I.

Kaufman, M., 1975, *The Housing of the Working Classes and of the Poor* (1907), new edn, E.P. Publishing, Wakefield.

Kay, Joseph, 1879, *Free Trade in Land*, 4th edn, C. K. Paul.

Kay-Shuttleworth, J. P., 1971, *The Social Condition and Education of the People*, I, new edn, Irish University Press, Shannon.

Kebbel, T. E., 1891, *The Old and the New English Country Life*, Blackwood.

Kellenbenz, H., 1974, 'Rural Industries in the West'. In P. Earle (ed.), *Essays in European Economic History 1500–1750*, Cambridge University Press, Cambridge.

Kelly, 1898, *Kelly's Directory of Bedfordshire, Huntingdonshire and Northamptonshire*, Kelly.

Kelly, 1891, 1905, *Kelly's Directory of Kent, Surrey and Sussex*, Kelly.

Kelly, E. R., 1879, *The Post Office Directory of the North and East Ridings of Yorkshire*, Kelly.

Kerr, B., 1968, *Bound to the Soil*, John Baker.

Kerr, Robert, 1864, *The Gentleman's House, Or How to Plan English Residences from the Parsonage to the Palace*, John Murray.

Ketteridge, C., and Mays, S., 1972, *Five Miles from Bunkum*, Eyre Methuen.

Kettle, L. J. (ed.), 1958, *The Material for Victory, being the Memoirs of Andrew J. Kettle*, Fellow, Dublin.

Kickham, C. J., 1879, *Knocknagow, Or the Homes of Tipperary*, James Duffy, Dublin.

Kieve, J. L., 1973, *The Electric Telegraph: A Social and Economic History*, David & Charles, Newton Abbot.

Kilby, K., 1971, *The Cooper and his Trade*, John Baker.

Killip, M., 1975, *The Folklore of the Isle of Man*, Batsford.

Kingsley, Charles, 1855, 'The Country Parish', *Lectures to Ladies at Working Men's College*.

Kingsley, Mrs, 1899, *Charles Kingsley: His Letters and Memories of his Life*, Macmillan.

Kitchen, F., 1940, *Brother to the Ox*, Dent.

Knightley, Lady Julia, 1915, *Journals 1856–1884*, ed. Julia Cartwright, John Murray.

Knoepflmacher, U. C., and Tennyson, G. B. (eds), 1977, *Nature and the Victorian Imagination*, University California Press, Berkeley, Calif.

Labourer's Friends, A Selection from the Publications of the Labourers Friend Society, 1835.

'Labourers in Council', 1872, *The Congregationalist*.

Lanceley, William, 1925, *From Hall-boy to House Steward*, Edward Arnold.

Land Enquiry Committee, 1913, *The Land*, vol. I, *Rural*, 5th edn, Hodder & Stoughton.

Lascelles, E., 1934, 'Charity'. In G. M. Young (ed.), *Early Victorian England 1830–1865*, II, Oxford University Press, Oxford.

Lawes, J. B., 1847, 'On Agricultural Chemistry', *Journal of the Royal Agricultural Society*, VIII.

Lawes, J. B., and Gilbert, J. H., 1851, 'On Agricultural Chemistry', *Journal of the Royal*

Agricultural Society, XII.

Lawes, J. B., and Gilbert, J. H., 1868, 'On the Home Produce, Imports and Consumption of Wheat', *Journal of the Royal Agricultural Society*, 2nd ser., IV.

Lawrence, Charles, 1865, 'The Royal Agricultural College of Cirencester', *Journal of the Royal Agricultural Society*, 2nd ser., I.

Lawson-Tancred, Mary, 1960, 'The Anti-League and the Corn Law Crisis of 1846', *Historical Journal*, III, 2.

Lawton, R., 1973, 'Rural Depopulation in Nineteenth Century England'. In D. R. Mills (ed.), *English Rural Communities: The Impact of a Specialized Economy*, Macmillan.

Leather, E. M., 1970, *The Folk-lore of Herefordshire*, S.R. Publishing, Wakefield.

Lee, J. J., 1969, 'Irish Agriculture', *Agricultural History Review*, XVII, 1.

Lee, J. J., 1973, 'The Ribbonmen'. In T. D. Williams (ed.), *Secret Societies in Ireland*, Gill & Macmillan, Dublin.

Lee, J. M., 1956, 'The Rise and Fall of a Market Town: Castle Donington in the Nineteenth Century', *Leicestershire Archaeological and Historical Society Transactions*, XXXII.

Lefevre, G. S. (Lord Eversley), 1894, *English Commons and Forests*, Cassell.

Lethaby, W. R., 1935, *Philip Webb and his Work*, Oxford University Press, Oxford.

Lewis, B., 1971, *Coal Mining in the Eighteenth and Nineteenth Centuries*, Longman.

Lewis, R. A., 1957, 'County Government since 1835'. In R. B. Pugh and Elizabeth Crittall (eds), *Victoria County History of Wiltshire*, V, Oxford University Press, Oxford.

Lewis, S., 1840, *Topographical Dictionary of England*, III.

Lindsay, J., 1968, *The Canals of Scotland*, David & Charles, Newton Abbot.

Little, Bryan, 1974, *Portrait of Somerset*, Robert Hale.

Little, E., 1845, 'The Farming of Wiltshire', *Journal of the Royal Agricultural Society*, V.

Little, H. J., 1874, 'The Future of Farming', *Journal of the Farmers' Club*.

Llewellyn Smith, H., 1904, 'The Influx of Population'. In Charles Booth, *Life and Labour of the People in London*, III, pt 1.

Long, Walter, 1923, *Memories*, Hutchinson.

Longmate, N., 1974, *The Workhouse*, Temple Smith.

Longrigg, Roger, 1972, *The History of Horse Racing*, Macmillan.

Longrigg, Roger, 1977, *The English Squire and his Sport*, Michael Joseph.

Longstaff, G. B., 1893, 'Rural Depopulation', *Journal of the Royal Statistical Society*, LVI.

Lorrain Smith, E., 1932, *Go East for a Farm: A Study of Rural Migration*, University of Oxford Institute for Research in Agricultural Economics, Oxford.

Loudon, J. C., 1833, *An Encyclopaedia of Cottage, Farm and Villa Architecture*, Longman.

Loudon, J. C., 1838, *Suburban Gardener and Villa Companion*, the author.

Loudon, J. C., 1840, *The Landscape Gardening and Landscape Architecture of the Late Humphry Repton* (reprinted 1970, Gregg International).

Loudon, J. C., 1845, *Self-Instruction for Young Gardeners . . .*, Longman, Brown, Green & Longman.

Loudon, J. C., 1846, *An Encyclopaedia of Cottage, Farm and Villa Architecture*, new edn, Longman, Brown, Green & Longman.

Lusk, Lewis, 1901, *The Life and Work of Benjamin Williams Leader, R.A.*, Art Annual, Virtue & Co.

McClatchey, D., 1960, *Oxfordshire Clergy 1777–1869: A Study of the Established Church and of the Role of its Clergy in Local Society*, Clarendon Press, Oxford.

McConnell, P., 1891, 'Experiences of a Scotsman on the Essex Clays', *Journal of the Royal Agricultural Society*, 3rd ser., II.

McConnell, P., 1910, *Notebook of Agricultural Facts and Figures*, Crosby Lockwood.

McCord, N., and Carrick, A. E., 1966, 'Northumberland in the General Election of 1852', *Northern History*, I.

McCrosty, H. W., 1903, 'The Grainmilling Industry: A Study in Organisation', *Economic Journal*, XIII.

McCulloch, J. R., 1837, *Statistical Account of the British Empire*.

McCulloch, J. R., 1839, *Statistical Account of the British Empire*, new edn, Charles Knight.

Macdonald, James, 1876, 'On the Agriculture of the County of Fife', *Transactions of the Highland and Agricultural Society*, 4th ser., VIII.

Macdonald, James 1881, 'On the Agriculture of the Counties of Forfar and Kincardine', *Transactions of the Highland and Agricultural Society*, 4th ser., XIV.

Macdonald, Stuart, 1975, 'The Progress of the Early Threshing Machine', *Agricultural History Review*, XXIII.

Macdonald, Stuart, 1976, 'The Diary of an Agricultural Apprentice in Northumberland, 1842', *Local Historian*, XII.

Macdonald, Stuart, 1979, 'The Diffusion of Knowledge among Northumberland Farmers, 1780–1815', *Agricultural History Review*, XXVII, 1.

MacDonnell, R. W., 1862, 'Statistics of Irish Prosperity', *Journal of the Statistical and Social Inquiry Society of Ireland*, III, pt XXII.

MacFarlane, J., 1976, 'Denaby Main Colliery', *Colliery Guardian*, March.

McIntosh, Charles, 1828, *The Practical Gardener and Modern Horticulturalist*, Thomas Kelly.

MacIver, Evander, 1905, *Memoirs of a Highland Gentleman*, T. & A. Constable, Edinburgh.

Mackay, Thomas, 1908, *The Reminiscences of Albert Pell, sometime M.P. for South Leicestershire*, John Murray.

Mackay, T., 1967, *A History of the English Poor Law*, Frank Cass.

Macrae, D., 1868, 'The Improvement of Waste Lands', *Journal of the Royal Agricultural Society*, 2nd ser., IV.

Maguire, W. A., 1972, *The Downshire Estates in Ireland, 1801–1845*, Clarendon Press, Oxford.

Malcolmson, R. W., 1973, *Popular Recreation in English Society 1700–1850*, Cambridge University Press, Cambridge.

Malet, Hugh, 1961, *The Canal Duke: A Biography of Francis, Third Duke of Bridgewater*, David & Charles, Dawlish.

Mann, H. P., 1904, 'Life in an Agricultural Village in England', *Sociological Papers*, I.

Mann, J. de L., 1971, *The Cloth Industry in the West of England from 1640 to 1880*, Clarendon Press, Oxford.

'Manufacturer, A', 1857, *The Manufacture of Agricultural Machinery Considered as a Branch of National Industry*, Stanford.

Marks, John George, 1896, *Life and Letters of Frederick Walker, A.R.A.*, Macmillan.

Marsden, R., 1895, *Cotton Weaving, its Development, Principles and Practice*.

Marshall, Sybil (ed.), 1967, *Fenland Chronicle*, Cambridge University Press, Cambridge.

Marshall, T. H., 1929–30, 'Jethro Tull and the New Husbandry', *Economic History Review*, II.

Marshall, W., 1817, *Review of Reports to the Board of Agriculture: Middlesex 1795*, York.

Martin, E. W., 1965, *The Shearers and the Shorn*, Routledge & Kegan Paul.

Martin, J. M., 1976, *The Rise in Population in Eighteenth Century Warwickshire*, Dugdale

Society Occasional Papers, no. 23, Oxford.

Mathew, W. M., 1970, 'Peru and the British Guano Market', *Economic History Review*, 2nd ser., XXIII.

Mathias, P., 1967, *Retailing Revolution*, Longman.

Matthews, A. H. H., 1915, *Fifty Years of Agricultural Politics*, P. S. King.

Mayes, J. L., 1960, *The History of Chairmaking in High Wycombe*, Routledge & Kegan Paul.

Mays, Spike, 1969, *Reuben's Corner*, Eyre & Spottiswoode.

Mechi, J. J., 1845, *Letters on Agricultural Improvement*.

Mechi, J. J., 1859, *How to Farm Profitably: Or the Sayings and Doings of Mr Alderman Mechi*.

Mee, G., 1975, *Aristocratic Enterprise: The Fitzwilliam Industrial Undertakings, 1795–1857*, Blackie.

Melling, E., 1964, *Kentish Sources: IV, The Poor*, Kent County Archives Office, Maidstone.

Melville, J., and Hobbs, J. L., 1947, 'Furness Travelling and Postal Arrangements in the Eighteenth and Nineteenth Centuries', *Transactions of the Cumberland and Westmorland Antiquarian and Archaeological Society*, n.s., XLVI.

Mendels, F., 1972, 'Protoindustrialization: The First Phase of the Industrialization Process', *Journal of Economic History*, XXXII.

Messenger, P., 1975, 'Lowther Farmstead Plans: A Preliminary Survey', *Transactions of the Cumberland and Westmorland Antiquarian and Archaeological Society*, n.s., LXXV.

Metcalf, D., 1969, 'Labour Productivity in English Agriculture 1850–1914', *Economic History Review*, 2nd ser., XXII.

Middleton, T. H., 1912, 'Early Associations for Promoting Agriculture and Improving the Improver', *Report of the British Association for the Advancement of Science*, John Murray.

Mill, J. S., 1873, *Autobiography*, Longman.

Millward, R., and Robinson, A., 1975, *The Peak District*, Eyre Methuen.

Minchinton, W., 1975, 'Cider and Folklore', *Folk Life*, XIII.

Mingay, G. E., 1963, *English Landed Society in the Eighteenth Century*, Routledge & Kegan Paul.

Mingay, G. E., 1975, *Arthur Young and his Times*, Macmillan.

Mingay, G. E., 1976a, *The Gentry: The Rise and Fall of a Ruling Class*, Longman.

Mingay, G. E. 1976b, *Rural Life in Victorian England*, Heinemann.

Mingay, G. E., 1977, *The Agricultural Revolution: Changes in Agriculture 1650–1880*, Black.

Ministry of Agriculture, 1968, *A Century of Agricultural Statistics*, H.M.S.O.

Mitchell, B., and Deane, P., 1962, *Abstract of British Historical Statistics*, Cambridge University Press, Cambridge.

Mitchison, R., 1959, 'The Old Board of Agriculture', *English Historical Review*, LXXIV.

Mitford, M. R., 1848, *Our Village*, Henry G. Bohn.

Moore, D. C., 1965, 'The Corn Laws and High Farming', *Economic History Review*, 2nd ser., XVIII.

Moore, D. C., 1976, *The Politics of Deference*, Harvester Press, Hassocks.

Moore, R., 1974, *Pit-men, Preachers and Politics: The Effects of Methodism in a Durham Mining Community*, Cambridge Univerity Press, Cambridge.

Moore, Thomas, 1830, *Letters and Journals of Lord Byron*, John Murray.

Moreau, R. E., 1968, *The Departed Village: Barrick Salome at the Turn of the Century*, Oxford University Press, Oxford.

Morgan, David, 1975, 'The Place of Harvesters in Nineteenth-Century Village Life'. In R.

Samuel (ed.), *Village Life and Labour*, Routledge & Kegan Paul.

Morgan, K. O., 1970, *Wales in British Politics 1868–1922*, revised edn, University of Wales Press, Cardiff.

Morgan, Raine, 1979, 'The Root Crop in English Agriculture, 1650–1870', unpublished Ph.D. thesis, University of Reading.

Morning Chronicle, 1849–50, *Letters from Rural Districts*.

Morris, M. C. F., 1922, *Yorkshire Reminiscences, with Others*, Humphrey Milford.

Morris, M. C. F., 1928, *The British Workman Past and Present*, Oxford University Press, Oxford.

Morton, J. C., 1856, *A Cyclopedia of Agriculture*, Edinburgh.

Morton, J. C., 1863, *The Prince Consort's Farms*.

Morton, J. C., 1865, 'Agricultural Education', *Journal of the Royal Agricultural Society*, 2nd ser., I.

Morton, J. C., 1868 edn, *Handbook of Farm Labour*, Cassell, Petter & Galpin.

Morton, J. L., 1858, *The Resources of Estates; being a Treatise on the Agricultural Improvement and General Management of Landed Property*, Longman.

Morton, J. L., 1863, 'Agricultural Progress: Its Helps and Hindrances', *Journal of the Society of Arts*, XII.

Moseley, A. F., 1968a, 'Black Country Chainmakers', *West Midlands Studies*, II (Wolverhampton Polytechnic).

Mosse, George L., 1947, 'The Anti-League: 1844–1846', *Economic History Review*, XVII, 2.

Mott, James, 1973. In Michael A. Smith, Stanley Parker and Cyril S. Smith (eds), *Leisure and Society in Britain*, Allen Lane.

Moule, Henry, 1870, *The Impossibility Overcome*, Cassell, Petter & Galpin.

Murphy, S. F. (ed.), 1883, *Our Homes and How to Make them Healthy*, Cassell.

Muthesius, H., 1904–5, *Das Englische Haus*, Wasmuth, Berlin.

Naismith, John, 1813, *General View of the Agriculture of Clydesdale*, Board of Agriculture.

Nash, Charles, 1845, *The Goodrich Court Guide*, 2nd edn, Hereford.

Neale, K., 1974, *Victorian Horsham: The Diary of Henry Michell 1809–1874*, Phillimore, Chichester.

New Book of Sports, reprinted from the *Saturday Review*, 1885, Bentley.

Newman, B., 1957, *One Hundred Years of Good Company: A History of Ruston & Hornsby 1857–1957*, Lincoln.

Nicholls, G., 1846, 'On the Condition of the Agricultural Labourer', *Journal of the Royal Agricultural Society*, VII.

Nicholson, John, 1890, *Folk Lore of East Yorkshire*, Simpkin, Marshall.

Norfolk Record Society, 1962, *The Ames Correspondence 1837–47*, Norfolk Record Society, Fakenham.

Northall, G. F., 1892, *English Folk-Rhymes*, Kegan Paul.

Nossiter, T. J., 1975, *Influence, Opinion and Political Idioms in Reformed England, Case Studies from the North-East 1832–74*, Harvester Press, Hassocks.

Obelkevich, James, 1976, *Religion and Rural Society: South Lindsey 1825–1875*, Clarendon Press, Oxford.

O'Brien, F. T., 1969, 'The Introduction of Steam Navigation in the Solent', *Mariners' Mirror*, LV, 3.

Bibliography

O'Brien, M., 1878, 'On Some of the Difficulties in the Way of Creating a Peasant Proprietary in Ireland', *Journal of the Statistical and Social Inquiry Society of Ireland*, VII, pt LII.

Ogle, W., 1889, 'The Alleged Depopulation of the Rural Districts of England', *Journal of the Statistical Society*, LII.

O'Gráda, C., 1973, 'Seasonal Migration and Post-Famine Adjustment in the West of Ireland', *Studia Hibernica*, XIII.

O'Gráda, C., 1974, 'Agricultural Head Rents, Pre-Famine and Post-Famine', *Economic and Social Review*, V, 3.

O'Gráda, C., 1975, 'The Investment Behaviour of Irish Landlords: Some Preliminary Findings', *Agricultural History Review*, XXIII, 2.

O'Gráda, C., 1977a, 'The Beginnings of the Irish Creamery System, 1880–1914', *Economic History Review*, 2nd ser., XXX, 2.

O'Gráda, C., 1977b, 'Some Aspects of Nineteenth-Century Irish Emigration'. In L. M. Cullen and T. C. Smout (eds), *Comparative Aspects of Scottish and Irish Economic and Social History, 1600–1900*, Donald, Edinburgh.

Ojala, E. M., 1952, *Agriculture and Economic Progress*, Oxford University Press, Oxford.

Oliver, Paul, 1975, *English Cottages and Small Farmhouses*, Barrie & Jenkins.

Olney, R. J., 1973, *Lincolnshire Politics 1832–1885*, Oxford University Press, Oxford.

Olney, R. J. (ed.), 1975, *Labouring Life on the Lincolnshire Wolds: A Study of Binbrook in the Mid-Nineteenth Century*, Society for Lincolnshire History and Archaeology, Sleaford.

Opie, I. and P., 1959, *The Lore and Language of Schoolchildren*, Oxford University Press, Oxford.

Orel, Harold (ed.), 1966, *Thomas Hardy's Personal Writings*, University of Kansas Press, Lawrence, Kans.

Orwin, C. S., 1929, *The Reclamation of Exmoor Forest*, Oxford University Press, Oxford.

Orwin, C. S., 1949, *A History of English Farming*, Nelson.

Orwin, C. S., and Felton, B. I., 1931, 'A Century of Wages and Earnings in Agriculture', *Journal of the Royal Agricultural Society*, XCII.

Orwin, C. S., and Whetham, E. H., 1964, *History of British Agriculture, 1846–1914*, Longman.

Osborne, B. S., 1978, 'Common Lands, Mineral Rights and Industry', *Journal of Historical Geography*, IV.

O'Súilleabháin, 1970, 'Irish Agricultural Output, 1868 and 1908', unpublished paper read at the Irish Economic History Group Conference, Dublin.

Owen, D., 1965, *English Philanthropy 1660–1960*, Harvard University Press, Cambridge, Mass.

Page, D., 1974, 'Commercial Directories and Market Town', *Local Historian*, II, 2.

Palin, W., 1844, 'The Farming of Cheshire', *Journal of the Royal Agricultural Society*, V.

Palliser, D. M., 1976, *The Staffordshire Landscape*, Hodder & Stoughton.

Parker, John Oxley, 1964, *The Oxley Parker Papers*, Benham, Colchester.

Parker, R. A. C., 1975, *Coke of Norfolk: A Financial and Agricultural Study, 1707–1842*, Clarendon Press, Oxford.

Parker, W. N., and Jones, E. L. (eds), 1976, *European Peasants and their Markets*, Princeton University Press, Princeton, N.J.

Parris, Leslie, 1973, *Landscape in Britain c. 1750–1850*, Tate Gallery.

Parry-Jones, D., 1972, *My Own Folk*, Gwasg Gomer, Llandysul.

Peacock, A. J., 1962, 'Land Reform, 1880–1914', unpublished M.A. thesis, University of

Southampton, Southampton.

Peacock, A. J., 1965, *Bread or Blood*, Gollancz.

Peel, L. J., 1976, 'Practice with Science: The First Twenty Years', *Journal of the Royal Agricultural Society*, CXXXVII.

Pelling, Henry, 1967, *Social Geography of British Elections 1885–1910*, Macmillan.

Perkin, H., 1969, *The Origins of Modern English Society, 1780–1880*, Routledge & Kegan Paul.

Perkin, H., 1970, *The Age of the Railway*, David & Charles, Newton Abbot.

Perkins, J. A., 1975a, 'Tenure, Tenant Right and Agricultural Progress in Lindsey, 1780–1850', *Agricultural History Review*, XXIII, 1.

Perkins, J. A., 1975b, *Working Class Housing in Lindsey*, Society for Lincolnshire History and Archaeology, Sleaford.

Perkins, J. A., 1976, 'The Prosperity of Farming on the Lindsey Uplands, 1813–37', *Agricultural History Review*, XXIV, 2.

Perren, Richard, 1970, 'The Landlord and Agricultural Transformation, 1870–1900', *Agricultural History Review*, XVIII, 1.

Perren, Richard, 1978, *The Meat Trade in Britain 1840–1914*, Routledge & Kegan Paul.

Perry, P. J., 1973, *British Agriculture 1875–1914*, Methuen.

Perry, P. J., 1974, *British Farming in the Great Depression, 1870–1914*, David & Charles, Newton Abbot.

Perry, P. J., 1977, 'Edward Girdlestone 1805–84: The Forgotten Evangelical', *Journal of Religious History*, IX, 3.

Peters, J. E. C., 1969, *The Development of Farm Buildings in the Western Lowlands of Staffordshire up to 1885*, Manchester University Press, Manchester.

Pevsner, Nikolaus, 1953, *The Buildings of England: Derbyshire*, Penguin, Harmondsworth, Middx.

Pevsner, Nikolaus, 1958, *The Buildings of England: North Somerset and Bristol*, Penguin, Harmondsworth, Middx.

Pevsner, Nikolaus, 1972, *The Buildings of England. Yorkshire: York and the East Riding*, Penguin, Harmondsworth, Middx.

Pevsner, Nikolaus, *et al.*, 1951–74, *The Buildings of England*, Penguin, Harmondsworth, Middx.

Philips, D., 1977, *Crime and Authority in Victorian England*, Croom Helm.

Phillips, A. D. M., 1969, 'Underdraining and the English Claylands, 1850–80: A Review', *Agricultural History Review*, XVII, 1.

Phythian-Adams, C., 1975, *Local History and Folklore: A New Framework*, National Council of Social Services Standing Conference for Local History.

Pinchbeck, Ivy, 1930, *Women Workers and the Industrial Revolution, 1750–1850*, G. Routledge & Sons.

Pine, L. G., 1961, 'Peerage in History and in Law', *Law Times*, 6, 13 October.

Plint, T., 1851, *Crime in England, its Relation, Character and Extent as Developed from 1801 to 1848*, G. Gilpin.

Plomer, W. (ed.), 1964, *Kilvert's Diary 1870–1879: Selections from the Diary of the Rev. Francis Kilvert*, Jonathan Cape.

Plowman, J., 1855, 'Oxford Farmers' Club Prize Essays', *Farmer's Magazine*, 3rd ser., VII.

Plowman, T. F., 1886, 'Agricultural Societies and their Uses', *Journal of the Bath and West Society*, XVII.

Pocock, D. C. D., 1959, 'England's Diminished Hop Acreage', *Geography*, XLIV.

Pollard, S., 1955, 'Barrow-in-Furness and the Seventh Duke of Devonshire', *Economic History Review*, 2nd ser., VIII.

Porter, A., 1907, *The Gamekeeper's Manual*, D. Douglas, Edinburgh.

Porter, G. R., 1912, *The Progress of the Nation*, ed. F. W. Hirst, Methuen.

Pratt, E. A., 1906, *The Transition in Agriculture*, John Murray.

Pratt, E. A., 1912, *Agricultural Organisation*, P. S. King.

Prest, J., 1960, *The Industrial Revolution in Coventry*, Oxford University Press, Oxford.

Price, Sir Uvedale, 1794–8, *An Essay on the Picturesque as Compared with the Sublime and the Beautiful: And on the Use of Studying Pictures of the Purpose of Improving Real Landscape*, Hereford.

Prince, H. C., 1959, 'The Tithe Surveys of the Mid-Nineteenth Century', *Agricultural History Review*, VII, 1.

Prince, H. C., 1967, *Parks in England*, Pinhorns, Shalfleet, Isle of Wight.

Prince, J., 1922, *History of Silkstone*, privately published, Silkstone.

Prothero, Rowland E., 1888, *The Pioneers and Progress of English Farming*, Longmans.

Prothero, Rowland E., 1901, 'Agriculture in the Reign of Queen Victoria', *Journal of the Royal Agricultural Society*, LXII.

Pugh, L. P., 1962, *From Farriery to Veterinary Medicine: 1785–95*, Heffer, Cambridge.

Pulbrook, Ernest C., 1922, *English Country Life and Work*, Batsford.

Pumphrey, Ralph Everett, 1934, 'The Creation of Peerages in England 1837–1911', unpublished Ph.D. dissertation, Yale University, New Haven, Conn.

Pumphrey, Ralph Everett, 1959, 'The Introduction of Industrialists in to the British Peerage: A Study in the Adaptation of Social Institution', *American Historical Review*, LXV, 1.

Pusey, Philip, 1842, 'On the Progress of Agricultural Knowledge during the Last Four Years', *Journal of the Royal Agricultural Society*, III.

Pusey, Philip, 1843, 'On the Agricultural Improvements of Lincolnshire', *Journal of the Royal Agricultural Society*, IV.

Pusey, Philip, 1850, 'On the Progress of Agricultural Knowledge during the Last Eight Years', *Journal of the Royal Agricultural Society*, XI.

Quinault, R., 1974, 'The Warwickshire County Magistracy and Public Order, *c.* 1830–1880'. In R. Quinault and J. Stevenson (eds), *Popular Protest and Public Order. Six Studies in British History 1790–1920*, Allen & Unwin.

Raistrick, A., and Jennings, B., 1965, *A History of Lead Mining in the Pennines*, Longman.

Randell, Arthur, 1969, *Fenland Memories*, Routledge & Kegan Paul.

Ransomes and Sim, 1862, *Reasons for not Exhibiting at the R.A.S.E. Meetings Canterbury 1860 and Leeds 1861*, Ipswich.

Ratcliffe, H., 1850, *Observations on the Rate of Mortality and Sickness Existing Amongst Friendly Societies ... Calculated from the Experience of the Manchester Unity ... of Odd Fellows*, Manchester.

Ravenstein, E. G., 1885, 'The Laws of Migration', *Journal of the Statistical Society*, XLVIII.

Raybould, J. T., 1973, *The Economic Emergence of the Black Country*, David & Charles, Newton Abbot.

Read, C. S., 1858, 'Recent Improvements in Norfolk Farming', *Journal of the Royal Agricultural*

Society, XIX.

Reaney, B., 1970, *The Class Struggle in Nineteenth-Century Oxfordshire*, History Workshop pamphlet 3, Ruskin College, Oxford.

Reckitt, B. N., 1951, *The History of Reckitt & Sons Ltd.*, Brown.

Redding, C., 1842, *An Illustrated Itinerary of the County of Cornwall*, How & Parsons.

Redford, A., 1926, *Labour Migration in England, 1800–1850* (new edn 1964, Manchester University Press, Manchester).

Rew, R. H., 1892, 'An Inquiry into the Statistics of the Production and Consumption of Milk and Milk Products in Great Britain', *Journal of the Royal Statistical Society*, LV.

Rew, H., 1897, 'British Agriculture under Free Trade, 1846–96', *Journal of the Farmers' Club*, December 1897.

Ribton-Turner, C. J., 1887, *A History of Vagrants and Vagrancy*, Chapman & Hall.

Richards, Eric, 1973, *The Leviathan of Wealth. The Sutherland Fortune in the Industrial Revolution*, Routledge & Kegan Paul.

Richards, Eric, 1974a, '"Captain Swing" in the Midlands', *International Review of Social History*, XIX.

Richards, Eric, 1974b, 'The Industrial Face of a Great Estate: Trentham and Lilleshall, 1780–1860', *Economic History Review*, 2nd ser., XXVII.

Richards, Eric, 1974c, '"Leviathan of Wealth": West Midland Agriculture, 1800–50', *Agricultural History Review*, XXII, 2.

Richardson, C., 1908, *The Complete Foxhunter*, Methuen.

Riches, Naomi, 1937, *The Agricultural Revolution in Norfolk*, University of North Carolina Press, Chapel Hill, N.C.

Ricks, C. (ed.), 1969, *Tennyson: Poems*, Longman.

Roberts, J. E., and Owen, R., 1924, *The Story of Montgomeryshire*, Educational Publishing Company, Cardiff.

Robertson, George, 1829, *Rural Recollections*, Cuninghame Press, Irvine, Ayrshire.

Robins, Mills, 1908, *Gleanings of the Robins or Robbins Family*, C. H. Woodward.

Robinson, David, 1826, 'Mr McCulloch's Irish Evidence', *Blackwood's Magazine*, XIX.

Robinson, J. M., 1974, 'Estate Buildings at Holkham—I', *Country Life*, CLVI.

Robinson, Peter Frederick, 1822, *Rural Architecture*.

Robinson, William, 1870, *The Wild Garden*, John Murray.

Robinson, William, 1883, *The English Flower Garden*, John Murray.

Rodee, Howard D., 1977, 'The "Dreary Landscape" as a Background for Scenes of Rural Poverty in Victorian Paintings', *Art Journal*, XXXVI, 4 (College Art Association of America).

Rogers, A., 1972, *This was their World: Approaches to Local History*, British Broadcasting Corporation.

Rollins, J. G., 1970, *The Needle Mills*, Society for the Protection of Ancient Buildings.

Rollinson, W., 1974, *Life and Tradition in the Lake District*, Dent.

Rolt, L. T. C., 1969, *Waterloo Iron Works: History of Taskers of Andover 1809–1968*, David & Charles, Newton Abbot.

Rose, M. E., 1976, 'Settlement, Removal and the New Poor Law'. In D. Fraser (ed.), *The New Poor Law in the Nineteenth Century*, Macmillan.

Rose, W., 1937, *The Village Carpenter*, Cambridge University Press, Cambridge.

Rose, Walter, 1942, *Good Neighbours: Some Recollections of an English Village and its People*,

Cambridge University Press, Cambridge.

Rosenblum, Robert, 1961, 'The Abstract Sublime'. In Henry Geldzahler, *New York Painting and Sculpture: 1940–1970*, Pall Mall Press.

Rossiter, M. W., 1975, *The Emergence of Agricultural Science: Justus von Liebig and the Americans, 1840–1880*, Yale University Press, New Haven, Conn.

Round, J. Horace, 1901, *Studies in Peerage and Family History*, Constable.

Rowlands, M. B., 1975, *Masters and Men in the West Midland Metalware Trades before the Industrial Revolution*, Manchester University Press, Manchester.

Rowntree, B. Seebohm, and Kendall, May, 1913, *How the Labourer Lives*, Nelson.

Royal Commission: Market Rights and Tolls, 1888–9, BPP 1888 LIII, LIV, LV.

Royal Commission: Poor Laws, 1834. Fifth edn, 1905 Cd. 2728.

Royal Commission: Poor Laws and Relief of Distress 1905–9. 1909 Cd. 4499.

Rubinstein, W. D., 1977, 'Wealth, Elites and the Class Structure of Modern England', *Past and Present*, LXXVI.

Ruddock, E., 1964–5, 'May-day Songs and Celebrations in Leicestershire and Rutland', *Transactions of the Leicestershire Archaeological and Historical Society*, XL.

Ruegg, Louis, 1854, 'Farming of Dorsetshire', *Journal of the Royal Agricultural Society*, XV.

Russell, E. J., 1937, 'Rothamsted Experimental Station', *Agricultural Progress*, XIV.

Russell, E. J., 1942, 'Rothamsted and its Experimental Station', *Agricultural History*, XVI.

Russell, E. J., 1966, *A History of Agricultural Science in Great Britain*, Allen & Unwin.

Russell, G. W. E., 1895, *Letters of Matthew Arnold, 1848–1888*, Macmillan.

Russell, Rex C., n.d. (*c.* 1956), *The 'Revolt of the Field' in Lincolnshire*, National Union of Agricultural Workers, Lincolnshire County Committee.

Russell, Rex C., 1965–7, *History of Schools and Education in Lindsey 1800–1902*, Lindsey County Council, Lincoln.

Russell, Rex C., 1975, *Friendly Societies in the Caistor, Binbrook and Brigg Area in the Nineteenth Century*, Workers' Educational Association, Nettleton Branch.

Ruston, A. G., and Witney, D., 1934, *Hooton Pagnell, The Agricultural Evolution of a Yorkshire Village*, Edward Arnold.

Rutherford, Mark, 1888, *Mark Rutherford's Deliverance*, T. Fisher Unwin.

Sage, Josiah, 1951, *Memoirs of Josiah Sage*, Lawrence & Wishart.

Saint, Andrew, 1976, *Richard Norman Shaw*, Yale University Press, New Haven, Conn.

Saint Maur, E. A. (12th Duke of Somerset), 1880, *Monarchy and Democracy, Phases of Modern Politics*, J. Bain.

Samuel Raphael, 1972, 'Comers and Goers'. In H. J. Dyos and M. Wolff (eds), *The Victorian City*, Routledge & Kegan Paul.

Samuel, Raphael, 1975a, 'Quarry Roughs: Life and Labour in Headington Quarry, 1860–1920. An Essay in Oral History'. In Raphael Samuel (ed.), *Village Life and Labour*, Routledge & Kegan Paul.

Samuel, Raphael (ed.), 1975b, *Village Life and Labour*, Routledge & Kegan Paul.

Samuel, Raphael, 1977, 'Mineral Workers'. In Raphael Samuel (ed.), *Miners, Quarrymen and Saltworkers*, Routledge & Kegan Paul.

Sands, T. B., 1959, *The Midland and South Western Junction Railway*, Oakwood Press, South Godstone, Surrey.

Sanford, John Langton, and Townsend, Meredith, 1865, *The Great Governing Families of*

England, William Blackwood & Sons, Edinburgh.

Saul, S. B., 1967, 'The Market and the Development of the Mechanical Engineering Industries in Britain 1860–1914', *Economic History Review*, 2nd ser., XX.

Saul, S. B., 1968, 'The Engineering Industry'. In D. H. Aldcroft (ed.), *The Development of British Industry and Foreign Competition, 1875–1914*, Allen & Unwin.

Saville, J., 1957, *Rural Depopulation in England and Wales 1851–1951*, Routledge & Kegan Paul.

Scharf, Aaron, 1974, *Art and Photography*, Penguin, Harmondsworth, Middx.

Scotland, Nigel A. D., 1977, 'Methodism and the "Revolt of the Field" in East Anglia, 1872–96', *Proceedings of the Wesley Historical Society*, XLI, 1.

Scott, G. G., 1857, *Remarks on Domestic and Secular Architecture*, John Murray.

Scott, J., 1882, 'Recent Advances in the Science and Practice of Agriculture', *Journal of the Farmers' Club*.

Scott Watson, J. A., 1937, 'The University of Oxford', *Agricultural Progress*, XIV.

Scott Watson, J. A., 1951, *Great Farmers*, Faber.

Selley, Ernest, 1919, *Village Trade Unions in Two Centuries*, Allen & Unwin.

Sellman, R. R., 1967, *Devon Village Schools in the Nineteenth Century*, David & Charles, Newton Abbot.

Seth-Smith, M., 1969, *The History of Steeplechasing*, Michael Joseph.

Shearer, E., 1937, 'The University of Edinburgh', *Agricultural Progress*, XIV.

Shearer, E., 1938, 'The School of Agriculture, Cambridge', *Agricultural Progress*, XIV.

Sheppard, J. A., 1958, *The Draining of the Hull Valley*, East Yorkshire Local History Society, York.

Shorter, A. H., 1938, 'Paper Making in Devon and Cornwall', *Geography*, XXIII.

Sidney, Samuel, 1848, *Railways and Agriculture in North Lincolnshire*.

Sigsworth, E. M., 1958, *Black Dyke Mills*, Liverpool University Press, Liverpool.

Silver, Allan, 1967, 'The Demand for Order in Civil Society: A Review of Some Themes in the History of Urban Crime, Police, and Riot'. In David J. Bordua (ed.), *The Police: Six Sociological Essays*, John Wiley & Sons, New York.

Simmons, J. (ed), 1974, *Memoirs of a Station Master*, Adams & Dart, Bath.

Simon, Brian, 1965, *Education and the Labour Movement 1870–1920*, Lawrence & Wishart.

Simon, Sir John, 1887, *Public Health Reports*, ed. E. Seaton.

Simpson, J., 1973, *The Folklore of Sussex*, Batsford.

Sinclair, Sir John, 1795, *General View of the Agriculture of the Northern Counties and Islands of Scotland*, Board of Agriculture.

Sitwell, Osbert, 1946, *The Scarlet Tree*, Macmillan.

Skirving, Robert S., 1873, 'On the Agriculture of East Lothian', *Transactions of the Highland and Agricultural Society of Scotland*, 4th ser., V.

Skirving, Robert S., 1878, 'Farm Labour and Labourers'. In *Report of the present state of the Agriculture of Scotland under the Auspices of the Highland and Agricultural Society*, William Blackwood & Sons, Edinburgh.

Smith, D. M., 1963, 'The British Hosiery Industry at the Middle of the Nineteenth Century', *Transactions of the Institute of British Geographers*, XXXII.

Smith, D. M., 1965, *Industrial Archaeology of the East Midlands*, David & Charles, Newton Abbot.

Smith, Henry Herbert, 1898, *The Principles of Landed Estate Management*, Edward Arnold.

Bibliography

Smith, S., 1971, 'Alfred Waterhouse', unpublished thesis, University of London.

Smith, Sydney, 1956, *Selected Letters of Sydney Smith*, ed. Nowell C. Smith, Oxford University Press, Oxford.

Solow, B. L., 1971, *The Irish Land Question and the Irish Economy*, Harvard University Press, Cambridge, Mass.

Soloway, R. A., 1969, *Prelates and People: Ecclesiastical Social Thought in England 1783–1852*, Routledge & Kegan Paul.

Somerville, A., 1852, *The Whistler at the Plough*, Manchester.

Somerville, Robert, 1805, *General View of the Agriculture of East Lothian*, Board of Agriculture.

Spearing, J. B., 1860, 'On the Agriculture of Berkshire', *Journal of the Royal Agricultural Society*, XXI.

Spence, C. C., 1960, *God Speed the Plow*, University of Illinois Press, Urbana, Ill.

Spencer, Earl, 1842, 'On the Improvements which have Taken Place in Norfolk', *Journal of the Royal Agricultural Society*, III.

Spring, David, 1951, 'The English Landed Estate in the Age of Coal and Iron: 1830–1880', *Journal of Economic History*, XI, 1.

Spring, David, 1952, 'The Earls of Durham and the Great Northern Coalfield, 1830–1880', *Canadian Historical Review*, XXXIII.

Spring, David, 1963, *The English Landed Estate in the Nineteenth Century: Its Administration*, Johns Hopkins University Press, Baltimore.

Spring, David, 1971, 'English Landowners and Nineteenth-Century Industrialism'. In J. T. Ward and R. G. Wilson (eds), *Land and Industry. The Landed Estate and the Industrial Revolution*, David & Charles, Newton Abbot.

Springall, L. Marion, 1936, *Labouring Life in Norfolk Villages 1834–1914*, Allen & Unwin.

Staehle, H., 1950–1, 'Statistical Notes on the Economic History of Irish Agriculture, 1847–1913', *Journal of the Statistical and Social Inquiry Society of Ireland*, XVIII.

Staley, Allen, 1973, *The Pre-Raphaelite Landscape*, Clarendon Press, Oxford.

Stanhope, Earl, 1938, *Notes of Conversations with the Duke of Wellington: 1831–51*, Oxford University Press, Oxford.

Stanton, A. W., 1902, 'Decadence of Agricultural Shows'. In A. J. Stanton (ed.), *Agricultural Annual and Mark Lane Express Almanac*.

Stanton, Phoebe, 1971, *Pugin*, Thames & Hudson.

Stedman Jones, G., 1971, *Outcast London: A Study in the Relationship between Classes in Victorian Society*, Clarendon Press, Oxford.

Steel, James, 1878, *Selection of the Practical Points of Malting and Brewing*, Glasgow.

Stephens, H. (ed.), 1858, *The Book of Farm Implements and Machines*, William Blackwood & Sons, Edinburgh.

Stephens, H. 1871, *The Book of the Farm*, 3rd ed., William Blackwood & Sons, Edinburgh.

Stephens, H. 1891, *The Book of the Farm*, 4th edn, William Blackwood & Sons, Edinburgh.

Stevenson, G. R., 1971, 'Open Village: Victorian Middle Barton', *Cake and Cockhorse*, III.

Stevenson, J. J., 1880, *House Architecture*, Macmillan.

Stewart, Robert, 1971, *The Politics of Protection: Lord Derby and the Protectionist Party 1841–1852*, Cambridge University Press, Cambridge.

Stirling, A. M. W., 1912, *Coke of Norfolk and his Friends*, new edn, John Lane.

Stone, Lawrence, 1965, *The Crisis of the Aristocracy 1558–1641*, Clarendon Press, Oxford.

Stone, Lawrence, and Stone, Jeanne C. Fawtier, 1972, 'Country Houses and their Owners in Hertfordshire 1540–1879'. In William D. Aydelotte, Allan C. Bogue and Robert William Fogel (eds), *The Dimensions of Quantitative Research in History*, Princeton University Press, Princeton, N.J.

Stone, Thomas, 1800, *A Review of the Corrected Agricultural Survey of Lincolnshire by Arthur Young*.

Stopes, H., 1885, *Malt and Malting*, Lyon, *Brewers' Journal* Office.

Story, Alfred T., 1892, *The Life of John Linnell*, Richard Bentley & Son.

Straker, E., 1931, *Wealden Iron*, Bell.

Street, A. G., 1932, *Farmer's Glory*, Faber.

Strong, H. W., 1971, *Industries of North Devon*, new edn, David & Charles, Newton Abbot.

Stroud, Dorothy, 1962, *Humphry Repton*, Country Life.

Sturge, W., 1879–80, 'Presidential Address', *Transactions of the Institute of Surveyors*, XII.

Sturgess, R. W., 1966, 'The Agricultural Revolution on the English Clays', *Agricultural History Review*, XIV.

Sturgess, R. W., 1967, 'The Agricultural Revolution on the English Clays: A Rejoinder', *Agricultural History Review*, XV.

Sturmey, S. G., 1968, 'Owner-farming in England and Wales, 1900–50'. In W. E. Minchinton (ed.), *Essays in Agrarian History*, II, David & Charles, Newton Abbot.

Sturrock, Archibald, 1867, 'On the Agriculture of Ayrshire', *Transactions of the Highland and Agricultural Society of Scotland*, 4th ser., I.

Sturt, G. (George Bourne), 1912, *Change in the Village*, Duckworth.

Sturt, G. (George Bourne), 1923, *The Wheelwright's Shop*, Cambridge University Press, Cambridge.

Surtees, R. S., 1854, *Handley Cross: Or Mr Jorrocks' Hunt*, Bradbury, Agnew.

Surtees, R. S., 1958, *Mr Sponge's Sporting Tour*, new edn, Oxford University Press, Oxford.

Taine, Hippolyte, 1957, *Notes on England*, trans. Edward Hyams, Thames & Hudson.

Tann, J., 1967, *Gloucestershire Woollen Mills*, David & Charles, Newton Abbot.

Tate, W. E., 1967, *The English Village Community and the Enclosure Movements*, Gollancz.

Tate, W. E., 1978, *A Domesday of English Enclosure Acts and Awards*, Reading University Press, Reading.

Taylor, A. J., 1960, 'The Sub-Contract System in the British Coal Industry'. In L. S. Pressnell (ed.), *Studies in the Industrial Revolution*, Athlone Press.

Taylor, D., 1971, 'London's Milk Supply, 1850–1900: A Re-interpretation', *Agricultural History*, XLV.

Taylor, D., 1976, 'The English Dairy Industry, 1860–1930', *Economic History Review*, 2nd ser., XXIX.

Taylor, F. D. W., 1955, 'United Kingdom: Numbers in Agriculture', *Farm Economist*, VIII.

Thackrah, C. T., 1832, *The Effects of Arts, Trades and Professions . . . on Health and Longevity* (reprinted 1957, E. & S. Livingstone, Edinburgh).

Theuriet, André, 1892, *Jules Bastien-Lepage and his Art: A Memoir*, T. Fisher Unwin.

Thirsk, Joan, 1957, *English Peasant Farming*, Routledge & Kegan Paul.

Thirsk, Joan, 1961, 'Industries in the Countryside'. In F. J. Fisher (ed.), *Essays in the Economic and Social History of Tudor and Stuart England*, Cambridge University Press, Cambridge.

Thirsk, Joan (ed.), 1967, *The Agrarian History of England and Wales, IV: 1500–1640*,

Cambridge University Press, Cambridge.

Thomas, A., 1978, *The Expanding Eye*, Croom Helm.

Thomas, Hilary, 1969, 'Margam Estate Management, 1765–1860', *Glamorgan Historian*, VI.

Thomas, J. A., 1939, *The House of Commons 1832–1901*, University of Wales Press, Cardiff.

Thomas, J. A., 1958, *The House of Commons 1906–11*, University of Wales Press, Cardiff.

Thomis, Malcolm I., 1968, *Old Nottingham*, David & Charles, Newton Abbot.

Thompson, E. P., 1965, *The Making of the English Working Class*, Gollancz.

Thompson, E. P., 1974, 'Patrician Society, Plebeian Culture', *Journal of Social History*, VII, 4.

Thompson, E. P., 1975, *Whigs and Hunters: The Origin of the Black Act*, Allen Lane.

Thompson, Flora, 1945, 1954, 1968, *Lark Rise to Candleford*, new edns, Oxford University Press, Oxford.

Thompson, Flora, 1971, 1973, *Lark Rise to Candleford*, new edns, Penguin, Harmondsworth, Middx.

Thompson, F. M. L., 1957, 'The Land Market in the Nineteenth Century', *Oxford Economic Papers*, 2nd ser., IX, 3.

Thompson, F. M. L., 1960, 'English Great Estates in the Nineteenth Century', *Contributions: First International Conference of Economic History*, Mouton, Paris.

Thompson, F. M. L., 1963, *English Landed Society in the Nineteenth Century*, Routledge & Kegan Paul.

Thompson, F. M. L., 1965, 'Land and Politics in England in the Nineteenth Century', *Transactions of the Royal Historical Society*, 5th ser., XV.

Thompson, F. M. L., 1968a, *Chartered Surveyors. The Growth of a Profession*, Routledge & Kegan Paul.

Thompson, F. M. L., 1968b, 'The Second Agricultural Revolution, 1815–1880', *Economic History Review*, 2nd ser., XXI.

Thompson, F. M. L., 1976, 'Nineteenth-Century Horse Sense', *Economic History Review*, 2nd ser., XXIX.

Thompson, F. M. L., 1977, 'Britain'. In David Spring (ed.), *European Landed Elites in the Nineteenth Century*, Johns Hopkins University Press, Baltimore.

Thompson, H. S., 1864, 'Agricultural Progress and the Royal Agricultural Society of England', *Journal of the Royal Agricultural Society*, XXV.

Thompson, R. J., 1968, 'An Enquiry into the Rent of Agricultural Land'. In W. E. Minchinton (ed.), *Essays in Agrarian History*, II, David & Charles, Newton Abbot.

Thomson, James, 1800, *General View of the Agriculture of Fife*, Board of Agriculture, Edinburgh.

Tibble, J. W. (ed.), 1935, *John Clare: Poems*, Dent.

Ticknor, George, 1864, *Life of William Hickling Prescott*, Routledge, Warne & Routledge.

Timmins, S., 1967, *Birmingham and the Midland Hardware District*, Frank Cass.

Topographical, Statistical and Historical Gazetteer of Scotland, 1842, A. Fullarton, Glasgow.

Torr, C., 1918, *Small Talk at Wreyland*, Cambridge University Press, Cambridge.

Tranter, N., 1973, *Population since the Industrial Revolution: The Case of England and Wales*, Croom Helm.

Trench, W. Steuart, 1869, *Realities of Irish Life* (reprinted 1966, MacGibbon & Kee).

Trinder, Barry, 1955. In *Victoria County History: Leicestershire*, III, ed. W. G. Hoskins and R. A. McKinley, Oxford University Press, Oxford.

Trinder, Barrie, 1973, *The Industrial Revolution in Shropshire*, Phillimore, Chichester.

Trollope, Anthony (ed.) 1868, *British Sports and Pastimes*.

Trollope, Anthony, 1869, *Phineas Finn, the Irish Member*.

Trotter, James, 1811, *General View of the Agriculture of West Lothian*, Board of Agriculture, Edinburgh.

Trow-Smith, Robert, 1959, *A History of British Livestock Husbandry: II, 1700–1900*, Routledge & Kegan Paul.

Turner, J. H., 1845, 'On the Necessity for the Reduction or Abolition of Hedges', *Journal of the Royal Agricultural Society*, VI.

Tyler, C., and Haining, J., 1970, *Ploughing by Steam, A History of Steam Cultivation over the Years*, Model & Allied Publishing, Hemel Hempstead, Herts.

Tyrrell, S. J., 1973, *A Countryman's Tale*, Constable.

Udale, J., 1908, 'Market Gardening and Fruit Growing in the Vale of Evesham', *Journal of the Royal Agricultural Society*, LXIX.

Unwin, T. Fisher, 1904, *The Hungry Forties: Life under the Bread Tax*, T. Fisher Unwin.

Vaizey, J., 1960, *The Brewing Industry 1886–1951*, Pitman.

Vallentine, R., 1866, 'On Middle-class Education', *Journal of the Royal Agricultural Society*, 2nd ser., II.

Vaughan, W. E., 1977, 'Agricultural Output, Rents and Wages in Ireland, 1850–80', unpublished paper read at the Franco-Irish seminar of economic and social historians, 1977.

Victoria County History: Bedfordshire II, 1908, ed. W. Page, Archibald Constable.

Victoria County History; Buckinghamshire, 1906, ed. W. Page, Archibald Constable.

Victoria County History; Cambridgeshire II, 1968, ed. L. F. Salzman, Dawsons Pall Mall.

Victoria County History: Dorset II, 1908, ed. W. Page, Archibald Constable.

Victoria County History: Essex II, 1907, ed. W. Page and J. Horace Round, Archibald Constable.

Victoria County History: Essex VI, 1973, ed. W. R. Powell, Oxford University Press.

Victoria County History: Gloucestershire XI, 1976, ed. N. M. Herbert, Oxford University Press.

Victoria County History: Leicestershire III, 1955, ed. W. G. Hoskins and R. A. McKinley, Oxford University Press.

Victoria County History: Lincolnshire I, 1906, ed. W. Page, Archibald Constable.

Victoria County History: Middlesex V, 1976, ed. T. F. T. Baker, Oxford University Press.

Victoria County History: Oxfordshire II, 1907, ed. W. Page, Archibald Constable.

Victoria County History: Oxfordshire VIII, 1964, ed. Mary D. Lobel and Alan Crossley, Oxford University Press.

Victoria County History: Oxfordshire IX, 1969, ed. Mary D. Lobel and Alan Crossley, Oxford University Press.

Victoria County History: Oxfordshire X, 1972, ed. Alan Crossley, Oxford University Press.

Victoria County History: Staffordshire XVII, 1976, ed. M. W. Greenslade, Oxford University Press.

Victoria County History; Suffolk, 1906, ed. W. Page, Archibald Constable.

Victoria County History; Wiltshire X, 1975, ed. E. Crittall, Oxford University Press.

Victoria County History: Yorkshire East Riding II, ed. R. B. Pugh, Oxford University Press.

Vince, J., 1975, *An Illustrated History of Carts and Wagons*, Spurbooks, Bourne End, Bucks.

Vincent, J. E., 1896, *The Land Question in North Wales*, Longman & Green.

Bibliography

Vincent, J. R., 1967, *Pollbooks: How Victorians Voted*, Cambridge University Press.

Wakelin, M. F., 1972, *English Dialects: An Introduction*, Athlone Press.

Walford, Edward, 1871, *The County Families of the United Kingdom or Royal Manual of the Titled and Untitled Aristocracy of Great Britain and Ireland*, 6th edn, Robert Hardwick.

Wallace, A. R., 1905, *My Life*, Chapman & Hall.

Walters, R. C. S., 1936, *The Nation's Water Supply*, Nicholson & Watson.

Walton, J. R., 1973, *A Study in the Diffusion of Agricultural Machinery in the Nineteenth Century*, University of Oxford School of Geography Research Paper no. 5, Oxford.

Wantage, Lady, 1907, *Lord Wantage, V.C., K.C.B.*, privately published.

Ward, J. T., 1971, 'Landowners and Mining'. In J. T. Ward and R. G. Wilson (eds), *Land and Industry. The Landed Estate and the Industrial Revolution*, David & Charles, Newton Abbot.

Ward, J. T., and Wilson, R. G. (eds), 1971, *Land and Industry. The Landed Estate and the Industrial Revolution*, David & Charles, Newton Abbot.

Ward, T. H. (ed.), 1887, *The Reign of Queen Victoria: A Summary of Fifty Years of Progress*, Smith & Elder.

Ward, W. R., 1965, 'The Tithe Question in England in the Early Nineteenth Century', *Journal of Ecclesiastical History*, XVI, 1.

Warwick, Countess of, 1898, *Joseph Arch: The Story of his Life told by Himself*, Hutchinson.

Watson, J., 1845, 'On Reclaiming Heath', *Journal of the Royal Agricultural Society*, VI.

Watson, J. A. Scott, 1939, *The History of the Royal Agricultural Society of England*, Royal Agricultural Society.

Watson, J. A. Scott, and Hobbs, M. E., 1937, *Great Farmers*, Selwyn & Blount.

Webb, S. and B., 1963, *English Poor Law History, Part II: The Last Hundred Years*, new edn, Frank Cass.

Weber, B., 1955, 'A New Index of Residential Construction 1838–1950', *Scottish Journal Political Economy*, II, 2.

Webster, C., 1868, 'On the Farming of Westmoreland', *Journal of the Royal Agricultural Society*, 2nd ser., IV.

Wells, W., 1860, 'The Drainage of Whittlesea Mere', *Journal of the Royal Agricultural Society*, XXI.

Welton, T. A., 1900, 'On the Distribution of Population in England and Wales 1801–91', *Journal of the Royal Statistical Society*, LXIII.

Whetham, E. H., 1964–5, 'The London Milk Trade, 1860–1900', *Economic History Review*, 2nd ser., XVII.

Whetham, E. H., 1968, 'Sectoral Advance in English Agriculture, 1850–80: A Summary', *Agricultural History Review*, XVI.

Whetham, E. H., 1978, *Agrarian History of England and Wales: VIII, 1914–39*, Cambridge University Press, Cambridge.

Whitaker, J., 1892, *A Descriptive List of Deer-parks and Paddocks in England*, Ballantyne.

White, Arnold, 1901, *Efficiency and Empire*, Methuen.

White, H., 1853, 'A Detailed Report of the Drainage by Steam-power of a Portion of Martin Mere, Lancashire', *Journal of the Royal Agricultural Society*, XIV.

White, R., 1939, 'The University College of North Wales', *Agricultural Progress*, XVI.

White, R. P., n.d., *The Standard Encyclopedia of Modern Agriculture*.

White, W., 1836, *History, Gazetteer and Directory of the County of Norfolk*, White, Sheffield.

Whitehead, C., 1883, 'Progress of Fruit Farming', *Journal of the Royal Agricultural Society*, 2nd ser., XIX.

Whitehead, C., 1889, 'Fifty Years of Fruit Farming', *Journal of the Royal Agricultural Society*, 2nd ser., XXV.

Whitehead, C., 1899, 'A Sketch of the Agriculture of Kent', *Journal of the Royal Agricultural Society*, 3rd ser., X.

Whitehead, R. A., 1964, *Garretts of Leiston*, Percival Marshall.

Wilkinson, Rupert, 1964, *Gentlemanly Power: British Leadership and the Public School Tradition; A Comparative Study in the Making of Rulers*, Oxford University Press, Oxford.

Willan, T. S., 1976, *The Inland Trade*, Manchester University Press, Manchester.

Williams, Alfred, 1912, *A Wiltshire Village*.

Williams, Alfred, 1913, *Villages of the White Horse*.

Williams, Alfred (ed.), 1923, *Folk-Songs of the Upper Thames*, Duckworth.

Williams, David, 1955, *The Rebecca Riots*, University of Wales Press, Cardiff.

Williams, L. A., 1975, *Road Transport in Cumbria in the Nineteenth Century*, Allen & Unwin.

Williams, M., 1970, *The Draining of the Somerset Levels*, Cambridge University Press.

Williams, Merryn, 1972, *Thomas Hardy and Rural England*, Macmillan.

Williams, R., 1973, *The Country and the City*, Chatto & Windus.

Williamson, Henry, 1941, *The Story of a Norfolk Farm*, Faber.

Wilson, Charles, 1954, *The History of Unilever, A Study in Economic Growth and Social Change*, I, Cassell.

Wilson, John, 1812, *General View of the Agriculture of Renfrewshire*, Board of Agriculture, Paisley.

Wilson, John, 1878, 'Farming of the East and North-Eastern Districts'. In *Report of the Present State of the Agriculture of Scotland Arranged under the Auspices of the Highland and Agricultural Society*, William Blackwood & Sons, Edinburgh.

Wilson, J. M., 1851, *The Rural Cyclopaedia*, Edinburgh.

Within Living Memory: A Collection of Norfolk Reminiscences, 1971, Norfolk Federation of Women's Institutes.

Wood, L. T., 1913, *A History of the Royal Society of Arts*, John Murray.

Woodbridge, K., 1971, *The Stourhead Landscape*, National Trust.

Woodroofe, K., 1962, *From Charity to Social Work*, Routledge & Kegan Paul.

Woodruff, D., 1934, 'Expansion and Emigration'. In G. M. Young (ed.), *Early Victorian England, 1830–1865*, Oxford University Press, Oxford.

Woods, K. S., 1921, *The Rural Industries Round Oxford*, Clarendon Press, Oxford.

Woods, K. S., 1975, *Rural Crafts of England*, new edn, E. P. Publishing East Ardsley, Wakefield.

Worsley, H. 1849, *Juvenile Depravity*, C. Gilpin.

Wright, Elizabeth Mary, 1913, *Rustic Speech and Folk-lore*, Humphrey Milford.

Wright, P. A., 1959, *Traction Engines*, Black.

Wrigley, E. A. (ed.), 1972, *Nineteenth Century Society*, Cambridge University Press, Cambridge.

Yelling, J. A., 1977, *Common Field and Enclosure in England, 1450–1850*, Macmillan.

Yonge, Charlotte, 1853, *The Heir of Redclyffe*, Macmillan.

Young, Arthur, 1804, *General View of the Agriculture of Norfolk*, Board of Agriculture.

Young, Rev. Arthur, 1813, *General View of the Agriculture of Sussex*, Board of Agriculture.

Zehr, H., 1976, *Crime and the Development of Modern Society*, Croom Helm.

Index

Main entries are in **bold**; plate numbers are in *italic*.

A

Abberley Hall (Worcs.), 400; *99*
Aberdeenshire: farm size, 87;
 labourer-farmers, 507; population
 levels, 181
Aberystwyth, college, 269
Absentee landlords, 77; agents for,
 439, 442, 453
Accidents: agricultural, 498, 518;
 industrial, 336
Acland, A.H., 123
Acland, Lady Anne, 422
Acland, Thomas Dyke, 251
Adam Bede, 138–9
Adams family, 447
Age: and disease, 501; and
 employment, 501–2, 593, 628; at
 marriage, 492
Agents, **439–55**; background, 443,
 444; and cottages, 536; duties,
 439–40, 441, 442, 445, 446, 452;
 effects, 454–5; incompetence, 441,
 443, 444; and landlords, 444, 445,
 446–7; and leases, 392; and
 legislation, 441–2; multiple
 estates, 442; political influence,
 445–6; power, 439–40, 444, 454–5;
 as profession, 444–5; prominent,
 447–50, 451–2; qualities, 440, 441,
 451, 454; and rents, 442, 444, 454;
 salaries, 441, 447, 449; status, 446,
 449, 453; and tenants, 442, 444, 446,
 448, 450–1; training, 443, 445
'Aggrieved Parishionership', 290
Agricultural Chemistry, 19, 194
Agricultural Children Act (1873),
 495, 527, 528
Agricultural colleges, 267–70
Agricultural Holdings Acts (1875,
 1883), 76, 392–3
Agricultural Labourers' Association,
 54
Agricultural Labourers' Protection
 Association, 582
Agricultural Organization Society,
 255
Agricultural Rates Act (1896), 600
Agricultural Union, 254
Agriculture and change, 110, 228,
 517–18; competition, 270–1; as
 consumer, 191–5; decline, 3–4, 5–6,
 15, 18, 20, 25, 103, 108, 179; and the

economy, 179–99, 243; and
 industrialization, 184–8;
 institutions, 245–6; Irish, 94–102,
 113–14; and Parliament, 15; and
 railways, 185–6; raw materials,
 186–8; revolution, 391; and
 science, *see* Science; Scottish
 practice, 83, 113; structure, 229;
 traditional, 11, 12–13; type, and
 migration, 120; Welsh, 71, 77,
 113–14
Agriculture and Horticultural
 Association, 255
Agriculture, Board of, 245; and
 education, 268, 269, 271; failure,
 245, 248, 250; machinery, reports
 on, 200, 202; on overcrowding, 536
Aintree racecourse, 482
Airedale Valley, in literature, 158
Aitkin, André, 194
Akenfield (Suff.), mobility, 31
Akroyden (Yorks), 419, 420
Albert, Prince Consort; as farmer,
 218–19; *51*; and model housing,
 417, 420
Aldeburgh (Suff.), in poetry, 157
Alderley (Ches.), suburb, 9
Aldermaston Court, Newbury, 408
Alexander II, Tsar of Russia, 387
Alexander, D., 301, 304
Alison, Archibald, 377, 380
Allchin & Co., of Newbury, 198
Allegory, in art, 172–4
Allen, William, 418
Allingham, Helen, 170
Allingham, William, 170
Allotments: and the clergy, 53–4,
 238; demand for, 67, 131–2, 608;
 and diet, 557, 564; pleasure of, 609;
 provision, 131–2, 334, 425–6, 570,
 575–6, 586
Allotments Extension Act (1882), 131
Allwood, Matty, *78*
Alnwick (Northumb.): Castle, 405;
 drainage, 435
Almshouses, 594, *164*
Alton (Hants), *144*
Altrincham (Ches.), growth, 9
Amcotts, Weston Cracroft, 434
Ames, Charles, 39
Amis, Arthur, 508

Ammonia, in fertilizers, 194
Ampleforth (Yorks.), trades, 302
Anderson, Dr, 215
Anderson, M., 125, 492
Andrew, Jenny, 145
Andrews, G.H., 222
Andrews, William, 158
Anglesey: diet, 559; game, 462; hours
 of work, 121
Anglican church: alienation, 48;
 income, 51–2; internal conflicts,
 238; and Nonconformism, 55;
 Oxbridge graduates in, 51; and
 recreation, 611; strength, 44–6; *see
 also* Church, the
Animals, *see* Livestock
Annual contracts, 508–9
Anti-Corn Law League, 46, 48, 385;
 and the Church, 48, 54
Anti-Tithe League (1886), 74
Apothecaries, 291–2, 293
Apperley, Charles (Nimrod), 476, 482
Apples, Kentish, 628–9
*Applicants for Admission to a Casual
 Ward*, 171
Apthorpe (Northants), 410
Arable farming: decline, 5, 18–19, 20,
 108, 111; labour, 201;
 mechanization, 206–7, 209; and
 migration, 120; profit, 4
Architecture: of cottages, 334,
 416–17, 418–20, 535, 537, 539; of
 country houses, 399–401; polite,
 532; vernacular, 399, 401, 419, 421,
 532, 535, 539
Arch, Joseph, 583; *161*; on
 allotments, 132; autobiography,
 56; on crime, 576; emigration, 130;
 game laws, 460; on landlords, 66;
 and Liberal Party, 587; rural
 relationships, 457–8; skills, 506;
 Union, 68, 110, 379, 569, 572, 584–6,
 589; vaccination, 292
Ardington (Berks), 419–20, 422–6
Aristocracy, **367–80**; and
 agricultural societies, 252–3;
 charity, 595; and colleges, 267;
 definition, 369, 370; and economic
 growth, 373–7; and elections, 61,
 379–80; elitism, 367, 380; as
 entrepreneurs, 373–7; families,

679

Blake, William, 138, 172
Blandford (Dorset), 523
Blaxall (Suff.), 510
Bledington (Gloucs.), 581
Bloomfield, Robert, 154–5, 173
Blore, Edward, 402
Blything (Suff.), women's outwork, 342
Boarding houses, and women, 309
Boards of Education, Diocesan: and schools, 543; and training colleges, 544
Boat-building, 13
Boby, Richard, corn screen, 196
B.O.C.M., 192, 193
Boer War, effects, 131
Bondagers, 494, 495, 507, 523
Bone-Lace, *see* Lace
Bones, *see* Fertilizers
Bonsall (Derbys.), 359
Bonus payments, 425
Booth, Charles, 502, 592
Boots, *see* Shoes
Boroughs: agricultural, 63–4; rotten, 371, 372, 386, 388
Borrow, George: on Breckland Heath, 24; on clergy, 290; on the land, 140–1
Bossenden Wood (Kent), 574
Boston (Lincs.), 528
Boulton & Paul, 195
Bourn (Cambs.), 574
Bournemouth, development, 184
Bourneville (Birmingham), 414, 420, 421
Boussingault, J. B., 194
Bowden (Ches.), growth, 9
Boycott, Capt., 440, 454
Bradfield (Berks.), Union, 600
Bradfield (Suff.), Young's farm, 216–17
Bradford (Yorks.), wool combers, 338
Bradshaw, R. H., 444
Bradwell (Derbys.), 358–9
Braiding, *see* Netmaking
Bramley, Joseph, 582
Brand, John, 195
Brandon, David, 406
Brass bands, 610
Brassey, Mr, 485
Braybrook, Lord, 497
Brazil, emigration to, 584
Bread: in diet, 522, 555, 558, 559, 560, 561, 563; flours, 189, 190, 558; home baking, 555, 558; ingredients, 556, 558; price, 562; white, 555, 558
Brecon, game in, 462
Brereton, R. M., 452
Breton, Jules, 173
Brett, John, 160
Brewing: and coopers, 317; development, 190–1; employment in, 126, 127; and imports, 190–1; and urbanization, 8, 283–4
Bricklayers' labourers, infant mortality, 492
Brickmaking: consumption of, 195; employment in, 124; mechanization, 195; works, 13
Brick tax, removal, 537

Bridgewater Canal, 451
Bridgewater, Dukes of, 373, 376; Trust, 441, 444
Bridgwater (Som.), allotments, 131
Bridlington (Yorks.): hirings, 508–9; mills, 283
Brightfield, Myron, 158–9
Bright, John, 460, 566
Brighton (Suss.), as resort, 10
Brindley, James, 373–4
Bristol: Bath and West Show (1874), 251; disease in, 292
Bristow, Samuel, 35
British Association for the Advancement of Science, 262
British Dairy Farmers Association, 255
British and Foreign Schools' Society, 544
British Produce Supply Association, 255
British Sports and Pastimes, 478
Brixworth (Northants.), Union, 600
Brocklesby estate, 433; hunt, 432, 436, 464, 469–70
Brodrick, G. C., 64, 222, 444, 500–1
Brontë family, and Haworth, 158
Brontë, Charlotte, 159
Brontë, Emily, romanticism, 136
Brooke (Norf.), 243
Brooks Co., of Manningtree, 235
Broughams, 32
Brown, Arnesby, 174
Brown, Capability, 415
Brown, Ford Madox, *see* Madox Brown
Brown, William Marshall, *15*
Bruce family, 64
Bryanston (Dors.), 401, 405, 410, 411; *109*
Buckinghamshire: elections, 446; game, 462; hiring, 508; iron foundries, 284; lace-making, 13, 343, 348; *89*; needle-making, 180; output, 115; straw plaiting, 342, 343; tambour work, 349
Budd, William, 291–2, 298
Buddle, John, 374
Building industry: and employment, 126, 317; growth, 537; materials, 11–12, 195, 406; in Tadcaster, 281; wages, 406
Building lease, 375
Builth (Brecon), mortality rates, 491
Bull-baiting, 604, 606
Bull, H., 446
Bulwer, Lytton, 386
Bunbury, Sir Charles, 481
Bunnington, Vale of Wrington, education, 123
Buntingford (Cambs.), migration, 126
Burford (Oxf.), 277
Burke, Edmund, 152
Burke, John, 383, 384, 385
Burke, John Bernard, 383, 385
Burne-Jones, Edward, 161, 173
Burnham Beeches, protection, 25, 26
Burns, Robert, 170
Burn, William, 405, 407
Burrell & Co., Thetford, 197, 198, 203

Burritt, Elihu, 6–7, 11
Burton-on-Trent (Staffs.), coopers, 317
Bury, Canon, 600
Buses, employment on, 126, 127
Butchers: employment, 301, 303, 309; shops, 279, 302; *75*; women, 309
Butt, Isaac, 96
Butter: demand, 21; in diet, 557, 561, 563, 565; imports, 187; Irish, 100–1, 187; prices, 109; substitutes, 187
Butterfield, William, 419
Buttonmaking: decline, 348; outwork, 341
Buxton, T. F., 407
Byerly, T. C., 271
Bylaugh Hall (Norf.), 408
By-products, manufacturing, consumption of, 191, 193, 195
Byron, George Gordon, Lord, 296, 298

C

C. & J. Clark Ltd., 421
Cadbury family, 421
Caernarvonshire, enclosures, 570
Caird, Sir James, 6; on Cirencester college, 268; on consumption, 105; on drainage, 21; on Essex milk, 22; on food supply, 4–5, 243; on free trade, 5; on hedgerows, 21; on high farming, 262; on imports, 243; on labourers, 500–1; on land agents, 443–4; on leases, 234; on Lilleshall and Trentham estates, 433; on machinery, 120, 207; on rents, 433; on wages, variations, 131, 497, 500, 558, 592; on wintering of cows, 11
Cairncross, A. J., 119, 120, 128, 129, 130, 133
Caistor (Lincs.), *138*
Calcium in diet, 559, 561, 565
Calcraft family, 64
Calendar, 619, 621, 623
Calories, in diet, 559, 561
Cambridgeshire: arable land, 20; close villages, 472; game, 462; gangs, 510; hiring, 508; migration to London, 127; women's work, 350
Cambridge University, agriculture at, 269
Canada, emigration to, 129, 130
Canals: and commerce, 33–4, 305; income from, 451; travel on, 33–4, 40
Candidates, electoral, selection, 60, 379, 436
Candleford (Oxf.), blacksmiths, 40, 324; crime, 573
Candles, saving, 632
Cane, crafts: employment, 316; outwork, 349
Canewdon (Essex), 606
Canning industry, 13, 187–8
Cannock Chase (Staffs.), clearing, 26; pit villages, 360
Canterbury (Kent), hiring fairs, 306; Royal Show (1860), 249

Index

430; food, 628–31, game, 461; hops, 22, 23, 524, 628, 635; industrialized villages, 354; living-in, 632; police, 465; prosperity 627–8; quality of life, 635–7; respectability, 632–5; trades unions, 582; vagrants, 573; wages, 627–8

Kent, Nathaniel, 409, 415
Kent and Sussex Union, 584, 585, 586, 587, 588
Kerr, Robert, 403, 405
Kesteven (Lincs.), *69*
Ketley (Salop.), 359
Kettering (Yorks.), 295
Kickham, Charles, 97
Kilburn (Lond.), Royal Show (1879), 249
Kilburn (Yorks.), trades, 302
Kilvert, Francis, 617
Kilvert, Robert, travel, means, 31, 32–3
Kincardineshire, farm size, 87
King, Gregory, 493
Kingsbridge (Dev.), 292
Kingsley, Charles: and the clergy, 53; and hunting, 486; and natural history, 291; realism, 146; and sanitation, 290–1
Kinross, decline, 92
Kirkburton (Yorks.), 357
Kirk Smeaton (Yorks.), 243
Knight family, and Exmoor, 25
Knitting: decline, 338, 349; growth, 355; machines, 330; mills, 13; outwork, 13–14, 330, 331, 333, 342, 346–7; villages, 354, 355; wages, 347; workers' housing, 333
Knocknagow, 97
Koch, Robert, 267

L

Labourers, agricultural, **491–503**, **627–37**; age, 501–2, 593, 628; aspirations, 502, 636; birth rate, 493; career, 12–13, 123–4, 231; casual, 121, 201, 207, 495–7; characteristics, 503; charity, 596; contracts, 508–10, 569; crime, 566–7; daily life, 6–7, 12–13, 86, 205, 606, 627–37; emancipation, 67–8, 69; family, workers, 123, 494, 510, 523; farmer-labourer relations, 78–9, 87, 95, 231, 457–8, 470; food, 6, 501, 522–3, 554–65, 628–31; harvest, 121; health, 501, 518, 524; hierarchy, 86–7, 507, 509; hiring, 508–10; hours of work, 121–2, 514, 583; housing, 414, 429, 470–1, 509, 539; industrial, 182; learning, 508, 523; and land, 231; and law, 571; life expectation, 492; living conditions, 122, 170–2, 470–1, 499–500, 533–4, 569; and machinery, 207–8, 517–18, 570, 574; marriage, 492–3; migration, 120–4, 125–6, 497–8; mortality rates, 491–2, 501; numbers, 493–4; perquisites, 498, 502, 555, 556, 560, 569, 595; poverty, 503, 561,

591–601; prosperity, 107, 115; protest, 566, 569–71, 573–6; recreation, 571, 603–14; redeployment, 207; regional variation, 500–1; religion, 633; rights, 570; self-sufficiency, 628; skills, 506–8; standard of life, 554–5, 558, 562, 564, 591; status, 507–8, 633–6; tasks, 511–16, 517–18; status, 507–8, 633–6; voting, 64, 67–8; wages, *see* Wages; in Wales, 78–9, 124; women, 120, 123, 492, 494–5, 510, 514, 515, 523, 527; work cycles, 511–16

Labourers, building, 406
Labourers' Friend Society, 596
Labourers, municipal, employment, 126, 127, 182
Labourers' Union Chronicle, 585, 587
Labour force, agricultural: age, 501–2; categories, 506–8; cost, 110, 111, 113, 200–1, 206; decline, 7, 18, 115, 120–1, 201, 243; effects, 501, 518, 524; housing, 414, 534, 538, 632; and mechanization, 120–1; and migration, 120; mobility, 181–2, 510, 583, 592; numbers, 3–4, 18, 118, 201, 243, 493–4, 592; productivity, 209–11; quality, 182; ratio to employers, 491, 493, 494; Scottish, 86; seasonal, 131; shortage, 121, 124, 131, 182, 498, 510, 592–3; surplus, 583, 592; use, 211
Labour force, industrial: housing, 333–5, 359, 414–15, 418, 421; outworkers, *see* Outwork; rural excess as reservoir, 181, 497
Labour force, national, agricultural workers in, 179
Labour Gazette, 513
Labour, Royal Commission on (1893), 37, 120–1, 498, 562
Labour, saving, 200–2, 206–8, 407
Lace-making, *88–9*; children at, 343, 344, 351; *89*; decline, 7, 13, 181, 285, 348; and disease, 345, 351; feast days, 350; instruction, 348, 351; outworkers, 341, 343, 348; payment, 347, 351; working conditions, 344–5
'Lady of Shallott, The', 161
Lake District: cottages, 532; folk medicine, 617; in literature, 154, 159; reservoirs, 25; tourists, 25, 159
Lambing, 516
Lamps, paraffin, 499
Lanarkshire, dairy farms, 87
Lancashire: child death, 525; clog making, 13; Depression, 112; diet, 560; drainage, 23; game, 461; hiring, 508; industry, 180; knitting, 13–14; mummers, 618; outwork, 331; rents, 106, 112; schools, 466, 467; shrimping, 341; wages, 565; weavers' cottages, 333; weaving, 331, 333
Land: agents, *see* Agents; and the Church, 43–56; concept of, 136–7; contraction, 243; flight from, *see*

Migration; in literature, 136–48; management, 440, 441; and migration, 131–2; and politics, 58–69; and power, 46–7, 58, 68, 137, 369, 391; premiums for, 232–3; reform, 59, 75, 587–8; selling, 297, 390; and the state, 392–3, 393–7; and status, 386–7, 391; surveys, 297; value, 115, 367, 374, 375, 378
Land Agents' Society, 444
Landaus, 32
Landed Gentry, 383–4, 385, 386, 390, 396
Land Enquiry Committee: on casual labour, 496; on land, access to, 132; on tied cottages, 123; on wages, 131, 498; on weather and work, 498
Landlords: bankruptcy, 95; and the Church, 47–50, 74–5, 469; decline, 15; definition, 369; in Depression, 115; duties, 14–15, 216, 223, 370, 378, 428–9, 458–9; and industrial development, 183; investment, *see* Investment; and leadership, 15, 49, 232, 378, 429–30; and model cottages, 417, 470; and model farms, 216, 217, 223; numbers, 390; and politics, 429–30, 436; power, 46–7, 368–9, 374–5, 387–8; profits, 14, 387–8; and railway promoters, 430; relationships, rural, 457–73; and schools, 465–9, 543, 546; sport, 464; and tenants, 14–16, 62, 66, 231–4, 376, 379, 391–3, 422–6, 428–37, 483; votes, 14, 59, 61–2, 73, 376, 378, 423–4, 436, 445–6
Land Restoration League, 67, 587–8; *160*
Landscape, rural, 17–27; in art, 166–74; decline, 3–4, 103; ideal, 153, 160, 161; in literature, 150–63; regional, 158–60; romantic, 159–61, 169–70
Landscaping, 408, 410, 415
Langley (Ess.), 571
Langley Marish (Bucks.), school excursion, 38
Language, local variation, 618–19
Lark Rise (Oxf.): girls at, 126; health, 501; mobility, 31; stage coaches, 32; women labourers, 495
Last Labourers' Revolt (1830–1), 574
Latchingdon (Ess.), 498
Lavatories, 290, 405, 420
Lavengre, 141
Lavenham (Suff.), food, 557
Lawes, John Bennet, 194, 271; and Liebig, 194, 262–3, 268; Rothamsted Experimental Station, 19, 223, 263, 264–5, 272
Lavoisier, A-L, 260
Lawton, R., 120
Lawyers: and estate management, 444; infant mortality, 492; rural, 294–5
Leader, Benjamin Williams, 168–9; *29*
Lead mines: and disease, 336; and education, 337; industrialized

690

Z